Romans

Romans

An Exposition of Chapter 12
Christian Conduct

D. M. Lloyd-Jones

THE BANNER OF TRUTH TRUST

THE BANNER OF TRUTH TRUST
3 Murrayfield Road, Edinburgh EH12 6EL, UK
P.O. Box 621, Carlisle, PA 17013, USA

*

© Lady Catherwood and Mrs Ann Beatt 2000

First published 2000
Reprinted 2005
Reprinted 2010

ISBN: 978 0 85151 794 0

*

Typeset in 10/12 pt Trump Medieval
at The Spartan Press Ltd,
Lymington, Hampshire

Printed in the USA by
Versa Press, Inc.,
East Peoria, IL

*The sermons in this volume
were originally preached at Westminster Chapel
between October 1965 and November 1966*

Contents

[vii]

Christian Conduct

Contents

[ix]

Christian Conduct

Contents

One

*

I beseech you therefore brethren, by the mercies of God, that ye present your bodies a living sacrifice, holy, acceptable unto God, which is your reasonable service. And be not conformed to this world: but be ye transformed by the renewing of your mind, that ye may prove what is that good, and acceptable, and perfect, will of God. For I say, through the grace given unto me, to every man that is among you, not to think of himself more highly than he ought to think; but to think soberly, according as God hath dealt to every man the measure of faith. For as we have many members in one body, and all members have not the same office: so we, being many, are one body in Christ, and every one members one of another. Having then gifts differing according to the grace that is given to us, whether prophecy, let us prophesy according to the proportion of faith; or ministry, let us wait on our ministering: or he that teacheth, on teaching; or he that exhorteth, on exhortation: he that giveth, let him do it with simplicity; he that ruleth, with diligence; he that sheweth mercy, with cheerfulness. Let love be without dissimulation. Abhor that which is evil; cleave to that which is good. Be kindly affectioned one to another with brotherly love; in honour preferring one another; not slothful in business; fervent in spirit; serving the Lord; rejoicing in hope; patient in tribulation; continuing instant in prayer; distributing to the necessity of saints; given to hospitality. Bless them which persecute you: bless, and curse not. Rejoice with them that do rejoice, and weep with them that weep. Be of the same mind one toward another. Mind not high things, but condescend to men of low estate. Be not wise in your own conceits. Recompense to no man evil for evil. Provide things honest in the sight of all men. If it be possible, as much as lieth in you, live peaceably with all men. Dearly beloved, avenge not yourselves, but rather give place unto wrath: for it is written, Vengeance is mine; I will repay, saith the Lord. Therefore if thine enemy hunger, feed him; if he thirst, give him drink: for in so doing thou shalt heap coals of fire on his head. Be not overcome of evil, but overcome evil with good.

Romans 12:1–21

As we resume our studies in Paul's Epistle to the Romans, we come to the beginning of the twelfth chapter. It has taken us some time to reach this point because it is such a rich Epistle.[1]

But, let me remind you again that an epistle is in itself a synopsis. People have sometimes playfully said to me that they are quite sure the Apostle Paul would be astonished if he could but know what I find in his epistles! But that is to display profound ignorance. Take this Epistle to the Romans: Why did the apostle write it? Well, he tells us at the beginning that he wrote it because he was not able to visit the Christians at Rome. He wanted to; he intended to. He tells us in the first chapter, in verses 12 and 13, that he had been hindered. In chapter 15 he tells us again, with more assurance, that he is hoping to call at Rome on his way to Spain. But as he is not yet able to be there in the flesh and talk to the Christians day by day and expound the glories and the mysteries of this Christian faith, he sends them this kind of synopsis. Remember, therefore, that this is nothing but a synopsis, and the business of an expounder of an epistle is not to give a synopsis of the synopsis, which is what many seem to do. Rather, it is to work out, to draw out, what the apostle has condensed in this particular manner. So that is how it has come to pass that we have been able to spend all this time in dealing with this great Epistle.

But now we come to a new section. I have often said that before, but I am saying it again for a very special reason. We have found many divisions and subdivisions in the first eleven chapters but between chapters 11 and 12 there is a division which is more significant than any of the others have been. Indeed, the nearest we have ever come to something like this has been away back at the first chapter, in verses 16 and 17. This is because the first fifteen verses are preliminary introductions and salutations and personal statements. Then at verses 16 and 17 Paul begins to expound his great doctrine, and from there right until the end of chapter 11 the letter is almost

[1] Dr Lloyd-Jones also commented as follows: 'Incidentally, for the sake of the statisticians, we are considering this Epistle for the 297th time. Now these statistics, I think, are interesting. If you include tonight and say 297, and then divide that by 11, because we have finished the first eleven chapters, you will see that, roughly speaking, it has been 27 addresses for each of the chapters. Of course, it has not worked out like that, some have taken longer than others, but it did strike me as being an interesting fact!

exclusively doctrinal. I say 'almost exclusively' because of course there have been applications here and there as Paul has gone along, but the main teaching has been doctrinal; and everybody grants that from the point of view of Christian doctrine, Romans is the greatest masterpiece ever written. It is a colossal and incomparable statement of Christian truth.

But now the apostle comes on here to the practical section. Having finished with his doctrine, he comes to his application, and continues with this from the very beginning of this twelfth chapter until he finally finishes the Epistle at the end of chapter 16. Now we must not make too much of this division. The Apostle Paul was an amazing man. He had a great intellect, and an unusual power and gift for teaching, but he was also a pastor with a very tender pastoral heart, so that he was all the time concerned with helping these people to whom he was writing. So while he does divide up his subject matter, all along these other aspects of the man keep breaking in.

I mention this in order to prepare you for the fact that though, as we said, from now to the end of the Epistle we are dealing mainly with practical matters – the outworking and the living of the Christian life – Paul constantly brings in doctrine; he cannot separate the two. So you must expect doctrine and argument, and doctrine and appeal. It is always fascinating to me to watch Paul in this respect. He is not one of these cold people who can divide a thing up mechanically. The burning heart is always there, in the most intellectual passages and in the most practical passages. It keeps on bursting forth upon us, as it were. This is characteristic of all Paul's epistles but it is very obvious, as we shall see, in the case of Romans.

Now I want to ask an important question, and I ask it particularly of those who have been following this whole series: How do you feel as we approach this new division? I am trying to be a pastor also and so I constantly emphasize this. I do not like the division of a man's ministry which leads him to say, 'Of course, on Sunday I do this, but Friday night is different; then I'm only a teacher.' That is a very artificial and, indeed, a very wrong division. There should be the same unity in our ministry as you find in the ministry of the Apostle Paul, and because of that, I put this question to you, to try to show you that it will tell you a great deal about yourself.

What is your reaction as we finish the great doctrinal section and come to these practical chapters? Do you have a feeling that they are going to be a bit of an anticlimax? Are you sorry you have finished with the first eleven chapters? Do you wish that Paul had gone on in that way instead of coming down to the practical application – is that your feeling? Do you in any sense feel like the Apostle Peter on the Mount of Transfiguration when he said, 'Let us make here three tabernacles' [*Matt.* 17:4]? Let us not go down again to the dull plains of life. It is so marvellous here on top of the mountain with this illuminated cloud and all the wonder and splendour of it all. Let us stay here. Let us make three tabernacles.

Is that your feeling? Do you want to stay in the realm of pure doctrine? Do you find it a little bit irksome and against the grain to have to come down to the level of the trivialities of the Christian faith? This is a most important question because if any of us feel that these remaining chapters are an anticlimax, then there is something wrong with us, something seriously wrong, as I shall try to show you. The same man who wrote the first eleven chapters is the man who has written the remainder of the Epistle; he goes on, so must we.

So let me introduce this great section to you. Why must we go on? My first answer is that that is what the Scriptures do, and in and of itself that ought to be enough for us. If we believe that the Scripture is indeed the Word of the living God, then we must read it all.

But is not the danger with many of us that we read certain sections only? Many people have their favourite passages; they are always reading them and they read nothing else. Or some only read certain books in the Bible and never the others. There is a tendency today among Christian people to discard the Old Testament, especially the historical portions. They say, 'That has nothing to do with me.' But that is quite wrong. If you believe that this is the Word of God, it *all* has something to do with you, and you must read it all. So we have no right just to enjoy the doctrine and not to worry about the practical sections.

Others, however, only enjoy the practical passages and do

not bother about the doctrine which they say they cannot follow. So in the same lazy way they divide up the Scriptures in a manner that should never be done. Scripture, being the Word of God, is to be read right through, because, of course, it is a whole and we must neither detract from it nor add to it.

You can detract from the Scripture by ignoring certain passages, or by saying, 'This is all that matters in Scripture.' Many people are teaching that at the present time. Some, for example, simply concentrate on our Lord's moral teaching, as if the whole of the Bible were just the Sermon on the Mount. But there are others who say, 'This has nothing to do with us now.' So they start in certain epistles and just concentrate on bits of them, and that is equally wrong.

The whole of the Bible is for us. It speaks to us and has a message to give us all as much today as at any other time. Therefore, because the Scriptures go on, so must we. It is not for any of us to say, 'I've had all I want out of the Epistle to the Romans, I'm a person who is only interested in doctrine. I'm not interested in the rest.' No, that is to do violence to the Scriptures and as I shall show you, it is also to do something extremely dangerous.

So I give as my second reason that we must go on because, after all, Christianity is not merely a teaching, but a life. There is a very beautiful description of Christian people – you find it two or three times in Acts – as the people of 'that way' [*Acts* 19:9, 23; 22:4], and that is a very good description. Christianity is not only a way of thinking but a way of living, a way of behaving. That is the essential characteristic of this Christian faith. It was never meant to be doctrine only. It *is* doctrine and the doctrine comes first; it is truth, and truth comes to the mind, and demands an intellectual response and assent. But Christianity does not stop there. Our artificial distinctions not only do violence to the Scriptures but also do harm to us. Christianity is primarily a way of life and the object of the doctrine is to enable us to live that life.

God made man and woman, and put them in the world, and intended them to live in fellowship with Him. But they sinned and fell. And the object of salvation is to restore them to that way of life. So doctrine is one part only. The whole person is involved, not only the understanding but the heart and

[5]

feelings, the will, conduct and behaviour. The Bible regards each man and woman as a whole, and we must always do the same. That is why these practical sections are as important as the doctrinal sections.

It follows that Christianity is not only an experience. There is a great and a glorious experience but the end and object of the Christian faith is not to give us experiences. It is most important that we should always remember that the purpose of the experience is to change our daily life and living. This is something that the Apostle Paul puts plainly when writing to Titus. He tells us that the Lord came from heaven and gave Himself for us on the cross on Calvary's hill to 'redeem us from all iniquity, and purify unto himself a peculiar people, zealous of good works' [*Titus* 2:14]. That is why He did it. That is what our Lord did by coming into this world, by living and teaching and dying on the cross, and by being buried and rising again. It was not just to give us intellectual interest, excitement and satisfaction, not merely to give us experiences. They are included, but the ultimate grand end and object is to purchase and to prepare and to train a people for God: God's people in the totality of their being and personalities and in all their activities.

God's people are not meant to be thinkers only, or people with fine sensibilities and nothing else, but whole men and women, redeemed and functioning as a people for God's own special possession. That is what the phrase 'a peculiar people' means: God's own, personal possession. And, therefore, you see that we have to emphasize the practical aspect as much as the doctrinal. As our Lord said, 'If ye know these things, happy are ye if ye do them' [*John* 13:17]. And we are reminded of that here in Romans 12 by this very introduction to the subject: 'I beseech you therefore, brethren, by the mercies of God . . .'

But there is a third reason for going on to the application, and it is because of the difficulties that inevitably arise in the life of the true Christian.

Here we are, we have become Christians, but we are still in this world. We are in it but we are not of it and the great problem of Christian living is that of coming to terms with the world in which we live.

We believe that when men or women become Christians they become new creatures: 'old things are passed away; behold, all things are become new' [*2 Cor.* 5:17]. But here they are, still in this world. What must they do now? Here they are with this new faith, this new belief, this new understanding, and they must obviously apply that to the whole of their life. They come up against difficulties and questions, and because they are now governed by an entirely new outlook, they now have a problem which they never had before, one which people who are not Christians do not have.

This, again, is a most important matter. If your becoming a Christian has not raised problems in your life which the non-Christian does not know about, then you can take it from me that you are not a Christian. Christians are not merely men and women who attend a place of worship on Sundays, go through a certain form of worship, and then go back into the world and live as they did before or as other people live. That is not the Christian. There is something wrong with people who are in that position. Christians, by definition, are men and women who are born again, who are regenerate, who have undergone the profoundest change people can ever undergo, and they now have a new outlook upon everything which is determined by this new belief. How are they going to relate to the world?

The New Testament epistles show us very plainly and clearly how the early Christians got into many difficulties at just this point. As I shall show you, there are difficulties on all sides and therefore we need guidance, we need help and instruction. As an unregenerate man, I lived to please myself; I lived to my own glory. As a Christian, I do not live for myself, but for the glory of God. Paul tells us that in detail in chapter 14: 'For none of us liveth to himself, and no man dieth to himself' [*Rom.* 14:7]. The Christian, by definition, is concerned about the glory of God and therefore I must know how I am to apply this great salvation to every single question and detail and problem. The apostle puts that in a picturesque way in writing to the Philippians: 'Only let your conversation' – your conduct and behaviour, your whole deportment – 'be as it becometh the gospel of Christ' [*Phil.* 1:27].

We must inevitably come up against these problems, and we

ought to be grateful to God that He ever put it into the mind of His great servant, this apostle, and inspired him with the Holy Spirit, to take up these questions, to deal with them and to resolve them for us, so that we have something to guide us in this tremendous process. I say again, if you say to me, 'Oh, I'm not concerned about that, I'm a theologian, a man who grapples with the great doctrines', my answer is: 'But, my dear friend, the question is: How are you living? It is no good being a great theologian if you deny it all by your behaviour. If you are rude to your wife or children or to your next door neighbours, you are a denier of the gospel and all your knowledge is of no value. The whole person is involved in the new birth, and, therefore, we need help and instruction at every single point.

The fourth reason for continuing to study the rest of Romans is the intimate connection between doctrine and practice, belief and behaviour. Each reacts upon the other and you cannot separate them totally. We analyse Paul's writing and make these divisions purely as a matter of convenience for understanding, but if we press them to a point at which we separate belief from behaviour, then we have misunderstood the doctrine. If you go wrong in your doctrine it will affect your life.

But, do not forget, it also works the other way round. The backslider will soon be compromising on doctrine. Why? Well, he does it to protect himself. As long as he holds on to the true doctrine, he will be very miserable as a backslider, so the devil persuades him to query the doctrine. The two must not be divided. 'What therefore God hath joined together, let not man put asunder' [*Matt.* 19: 6]. So you must take the whole Epistle, the second half as well as the first.

Then, lastly, we are always confronted by an adversary, a brilliant, able, subtle, knowledgeable adversary. Paul reminds the Corinthians that the devil can transform himself into 'an angel of light' [*2 Cor.* 11:14], and we know that he can. We see him tempting our Lord, and quoting Scripture to Him, in order to try to trip Him and to trap Him, and to make Him mis-understand and misapply God's Word. Satan is there always facing us and you will see, as we argue our way through this practical section, that he deceives us in two main ways.

The first is by telling us that this practical section does not matter at all. He says that it is all right, of course, for those unintelligent people who cannot read books of theology and who cannot be bothered with doctrine. They are only interested in the practicalities – that is all right for them – but for you, these things are of no importance. So he turns you into a kind of pure intellectual. But, I repeat, if you ignore the practice, you will soon make shipwreck of your faith. That is why Paul had to write these epistles.

But there is another side and it is equally important. When the devil fails to make a man ignore practicalities and just live in this delightful, rarified, intellectual atmosphere, he then comes to the same man and tries to make him overdo the practical aspect. He makes him become over-scrupulous and legalistic. There are examples of this further on in Romans. Chapter 14 deals with it almost exclusively – the question of meats offered to idols, and the observation of days, and so on. The devil is so subtle that he will change right over from one extreme to the other. He will either make you ride cavalierly over the whole question of conduct, or he will make you become so punctilious and careful and so engrossed with details and minutiae, that you have lost your liberty as a Christian man or woman and have become a legalist, back under the law once more. So we are always confronted by the devil and we should be very grateful to God that He ever caused His servant to take up these various problems. For you and I are still confronted by the same problems and questions that confronted the Christians of the first century.

There, then, is my general introduction to this whole matter. Now I think it would be good for us to have a general analysis of the whole of this practical section so that we may see how the principles I have been putting before you are actually worked out by the great apostle. I suggest some such analysis as this:

Chapter 12:1-2 is a general introduction to the whole section. In these verses the apostle shows us why we must turn to the application. Here the whole case is stated. Then, having done that, Paul proceeds to take up a number of separate problems.

Now these problems were obviously troubling the church of Rome at that time. The apostle knew that. He had received messages from churches; he was in touch with them all. He talks about 'the care of all the churches' [*2 Cor.* 11:28] – and he knew that certain things were threatening the life of the church both at Rome and throughout the Empire, problems which arose simply from the attempt of these early Christians to apply their new-found faith. So, in order to help them, he takes up these problems one by one. He lays down his principles and deals with them, and, I emphasize again, we should thank God for this because you and I are still confronted by the same problems. Sometimes they take a slightly different form, but that is the mere dress; the essential problem is still exactly what it was at the very beginning. Christians are 'new creatures' in Christ in both the first and the twentieth centuries.

In *Chapter 12:3–21* he deals with Christians in their relationship to the church, which Paul divides into two sections, as we shall see.

In *Chapter 13* he takes up the question of Christians in their relationship to the world, to the state, to magistrates and 'the powers that be'. These Christians in Rome were born again but they had to grapple with the problem of the Roman Empire. The devil would often come to the early Christians and say, 'Because you are Christians now, you have nothing at all to do with the state, pay no attention to it whatsoever.' They got into trouble because of that and they brought the whole gospel into disrepute. Is this not a contemporary question facing us all? In this century there have been countries where Christian people have had – and are having – to face this issue very acutely. What do Christians do if they are in a dictatorship? What is the relationship of the Christian to the state? It is a very urgent problem. It is a problem for the non-Christian, but not in the way that it is for the Christian. Christians have a greater tension here.

Chapter 13 also concerns Christians in their relationship with non-Christian people. How do you live with them? How do you get on with them? How are you to conduct yourself with respect to them? These were tremendous difficulties in the early church, and are they not difficulties for us also? But, thank God, we have help here.

In *Chapter 14* he brings us back into the realm of the church. There are always things that tend to break up the unity of the church. The devil always wants to do that. The church is God's creation, 'created in Christ Jesus' [*Eph.* 2:10]. It is God's masterpiece. Therefore the devil, as he tried to ruin, and so marred, the original creation, is now trying to spoil and ruin this new creation. He strives therefore to upset the life of the church.

How does he do it? Well, by causing misunderstandings. He creates differences and quarrels with regard to the problems that arise in the application of our Christian principles even down to the details of our lives: 'Which day should you observe as the Lord's day? Should it be the Jewish Sabbath or should it be the first day of the week – the Lord's day? And they were quarrelling. They were getting into trouble over those issues and others – eating meat sacrificed to idols, the relationship of masters and slaves, and so on.

And Paul points out that there were two main difficulties. Some of the more enlightened members of the church in Rome were condemning and despising their weaker brethren who would not eat meat offered to idols. These 'stronger' Christians were saying, 'This is no problem; this is quite clear. Those idols are only things, and therefore the meats are quite irrelevant and unimportant. We can eat what we like.'

But the apostle corrects them for taking that attitude. You are wrong, he says, in disregarding your weaker brother. Christ died for him as much as for you. Whatever may be true about meat, your attitude to your brother is wrong. You are misusing, indeed, you are abusing the liberty of the Christian.

So this is a highly practical question and when we come to deal with it, we shall apply it in its modern setting. It is not meat offered to idols with us, but there are many such problems and we very much need guidance along these lines, not only for our own peace and happiness, but for the sake of the life of the church, and because of maintaining the unity of God's people.

In *Chapter 15:1–13* he continues with this question of the unity of God's people, especially in terms of the relationship of the Jew and the Gentile as Christians together in the church of God. Of course, that was a tremendous problem in the first century. Jew and Gentile, the ancient division, the feud, the hatred, but now the 'middle wall of partition' [*Eph.* 2:14] has been broken down. Yes, it is all right to say that in theory, but when you have to live it out in practice, oh, what a problem! Not so much Jew and Gentile today, perhaps, as white, black and yellow, so called. How are these divisions to be worked out? Thank God, here we are given practical help and guidance.

In *Chapter 15:14–33* the apostle is finishing his letter and is speaking in a purely personal manner. He says in effect, 'I am concerned with all these questions, and I have written to you because of that. I have been given the honour of being called to be the apostle to the Gentiles in particular.' He has already told us that, but he 'magnifies his office' again, in order to help these Christians in Rome. Way back in the first chapter, he wrote, 'For I long to see you, that I may impart unto you some spiritual gift, to the end ye may be established' [*Rom.* 1:11]. He speaks as a Christian, as an apostle and as a teacher. He wants to help them; his heart yearns for them. He says in effect, 'I wish I could have been with you. I am hoping to come on my way to Spain, but in the meantime, I am sending you this letter, and I do hope this is going to help you. I am not interfering in your lives. I am not building on other people's work. I am really just out to try to bring you to an understanding, to increase your joy, so that the church in Rome may be entirely to the glory of God.' That is the remainder of chapter 15.

Chapter 16:1–16 is a series of wonderful greetings, good wishes and salutations to various people. It is marvellous that this astounding genius, this brilliant brain, this great man of God, should come down to details, to persons, to individuals. Thank God that we all count in His economy. Paul is a great man, yes, but he is as interested in the most unimportant person who is a true Christian as he is in this world's powerful people, more interested in them than in the emperor. This is how Christians show themselves in everything. So Paul sends his regards, as it were, to slaves, and to a number of people who had been kind to him, and who had helped him at various times, and who were playing a part in the life of the church.

Chapter 16:17–20 has a final warning against false brethren. The Apostle Paul, you see, not only preached at great length –

you remember how he once preached until midnight and a poor young man dozed and then fell down from his seat on a window sill [*Acts* 20:9–12]! – but he found it difficult to stop preaching, and equally difficult to stop writing. He has really finished but he is so concerned that his pastoral heart is moved and in verses 17 to 20 he warns against false brethren, encouraging the Christians and showing them how to deal with such people.

Chapter 16: 21–24 gives greetings from the people who were with Paul to the church at Rome and to various members in particular. Probably the apostle dictated a good deal of his letter. His amanuenses were with him and he did not ignore them – they were all playing a part. If you merely take down a dictated letter you are serving God, because you are helping His servant. And so Paul says, 'These people who are here with me send their regards also.' What a life this Christian life is. You soar in the Empyrean, as it were, but your feet are always firmly on earth, and nothing is too small to do for God. It is a great life, a supernatural life, but also a natural life. It includes, as I have said, the whole person. So there, in verses 21 to 24, you get these special greetings.

In *Chapter 16:25–27* Paul, as he usually does, seems to stand back and, looking upon it all once more, finds that there is only one thing to do, and that is to burst forth into a great doxology. And so he ends his mighty Epistle.

There, then, is the general analysis of the remainder of this majestic Epistle to the Romans. Let me finish with a brief analysis of chapter 12.

Verses 1–2 – a general introduction, as I have already pointed out.

Verses 3–8 – the Christian life of service in the church; Christians exercising the gifts that have been given to them; Christians as people who work in the church.

Verses 9–21 – Christians in their relationship with their fellow members in the church. We all have a gift and Paul tells us how to exercise it. But, in addition, and just as important, we must live with one another. It does not matter how gifted you are, if you are difficult to get on with, your gifts are of no value. It is always this balance.

So in this twelfth chapter I am hoping to show you that we

have a view of Christian men and women living their life in the church. But we must start, of course, with the general introduction to Christians living the whole of their lives while they remain in this world: their life in the church; their life in the world. The apostle shows us that there are great principles that cover it all and in various and varied ways Christians have to apply the doctrine they have received. And the apostle was raised up by God and called to be the apostle to the Gentiles in order to help us and to aid us in that application and outworking. Blessed be the name of God!

Two

*

> *I beseech you therefore, brethren, by the mercies of God, that ye present your bodies a living sacrifice, holy, acceptable unto God, which is your reasonable service. And be not conformed to this world: but be ye transformed by the renewing of your mind, that ye may prove what is that good, and acceptable, and perfect, will of God.*
>
> Romans 12:1–2

We are now in a position to start examining in detail the first two verses of the twelfth chapter of Paul's Epistle to the Romans. They are a most important statement from many standpoints, chiefly because they lay down for us the great principles which govern Christian conduct. The Bible gives great attention to this subject, as I have reminded you, and there is no doubt at all but that this is a most important question especially at the present time when there is a good deal of misunderstanding about the way Christians should behave.

But apart from that – and this is my chief reason for emphasizing it – I believe that from the standpoint of evangelism there is nothing more important than the life lived by Christian people. The world has been saying this for years; it has always said it, but it is saying it particularly at the present time. 'It's easy for him to talk,' people say, 'but how does he *live?* How does he put his faith into practice?'

I am certain that amidst all the confusion in the contemporary world there is one thing that still speaks to people in a way that nothing else does, and that is the quality of a life lived – people are always ready to listen to that. That is why it behoves us as Christian people to attach great significance to our practice, our conduct, and our behaviour. So in these two verses, in which the apostle introduces the whole of the next section, with all its detailed treatment of particular problems, he lays down the general teaching governing this entire matter.

Now I have tried to divide up his teaching under a number of headings or principles. The first is quite simple and yet very interesting. Notice the way in which the apostle introduces the subject to these members of the church at Rome. He starts by calling them 'brethren': 'I beseech you therefore, brethren, by the mercies of God . . .' 'Brethren'! The apostle was a great man, endowed with unusual abilities, brilliant as a student, and holding a prominent position as a Pharisee. But here he is, an apostle of Jesus Christ, commissioned by the risen Lord Himself on the road to Damascus. He had seen the risen Lord with his naked eyes and had been given a commission. Revelations had been granted to him in a most exceptional manner and he was a man who had been used in the working of miracles and in many other respects. And yet you notice his humility. He does not talk down to these people. Most of the members of the church at Rome were not only very ordinary people, but the probability is that most of them were slaves and servants and soldiers. Paul refers in the Epistle to the Philippians to those who are in 'Caesar's household' [*Phil.* 4:22] and makes references in other epistles to them. There is no question but that the church began among the common, ordinary people. It could be said of Rome as of the church at Corinth, 'Not many mighty, not many noble are called' [*1 Cor.* 1:26]. Yet he writes to them as 'brethren' – he puts himself on the same level with them.

Paul does this continually. In the very first chapter of Romans we read, in verses 11 and 12: 'For I long to see you, that I may impart unto you some spiritual gift, to the end ye may be established; that is, that I may be comforted together with you by the mutual faith both of you and me.' He says in effect, 'We are all Christians together. I may have been privileged to have these gifts and revelations, but I am only a brother like the rest of you. I am a sinner saved by the grace of God, as is every other Christian.'

Now this is truly interesting. You will find the other

apostles doing exactly the same thing. The Apostle Peter says, 'The elders which are among you I exhort, who am also an elder, and a witness of the sufferings of Christ, and also a partaker of the glory that shall be revealed: Feed the flock of God which is among you, taking the oversight thereof, not by constraint, but willingly; not for filthy lucre, but of a ready mind; neither as being lords over God's heritage, but being ensamples to the flock' [*1 Pet.* 5:1–3]. Again, he writes: 'Simon Peter, a servant and an apostle of Jesus Christ, to them that have obtained like precious faith with us through the righteousness of God and our Saviour Jesus Christ' [*2 Pet.* 1:1]. The apostles do not have a special faith; there is only one faith. We are all saved by faith and it is the same faith: the 'like precious faith with us'. Peter does not lord it over his fellow Christians; nor does the Apostle Paul.

And John writes in exactly the same way. He introduces his Epistle like this: 'That which was from the beginning, which we have heard, which we have seen with our eyes, which we have looked upon, and our hands have handled, of the word of life' [*1 John* 1:1]. And in verse 3 he gives his reason for writing: 'That which we have seen and heard declare we unto you, that ye also may have fellowship with us: and truly our fellowship is with the Father, and with his Son Jesus Christ.'

Now you may say, 'What is the importance of that to me?' Well, to me it is very important. These days we hear a great deal about dignitaries and hierarchies. We hear about various ecclesiastical offices ruled over by great men who are called Lords. You only have to look at them at a distance, to see them there, 'being lords over God's heritage' [*1 Pet.* 5:3]. But that is not New Testament; it is not apostolic. They talk about 'apostolic succession'; they talk about being 'the successors of Peter'; but they are not, they are contradicting Peter's words. They are lords; they are princes; they are heads of states. You do not get that in the New Testament. 'I beseech you, brethren . . .' Here is the apostolic manner.

How far the church has wandered from the original pattern! It is good for us to notice these things as we go along. When the church begins to imitate the state – she began doing it, of course, at the time of Constantine and has done so ever since – when the church models her government, or anything else, on the state, she has violated the New Testament principle. The great apostle sits down on the bench, as it were, with the humblest Christian and he says: We are brothers together. We are sharers of the same 'common salvation'. We have the same 'precious faith'. We are all one in Christ Jesus.

Paul does not mean that they are all absolutely equal. Of course the Apostle Paul had gifts and abilities that they did not possess, but that does not matter. The point he is making is that fundamentally we are all one. The Apostle Paul, like everybody else, was nothing but a sinner saved by the grace of God. Indeed, he speaks of 'sinners of whom I am chief' [*1 Tim.* 1:15]. Because he never forgot that, this element of humility always appears.

Then again – these are just preliminary points – Paul says, 'I beseech you.' He does not command them, he pleads with them. 'I beg of you,' he says. 'I entreat you.' That, again, is a characteristic note of the New Testament, and in that it differs in some vital respects even from the Old Testament. Moses 'commanded', the apostle 'beseeches'. And, again, you can see the relevance of this in the history of the church. There should be no lording it, no commanding, no insisting.

Do you understand what I have in mind? There are sections of the church which are governed and controlled by a priesthood. There is a priestcraft, and there are priest-ridden nations and people who just take orders – the common people. They do not know. They are told what to do and what not to do and they dare not disobey. But that is not New Testament. 'I beg of you,' says the apostle, 'to listen to what I have to say to you.' How easily the church forgets the primitive, original pattern and turns herself into something that is quite different, something that is altogether remote from the ethos, the atmosphere, which you find here in the New Testament. So that is the first point: the way in which the apostle introduces his subject and addresses the members of the church at Rome.

But now, secondly, why should we live the Christian life? What are our motives? What persuades us to live as Christians? I feel that this has a vital relevance for us, because here the apostle shows us the essential difference between Christian conduct on the one hand, and all ethical systems on the other.

This is important because there are many people in the world today who are concerned about living a good life. It is not confined to Christians. You hear a great deal at the moment about the 'humanists' as they are called, and at the present time humanism poses perhaps one of the most serious of the attacks made upon the Christian faith. The argument of these people is that you can live a good life without being a Christian. They say it is about time people grew up and began to think and gave up this nonsense about God and an unseen world, and all this talk of a so-called incarnation and redemption and all the rest of it. So they are 'humanists'.

Now humanists claim that they are living a good moral life and many of them do, though that is not true of all of them, of course – there are talkers among them as everywhere else! But let us grant them that. There are many among them who really do live a good life. But they attack the Christian faith, and not only that, they often trouble simple Christian people, who do not know how to answer them. Christians say, 'There are these humanists and we have to admit that they are living good lives. Yet they deny all that we believe in.'

A further important reason for being clear about this is that there is a tendency today, among many in the church who call themselves Christians, to elevate behaviour to the supreme position and to say that it does not matter very much what people believe as long as they live good lives. We come across this attitude almost daily. People die and when you read the obituary notices you sometimes find, even in evangelical circles, that great praise is lavished on men and women who have denied most of the vital elements of the Christian faith. Why are they praised? Because they 'did good'. This is a very serious matter. If you are to say that everybody who lives a good life is a Christian, then you must scrap the New Testament and do away with the Christian church since it is not necessary.

So, then, the apostle's teaching here can be put like this: What really matters is not *what* we do, but *why* we do it. In other words, you may show me two people who appear to be living the same kind of life, who perform the same good actions, so that if you looked at them externally, you would say, 'There is really no difference between these two people –

both are highly moral, both give their time and their energy to helping others, they are always doing good – both of them.' And yet it is possible that one may be a Christian while the other is not and may even be an opponent of Christianity. He may be a humanist, whether scientific or classical, that does not matter. So how do you tell the difference between the two? Here is the answer: the vital question, I repeat, is not what people do but why they do it.

What, then, is the essential difference between Christians in their living and all others? Sometimes it is this. Take humanists. Their conduct has no reference whatsoever to God. They do not believe in God. They regard Him as a product of folk-lore, as superstition, something we ought to get rid of. So why do they live good lives? It is for reasons of prudence, what some of the great philosophers of the nineteenth century called 'utilitarian' reasons – *Utilitarianism*.

John Stuart Mill[1], for instance, has many followers at the present time who have never heard of him. Their reason for living the good life is entirely, they say, common sense. Common sense indicates that if you want to be happy, then you must not be a fool. If you want to be happy, you do not go and get drunk because you will have to suffer if you do and it will land you in difficulties. If you want to be truly happy, you must not be promiscuous because that, again, will get you into trouble. Utilitarianism! Prudence! Common sense! They say, 'You have only to think these things through to see that everyone ought to live by a good moral code. It is better for the whole of the human race; it is a better kind of life.' Those are their reasons and there is no reference to God. So there, at once, you see an essential difference between the humanist, the good moral man, the good pagan, and the Christian.

But let me go further. There are others who are living this good life who *do* refer it to God – they are not all humanists. Take, for instance, people like the orthodox Jew, the Muslim, and many others. These people often have a very high ethical standard and they say that their reason for living this life is because they believe in God. God commands it, and this is

[1] English philosopher (1806-73), a major proponent of the ethical theory of Utilitarianism.

their way of worshipping Him. So there is a reference to God as the basis of their life, and yet, according to the apostle's words here, it is not Christian. They do not have the same motives; they are not moved by the same considerations and persuasions, as the Christian.

Why, then, do they live the good life? It is very largely because they are afraid of God. It is out of fear, a craven fear. It is the fear of punishment. It may be that they are living this good life because they say to themselves, 'If we do not live like this, we shall be punished, but on the other hand, if we do, we will accumulate merit and God will be well pleased with us. That will lead Him to forgive us our occasional failures and sins, and faults and blemishes, and it will ensure that we will go to heaven when we die.' They are trying to build up a great mound of righteousness which will satisfy God and ensure their salvation.

Now the Apostle Paul, you remember, was once like that himself. That is exactly what he tells us in that piece of autobiography in the third chapter of the Epistle to the Philippians. He was living a godly life according to the law and he thought he was wonderful. He was quite self-satisfied, quite pleased with himself. He thought he was pleasing God, and that all was well. But then he came to see it was all 'dung' and 'refuse' and 'loss'. Do you not see how tremendously important all this is? To say that it does not matter what people believe and that we must look at the life they live, at the sacrifices they have made and the tremendous good they have done, is to deny these two verses in Romans 12. It is really to be anti-Christian. Again, I repeat, what determines whether or not men and women are Christians is not what they do, but why they do it. And so that is the apostle's emphasis here.

In other words, here, in these two verses, we have the principles, a perfect summary, of the true biblical doctrine of sanctification. Let us see, then, how the apostle divides it up. We look first of all at the word 'therefore': 'I beseech you therefore, brethren.' There is our first division. The second will be 'by the mercies of God'. Now here, as we have said, we are dealing with the realm of motive, with what persuades us to live the Christian life. And I am not sure but that the great fight for the Christian faith over the next years is not going to be over this very thing. We are up against a great emphasis on conduct, activity, behaviour. This is where the confusion comes in and here is the only answer – the motive.

Paul divides the subject into two sections. The first is the appeal to the mind, the appeal to the understanding – 'therefore'. Now what does he mean by this word? Let me first put it negatively. Paul says that the Christian does not live the good life as a kind of mechanical obedience to a law. This, again, is a crucial point. Christians live as they do, not merely to conform to a pattern, not simply because others are doing so, or because others have told them to do so. There are many Christians who do that, are there not? They are taken to a meeting, they claim to be converted, and then they are told, 'Well, then, now you have been converted, and you are a Christian, stop doing this, and start doing that.' And they obey.

But they do not know why they are obeying. They do not understand. They have been given a number of rules and regulations. They have been told that all who belong to this particular group live in this way. So they fall into the same pattern of behaviour, and they cannot give a reason, except that this is the thing to do in this circle. They used to belong to other circles and conformed to other patterns. Before conversion, in the world, they did all the things the world does, they drank, they danced, they even did terrible things, but now they have taken up this other way of life. They have switched over from one behavioural pattern to another.

But that, according to the apostle, is all wrong. You should never act unintelligently. You should never live in a certain way without understanding why. *Therefore*, says the apostle. You must have a reason; your mind must be in control. Paul's 'therefore' means that our behaviour is to be rational. So do not live the Christian life mechanically. Do not allow anybody to put you back under the law.

The law says, 'Do this.'

You say, 'Why should I?'

The law answers, 'Do not ask questions.'

There are many parents who answer their children like that, are there not? 'Because I say so.' Perhaps up to a given age that is all right, but if you go on doing that you will get disaster.

You must explain. You must give reasons. So that is one of the negatives.

But let me take another negative. The word 'therefore' also tells us that the Christian life, the life of sanctification, is not an experience to be received. This, again, is a popular teaching. There are people who say, 'You have received your justification by faith, now take your sanctification by faith also.' They say, 'You can get it. You can go into a meeting unsanctified and come out sanctified. You receive it in an experience.' That kind of teaching is not recent – John Wesley started it and it has continued in various forms ever since. I think it is simply an intellectual confusion. People have had a genuine experience but they should not call it sanctification.

Now let us be clear about this. Experiences can, of course, be a tremendous help to sanctification. Every rich experience promotes sanctification, but it is not sanctification itself. You must not say that you 'receive' your sanctification. Paul's word 'beseech' negates that immediately, and the 'therefore' does the same.

But let us go on. We also see in the third place under this negative heading that the living of the Christian life must never be represented as a passive abiding in Christ. Here again is another popular teaching. People say, 'The mistake you make, you see, is to make an effort. You are striving. You are struggling. You must not do that. You must do nothing. Hand everything over. Let go. Be passive. Let it all be done for you. *You* cannot do it – you have nothing. Indeed, you are not asked to do anything.'

Now that teaching has been very popular but where does the 'therefore' come in? It is excluded. That is why I feel these negatives are so important. If those teachings were right the apostle would never have used the words 'I beseech you' or 'therefore'. There is no room for them in those various teachings, but here, they are at the very centre, they are the foundation of the apostle's presentation of the doctrine of sanctification.

Indeed, I can go further. If those other teachings were true, then the apostle would not have written Romans chapters 12 to 16. Having finished chapter 11, he would merely have said, 'Very well; now that you have got all that by faith, there is only one other step for you to take. Take your sanctification by faith also. Stop doing anything.' And he would have finished his letter. But here he is – 'therefore'. And he works out in detail how the Christian life must be lived, with argument, logical deduction and pressure. So these principles are of very great importance. Our business is to be guided by the Scripture and this is the scriptural way of sanctification.

What, then, is sanctification, positively? It is all in this word 'therefore' and it means that Christian conduct must be the outworking of the teaching: always, invariably. 'I beseech you therefore' – in the light of what? And this is interesting. 'I beseech you therefore, brethren, *by the mercies of God* . . .' Now there are some who seem to think that the apostle by his 'therefore' is only referring to what he has just been saying in chapter 11, but that is patently wrong. He does include that chapter but what he is saying is this: 'In the light of all I have been saying to you since verse 16 in chapter 1, now then, "I beseech you." ' The word 'therefore' looks back to the whole of the great doctrinal teaching that we have been considering in the first eleven chapters. And this is what marks off Christian behaviour from every other kind of ethical living. It is all the result of this great doctrine.

Let me summarize that doctrine for you: it is the doctrine of the fall; the doctrine of man made in the image of God and falling, sinning against Him. That was the first chapter of Romans, that is the condition of the Gentiles. 'Because that, when they knew God, they glorified him not as God, neither were thankful; but became vain in their imaginations . . .' [*Rom.* 1:21]. Why is the world in a mess? That is the whole answer: they 'worshipped and served the creature more than the Creator' (verse 25). So this is what determines how I live and how I behave. I see at once, because of this doctrine, that I have been living the life I have been living because I am a fallen creature, because I have sinned against God, because Adam sinned and fell.

Had you ever realized that before? You must realize, first and foremost, why you have ever sinned, why you have ever lived that old worldly life. According to the apostle, it is that realization that brings you to Christian living. And then you realize that men and women are awakened by the law to see that they are under condemnation. They try to live a better life, and they try to save themselves and to reconcile themselves to God, but they cannot do it. As long as they think that they can, they are not Christians and they are not living the Christian life. No, no, Christians are people who come to understand that there is only one way of salvation – 'But now . . .' [*Rom.* 3:21]. Justification by faith only. It is the only way.

Justification means that now God has taken our sin, and our failure, and put it on His Son and punished Him for it. In the light of that, He can graciously and freely pardon us and reconcile us unto Himself. We do nothing, we only believe. We are 'justified by faith without [apart from] the deeds of the law' [*Rom.* 3:28].

So the apostle's contention, and it is the simple truth, is that men and women can never live the Christian life unless they understand justification by faith only. It is only those who are justified by faith who can live this life. As he says in Ephesians 2:10: 'For we are his workmanship, created in Christ Jesus unto good works.' That is the order. But then, as we have seen, Paul does not stop with the doctrine of justification. Having dealt with that, he goes on to deal with the doctrine of our union with Christ. We were in Adam and we failed in him, but as we were in Adam, even so we are in Christ. Joined to Adam, joined to Christ; dead with Adam, alive with Christ. You remember chapters 5 and 6 – oh, the wonder of it all!

So Christian men and women live the Christian life because of all this. It is this that gives them their motive. They are now 'in Christ' and they know they have got there because they have been chosen. So Paul gives us the great doctrines of predestination, calling and sanctification – they are all here in Romans. The apostle says, 'In the light of all that . . .' But he does not stop at sanctification. He goes on to sonship. 'For as many as are led by the Spirit of God, they are the sons of God' [*Rom.* 8:14]. God has put His Spirit in our hearts, 'whereby we cry, Abba, Father' [8:15]. Here is 'the new man' in Christ Jesus. Christians are born again, they have this new nature. The Spirit of God is in them, and working in them, and they are led by the Spirit. This is why they want to live the good life, and this is how they live it.

And then Paul writes about how we will be kept going. He

says that we will be preserved: 'the final perseverance of the saints'. 'Whom he justified, them he also glorified' [8:30]; nothing 'shall be able to separate us from the love of God' [8:39]; 'The sufferings of this present time are not worthy to be compared with the glory which shall be revealed in us' [8:18]. We are 'the children of God'; we are 'joint-heirs with Christ' [8:17]. We are being prepared for glory. There is a glorious inheritance beyond death and the grave. Christ is coming again. He will establish His kingdom and we will be in it. That is what Paul has been putting before us. And then he has worked out how this will happen to the Jews and to the Gentiles – by means of God's great plan of redemption in our blessed Lord and Saviour Jesus Christ. That is the content of the word 'therefore'. Paul has been laying it out, opening it out for us. Then he says: Well then, in the light of that, 'I beseech you . . .'

Let me put it, then, in the form of some principles. Our conduct as Christians is always a deduction from our doctrine. Now this apostle is very fond of saying that. He says it in a most beautiful manner in Philippians 1:27: 'Only let your conversation be as it becometh the gospel of Christ.' 'Becometh' there means, 'Let it be fitting'. One thinks of the illustration of a lady's dress. One asks: Is it becoming? Is it appropriate? It is not fitting for an older lady to dress like a young girl. Do the different parts of the outfit match? Paul says: Only let your conduct, your behaviour, 'be as it becometh the gospel of Christ.' Let it be an indication of it; let it match it.

Or take the way our Lord Himself put it. He said, 'The truth shall make you free' – and it is only the truth that does set us free, nothing else. 'If ye continue in my word, then are ye my disciples indeed; ye shall know the truth, and the truth shall make you free' [*John* 8:31-32]. Or take His prayer in John 17: 'Sanctify them through thy truth: thy word is truth' [*John* 17:17]. That is the way to be sanctified; it is always by the truth. So, I repeat, conduct is always a deduction from doctrine.

Secondly, conduct and doctrine must never be separated. This is most important from the standpoint of evangelism. There is a form of evangelism that divides these off from one another and says, 'Now all you must do tonight is come to Christ and get forgiven.' You can have that alone, as it were.

There is no mention of anything else. That is false evangelism because it does not include any law. True evangelism always suggests the whole of the doctrine. It always has an element of law and of condemnation. It always has a reference to God. There is a superficial evangelism which puts the gospel entirely in terms of human beings. Are you unhappy? Are you worried? Do you want this or that? Come to Christ and you will get it. And so people come. They have never trembled under the holy law of God, and that is because they were never taught it. 'Well,' they say, 'I'm all right now, I'm forgiven.' And they are negligent about their conduct. They have not realized its importance because they do not know why a person is saved.

Thirdly, the conduct of Christian men and women should always be inevitable in the light of their doctrine. The 'therefore' suggests that. Let me put it like this to you. There is a term we sometimes use called *antinomianism*. People who are content only with an intellectual understanding of the gospel are guilty of antinomianism. They say, 'I see the truth, I believe it, I'm saved now. It doesn't matter, in a sense, what I do. If I'm saved, I'm saved.' People who believe in election are particularly prone to fall into this terrible sin.

And the trouble with such people is that they have never really understood the doctrine. The fact that they can say that they know the doctrine of God and the doctrine of the fall and the doctrine of justification by faith only, and election and all the other great doctrines, while their conduct is not affected to the slightest extent, means that either they have not understood the doctrines or they are lunatics! Fancy glorying in a knowledge of doctrine which does not affect your life! The thing is ludicrous.

Now the apostle has dealt with all this in chapter 6. He has been laying down his great doctrine and he imagines somebody saying, 'What shall we say, then? Shall we continue in sin that grace may abound?' 'God forbid,' says the apostle. 'How shall we that are dead to sin, live any longer therein?' [*Rom.* 6:1–2]. If you so twist your doctrine as to excuse bad behaviour, then, my dear friend, you need to be taught about doctrine. You have not understood it. You have taken it up in a kind of detached, theoretical manner, but it has never laid hold of you.

No, no, conduct should be inevitable. Antinomianism is excluded.

But another way I would like to put it is this, and here is a very good test of our position. Do you resent the New Testament teaching on sanctification? Do you tend to kick against the discipline of the Christian life? Do you feel that it is a rather hard and narrow life? You say, 'I want to be a Christian. I want to be forgiven. Of course, I want to go to heaven. But I cannot see that I must not do this and must do that.' At the present time, we frequently come across a whittling down of the high moral standards of the New Testament and the excusing of undisciplined conduct in many realms and departments. People apparently find the commandments of God grievous. But the Christian should not. The Christian says, 'It is inevitable, therefore I must live like this. I don't argue about this. I can see that one follows the other as night follows day.'

The Apostle John says, 'His commandments are not grievous' [1 John 5:3], and if we find them so, are we Christians at all? What is the matter with us? Are we born again? Have we understood the doctrine? Have we understood the real reason for salvation? These things are very important. You say, 'I've got the doctrine taped. I've got it all.' Have you? I will soon tell whether you have or not. There is never anything glib about the understanding of doctrine. True doctrine inevitably shows itself in the way we live.

And, fourthly, the doctrine always determines in detail the exact nature of our conduct. Christians always know why they must behave in a given manner. It is always a deduction from the truth.

Then, lastly, it is this doctrine alone that shows me two things: first, why I should live this good life. My motives are not utilitarian or prudent. No, no! These are the reasons for trying to live a Christian life: I am a child of God and I have the hope of glory. The Apostle John says, 'And every man that hath this hope in him purifieth himself, even as he is pure' [1 John 3:3]. If I say that I am looking forward to meeting Him and seeing Him as He is and then still go on living anyhow, somehow, I am contradicting myself. Doctrine! All the mighty doctrine of these early chapters shows us why we should live this Christian life.

Secondly, the doctrine shows us the only way in which this life can be lived. Because if you set up the Sermon on the Mount and try to live it in your own strength, you will soon find you cannot do it. The doctrine tells us that the Spirit is in us. The apostle has put it for us in chapter 7 in these words: 'When we were in the flesh, the motions of sins, which were by the law, did work in our members to bring forth fruit unto death. But now we are delivered from the law, that being dead wherein we were held; that we should serve in newness of spirit, and not in the oldness of the letter' [*Romans* 7: 5-6]. Again, in chapter 8 he says: 'The law of the Spirit of life in Christ Jesus hath made me free from the law of sin and death' (verse 2). Christ has died 'that the righteousness of the law might be fulfilled in us, who walk not after the flesh, but after the Spirit' (verse 4). We are 'led by the Spirit of God' (verse 14), and the power of the Spirit of God is in us. 'If ye through the Spirit do mortify the deeds of the body, ye shall live' (verse 13).

There, then, are the first principles, or the first subdivision of this first great principle. Here is the motive for living this life. My mind sees it in the doctrines; it is inevitable in the light of those. I have not seen the doctrine clearly unless it has led to this 'therefore'. My understanding of the doctrine is the motive and the controlling power in my living of the sanctified life in Christ Jesus.

Three

*

> *I beseech you therefore, brethren, by the mercies of God, that ye present your bodies a living sacrifice, holy, acceptable unto God, which is your reasonable service. And be not conformed to this world: but be ye transformed by the renewing of your mind, that ye may prove what is that good, and acceptable, and perfect, will of God.*
>
> Romans 12:1–2

We ended the last study by saying that it is the doctrine alone which shows us why we should live the Christian life, and how it is possible to live it. This is our contention as Christian people – that nobody can live this kind of life except the Christian. That is our answer to the humanists. Humanism is bound to fail, indeed it is failing, and herein lies our opportunity. Our contention is that it is no use telling men and women what they are to do, for they cannot do it. What humanity needs is not knowledge and information, it is power.

There are people who know exactly what they ought to be doing but they do not do it. I have often put the argument like this. Any doctor knows all about the evil effects of the over-consumption of alcohol, but that does not mean that there has never been a doctor who has not been guilty of taking too much alcohol; often it is quite the reverse. Knowledge is essential, but it is not enough. The whole problem of the human race is not the problem of knowledge, it is the problem of power, and here is the only answer. Here alone are we shown why we *should* live this kind of life and here alone are we shown how we *can* live it.

So it all comes to this: we must start by realizing who we are and what we are. It is the old story of the message of Horatio Nelson on the morning of the Battle of Trafalgar: 'England expects that every man this day will do his duty.' Duty is something that is applied; the honour of the school, the honour of the family. As a Christian you are a child of God. You are not only reconciled to God and forgiven, you have been 'born again', you are 'in Christ', you have a new nature, a new outlook and the Spirit of God is in you. Paul has been telling us all this.

That, then, is the way to approach the question of conduct and behaviour. You do not just start with individual problems or questions, you start by reminding yourself who you are, and then you deduce your doctrine from that. That is the first thing.

In other words, the first great motive for Christian living is intellectual; it begins with the mind. Christians do not merely live according to their feelings and impulses; they are governed by their understanding of truth. They know who they are, and they realize that they must behave accordingly. That is the 'therefore', the intellectual argument for living this life.

But there is a second great motive here. 'I beseech you therefore, brethren, *by the mercies of God*'. Here is a motive which is not intellectual; here is one which appeals to the heart. The appeal of the gospel is never only to the intellect, it always includes the emotions – the heart. And how essential it is that we should emphasize this. People who give the impression that theology is as dry as dust show either that they do not know their theology or that they are very bad teachers. There is no such thing as dry-as-dust theology. True theology always moves the heart, it always brings this second great appeal, this second great motive for living the Christian life.

Here, again, is something that is unique to the Christian faith and that, once more, is where humanists are shown to be so defective. They have no emotional appeal; theirs is a purely intellectual attitude. They are the learned people, the people with brains, as they are never tired of telling us. They look out upon life and they say, 'It's common sense not to get drunk; it's common sense not to fight; it's common sense not to do this and that.' That is their diagnosis, which they come to with an intellectual detachment.

[31]

The final trouble with the humanists is that they are cold; there is no warmth about them and they cannot help a poor sinner because they have no sympathy. They despise him because he is not using his brains. They are what they are because they apply their intellects. There is never anything about them at which a poor sinner can warm the hands of his soul. There is no heart in their pronouncements, and that is why we are eventually going to show them that their whole position is wrong, even intellectually. It does not merely break down in practice, it is wrong in its theory because it does not take up the whole person. But Christianity does. Christianity is concerned as much with the heart as with the head.

You find an illustration of the Christian's reaction in the Old Testament, in Psalm 116:12: 'What shall I render unto the Lord for all his benefits toward me?' That is a man speaking not from his head, though that is included, but from his heart. Really, it is the Old Testament summary of what the apostle is saying here, especially in the phrase, 'by the mercies of God'.

Now it is interesting to notice that the apostle puts the word in the plural: not 'by the *mercy* of God' but 'by the *mercies* of God' and I think his reason is that though ultimately the mercy of God is one, yet it manifests itself in many different ways. So as we look at God's mercy in terms of the benefits that we receive, we regard it as something plural and we talk, therefore, about 'the mercies of God'. Not only does it come in different ways, it comes at different times. It comes every day, it comes repeatedly. So it is quite natural that Paul should have used the plural instead of the singular.

But what is mercy? You constantly find this word in the Bible and, perhaps, the best way of approaching it is to turn to the salutations in the epistles and particularly in the so-called 'pastoral epistles' to Timothy and Titus, where there is a kind of formula: 'Grace, mercy, and peace from God the Father'. What is the difference between grace and mercy? It is an important distinction. Grace is that quality in God that disposes Him to be kind to people who do not deserve kindness. Grace is gratuitous kindness, and it is because God is a God of grace, 'the God of all grace' that there is any possibility at all of a way of salvation.

Alongside this, mercy means the pity of God for our

condition. Grace is that disposition that enables God to do anything for us, who do not deserve anything good, but mercy means that God, having looked upon our state and condition, is sorry for us and pities us. John Milton wrote:

> *He hath, with a piteous eye*
> *Looked upon our misery.*

That is exactly what is meant by mercy. The whole hymn, the whole paraphrase, is on this question of mercy.

> *For His mercies aye endure,*
> *Ever faithful, ever sure.*

This is a perfect definition. The great eternal God has looked down upon His creation, and upon humanity in particular. He has seen not only our folly and our sinfulness and our rebellion, but has seen that we have brought our miserable condition upon ourselves, and He has had pity upon us. So the apostle is here reminding us that all the benefits of salvation which we enjoy are entirely and solely the result of this pity, this mercy.

Paul has been making a point of this at the end of the eleventh chapter and that is undoubtedly why it is in his mind here in verse 1 of chapter 12. Take, for instance, verses 30 and 31 of chapter 11. The apostle says, 'For as ye in times past have not believed God, yet have now obtained mercy through their unbelief: even so have these also now not believed, that through your mercy they also may obtain mercy.' Paul describes the Christian as one who has obtained mercy. Christians are those upon whom God has looked 'with a piteous eye'. He has felt sorry for them, and has delivered them. And this is not all. Our justification is the result of God's mercy; our sanctification and our future glorification will be entirely the result of God's mercy; and so are all the other benefits and blessings of salvation which are summarized in this one word 'therefore'.

All the doctrine that we have considered comes out of this mercy. The argument is stated very frequently in the Old Testament, as I have already reminded you, and particularly in the psalms. Take Psalm 103, where it is put like this: 'Like as a father pitieth his children, so the Lord pitieth them that fear him. For he knoweth our frame . . .' (verses 13–14). 'He hath not dealt with us after our sins; nor rewarded us according to our iniquities. For as the heaven is high above the earth, so great is his mercy toward them that fear him' (verses 10–11).

You find the same thought again in Psalm 130:3–4: 'If thou, Lord, shouldest mark iniquities, O Lord, who shall stand? But there is forgiveness with thee' – and this, again, is the result of the mercy – 'there is forgiveness with thee, that thou mayest be feared.' Now you notice that there are two statements – and that is what is so wonderful. These two things always go together. 'There is forgiveness with thee'; 'that thou mayest be feared'. 'By the mercies of God I beseech you,' says Paul, to live this kind of life. It is exactly the same argument. Those who truly realize the mercy of God are those who will show it.

This is the whole appeal of the apostle here. He says in effect, 'If you want to show your gratitude to God for His many mercies towards you, this is the way. You thank Him not only with your lips, but still more with your lives. There is nothing that pleases God more than to see His people giving proof of the fact that they are His people, demonstrating to the world the power of God unto salvation. It rejoices the heart of God.' And this is the way that we must look at the demands of the New Testament teaching for good conduct and for holiness. It is not merely that we should see that sin is irrational, and that it is a contradiction of what we claim to believe, but we must increasingly think of sin as base ingratitude. It just means that we are ready to take everything but do not even thank God for it.

So there is a double argument here and it is very powerful. The will is determined ultimately by the mind and by the heart. There is no need to make too direct an appeal to the will because a changed will is the outcome of having understood the truth and having felt it. Here are the motives, the mind and heart motives, and if we are deficient in one or the other, it is very serious. So the apostle is saying that our minds and our hearts, in unison and jointly, should be urging us to live this Christian life to the glory of God and thereby we show our understanding and our gratitude.

This can never be emphasized too strongly. What a tragedy it is that so often we deal with these problems of conduct in a piecemeal, almost legalistic manner. I have to say this in private as much as I have to say it from the pulpit. The great thing with all these problems is to put them into their setting, into their context. The way to overcome temptation and sin is, primarily, to realize who you are and what you are, and what you owe to God. Those are the grand motives whereby you can deal with any sin.

And so the gospel lifts up the whole problem of conduct to a high spiritual level. Nothing and no one else does that at all: not humanists, not moralists, not philosophers, not sociologists, not educationalists – none of them. They know nothing about these two grandest motives. That is why all their systems fail. The world today gives absolute proof of this. Look at Britain and look at America. Their moral deterioration is becoming increasingly evident. What is the cause? There is only one explanation: about the middle of the nineteenth century men and women, in their cleverness, turned their backs on God and have done so in increasing numbers ever since. 'We can achieve everything,' they said, 'by education. We need not believe in God. Tell man what to do and he will do it. Man has it in him. Believe in man!' And you see the result. The two great motives for true living are entirely ignored and the world today is proving the truth of the apostle's words in these two verses.

So, having seen our motives, having listened to Paul's appeal to us as 'brethren', we now come to the next division, which is this: How are we to live this Christian life? That is the great question that every true Christian invariably asks. What is the manner of this life? How is it to be carried out in practice? And here, again, the apostle has a complete answer for us: '. . . that ye present your bodies a living sacrifice, holy, acceptable unto God, which is your reasonable service. And be not conformed to this world: but be ye transformed by the renewing of your mind.'

The first thing we must realize about the practical out-working of this argument, this great motive, is the principle that we must make a complete surrender of ourselves, body, soul and spirit, to God. Here is how Paul puts it: 'present your bodies'; then, 'be not conformed to this world' – that refers to what I would call the mind, or, if you prefer, the soulish part of man – 'but be ye transformed by the renewing of your mind', which is the spirit, as I shall show you. So it is a totalitarian demand. We must yield ourselves entirely to God. And the words 'reasonable service' – suggest exactly the same thing.

Half the battle is to grasp this great principle. Notice that the apostle puts it to us by using an Old Testament analogy: you present, he says, a sacrifice, and this is your worship, this is your service. Now in the Old Testament, in the book of Leviticus in particular, there is a great deal about the worship of God and the presentation of offerings and sacrifices. Paul, writing to the Thessalonians, reminds them 'how ye turned to God from idols to serve the living and true God' [*1 Thess.* 1:9]. It is the same idea – our new life is a life of service and of worship. The apostle takes up the Old Testament analogy of the offerings in order to make his point plain.

Paul is rather fond of this analogy. Let me give you one other example from his letter to the Philippians. In chapter 2 verse 17 Paul writes, 'Yea, and if I be offered upon the sacrifice and service of your faith, I joy, and rejoice with you all.' Now the language which he used in the original is this: 'If I am to be poured out [if my blood is to be poured out] upon the sacrifice and service of your faith, I am very happy about it all.' Paul is speaking in terms of the Old Testament analogy of what happened when certain offerings were made. The priests would prepare the offering, and then would pour oil and wine upon it. So Paul says that he is ready to be 'offered' in that way upon their sacrifice. That is an illustration of how the apostle takes up terminology that would be familiar to Jews who had become Christians, and was perhaps becoming familiar to Gentile Christians too as they went on in their lives in the Christian church.

So what does it mean? We must start with this great word 'present': 'that you present yourselves'. The apostle has already used this Greek word but it has not been translated as 'present' in our previous encounters with it. Go back to Romans 6 and there you will find him using this same word in verses 13, 16 and 19. In verse 13 the Authorized [King James] Version reads: 'Neither *yield* ye your members as instruments of unrighteousness unto sin: but *yield* yourselves unto God, as those that are alive from the dead, and your members as instruments of righteousness unto God.' An even better rendering is: 'Do not *present* your members as instruments of unrighteousness unto sin, but *present* yourselves unto God, as those that are alive from the dead, and *present* the members of your body as instruments of righteousness unto God.'

Then take verse 16: 'Know ye not, that to whom ye *yield* yourselves servants to obey, his servants ye are to whom ye obey; whether of sin unto death, or of obedience unto righteousness?' Paul is saying, 'Do you not know that to whomsoever you *present* yourselves as servants to obey, you are his servants, you are the servants of the one whom you are thus obeying, whether it is sin unto death, or obedience unto righteousness.' You present yourself as a servant to a master.

And you have the word again in verse 19: 'I speak,' Paul says, 'after the manner of men because of the infirmity of your flesh.' He is saying: Because of your difficulty in following what I am saying, I am going to use a simple illustration. 'For as ye have *yielded* your members servants to uncleanness and to iniquity unto iniquity; even so now *yield* your members servants to righteousness unto holiness.' Again, the translation should be 'present': 'For as you have *presented* your members servants to uncleanness and to iniquity unto iniquity; even so now *present* your [these same] members servants to righteousness unto holiness.'

Present! It is a most interesting word. It recalls the Old Testament practice regarding the burnt offerings and sacrifices. It is the classical term used to denote the laying of the sacrificial animal upon the altar. But it is used not only in the Old Testament but also in the so-called mystery religions. As you know, there were many other religions besides Judaism that had burnt offerings and sacrifices. In these religions, too, priests would take an animal and kill it and lay the body upon the altar. So the word came to have the meaning of putting oneself at somebody else's disposal. As you put the animal's body on the altar, so you put yourself upon the altar of God.

So the word 'present' in Romans 12:1 means that we put ourselves unreservedly at God's disposal; that as this animal's body was put upon the altar for an entire offering to God, so we must offer ourselves entirely to God. We must make a sacrifice of ourselves to God in the sense of presenting ourselves to Him.

This is a wonderful picture, as I think you will see. But, of course, as with every picture, it has its dangers and pitfalls and we must be careful that we do not abuse, misinterpret or misunderstand this word. It must not be taken in a literal sense to mean that I can propitiate God by offering myself. It is the exact opposite of that. The New Testament teaching is that Christ is the one and only sacrifice and offering, and that He has offered and presented Himself once and for ever to God on the cross on Calvary's hill. 'There remaineth no more sacrifice for sins' [*Heb.* 10:26].

So we must not err in this, as people have often done in the long history of the church. There have been people who have said that we are told quite plainly that if we only make this sacrifice of ourselves, God will be propitiated and will be well pleased with us. That is to deny the whole of the New Testament teaching. There are many people doing that today, but that is justification by works, the kind of thing that the apostle is answering in 1 Corinthians 13:1: 'Though I speak with the tongues of men and of angels . . . though I give my body to be burned . . .' No, it is no good, says Paul, unless I have love. Indeed, your whole motive is wrong. There has been one sacrifice for ever.

So the apostle is not telling us here that we can save ourselves by offering ourselves to God. This is an illustration; the apostle is using figurative language. He says in effect, 'Now I am taking this idea of sacrifice, and I want to use it. I want you to see that you must now do something comparable with yourselves. Because of the mercies of God, because Christ is the one and only offering, because everything has been done, now you must present yourselves in this way to God.' With that in mind, what is the argument, what is the appeal? It is a very important one. Indeed, I venture to say again that it is one of the most vital of all, not only with regard to daily conduct, but also with regard to the whole question of ecumenicity and fraternizing with Rome in particular. We must be very careful.

So let us be clear about the argument. It is that we are always 'slaves'; there is never a time in our lives when we are not slaves. We have already considered this in chapter 6 verse 17: 'But God be thanked, that ye were the servants [the slaves] of sin, but ye have obeyed from the heart that form of doctrine which was delivered you.' The apostle, you see, has said it all before but here he is saying it again. That is the essence of teaching. We are so dull that it has to be repeated. 'God be thanked, that ye were [once] the slaves of sin' – what has happened to you? – 'but ye have obeyed from the heart that form of doctrine which was delivered you.'

I say, therefore, that we must realize that we are always slaves. It is very difficult for us to realize this, is it not, but it is the truth. By nature we are all the slaves of sin and the slaves of Satan, every one of us. 'You were the servants [the slaves] of sin.' We were under the dominion of Satan. That is true of the whole of humanity. The chief consequence of the Fall was that men and women became the slaves of the devil and of evil and of sin; so we are born slaves. But the apostle's argument here is that we now enter into a new slavery.

Now I need not stop, need I, to prove that first contention that we were always slaves? Our Lord taught exactly the same thing: 'Ye are of your father the devil' [*John* 8:44]. 'When a strong man armed keepeth his palace, his goods are in peace' [*Luke* 11:21]. That is the slavery, and humanity is in slavery to the devil. But here the apostle says that something has happened; we are in a new position. He is telling us here that as we were once the helpless, hopeless slaves of sin and evil and the devil, we are now to become the voluntary slaves of God and of His Christ. We are still slaves but it is an entirely different form of slavery. If you read Paul's epistles, you will find that he is very fond of referring to himself like this: 'Paul, a servant of Jesus Christ' [*Rom.* 1:1]. That is the Authorized Version, but the correct translation there is this: 'Paul, the bondslave of Jesus Christ'. That is how he likes to describe himself.

And it is the simple truth concerning us. We are never free. Everybody in the world tonight is either the slave of sin and Satan or else the slave of Jesus Christ. Paul says to the Corinthians, 'Know ye not that . . . ye are not your own? For ye are bought with a price' [*1 Cor.* 6:19–20]. You have been bought from one master; you now are the possession of another

Master. You are the slaves of Jesus Christ. He has redeemed you. He has purchased you. He has bought you out of the market. He has bought you at the price of His own precious blood, and you belong to Him. You have no right to go on living that life. You are not your own; you are a slave. That is the argument.

Of course, we must put this in the right way. There is one vital difference, and this is why Paul 'beseeches' them. As I indicated above, this is a voluntary slavery, a slavery in which one delights. You are not forced into this slavery, but you want it. That is Paul's argument. As a famous phrase in the Prayer Book puts it, 'Whose service is perfect freedom' – or, if you like, 'Slavery to whom is perfect freedom.' Present yourself, argues Paul at this point – hand yourself over. That is, put yourself in the position of being a slave. You are renouncing your right to yourself. It now belongs to somebody else.

Let me put this to you in the form of a story. There was once a godly Christian physician here in London, a Dr A.T. Schofield, and I think he put this truth very well in an incident that he wrote about in one of his books. He tells us that he once owned a dog which he used to take out for walks. The dog was young and, of course, he was on a leash. There was the dog straining at the leash, wanting to get free. After training the dog for some time, Dr Schofield felt that he could now allow him a little freedom. So one day, after they had walked for a certain distance, he unfastened the leash and off went the dog. In his new-found freedom, he rushed about wherever he liked, and soon raced right out of sight. But he did not remain long out of sight; he came back to Dr Schofield and then continued to trot by the side of his master.

There was no leash, the dog was absolutely free, but in that escapade, in that great thrilling moment of absolute freedom and independence, the dog had made some great discovery. Perhaps he had been frightened by other dogs, or perhaps somebody had cursed at him or thrown a stone at him or beaten him with a stick, I don't know, but the dog, somehow or other, had come to the conclusion that the essence of wisdom as far as he was concerned was to trot by the side of his master – he was choosing to do it. That was a voluntary slavery. He wanted to be there under his master's control and guidance. Somehow he had come to understand that it was the best thing for him.

That is exactly what the apostle is saying here. 'I beseech you,' he says. In a sense you are free, but then in this other sense you go into a voluntary submission and hand yourself over to God because of His great mercy with respect to you, and because this is right for you, and best for you. All that is in this wonderful word 'present'.

Now we come to our next word, which at this point I shall just introduce. 'That ye present your *bodies* a living sacrifice, holy, acceptable unto God.' What does Paul mean by 'bodies'? The commentators are disagreed. Charles Hodge is quite sure that here the word 'body' does not mean literal body. When you talk about the body, he says, you are really referring to the whole person. You may sometimes say that there were a given number of bodies at a meeting, meaning a given number of people. The body is the whole personality, represented by, and in and through the physical body. But Robert Haldane disagrees and says that Paul means the literal body, and I myself, without any hesitation, am in entire agreement with Robert Haldane.

Why? Well, I feel that Paul's words in verse 2 make this view imperative. In that verse Paul goes on to say, 'Be not conformed to this world.' Now the part of us that is related to the world and its people is not the body but the soul. Our relationships with other people, and with animals even, is a matter of the soul; so I suggest that in verse 2 Paul is talking about the soul. And then when you come to 'be transformed by the renewing of your mind', I suggest, as I shall try to prove to you, that there Paul is dealing with the spirit. The same apostle, in Ephesians 4:23, talks about being 'renewed in the spirit of your mind', and that is undoubtedly a reference to our spirit. So I argue that the sense of verse 2 and the analogy of Scripture insist upon our interpreting 'body' here in verse 1 as the literal body.

We have already seen, away back in chapter 6, that the apostle talks about the body as a physical body and he is concerned about it and interested in it. Take, for instance, chapter 6 verses 12 and 13: 'Let not sin therefore reign in your mortal body' – he does not mean your total personality, he literally means your flesh – 'that ye should obey it in the lusts

[41]

thereof. Neither yield ye your members . . .' – he is talking about the parts of the physical body.

Then in Romans 8 verses 12 and 13 we find exactly the same thing. Paul says, 'Therefore, brethren, we are debtors, not to the flesh, to live after the flesh. For if ye live after the flesh, ye shall die: but if ye through the Spirit do mortify the deeds of the body, ye shall live.' Paul is talking there specifically about the body. It is the same in Colossians 3:5 – 'Mortify therefore your members which are upon the earth.' That is a direct reference, as the context proves, to the body. The apostle is very interested in the body, and later on I shall give you, God willing, the reasons for this.

Again an explicit statement with respect to the physical body appears in 1 Corinthians 6: 'What? know ye not that your body is the temple of the Holy Ghost which is in you, which ye have of God, and ye are not your own? For ye are bought with a price: therefore glorify God in your body, and in your spirit, which are God's [*1 Cor.* 6:19–20]. Beyond any question 'body' there means the physical body. Paul's whole argument is about that. 'Know ye not that your bodies are the members of Christ? shall I then take the members of Christ, and make them the members of an harlot? God forbid' [verse 15]. And he goes on to show what is really involved in the sin of fornication and it is purely a question of the physical body.

And then my last quotations are to be found in the First Epistle to the Thessalonians, in chapters 4 and 5. Look at it first in 1 Thessalonians 4:1-5. Here again Paul is dealing with conduct: 'Furthermore then we beseech you, brethren, and exhort you by the Lord Jesus, that as ye have received of us how ye ought to walk and to please God, so ye would abound more and more. For ye know what commandments we gave you by the Lord Jesus. For this is the will of God, even your sanctification, that ye should abstain from fornication: That every one of you should know how to possess his vessel in sanctification and honour; not in the lust of concupiscence, even as the Gentiles which know not God.' That is a reference to the physical body.

And then in chapter 5 verse 23 Paul has this important distinction: 'And the very God of peace sanctify you wholly; and I pray God your whole spirit and soul and body be preserved blameless unto the coming of our Lord Jesus Christ.' There is the threefold division. Here in Romans 12 we have exactly the same division, only the apostle has put it the other way round – 'body' first, 'soul' second, 'spirit' third.

Those are my reasons for saying that on this occasion I am in entire agreement with Robert Haldane as against Charles Hodge. And if you want a final proof, it is that, as we have seen, the apostle is using here an analogy from the Old Testament sacrificial system, and there you will remember that the priests not only offered the blood – 'For the life of the flesh is in the blood' [*Lev.* 17:11] – but they also offered the body. The body of the beast was put upon the altar: it was a whole burnt offering, not only the spiritual element, as it were, but the physical body. And as that is the analogy which is in the apostle's mind, it seems to me that that is the final proof and confirmation of the rightness of the interpretation which says that here he is telling us, and exhorting and beseeching us, to present our literal, physical body as a living sacrifice upon the altar of God, the God whose mercy towards us has been so great as to make us participators in this glorious salvation.

Four

> *I beseech you therefore, brethren, by the mercies of God, that ye present your bodies a living sacrifice, holy, acceptable unto God, which is your reasonable service. And be not conformed to this world: but be ye transformed by the renewing of your mind, that ye may prove what is that good, and acceptable, and perfect, will of God.*
>
> Romans 12:1–2

We have been considering this great word 'present': 'present your bodies'. The word 'present', as I told you, is a technical term for the offering of sacrifices to God. Paul is, therefore, telling us to offer ourselves to God, to hand ourselves over as slaves to Him.

But then we saw that Paul takes this in detail. He starts by saying that we must offer our bodies to God, and we ended the last chapter by arguing that when the apostle says here 'bodies' he means our physical bodies. But why should we stress this? Why is it important that, in addition to saying that I surrender myself to God, I must, in particular, surrender my body, my physical frame, to God?

Let me give you some reasons, which I think are most important, and which will help us all in the great fight of faith, this endeavour to live the Christian life to the glory of God who has been so merciful towards us. Why, then, the body? First, I think the apostle divides it up like this, and puts emphasis on the body, in order to stress the fact that in the Christian salvation the whole person is to be saved. It is not merely our minds that are saved, it is not merely our spirits or our hearts, the body is also saved. It is a complete salvation, and I think that this is of tremendous importance.

Some of you will remember that when we were studying some of these earlier chapters, we were at great pains to emphasize that. For instance, when we were in chapter 8, we read this in verse 11: 'If the Spirit of him that raised up Jesus from the dead dwell in you, he that raised up Christ from the dead shall also quicken your mortal bodies by his Spirit that dwelleth in you.' Now that is a clear statement that the body is also to be saved. Paul was really saying the same thing in verse 10 of chapter 8: 'If Christ be in you, the body is dead because of sin; but the Spirit is life because of righteousness.' That is the position now. But, he says, it is all right, for, 'If the Spirit of him that raised up Jesus from the dead [does] dwell in you, he that raised up Christ from the dead shall also quicken your mortal bodies by his Spirit that dwelleth in you.'

Again, in the twenty-third verse of that eighth chapter you have the same emphasis: 'And not only they,' Paul says, 'but ourselves also, which have the firstfruits of the Spirit, even we ourselves groan within ourselves, waiting for the adoption' – what is that? – 'to wit, the redemption of our body.' Now there 'body' means the literal, physical frame, the flesh in which we dwell, because the apostle has earlier been dealing with other aspects of the person, and yet he now says that that adoption, that 'redemption of the body', is the ultimate, the final state.

So this is a very important point and Paul really wrote the great fifteenth chapter of the First Epistle to the Corinthians to establish this same truth. There were people in the church at Corinth teaching that the resurrection was already past. They said, 'Don't be interested in the body, it doesn't matter. The important thing is that the soul and the spirit go on. The body is nothing. A man is resurrected when he becomes a Christian; the rebirth is the only resurrection.' The apostle writes that great long chapter in order to controvert that, and to point out that the Christian teaching is that the body will be raised, the body will be glorified, the body will be redeemed – our physical bodies.

When Adam fell in the Garden of Eden his body fell as well as his soul and spirit. So it is an essential part of this great salvation that the entire person is going to be saved. And the great promise we are given is that we shall be completely redeemed. At the end of Philippians chapter 3 Paul says, 'For our conversation [citizenship] is in heaven; from whence also we look for [and expect] the Saviour, the Lord Jesus Christ: who shall change our vile body [the body of our humiliation], that it may be fashioned like unto his glorious body [or the body of his glorification], according to the working whereby he is able even to subdue all things unto himself' [*Phil.* 3:20–21]. You must, therefore, never leave out the body in your ideas of redemption, so it naturally comes in here in Romans 12.

A second reason for putting an emphasis upon the physical body, I suggest, is to remind us of the inter-relationship, and the unity, of the different parts of our being. This emphasis is very necessary today and it was very necessary in the first century. There were teachers then, as there are now, who said that the body did not matter at all. 'Asceticism' is the technical term given to this teaching. Ascetics taught, and still teach, that the body in and of itself is irrelevant. They said that what really matters is I myself, as a person, a being, and they pressed this idea as far as to say that as long as I am saved, then what I do in the body does not matter at all, because the body is going to die and I will leave it. And so they excused sin in the body.

This terrible teaching was dealt with in the First Epistle of John. A man called Cerinthus, who was a famous teacher in the second half of the first century, taught this doctrine. There is a legend that the Apostle John so hated Cerinthus' teaching that once, when John was told, as he was going into the baths, that this man was also in the building, he immediately turned round and walked out. He would not even be in the same building with such a man, leave alone in the same church.

This teaching, that though I may do things that are wrong in the body, it has nothing to do with my soul, the apostle answers by showing that you must 'present' your body. Paul also, of course, makes a great point of this in many other places. He tells the Corinthians, for instance, 'Know ye not that your body is the temple of the Holy Ghost which is [dwelleth] in you' [*1 Cor.* 6:19]. That, he says, is the right view of your body. You must not despise it or say that it does not matter. Nor must you say that it does not matter what you do with your body nor say that the only sin that really counts

[46]

in the sight of God is a sin in the realm of the spirit. You must not say that, says Paul, for your body is the temple of the Holy Spirit. And once you realize that the Holy Spirit dwells in your body as a temple, then, of necessity, you will be careful what you do with that body.

But let me give you a third reason why Paul emphasizes the body. It is important that we should realize that the body, after all, is the instrument through which our souls act. The soul is not something that dwells in a vacuum. You may say, 'The important thing about me is that I am a living soul.' All right; but how is that soul going to express itself? And the answer is, of course, that the soul, the personality, the being that each one of us is, expresses itself through the body, the physical frame – through the brain, the understanding; through the organs of speech; through the eyes; through the hands and feet. We do not have a soul without a body. No, they always belong together.

Now we have seen the apostle saying all this back in chapter 6, where he puts it like this: 'Let not sin therefore reign in your mortal body, that ye should obey it in the lusts thereof.' Then notice: 'Neither yield ye your members as instruments of unrighteousness unto sin: but yield yourselves unto God, as those that are alive from the dead, and your members' – that is to say, your faculties: hands, feet, eyes, brain, all that you have in your body, yield all these – 'as instruments of righteousness unto God' (verses 12-13).

Then the fourth – and very powerful – reason is that the body is after all one of the chief sources of temptation and sin. This is what makes this subject so tremendously important and serious. People glibly say, 'I'm saved now, therefore it doesn't matter what I do in the body.' But it does. You cannot divide yourself up like that. If you start regarding your body loosely, you will soon find that your soul will be in trouble, because sin takes advantage of the body, and the greatest fight of every Christian, every born again person, is this fight against sin as it ever threatens to take over.

Now I must go back once more to the sixth chapter because it is so important. The apostle has given us a tremendous statement of our union with Christ: how we have been crucified with Him; how we have died with Him; how we have been buried with Him; how we have risen with Him, all this wonderful teaching which he sums up in verse 11 when he says, 'Likewise reckon ye also yourselves to be dead indeed unto sin, but alive unto God through Jesus Christ our Lord.' But he does not leave it at that, he does not stop there. He does something which people today would often regard as an anticlimax. It is always true of this apostle that he never leaves us with some general principle only, but brings us down to earth. So immediately he goes on in verse 12: 'Let not sin therefore reign in your mortal body, that ye should obey it in the lusts thereof.' Now I must not go back over the exposition which we gave of that great statement[1] but it means that sin is always there lurking in the body.

This, of course, is a result of the Fall. When Adam fell, as I have already reminded you, he fell totally. He fell in spirit, soul, and body; body, mind, and spirit. The whole person fell. Now in our salvation the soul and the spirit are redeemed, and, I venture to say, they are as much redeemed now as they will ever be: '. . . whom he justified, them he also glorified' [*Rom.* 8:30]. But the body is not yet redeemed. That is why the apostle says, 'We ourselves also, have the firstfruits of the Spirit, even we ourselves groan within ourselves, waiting for the adoption, to wit, the redemption of our body' [*Rom.* 8:23].

It is a great mystery, but it is a fact, that the chief seat of sin in the redeemed person is in the body. It is always there and it always wants to control us. It always wants to be 'reigning' in us, in our mortal body. So I repeat that the principle which we lay down is that if we think we can neglect presenting our bodies as a living sacrifice to God, we shall soon find that we have fallen into sin through the body, and the soul is again brought into a captivity, and sin is reigning over us.

You find the same thought in Romans 7:5: 'For when we were in the flesh, the motions of sins, which were by the law, did work in our members to bring forth fruit unto death.' And even after you are redeemed, remember that sin, 'the motions of sins', the energies of sin, are still there and they are ready at any unguarded moment to 'work in our members' – the parts of our body – 'to bring forth fruit unto death'. Sin is always there

[1] Romans: An Exposition of Chapter 6: The New Man

[48]

waiting for its opportunity to assert this mastery, ready to stir us up, as it were.

Indeed, you find the same teaching in Romans 8:12-13. Having just told his readers that the Spirit in them is a guarantee of the future resurrection of their bodies, the apostle says, 'Therefore, brethren, we are debtors, not to the flesh, to live after the flesh. For if ye live after the flesh, ye shall die: but if ye through the Spirit do mortify the deeds of the body, ye shall live.' Now when Paul says 'body' there, he means the physical body, and you notice what he says. He is writing to Christians and he is appealing to them to 'mortify', to put to death through the Spirit, 'the deeds of the body'. The body needs to be mortified because sin is ready, at any moment, to lift up its head and to gain the mastery; and we are in slavery again.

And, of course, Paul teaches this not only in the Epistle to the Romans, but in other epistles also. Notice, for instance, what he says at the beginning of the Epistle to the Ephesians, in chapter 2:1-3: 'And you hath he quickened, who were dead in trespasses and sins: wherein in time past ye walked according to the course of this world, according to the prince of the power of the air, the spirit that now worketh in the children of disobedience: among whom also we all had our conversation in times past' – notice! – 'in the lusts of our flesh, fulfilling the desires of the flesh, and of the mind.'

Now when a man or woman is born again and redeemed, the 'desires of the flesh, and of the mind' still remain and they must be watched. And that is why the apostle gives us here in Romans 12 this kind of general instruction: 'Present your bodies [as] a living sacrifice . . . ' It is the way to counteract this tendency. It is a strange thing in God's wisdom and economy that He should have left us like this, but He has. He did exactly the same with the children of Israel. When He took them from Egypt and its bondage into the land of Canaan, He did not destroy all their enemies. He left the enemies as 'pricks in your eyes' and 'thorns in your sides' [*Num.* 33:55]. He left those people there for the children of Israel to contend with. He does exactly the same with us. We are not made perfect, and, in particular, sin remains like this in the body – 'the desires of the flesh and of the mind' [*Eph.* 2:3].

Now do not misunderstand this. There is nothing wrong with the natural instincts, they are given to us by God, but because of the Fall they have a mastery over us. Look at the world as it is, dominated by sex. There is nothing wrong with sex, but it is very wrong to be dominated by it as the newspapers and television are. There the perversion comes in; it becomes a tyranny, and that is where the sexual instinct has gone wrong. The Apostle James also shows how sin attacks the Christian through the body. In his third chapter he puts it in terms of the tongue: 'Even so the tongue is a little member, and boasteth great things. Behold, how great a matter a little fire kindleth! And the tongue is a fire, a world of iniquity: so is the tongue among our members, that it defileth the whole body, and setteth on fire the course of nature; and it is set on fire of hell' [*James* 3:5-6].

You may say, 'I needn't watch my tongue. I'm redeemed now. I needn't be careful about my conversation.' But the answer given is, 'Watch this little member.' Oh, the havoc it makes! How many a soul has got into bondage again through injudicious, undisciplined talk. It is the same argument. You must watch your tongue as a Christian; you do not stop at general principles. You do not say, 'Surrender yourself now to God and leave all the rest.' Not at all. You must come down to these details.

Peter, also, writing to saints, to redeemed people, puts it in this way: 'Dearly beloved, I beseech you' – the same language as Paul uses – 'as strangers and pilgrims, abstain from fleshly lusts, which war against the soul' [*I Pet.* 2:11]. That expresses it perfectly. He is writing to Christians, remember. 'Abstain from fleshly lusts' – why? – because they 'war against the soul'. You must not neglect your body. You must not say that the body does not matter. 'Be careful,' Peter says in effect, 'abstain from fleshly lusts because if you don't they will get your soul down, they will war against it and its well-being and its knowledge of God and its receiving of blessings from Him.' So this warning is put as strongly as possible by these various writers.

But now let me put it all positively to you and sum it up as I do so. Why must I present my body as a living sacrifice? It is because I am meant to glorify God with the whole of my being,

with each and every part of it. In 1 Corinthians 6:20 the apostle
puts that even more plainly than he does here: '. . . therefore
glorify God in your body, and in your spirit, which are God's.'
You are not to glorify God only in your spirit or with your
understanding only but with your body also. The body as much
as the spirit. The whole person, the entire being, is to live and
to minister to the glory of God. The psalmist had anticipated
this: 'Bless the Lord, O my soul: and all that is within me, bless
his holy name' [*Psa.* 103:1]. Everything that is in you; it is all to
bless His holy name.

Those, it seems to me, are the five main reasons why the
apostle, after giving the general injunction, brings it down to
the particular and emphasizes the body and the importance of
surrendering the physical body to God. Oh, what shipwreck
many have made of their Christian life because they have
ignored this! The history of the church is full of the most tragic
examples and illustrations of this very thing, and yet people
still dislike and resent it. Some are only interested in doctrine,
and some only want to do the things which they feel like
doing, and are unhappy with this pressure that is brought to
bear upon them. But the pressure is here and it is the pressure
of God Himself through His servant, the Apostle Paul.

There, then, we see why Paul singles out the body. But he
does not leave it at that. He again amplifies his words, and now
tells us, in detail, about the character of the offering. 'I beseech
you therefore, brethren, by the mercies of God, that ye present
your bodies a living sacrifice.' Why does he define it as 'a living
sacrifice'? This is a most profound statement. Paul is obviously
contrasting what you and I must do, with what was done by
the children of Israel under the old dispensation. He has
borrowed the idea of sacrifice because it gives him a perfect
picture. But, of course, he is now at great pains to show that
though the general principle is the same, yet what you and I
actually have to do is very different indeed from the old way.

This is one of the differences between the old dispensation
and the new, and Paul often deals with it. The old, he says, was
in the 'letter', whereas this is 'in newness of spirit' [*Rom.* 7:6].
But in addition to that, in the old dispensation the priests used
to kill the animal and then put its dead body upon the altar.
And the apostle is telling us here that we do not present dead

bodies, but we present our living bodies – 'a living sacrifice'. Paul has to point out this difference; it was misunderstood and it is still misunderstood.

There are some people who think that if they sacrifice their body – as Paul puts it in 1 Corinthians 13:3: 'If I give my body to be burned' – then they will put themselves right with God. People have done that sort of thing but if it is not done in the right way with charity, it is useless. There were many Japanese in the Second World War who were very ready to sacrifice their bodies – *hara-kiri* they called it – and they thought that it was wonderful, this sacrifice of the body, a dead body. But, no, it is not that, says Paul; God wants a *living* sacrifice.

And again, scripture throws light upon scripture. Peter says exactly the same thing: 'If so be ye have tasted that the Lord is gracious. To whom coming' – note this – 'as unto a living stone, disallowed indeed of men, but chosen of God, and precious, ye also, as lively stones [living stones], are built up a spiritual house, an holy priesthood, to offer up spiritual sacrifices, acceptable to God by Jesus Christ' [*1 Pet.* 2:3–5]. The Apostle Peter here has got hold of this idea that the church is a temple, the temple of the Holy Spirit, the temple in which God dwells, so he says: Now I am going to compare you to a temple, to a building.

But then Peter immediately adds, in effect, 'Do not misunderstand this. I am not going to say that the members of a church are like a collection of stones. Obviously that is no good because a stone has no life in it. So you must not think of yourself like that. Though I am comparing you to a building – and it is a very useful analogy which helps us to see different aspects of this whole truth – and say that you are stones, I do not mean that you are dead, lifeless people who always just sit down, and do nothing at all. You are to be *living*. We are living stones in this temple of God, as our Lord Himself is a living stone. He is a stone, a foundation stone, but there is life in Him.' Peter makes the same kind of contrast that the Apostle Paul is reminding us of here when he talks about our presenting our bodies as a 'living' sacrifice.

Then, secondly, Paul wants to remind us that we must go on offering our bodies. When, under the old dispensation, the priests killed the animal and put the body there upon the altar, they could only kill that animal once. And there are people who think like that in the Christian life. They make one great decision and they put themselves on the altar, and having done that, they say, 'All's well now. I've made my offering.' And they continue to live their own selfish lives. But that is a very pernicious view. The body is a living sacrifice. You go on presenting day by day, hour by hour, and you never stop. This is the difference between a dead animal and a living man; the difference between a stone and a 'living' stone.

So Paul is emphasizing the element of continuity and persistence. Again, of course, he is just putting, in another way, what he has already told us in the sixth chapter. I have quoted parts of that chapter already, and I trust you do once more see what a key chapter that is; we spent time on it for that reason. In that chapter, Paul constantly repeats this truth. He writes, 'Therefore we are buried with him by baptism into death: that like as Christ was raised up from the dead by the glory of the Father, even so we also should walk in newness of life. For if we have been planted together in the likeness of his death, we shall be also in the likeness of his resurrection' [verses 4-5].

Then Paul continues, 'Now if we be dead with Christ, we believe that we shall also live with him: Knowing that Christ being raised from the dead dieth no more; death hath no more dominion over him. For in that he died, he died unto sin once: but in that he liveth, he liveth unto God. Likewise reckon ye also yourselves to be dead indeed unto sin' – that is the slaying, but you do not stop there – 'but alive unto God through Jesus Christ our Lord' (verses 8-11). And he is so concerned about this that he repeats it in the thirteenth verse: 'Neither yield ye your members as instruments of unrighteousness unto sin: but yield yourselves unto God, as those that are alive from the dead' – a living sacrifice! – 'and your members as instruments of righteousness unto God.' And he repeats all that again from verse 18 to the end of the chapter. It is this principle; it is a 'living sacrifice'. We go on presenting our living bodies to God because we are no longer dead. We have become alive and this is a living activity.

Then the next word is the word 'holy' which means 'set apart'. But not only that. Take the Old Testament analogy. If you read the book of Leviticus, you will find that the priests are told to collect the blood of certain animals and to present the body. And every time they are told, very particularly, that they must never offer as a sacrifice an animal that has any blemish whatsoever. You might look at a lamb in the distance and it might appear to be perfect, but when you examine it you find that it has a broken leg or has some defect. Then you must not use it. You must always have a perfect offering; it must be a spotless lamb.

Now all this is summed up in this one word 'holy'; and Paul is telling us that we must constantly present our bodies, without blemish, spotless, to God. We must present them to God free from anything that is in any way unworthy: the *body*, remember. Had you realized the material element in Christianity? But this is the apostle's great appeal: 'present your bodies a living sacrifice, holy . . .'

And, lastly, 'acceptable unto God'. This, again, is not a difficult statement at all. It is something that is explained in the regulations about those burnt offerings and sacrifices in the Old Testament. One was called, 'the sweet smelling savour'. The priests took fine flour and put oil and incense on it. Then when the smoke went up there was a pleasant aroma. Now that was just a picture, a symbol, of presenting to God something that would be acceptable to Him, something that would be well pleasing in His sight. And that is exactly what the apostle is saying here. You must so present your body, he says, that it will come up with a most beautiful aroma to God. Because you are a Christian, and because you want to show your gratitude to God, you should keep your body in such a condition that as you present it day by day there will be 'a sweetsmelling savour' that will go up, as it were, to God, and He will be very happy to accept your offering.

Paul uses exactly the same expression in Ephesians 5:1-2: 'Be ye therefore followers of God, as dear children; and walk in love, as Christ also hath loved us, and hath given himself for us an offering and a sacrifice to God for a sweetsmelling savour.' Our Lord did that, and you and I are to do the same thing. 'Oh,' says the apostle in effect, 'you are to glorify God and to worship Him and to praise Him and show forth His excellencies, not only with your spirit and your soul but also with your body.

Present it to Him, therefore, as a living sacrifice, as a holy sacrifice, as something that will be sweetly acceptable in His most holy sight.'

We shall go on, God willing, with this and see how it is to be done in practice. I have a most uncomfortable feeling that most of us modern Christians need this very exhortation. In much that is being written at the present time it is evident that there is a loosening, even in evangelical circles, along that very line. I read an article not so long ago which was virtually exhorting young Christian men to take alcoholic drink. I cannot imagine anything more dangerous than this new idea that seems to be creeping in that we are to be modern and up to date and that we are to recommend the gospel by being like everybody else. I regard it as of the very devil, dangerous to the individual soul, dangerous to the life of the church, dangerous to those who are outside. These matters are of great urgency and acute present relevance. That is why we must continue to examine the apostle's statement with great care, and in humility, under the guidance of the Holy Spirit.

Five

*I beseech you therefore, brethren, by the mercies of God, that ye
present your bodies a living sacrifice, holy, acceptable unto God,
which is your reasonable service. And be not conformed to this
world: but be ye transformed by the renewing of your mind, that
ye may prove what is that good, and acceptable, and perfect, will
of God.*

Romans 12:1–2

Some of the greatest tragedies in the history of the church, and
in the lives of individual Christians, have been entirely due to
the fact that people have never grasped the teaching of these
two verses; they have never understood the meaning of Paul's
'therefore' and 'by the mercies of God'. This is one of those
junctions, or links, which connect the great doctrines of the
Christian faith with the living of the Christian life. Railway
junctions are always important and always dangerous places.
You can foul the lines and it can lead to endless and grievous
trouble. In the Scriptures, a junction is particularly important
and nowhere more so than here, where we are being introduced
to the living of the Christian life. These two verses are the
introduction to the remainder of this great Epistle.

So we have been considering Paul's words and we have seen
that the motive for living this life is the great doctrine of the
first eleven chapters of Romans. The words 'therefore', and 'by
the mercies of God', bring out the element of gratitude. We
have seen, too, the importance of the word 'present' as we
consider how we should live the Christian life. You are to
present your literal, physical body as a sacrifice to God, and it
is not a dead sacrifice but a living and continuing offering. It

[56]

must also be a 'holy' sacrifice, one that is acceptable to God and pleasant in His sight, a kind of 'sweetsmelling savour' rising up into the presence of God and giving Him pleasure and satisfaction.

We resume at this point, and here the apostle goes on to say something further. He says, 'which is your reasonable service'. Here, again, is a most interesting statement and we must be clear about it. The word 'service' is one of the technical terms that are used in Scripture. It can be translated by the word 'worship'. The 'service' of God means the worship of God, as Paul indicated in writing to the Thessalonians: '. . . how ye turned to God from idols to *serve* the living and the true God' [*1 Thess.* 1:9]. And you worship the living and the true God not merely in public services – that is a part of it – but by the whole of your life.

Writing to the Philippians, Paul says, 'Yea, and if I be offered upon the sacrifice and service of your faith' – 'service' here is exactly the same idea – 'I joy, and rejoice with you all' [*Phil.* 2:17]. Paul is using a picture and he says, in effect, 'All right, you have your sacrifice ready to offer to God. Now under the old dispensation it was the custom to pour wine or oil on the various offerings, and,' says Paul, 'if necessary, I am ready for my blood to be poured out and offered upon your sacrifice and service.' They are bringing their sacrifice, which is themselves, to offer to God as an act of worship and of praise, and Paul is ready to be the libation, if you like, the poured out substance, on the offering.

Then there is another interesting example, again in Philippians, where Paul says, 'For we are the circumcision, which *worship* God in the spirit . . .' [*Phil.* 3:3]. The word translated 'worship' here is the same Greek word as the word translated 'service' in Romans 12:1. So the translation might very well have been 'who serve God'. Worship and service are interchangeable terms. Indeed, we ourselves say both that we are going into the house of God to worship God, and that we are going to a service in the house of God. So that is Paul's idea here. This offering of our bodies to God as living and holy and acceptable sacrifices, is an act of worship. The whole of my life is to be a worship of God.

But Paul also describes this offering as a 'reasonable' service.

Christian Conduct

Now if you just take that term as it is in the Authorized Version (the King James Version), you might come to the conclusion that he is saying, 'Now what I am asking you to do is something which is not unreasonable; in fact, it is very reasonable. In the light of what God has done for you, in the light of the mercies of God, in the light of the sacrifice of His Son, what is more eminently reasonable than that God should ask you to give yourself to Him, in order that you may live a life in His service and to His praise.'

Well, you can include that, if you like, in the meaning of this word 'reasonable', but it actually does not mean that. Paul uses the term to describe further the character of this offering of our bodies. He has told us that it is 'living'; he has told us that it is 'holy'; he has told us that it is 'acceptable to God'; and now, in addition to that, he says it must be 'reasonable'.

This is a most interesting word. It means something that is rendered by the mind, something mental, something spiritual. Let me again illustrate it to you by noting the use of the same word somewhere else. I do trust that as we do this you are being introduced to a method of studying the Scriptures. There is nothing better than to explain scripture by scripture. Always get an analogy in the Scriptures and then you will always be safe. Always compare scripture with scripture. That is the supreme way, it seems to me, of studying and of expounding the Bible.

So I take you to the First Epistle of Peter and to the second chapter and the second verse. We considered that chapter earlier, but we did not include these words: 'As newborn babes' – I am reading here from the Authorized Version – 'desire the sincere milk of the word, that ye may grow thereby.' But that is not a very accurate translation. It is all right, what it says is perfectly true, it is 'the sincere milk of the word' that Peter is talking about. But he did not actually say that. What he said was, 'the spiritual, sincere [unmixed, unadulterated] milk'. Not 'milk of the word' but 'spiritual milk'. The word translated 'spiritual' here is the same Greek word as the word translated 'reasonable' in Romans 12:1.

So to put it in another way, Peter says, 'Desire the thought-nourishing sincere milk'. In other words, the Word is something mental, something spiritual. Paul is contrasting it, of course, with the ordinary milk which nourishes the body. So in effect he says: 'I am telling you to take not a material milk but a spiritual milk which nourishes the mind.' That is the contrast. So here, in Romans 12:1, Paul is saying: Your offering is to be a spiritual or a mental service or worship of God.

Now you see the significance of this? Again, the apostle uses these words in order to present us with a contrast. He did that, as we saw, in connection with the word 'living': not a dead animal, not a dead body, but a living and continuing sacrifice. And here the contrast is with something which is merely external. The offering is not to be that. It is not to be outward but inward. It is not to be merely a part of a ceremony or a ritual but its whole characteristic is inward, mental, spiritual. This is a point that needs to be emphasized very much at the present time. There is undoubtedly a tendency for people to multiply the external forms in connection with religion. People always like something spectacular, something visible. A great battle that the Christian faith has had to fight from its very beginning has been against the perpetual tendency to externalize worship.

It is fascinating to read the story of that fight throughout the running centuries. It begins in the New Testament with the so-called Judaizers. Their response was quite natural. They had been brought up as Jews and they were accustomed to the ritual and the externals of the worship of God in the temple. They found it very difficult to break with that and to come to a more spiritual worship. So you find the fight even in the New Testament itself. And it continued in the subsequent history of the church.

At the present time, too, we really should know something about this. Take, for instance, the Roman Catholic Church – and at the moment I am not saying all this primarily with the intention of criticizing what she has done, but am simply giving you historical information. Even before the church became Roman Catholic, but still more after that, she was face to face with this problem. As Christianity spread, it grew, of course, among people who had been brought up in pagan circumstances. They all had their religions – everybody has a religion – and there were many pagan religions including the mystery religions. All these pagan religions laid great emphasis upon the spectacular, upon the visible, upon the external.

Many of these pagan people became Christians as a result of a kind of mass movement. When the emperor Constantine decided to become Christian and to make the Roman Empire Christian, all his people came into the church automatically. It was not that every one of them was individually converted, not at all! And when they were confronted by the simple, un-adorned, spiritual, inner worship of the Christians, they felt lost. They felt they were missing something. And the result was that the leaders of the church made a compromise. They said, 'We must give these people something to look at, they have been accustomed to it.'

So you can trace the story of how, increasingly, Christians departed from the simple worship, the spontaneous, simple worship of the New Testament, to an increasingly elaborate ceremonial with a priesthood. The altar, which had been among the people, was removed far away, and only certain special people were allowed to offer the worship to God, while the rest sat back and watched the spectacle.

That is how it all happened. Christian people even took over many of the pagan ceremonies and dressed them up in a Christian form. They took up many of the pagan days, these 'holy days' that are referred to in Colossians and other epistles. They said that they had 'baptized them into Christianity'. That was the term they used, and that was the argument. But what were they really doing? Were they baptizing these pagan practices into Christianity, or were they degrading and debas-ing Christianity and turning it into a sort of semi-paganism?

Well, we all have our views on these subjects, have we not? All I am trying to show is that these dangers are implicit in the apostle's use here of this word translated 'reasonable'. This is mental; this is spiritual; this is internal. This is the antithesis, in a sense, of the external ceremonial. It is a service to God such as befits the reason. It is a spiritual offering, the worship of a rational human being as distinct from the offering of an irrational animal.

There are many other contrasts here, too. The apostle is fighting against a legalistic attitude towards the worship of God. This, I think, is still one of the major battles today, and it will certainly continue in these coming years. You are aware of all these trends – the new interest in Rome, for example. 'Isn't Rome changing?' people say. And she is, of course. She is trying to bring these ceremonies of hers to us in a manner that will be more appealing. The leaders have decided, for instance, no longer to conduct services in Latin, but to use the vernacular. That is the bait, and there is a hook inside it. This hook is the ceremonial, this external worship, which is, ultimately, legalistic.

In the Epistle to the Colossians, the apostle puts the danger of legalism in a very striking form. Having given again the great doctrine of salvation and the work upon the cross, he says in Colossians 2:16–23: 'Let no man therefore judge you in meat, or in drink, or in respect of an holyday, or of the new moon, or of the sabbath days: which are a shadow of things to come; but the body is of Christ. Let no man beguile you of your reward in a voluntary humility and worshipping of angels, intruding into those things which he hath not seen, vainly puffed up by his fleshly mind. And not holding the Head, from which all the body by joints and bands having nourishment ministered, and knit together, increaseth with the increase of God. Wherefore if ye be dead with Christ from the rudiments' – by which Paul means elemental principles, or the kind of coarseness which belongs to everything primitive – 'of the world, why, as though living in the world, are ye subject to ordinances, (touch not; taste not; handle not; which all are to perish with the using;) after the commandments and doctrines of men? Which things have indeed a shew of wisdom in will worship, and humility, and neglecting of the body' – notice that – 'not in any honour to the satisfying of the flesh.'

Now that is nothing but a kind of disquisition on this theme that we are considering here in Romans 12. There was a fight in the church at Colosse and in the neighbouring churches. These other men had come along with an admixture of Christianity and philosophy and those old mystery religions, with a bit of Judaism mixed in. It was a most extraordinary hotchpotch of different teachings and religions. It sounded very wonderful, of course, as these quack religions always do, and there were people who were tending to take it up, feeling that they had something extra here. They were being told, 'You only need to do this, you see, and carry out these rules and regulations, and all will be well with you.'

That is always the charm of that kind of religion. That is why so many people have from time to time gone into the Roman Catholic Church – you can read the autobiographies of people who have given this as one of their reasons. They say, 'Your Protestant evangelical faith in particular seems to leave it all to me, and who am I? I find this too much for me. But Mother Church says, "Come to me, we will conduct the worship for you."' So you sit back and you look on at the great spectacle and you are assured that everything is being put right for you. Now that is what the apostle is dealing with here. That is legalistic, he says, and we must never view our services in that way.

Then let me give just one other quotation so that we may see this quite clearly. At the beginning of 1 Timothy 4, Paul says, 'Now the Spirit speaketh expressly, that in the latter times some shall depart from the faith, giving heed to seducing spirits, and doctrines of devils; speaking lies in hypocrisy; having their conscience seared with a hot iron; forbidding to marry, and commanding to abstain from meats, which God hath created to be received with thanksgiving of them which believe and know the truth. For every creature of God is good, and nothing to be refused, if it be received with thanksgiving: for it is sanctified by the word of God and prayer. If thou put the brethren in remembrance of these things, thou shalt be a good minister of Jesus Christ, nourished up in the words of faith, and of good doctrine, whereunto thou hast attained' (verses 1–6).

Now I am trying at this point to be a good minister of Jesus Christ by calling your attention to these very things, and what I am saying comes to this: Paul is dealing with what you do with your body and he is telling the Christians in Rome not to listen to the words of these false teachers because they will tell you to do things which are quite irrational and unreasonable, things that your mind should reject. Paul says: I want you to offer a spiritual worship which is offered with the reason. That is the kind of offering that befits a man or woman.

Paul contrasts 'reasonable worship' with this wrong, false teaching. There are those who would even tell you to inflict pain on your body. It has often been taught: the wearing of a hair shirt, for example. Some would even carry this teaching to the extent of literally scarifying the body. Others have so misunderstood the whole teaching that they have almost starved themselves to death. What they were trying to do was to deal with the impulses and the drives that come up out of the body, which we considered earlier, but their method of doing that was to starve the body until some of them became seriously ill.

But that is irrational; that is not New Testament teaching. Again, some went so far as to say quite seriously that whether you were a man or a women, if you wanted to be a true Christian, you must never get married. And they were not allowed to eat any meat at all. Why? Well, they said that if you eat meat you are not only doing what the world does, but meat is dangerous because it stimulates certain parts of your body and your appetites. So if you really want to live the Christian life and to present your body to God, you must only eat herbs and vegetables with your bread. That is the sort of thing that Paul is dealing with in Colossians 2 and in 1 Timothy 4, and that is what he puts in the one word 'reasonable' here in this chapter. In chapter 14 he works it out and expands it, and then sums it up in that great statement in the seventeenth verse: 'The kingdom of God is not meat and drink; but righteousness, and peace, and joy in the Holy Ghost.'

So here Paul is emphasizing that presenting your body must always be rational. You must be able to justify it. It must be consistent with the picture of the Christian that is given in the New Testament. Throughout the centuries, some people in the church have needed to be told that sacrifice in and of itself must never be an end. There are always people who are ready to 'give their body to be burned', and they feel that there is some merit in the sacrifice *per se*. Only recently, we read in our newspapers of some poor man doing that, I think outside the Pentagon in New York. He threw petrol or whatever it was, over his body and burnt himself to death for his religion, as he thought, for his principles. And people have done that, not in such an extreme form, but in various other ways. But that is irrational and unreasonable and the apostle is saying that true worship is a complete contrast to all that. So he puts his emphasis on this positive, spiritual presentation of our bodies to God, that He may use them to His glory and to His praise.

Let me sum all this up by reading from John chapter 4 which describes our Lord's conversation with the woman of Samaria. This makes exactly the same point. 'The woman saith unto him, Sir, I perceive that thou art a prophet. Our fathers worshipped in this mountain; and ye say' – that is, the Jews – 'that in Jerusalem is the place where men ought to worship' – or, to serve God – 'Jesus saith unto her, Woman, believe me, the hour cometh, when ye shall neither in this mountain, nor yet at Jerusalem, worship [serve] the Father. Ye worship ye know not what: we know what we worship: for salvation is of the Jews. But the hour cometh, and now is, when the true worshippers' – the true servants of God – 'shall worship the Father in spirit and in truth: for the Father seeketh such to worship him. God is a Spirit: and they that worship him must worship him in spirit and in truth' [verses 19–23].

That is exactly the contrast that the apostle has in his mind here. The Samaritan woman was thinking in those old terms: you worship God in this mountain, or you must be in the temple in Jerusalem. That was the whole trouble with the Jews at that time. That is what they could never grasp from our Lord. They felt that He was against God, that He was a blasphemer and an impostor. Why? Because he was teaching that you could worship God without the temple, without priests and high priests, that was the scandal.

And it was the scandal, too, of the Apostle Paul and all the apostles and the early Christians. The Jews said, 'These people are irreligious.' It was simply because they did not worship in the old visible, external, ceremonial manner, but said that worship was entirely inward and spiritual. 'God is a Spirit: and they that worship him must worship him in spirit and in truth.' Mountain, temple, Jerusalem, none of these things matter; *spirit and truth* are what matter.

It is very interesting to observe that in the second century AD the most common charge that was brought against the Christians was that they were atheists! And the explanation for that was that while the pagans worshipped a multiplicity of gods, the Christians did not; they only worshipped one God and they did it in this inner manner, without temples, without burnt offerings and without making sacrifices. They seemed to be worshipping God altogether inside themselves and in their minds; they did not need ornate buildings and all the ritual.

There, then, is the principle; but how is this to be done? Let me divide it up into its negative and positive aspects. Remember, we are dealing with practicalities here. We are dealing with our use of the body that God has given us. How do I carry out all this?

The first point, obviously, is that I must refrain from sin. I must not sin with my body. I need not elaborate that; it must be clear to everybody. But let me go on to certain other negatives. I must not use my body selfishly. Now here we are coming to the heart of it. I must not regard my body even as my private property. That is what Paul is saying in 1 Corinthians 6:19–20: 'Know ye not that . . . ye are not your own? For ye are bought with a price.' Your body is 'the temple of the Holy Ghost' (verse 19). So I must learn that my body is not at my disposal. I must not use it for my own ends. You must work this out for yourself in the details; I am simply putting down the principle.

It can be put like this: you must not pamper your body, because if you do, you are taking a wrong view of it. The body is not meant to be pampered. It is given us in order that we may express ourselves and the personalities and the powers that God has given us. The moment you pamper your body you are paying too much attention to it, you are elevating it, you are putting it in the first position and it was never meant to be there. So in the Scripture we find a statement like this: 'Whose adorning let it not be that outward adorning of plaiting the hair, and of wearing of gold, or of putting on of apparel; but let it be the hidden man of the heart, in that which is not corruptible, even the ornament of a meek and quiet spirit, which is in the sight of God of great price' [*1 Pet.* 3:3–4]. It is often read in the marriage service, and very rightly so. That is the right kind of adorning.

There is, as I have explained before, an order in these matters – spirit, soul, body. You do not live for the body, and you do not live for the glory of the body. Some people have greater temptations than others at this point. We all have our own

[65]

particular temptations, but if you have been given a shapely, comely body, be careful that you do not turn it into an idol, that you do not begin to worship it, and that you do not pamper it. All that is involved here. Remember, it is not yours, it is God's, and the moment you tend to live for the glory of your own body you are transgressing this very appeal, this exhortation which we are considering together here.

Then, of course, it is important that still less must we abuse the body. The abuse of the body is a grievous sin because it is not ours, it is 'the temple of the Holy Ghost'. Therefore, if I am to offer my body to God as a sacrifice which is living, holy, pure and acceptable in His sight; if nothing is to come up to God but 'a sweetsmelling savour', and if I am to be reasonable in all this, then, clearly, I must not abuse my body in any way. We have already touched on this subject. The body must not be mistreated. Alas, we can abuse it in many ways. You can abuse it by neglecting it. It is not ultra-spiritual to neglect the body. Many saints have done that and their work and their ministry have suffered as a result. As Robert Louis Stevenson put it, the body is regarded as 'brother ass' and is treated as such. That is wrong. You must not regard your body with contempt. You must not say, 'I'm such a spiritually-minded person that I've got no time to pay any attention to my body.' It may sound unspiritual, but it is what the apostle is saying.

You can also abuse your body by giving it too much food. You must give it food, the body cannot live without it, but if you give it too much, you are mistreating it, you are again allowing it to become too important. You are allowing it to dictate. You are allowing the appetites to take control. They are never meant to do that in a rational being, and 'the new man in Christ' is rational. So we must treat our bodies in a rational manner: sufficient food but not too much. Our Lord dealt with this: 'And take heed to yourselves lest at any time your hearts be overcharged with surfeiting' [*Luke* 21:34]. You must eat according to necessity.

And then, of course, the same applies to drink – any sort of drink. Alcoholic drink in particular can be a terrible abuse of the body; not in 'surfeiting, and drunkenness', says our Lord [*Luke* 21:34]. If you drink too much alcohol you violate your body, you knock out the highest part of it that God has given you, your higher centres which should be in control. So you are then no longer able to offer your body as a sacrifice of the type described by the great apostle here.

And may I add – and it has to be added at a time like this – the same applies to sex. There is nothing wrong in sex, but, again, if the element of excess comes in, it is bad. The world today is living for sex and nothing can be more terrible. It is worse even than the worship of the body. The ancient Greeks worshipped the physical form. Their games were designed to glorify the human body. You see sculptures in the British Museum and elsewhere of this perfect human frame. They were wrong. The body is not to be worshipped. The body is to be presented to God and used entirely to His glory and to His praise.

To put it bluntly and plainly, sex is given to you by God, but if you use your body and your sexuality to indulge yourself and your own appetites, you are not only violating your body, you are violating your human constitution. You must not use the body or any part of the body for your own selfish gratification. Do all things to the glory of God, says the apostle: 'Whether therefore ye eat, or drink, or whatsoever ye do, do all to the glory of God' [*1 Cor.* 10:31].

And the same applies even to sleep. We cannot go on without sleep, and if you do not get proper sleep, then every part of you will suffer. Your work will suffer and above all your worship of God will suffer. So sleep is essential. But, again, too much sleep is bad for the body, and therefore prevents your presenting it to God as this living, holy sacrifice which is acceptable in His most holy sight. Christian people, we have been rather tending to forget these matters, have we not? There is a sense in which you can become too spiritual. In one sense, of course, you can never be too spiritual, but if you isolate the spiritual and cut it off from the physical, you have fallen into very grievous error.

Then, positively, Paul's teaching in Romans 12:1 means that we keep our bodies in as healthy a condition as we can. You are not being very spiritual if you do not take any exercise. You should take exercise. The fitter your body, the fitter will be your mind and understanding. *Mens sana in corpore sano* – that is it – 'A healthy mind in a healthy body.' These things

[67]

interact. You must present your body holy to God, not crippled, not only working fifty per cent, not struggling and failing. No; let it be as fit as you can make it. But do not live for physical fitness; be fit in order that you may serve God, and in order that He may use you to His glory and to His praise.

The apostle has said this in detail in Romans chapter 6 – I quoted this earlier: 'Neither yield ye your members as instruments of unrighteousness unto sin: but yield yourselves unto God, as those that are alive from the dead, and your members as instruments of righteousness unto God' [verse 13]. And in that same chapter, later on, Paul repeats it all: 'Being then made free from sin, ye became the servants of righteousness. I speak after the manner of men because of the infirmity of your flesh: for as ye have yielded your members servants to uncleanness and to iniquity unto iniquity; even so now yield your members' – the same members – 'as servants to righteousness unto holiness' [verses 18–19].

In other words, the principle is that we give our bodies to God and put them at His disposal for His service. And you can do this. You can use every part of your body, sex included, to the glory of God. Sex can be used to the glory of God, just as you can eat and drink to the glory of God, and walk to the glory of God. If you think that sex cannot be used to the glory of God, you have misunderstood the whole of this teaching and you are not in a Christian position. Never abuse, but always use, to the glory of God. 'Use . . . as not abusing,' says the apostle in 1 Corinthians 7:31. That is the principle. And you will find that it runs as a theme and a motif right through the New Testament epistles.

Finally, let me give you a quotation from that great preacher in the early centuries of the Christian era, John Chrysostom, 'the golden-mouthed orator' as he was sometimes called. He expresses all this in a very beautiful way in these words: 'How can the body become a sacrifice?' And here is the answer: 'Let the eye look on no evil, and it is a sacrifice.' It is, is it not? Our eyes have become accustomed to look at evil as we walk about the streets and see people and hoardings and as we pick up the newspaper. The eye has become accustomed to look at evil, and by nature we enjoy that, so when the eye does not look on evil, it is a sacrifice. Job, that wise man in the Old Testament, put it like this: 'I made a covenant with mine eyes; why then should I think upon a maid?' [*Job* 31:1]. 'I came to this decision,' says Job in effect. 'I made a covenant with my eyes that I would always look straight ahead. I would not look to the right nor to the left. I would not squint, as it were. I would not use even the corner of my eye to look at evil.'

Then Chrysostom continues: 'Let the tongue utter nothing base, and it is an offering.' The tongue likes to utter base things. 'Neither filthiness, nor foolish talking, nor jesting,' says Paul, 'which are not convenient' [*Eph.* 5:4]. What evil is wrought by the tongue! James tells us, 'The tongue is a little member . . . Behold, how great a matter a little fire kindleth!' [*James* 3:5]. Oh the trouble it can cause, and what harm is done by speaking evil things! Not only speaking evil about other people, but speaking evil, suggestive things. 'No,' says Chrysostom, 'let the tongue utter nothing base, and it is an offering.' You are presenting it as an offering to God.

Chrysostom continues, 'Let the hand work no sin, and it is a holocaust.' In other words, it is such a tremendous thing, it is as if you were taking a great offering and burning it up.

'But more: this suffices not,' says Chrysostom. That is not enough. That is negative. Chrysostom is using the division that I have been trying to use. 'But more: this suffices not, but besides, we must actively exert ourselves for good, the hand giving alms, the mouth blessing them that curse us, the ears at leisure for listening to God.' We must stop listening to the raucous voices of the world. You stop listening to the world in order that you may begin listening to God. That is presenting your ears, your organs of hearing, as a sacrifice to God. Is not that beautiful?

That is presenting your bodies 'a living sacrifice, holy, acceptable unto God', which is your 'service with reason', your 'mental service', your 'spiritual worship', a truly spiritual offering to God.

> *Take my hands and let them move*
> *At the impulse of Thy love;*
> *Take my feet, and let them be*
> *Swift and beautiful for Thee.*

Christian Conduct

Take my voice, and let me sing
Always, only for my King;
Take my lips, and let them be
Filled with messages from Thee
Francis Ridley Havergal

And so you go through every member of your body and present it to God in this way. Then you are living a spiritual life, with nothing irrational, nothing mutilated; not regarding the body as evil and as something which has to be destroyed, no, no, but regarding it as a gift for God; not using it for yourself, but offering it to Him to use for His glory and His praise.

And the apostle puts all that in one word – 'reasonable'. Reasonable! May God give us grace to work it out in our understandings and then put it into practice in detail in our daily lives.

Six

*

> *I beseech you therefore, brethren, by the mercies of God, that ye present your bodies a living sacrifice, holy, acceptable unto God, which is your reasonable service. And be not conformed to this world: but be ye transformed by the renewing of your mind, that ye may prove what is that good, and acceptable, and perfect, will of God.*
>
> Romans 12:1–2

We move on now to the second verse where the apostle takes this great statement in Romans 12:1 a step further. He illustrates what he has already been saying and puts it from another angle, showing us why we ought to present our bodies as living sacrifices to God. And as we follow these further arguments, we shall see still more clearly why we are called upon to live in this way.

I suggested in my original analysis of these two verses that here we are moving from the realm of the physical body to the realm of the soul. Now I do not know what division you accept of a human being, but I would suggest that there are three aspects: body, soul and spirit. There are those who say that the soul and spirit are one and, in a sense, I agree; yet I think there is an important distinction between them. It is a distinction which is drawn in several places in the Scripture itself, as we have already seen. So here we are moving on to the realm of the soul, or that part of human life which is expressed through the psyche.

Now this is the part in man or woman in which they are related to life in this world. Through the psyche, through the soul, people are related to their fellow men and women. But not only that: by the psyche they are related also to the animal kingdom and to the inanimate part of creation. The psyche is pre-eminently the realm of relationships, all relationships, short of our relationship with God.

Now in Romans 12:2 the apostle gives us an important principle which is taught right through the New Testament. It is one of the controlling principles about which we must be clear. You cannot read the New Testament, even in a cursory manner, without noticing frequent references to 'the world', or to 'this world', or to 'this present evil world', or to 'this age', with an explicit or implicit contrast with the age or the world which is to come.

Take, for instance, the apostle's words right at the beginning of the Epistle to the Galatians: 'Grace be to you and peace from God the Father, and from our Lord Jesus Christ. Who gave himself for our sins, that he might deliver us from this present evil world' – there it is – 'according to the will of God and our Father' [*Gal.* 1:3–4].

Then there is a statement, which is probably more familiar, in the First Epistle of John: 'Love not the world, neither the things that are in the world. If any man love the world, the love of the Father is not in him. For all that is in the world, the lust of the flesh, and the lust of the eyes, and the pride of life, is not of the Father, but is of the world. And the world passeth away, and the lust thereof: but he that doeth the will of God abideth for ever' [*1 John* 2:15–17]. And again, there is another reference in the fifth chapter: 'Whatsoever is born of God overcometh the world: and this is the victory that overcometh the world, even our faith' [*1 John* 5:4]. And the writer to the Hebrews has the same teaching. He says that the men and women of faith considered themselves to be 'pilgrims and strangers' [*Heb.* 11:3] in the world.

Now as we have seen, Paul gives us, in these two opening verses of Romans 12, the principles controlling Christian conduct, and we have arrived at a most vital one: we must not be controlled by, we must not conform to, 'this world'. But what does the apostle mean by 'the world' and what does the New Testament mean as it constantly uses this term? It is important, of course, that we should realize that the New Testament writers are not usually referring to the physical universe. Sometimes they do use the word in that sense, but when they do the context generally makes it abundantly plain. There is nothing inherently wrong with the material universe, and in any case nobody conforms to that. No, in the first place, by 'world' the New Testament means life as it is thought of, organized, and lived apart from God, without reckoning on God, without being governed and controlled by Him. So there is a great dichotomy, a great division. We all either belong to the world, or we belong to the kingdom of God.

Then, secondly, the word 'world' can be defined as life and activity which, as the result of the Fall, is controlled by the devil. In 2 Corinthians 4:3-4 we read: 'If our gospel is hid, it is hid to them that are lost: in whom the god of this world hath blinded the minds of them which believe not, lest the light of the glorious gospel of Christ, which is the image of God, should shine unto them.' There it is, this reference to 'the god of this world'. He controls it, and he controls the minds of those who reject the gospel. So, 'world' means the outlook, the way of living which is not only apart from God, but is positively controlled by the devil.

Again, the Apostle Paul puts this clearly in the second chapter of the Epistle to the Ephesians. Here he is describing people who are not Christians: 'And you hath he quickened, who were dead in trespasses and sins: wherein in time past ye walked according to the course of this world, according to the prince of the power of the air, the spirit that now worketh in the children of disobedience: among whom also we all had our conversation in times past . . .' [*Eph.* 2:1-3]. Now that is to be conformed to the world. It is the kind of life which is governed, in every respect, by this 'prince of the power of the air, the spirit that now worketh in the children of disobedience'. That is another description of the devil and the forces of evil.

But there is still another, a third, definition of 'world', one which we have already found many times in working our way through this Epistle to the Romans. This definition is subsumed under the term 'flesh', which is a technical word in the Bible and generally means this worldly outlook and a worldly type of life. Of course, you will sometimes find that the word is used of the body, or it is even used of a number of people, or of a single individual, but, speaking generally, the term as used in the New Testament, and particularly in the Pauline epistles, is virtually synonymous with the word 'world'.

Let me remind you of how we saw the word 'flesh', for instance, in Romans 8:3–12. Here the apostle is giving another great summary of the gospel: 'What the law could not do, in that it was weak through the flesh' – Paul does not merely mean the physical body, you see – 'God sending his own Son in the likeness of sinful flesh' – He did send His Son in a body, but Christ did not come 'in sinful flesh' but 'in the likeness of sinful flesh' – 'and for sin, condemned sin in the flesh: that the righteousness of the law might be fulfilled in us, who walk not after the flesh, but after the Spirit.'

Now there the gospel is clearly put in the form of an antithesis. 'The world' is that which walks 'after the flesh', and not 'after the Spirit'. Paul continues, 'They that are after the flesh do mind the things of the flesh; but they that are after the Spirit the things of the Spirit.' Then he adds another term – 'For to be carnally minded is death' – that is to be in the flesh – 'but to be spiritually minded is life and peace. Because the carnal mind is enmity against God: for it is not subject to the law of God, neither indeed can be. So then they that are in the flesh cannot please God.'

Now in a physical sense we are all in the flesh, but as Christians we are not, for 'they that are in the flesh cannot please God'. And Paul adds in verse 9: 'But ye are not in the flesh, but in the Spirit, if so be that the Spirit of God dwell in you.' And then Paul continues with the argument until he comes to the appeal of verse 12: 'Therefore, brethren, we are debtors, not to the flesh, to live after the flesh. For if ye live after the flesh, ye shall die: but if ye through the Spirit do mortify the deeds of the body, ye shall live.' A good way, therefore, of looking at this term 'world' is to say that it means 'walking after the flesh', rather than 'walking after the Spirit'.

This is absolutely crucial. No one can possibly understand the New Testament teaching about conduct and morality without grasping the New Testament teaching about the world. This is the controlling principle, and it is just here that we see the uniqueness of the Christian teaching. Philosophers who are not Christians know nothing about this. They do not draw a distinction between the world and the kingdom of God, nor between the flesh and the Spirit, and being in the flesh and being in the Spirit. They neither know nor understand it. That is where they are blind.

Moralists and humanists, too, know nothing about this distinction. They not only fail to understand, but this is the reason why all their schemes and proposals never come to anything. It is the cause of the utter failure of education to solve our problems. Education knows nothing about the meaning of the words 'world' and 'flesh'. It does not believe in the devil so it misses the whole point. It does not see why things are as they are. It does not see the depth of the problem or comprehend the reason why only one solution can possibly deal with it.

Statesmen do not understand, either. A Christian statesman does, of course, but a statesman who believes that the problem can be dealt with by acts of Parliament does not understand this, and neither, indeed, does the whole legal system of our country. That is why judges, lawyers and magistrates also tend to fail completely in dealing with the moral problems confronting us in such a glaring manner in this and in other countries at the present time.

Christians look at life and its problems in a unique manner. Now this is, of course, important for many reasons and if we do not grasp this as we should, we Christians may also get into trouble. The moment we begin to expect Christian behaviour from people who are not Christians, we have ourselves fallen into the very muddle we have just been considering. At various points in its long history, the church foolishly tried to impose upon men and women who were not Christians, the Christian teaching with regard to conduct. I believe, and I say so with great regret and reluctance, that that was one of the cardinal errors of the Puritans of three hundred years ago, as it is still the error in the thinking of many of their blind followers today.

So, whichever way you look at it, this teaching of the Bible is important. It can be put like this: the devil and the forces of evil are exercising a pervasive and a controlling influence and power upon the whole of the life of humanity. The world is being governed by a malign power, the head of which is the devil, 'the god of this world', 'the prince of the power of the air, the spirit that now worketh in the children of disobedience' [*Eph.* 2:2]. Ephesians 6:12 and other passages make this clear: 'We wrestle not against flesh and blood, but against principalities, against powers, against the rulers of the darkness of this world, against spiritual wickedness in high places.' This is a primary, fundamental principle of biblical teaching. You cannot follow biblical reasoning unless you grasp this principle. You must start with it. You do not understand the Bible's doctrine of salvation, or any other of its doctrines, unless you are clear about this.

So the devil and his powers control the life of this world, its politics, its art, its pleasure and its view of everything that happens, as men and women live the life of the soul in this world of time. Whatever the international problems, you do not begin to understand them unless you have grasped this particular key. It is this that enables you to understand it all: the clashes and the turmoil, the pain and the agony. This is the one and only adequate explanation. How pathetic it is that people should have thought that they could explain all the events of the First World War in terms of the Kaiser, and then should have repeated the same error in thinking that Hitler alone explained the Second World War. Such thinking is childish in its superficiality. Because people took that wrong view, they said, 'If only we can get rid of this evil thing, then everything will be all right.' But before the war ended they discovered that though they had got rid of Hitler, there was somebody else rising – Stalin – and on and on it goes. That is the tragedy of having the mind of the world and failing to understand the biblical connotation of this most important term.

How does this 'mind of the world' reveal itself? Again, there are many statements about this in the New Testament. The Apostle John says, 'Love not the world, neither the things that are in the world' – but what are they? – 'the lust of the flesh, and the lust of the eyes, and the pride of life' [*1 John* 2:15–16]. That is a very good summary, but it is not enough, we must say more.

Now here, I think, it is the appropriate point to issue a warning. Many of us confine the meaning of this term 'the world' within limits that are too narrow and this is a grave danger. Many people seem to think that when the Bible tells us, 'Be not conformed to this world,' it is only telling us not to participate in certain so-called worldly pleasures. There are those who think that as long as they do not go to a cinema or a theatre, or a public house or something like that, then they are not guilty of worldliness; some almost reduce it to not having a television set! You probably know such people and can see how small their whole conception is of this term 'world'.

Others think worldliness is purely a matter of money. I remember quite well that when I was a boy this was the word that I used to hear quite often, particularly in Welsh. Worldliness was synonymous with love of money, or with having money and possessions. We would say, 'He's a worldly man', when we simply meant that he was very fond of money and wanted more of it. Because he lived for amassing money and possessions, he was called worldly. Of course, that is included, but you must not confine worldliness to that; you must not confine it to just a handful of things which should not be done. This term, 'the world', is much bigger than that. As we have seen, it is something that takes in the whole of a man or woman, thinking as well as practice: it is a large and comprehensive term.

So we are told not to be conformed to this world, and I want to put it to you, as strongly as I can, that there was never greater need of this particular injunction than at this moment. Indeed, I am almost coming to the conclusion, as I said earlier, that the key to most of the situations in which we find ourselves as Christians at the present time is to be found in this one phrase. Let us look at these words, therefore, and see exactly what they are telling us not to do.

The danger here – and I hope to elaborate upon it later – is that in our attempt to carry out this injunction, we should fall into one of two extremes. One is a legalistic narrowness, and the other, in reaction to that, is conformity to this world. It is surprising to notice the number of Christians in one extreme or the other. It is always easier to be at an extreme than to hold the balance which characterizes the Bible itself and has been the mark of the true saint throughout the centuries.

So let us keep that in mind and go on now to look at this exhortation and see it with respect to our thinking. Notice that

I start, not with whether or not we go to a cinema, but with our thinking. It is most interesting, and sometimes can be very amusing, to notice the worldliness of people who think they are not worldly just because they do not do this, that or the other. They can sometimes be much more worldly than the people who are guilty of those particular activities. And that is because worldliness is, in the first place, a matter of thinking, a matter of the mind.

Now we, of course, are concerned with this primarily in the realm of the church, and I want to try to show you that the tragedy of the church today, speaking generally, is that it conforms to this world in its thinking. How is it doing that? It is in its theology. This is most amazing. Take the popular theology, the theology that sells on the bookstalls. Look at the phenomenal sales, for instance, of *Honest to God* and its successor *The New Reformation*, or a book like *Down to Earth*, all that goes by the name of South Bank theology, this theology that has achieved such popularity in the last few years.

Now quite apart from the details in which this theology is so wrong, and the fact that it denies every cardinal article of the Christian faith, you can see, even on the first page of such books, generally even in the introduction or the preface, that the theology is going to be all wrong. Why? Because the real trouble with it is that it is entirely based on conforming to the thinking of this world. This is how it starts; this is always the presupposition.

Why do we need a new theology? The answer we are given is: 'It's no use telling the modern man . . .' But the moment we have heard that, we have heard enough. The theologians who say this have revealed their whole position. If they stand in a pulpit or write and say words like that, they have already put themselves out of true Christian theology because they are saying exactly what the world is saying. The world says, 'We today are entirely different from all who have ever gone before us and we're different because of our great knowledge. We're twentieth-century men and women; we've come of age; we're grown up; we're living in this scientific age, this 'atomic' age, and, of course, the latest knowledge has revolutionized every-thing. In their ignorance and simplicity people used to believe in a sort of three-storeyed universe, but of course we know now that that is no longer possible.'

Now I am repeating their statements. Modern theologians say, 'It's impossible for scientific men and women to believe in the supernatural, or the miraculous. So if you are going to try to teach them a theology or a view of life which still goes on in that way, then your position is hopeless. The world will not listen to you and you might as well shut your buildings, shut your books and shut your mouths. We must reconstruct the whole thing. We need a new Reformation. We must start afresh. We must discover a truth that will be acceptable to people today.'

Now can you not see that that is nothing but conforming to this world? It is saying that the man in the street decides what is to be believed and accepted. You no longer approach him saying, 'Thus saith the Lord.' You look at him and analyze him. You discover what he believes, what he reads, what he thinks. You go and work with him and drink with him. Having mixed with him in work and pleasure, and having discovered where he is and how he thinks, you present him a gospel that he will be able to understand and accept. He determines and controls your teaching.

There is a German theologian called Bultmann, who is a very great theologian, and he starts with a very good and practical intention, but that modern approach is the whole basis of his teaching. It is true also of another well-known man called Dietrich Bonhoeffer. He is not so extreme, I agree, but he virtually says the same thing – that people today, because of their knowledge and learning, cannot take this gospel as it stands. So Bultmann teaches that you must 'demythologize' the gospel and take out all the miracles. The only one thing you can be certain of, he says, is that a man 'Jesus' died upon a cross. Certainly not the resurrection of the body; certainly not the virgin birth; certainly not the miracles: all that is first century and must be shed. Bultmann said all this in the interests of giving a message to the modern man. He was honest and sincere. He wanted to do good and to help people, but he was conforming to the world.

Now the Bishop of Woolwich, the imitator of Bultmann and others, says the same thing – a kind of muddled gramophone record of their teaching. Let us grant that he is concerned to help others. All these people are. That is the extraordinary thing about them. They say that if you really want to help people, then this is the only way to do it, and they say that those of us who go on preaching the old gospel in the old way are foolish. Incidentally, there is one interesting, practical comment that one could make – the more they preach and teach in that way, the fewer the people who listen to them. It is still a fact that it is the old supernatural gospel that assumes nothing about modern men and women, except that they are the same as human beings have always been – that they are sinners controlled by the devil, who need to be born again and can only be saved by the blood of Christ – it is such preaching that still appeals to them because it is the only truth.

There is a second way of being conformed to this world in one's thinking, and this is found even in the realm of evangelism. It is very subtle. The apostle's exhortation, re-member, means: Do not allow yourself to be controlled by the outlook and the thinking of this world, apart from Christ and without the Spirit. What, then, about a kind of evangelism which says, 'Modern men and women no longer like preaching and long services, but they do like films. So don't preach, especially don't preach long sermons, but show films.' What about that? The world says, 'We like everything to be bright and breezy. We don't like solemnity. We don't like too much seriousness.'

So what about an evangelism which says: 'Well now, that's what the world likes. It likes colour and glamour and a lot of singing. It doesn't like too much reasoning but it does like stories and illustrations, so let's give people that.' Is not this conforming to the world? The moment you allow the world – men and women without the Spirit and without Christ – the moment you set them up as a standard, and not the truth itself as revealed, then, I say, you have already violated this principle.

Here, again, of course, we must not go to extremes. Some-body may think that I am arguing for solemnity or a lack of liveliness, or a miserable, droning service. I am doing nothing of the sort. All I am saying is that if you once grant the principle that people who are not Christians are to control your message or your method, then you are conforming to this world.

But come on to the realm of morals, for, of course, these things all go together. If you go wrong in your theology and in your evangelism, then your morals will inevitably follow suit, and we are seeing that at the present time. Here we find the basis of what is called 'the new morality'. This teaching is nothing but a blank contradiction of Paul's exhortation not to be conformed to this world. Its whole basis is, again, that it is the people in the world who decide what is right and wrong. This is a most solemn and serious matter. It is the basis of the law of this land as it is being taught at the present time. We are told that we must never legislate against the will and the opinion of the majority of the people.

This was the argument behind the Wolfenden Report[1] which has now been passed in the Houses of Parliament. The argument is that if the majority of enlightened people hold the view that this perversion should not be regarded as a crime, then you must not regard it as such. I could mention books which deal with this in a very learned manner and which were the basis of the Wolfenden Report. If the majority opinion has changed, it is said, then you must change your law accordingly. And exactly the same thing has happened on the issue of capital punishment for the crime of murder. The argument has simply been that modern men and women with their enlightened minds cannot accept this. So our laws are to be decided entirely by majority opinion and that, again, is conforming to this world.

But it is much more serious when that kind of argument comes into the realm of the church and her moral teaching, and that is the very thing that is done by this so-called South Bank school of theology. Let me give you a quotation. In Sweden the main church is the Lutheran Church. You may have read during the last few years about the state of that country. Sweden was not involved in either of the two world wars, and is now one of the most prosperous countries in the world. However, morally it is in an increasingly deplorable

[1] The Wolfenden Report proposed the relaxation of laws against homosexuality.

condition, and what is so terrible is that the Lutheran Church in Sweden is, at the present time – I am quoting – 'discussing seriously whether pre-marital intercourse must, in view of the facts of present Swedish life, be regarded as sin under all circumstances'.

Now you notice what is being said. The Lutheran Church is not arguing about whether pre-marital intercourse is wrong in and of itself according to the law of God. No, it is raising the question 'in view of the facts of present Swedish life'. Morals in Sweden have gone down and down and the church is now seriously debating whether or not it has a right to maintain that old standard which the church has always maintained. That, again, is 'conforming to this world'. It is basing teaching upon popular opinion and not upon God's revealed, holy will. To throw the apostle's teaching overboard in this way is not only wrong in and of itself, but it means that the laws will constantly have to be changed. People say, 'Oh, under certain conditions homosexuality is not a sin, it is not a crime, so change the laws.' But then something else may happen, causing the laws to be changed again. So there is no stability and nobody knows exactly what they should do.

But apart from all that, I repeat that the big principle is that biblical teaching starts with the fundamental postulate that popular opinion is not the determining factor. Our theology tells us – Paul starts doing this in Romans 1:18 and continues in the following chapters – that men and women are fallen and perverted. They are not capable of judging in a true way. They are unreliable. They are governed by 'the prince of the power of the air, the spirit that now worketh in the children of disobedience [*Eph.* 2:2]. Their opinion is, therefore, of no ultimate value. In these matters the world does not decide because it cannot do so, and we must never therefore allow our thinking to be determined and controlled by the world and its opinion.

Now I do hope that nobody is imagining that all this merits the designation of obscurantism. It is not that. I am not saying that you should bury your head in the sand and just maintain some status quo over and against changes that are taking place in the world. I am not saying that for a single second. What I am saying is that we have a great, basic, fundamental position, which the advance of science and knowledge does not change to the slightest extent. Therefore, while we are open to any fresh light or knowledge that comes in any realm, in our assessment of men and women and their conduct, we start by saying that we cannot get any help from that direction, for it is 'the world', and we are told, 'Be not conformed to this world.' Our thinking, our ideas, our practice, our everything, are controlled from above by the revelation which we have in God's Word, and in that alone.

Seven

*

I beseech you therefore, brethren, by the mercies of God, that ye present your bodies a living sacrifice, holy, acceptable unto God, which is your reasonable service. And be not conformed to this world: but be ye transformed by the renewing of your mind, that ye may prove what is that good, and acceptable, and perfect, will of God.

Romans 12:1–2

We have seen that, speaking generally, the thinking of the church and the world today are governed by the mind of this world, which is a direct contradiction of what the apostle tells us here in Romans 12.

But having made that statement, I feel constrained to issue a word of warning. In my last study I had to leave my statement incomplete, owing to the exigencies of time and it would be very wrong indeed if we were to leave it at that point. I have stated the principle, and I repeat it. It is wrong for the church to allow her thinking about theology, her evangelism and ethics to be governed by the mind and outlook of the world. But having established that general principle, I must go on to point out that we are doing something reprehensible if we interpret that in terms of becoming obscurantist. We react so violently, and move so easily from one extreme to the other that the danger confronting Christian people – it is always a danger and especially in the more conscientious – is of swinging right over from the extreme of being governed by the mind and outlook of the world to the exact opposite, which is obscurantism.

Let me illustrate this. You have no doubt often seen references in the newspapers or in other places to the Roman

Catholic Church and her opposition to Galileo. This is often used as a reason for dismissing the whole of Christianity. 'But', people say, 'look at the Roman Church, how she opposed the teaching of that new astronomy.'

Now we must face this quite honestly. When the Church opposed Galileo, she was doing something that was wrong; she was guilty of obscurantism. But the important thing for us to discover is why she ever fell into that error, because you and I can fall into the same error unless we are clear about it. Now what happened was that the Roman Catholic Church, instead of having her thinking determined solely by the Bible, was being governed by the Bible plus the philosophy of Aristotle. She had made Aristotle's ideas a fundamental part of her dogmatic teaching. She had gone beyond the Bible.

In other words, there is nothing in the Bible itself which is opposed to the new teaching concerning astronomy which came in about the end of the sixteenth and the beginning of the seventeenth centuries. When the Roman Catholic Church said that it was wrong and contrary to her teaching, she meant the Bible plus her own philosophical thinking. Because the new astronomy did not fit in with what the Church had always taught about the universe, it was condemned. But now Roman Catholics have had to admit that it was the Church that was wrong.

So we must always be governed by the clear teaching of the Bible. If the Bible does not teach us about a certain matter, then we must not say that this is the biblical teaching. We must realize that it is our opinion, and our opinions can be wrong, though we are Christians. Let me put it to you like this: while we must never submit to the outlook of the world, we must be equally careful never to become traditionalists. There is a difference between tradition and traditionalism. Thank God for every good tradition, but God preserve us from traditionalism! A person who is guilty of traditionalism is someone who starts by saying, 'Everything new is wrong. Anything I have never heard before is certain to be wrong.' And the moment you get into that position, you are in as bad a position as the man who is submitting, on the other extreme, to the mind of the world. As we have seen, there are two extremes here: worldliness and traditionalism, and my principle is that we are never to be at either of these extremes; we are always to be in the biblical position.

Of course, it is more difficult to be in the biblical position than it is to be at the extremes. Extremes are always easy. There is a craving in us all for a sort of ready-reckoner Christianity. Problem? Turn it up. Here you are, you cannot do that! But that is not biblical. If you have a biblical attitude, you will be aware of certain tensions; everything will not be cut and dried.

That is not only true in the realm of theology, we need the same sort of warning in the matter of evangelism. There is a good deal of talk about this and, I think, a good deal of confusion also. Again, I have laid down the principle that our evangelism must never be governed by the outlook of the world. But once more we must be very careful that we do not react so violently to that as to go to the other extreme, which is equally wrong and harmful. We must be very careful lest, in our desire not to be worldly in our evangelistic methods, we put ourselves into a position in which we lose any point of contact whatsoever with the world which is round and about us, and again become guilty of another form of traditionalism, or, indeed, a form of legalism.

There are many people who are in great trouble about evangelistic methods and it is quite right that we should consider these. That is why I mentioned it earlier. But God forbid that I should be misunderstood. There are people who object to the singing of hymns and regard it as virtually sinful, and there are others who object to certain forms or methods of evangelism. Now that is the sort of thing that needs to be examined.

I happen to have had this problem put to me a number of times quite recently. Some Christian people in different parts of this country are beginning to use what is called (I believe I am using the correct term) 'Coffee bar evangelism'. I know of one instance where a group of Christian men have taken over a building, and every evening invite people in off the street, particularly young men and women who are leading the sort of life that we read about in the newspapers but which many of us know nothing at all about in practice. It is all done on a voluntary basis. They are concerned about these young people so they invite them in and give them coffee or tea, and then address them on the subject of their souls and the way of salvation. Now this is subject to a great deal of criticism from many people who say, 'This is a worldly method. Fancy supplying coffee!' It is regarded as something terrible which should not be done. Similar criticism is levelled at other voluntary evangelistic activities.

I am raising this question to show you that we must be very careful, as we interpret Paul's instruction here, that, firstly, we do not develop a hyper-critical spirit. We must never allow ourselves to get into a position in which we react so violently to what people are doing that we turn ourselves into spiritual detectives and inspectors waiting for things on which we can pounce and which we can denounce simply because they have not been done in the past, simply because they are new, and simply because they are the sorts of things that we would not instinctively do ourselves.

Now is this just my personal opinion? Let me show you that it is not, but that it is biblical teaching. There is a great warning to us at this point from the Scriptures and from history. My dear friends, we must watch our spirits. We may be very clear about refusing worldly methods – all right, I myself have laid that down as a principle and we must always adhere to it – but let us be very careful that we do not develop a false spirit.

So what is my warning from the Scriptures? It is the way in which the Pharisees and scribes reacted to our blessed Lord and Saviour. They saw the tax-collectors and the sinners drawing near to Him, and they saw that He was ready to receive them, that He was ready to sit down with them and to eat and drink with them, and they turned on Him aghast and said, 'This man receiveth sinners' [*Luke* 15:2]. 'This man is a wine-bibber, a friend of publicans and sinners!' [*Luke* 7:34]. They were amazed. Fancy our Lord mixing with people like that and sitting down and eating and drinking with them! To the Pharisee this was dreadful, unthinkable. Yes, but remember this outcry was the measure of their complete failure in the realm of the spirit, to understand the whole object of the coming of our blessed Lord into this world. That was the terrible thing about the Pharisee.

Again, in exactly the same way, you find that these same kinds of people, who are called 'Judaizers' later on in the New Testament, followed the Apostle Paul everywhere and were highly critical of his methods and his dealings with the Gentiles. They said, 'This man is quite wrong. He's doing something that has never been done before. He does not compel these people to submit to circumcision.' Now that was the whole error. They thought that the Apostle Paul was being lax in his evangelism.

And then, to turn to history, the great George Whitefield, for example, got into trouble because of his open-air preaching. John Wesley stumbled at this, and could not understand it. George Whitefield was preaching in the open air, but it was thought that you should not preach and evangelize anywhere except in a consecrated building. What right has a man to preach in a building which has not been consecrated, or to stand on a table or on a stone in the open air? Now this was a genuine objection. At first Wesley thought that he was being biblical when he opposed Whitefield. And he was not the only one, of course. There were many who thought that this was a terribly wrong thing for a man to do. It was something new. So the question was, 'Can this be right?' Wesley, however, quite soon became convinced about open air preaching and began to preach in this way himself.

I could give you other examples. Those of us who are so clear about not being governed by the mind and the thinking of the world must always be aware of the danger, the great and very real danger, of becoming guilty of the spirit of the Pharisees and scribes, the traditionalists. We must be quite certain that we are being controlled by biblical teaching and thinking and not by our own personal prejudices or tradition. If we are not governed by biblical thinking, we shall soon find ourselves resisting some new thing that God is doing in a difficult age such as this. This is a very subtle matter, but if we cannot prove that our opinion is biblical, then we must be very careful in what we say.

And so I have often had to say to our friends who are opposed to singing hymns and who say you should sing nothing but psalms that they should prove it from the Bible. But they cannot. Take the passage from Ephesians 5:19. What are those 'spiritual songs'? I have no doubt whatsoever but that it means singing under the direct inspiration of the Spirit, exactly as you have it in 1 Corinthians 14:15. I shall not go into detail about that now – I am only showing you the danger of being governed by a rigid traditionalism.

Secondly, we must never be governed by the spirit of fear. This is a dreadful thing and terrible crimes have been committed as a result of it. A man can be very honest, but if he is governed by the spirit of fear and concerned only about his own correctitude, he puts himself in a dangerous position. So if ever, in these matters, we find ourselves primarily concerned about ourselves and our own correctness, we are already in danger.

Let me put that positively. If a concern for the souls and the salvation of others is not my leading motive, I must be very careful what I say about evangelism. I should always maintain my evangelistic concern. If that is not primary, there is something wrong with me. The foremost task of the church is to evangelize, to preach the gospel of salvation that the souls of men and women may be saved. The primary business of the church is not to be always guarding her own correctness and her own perfection. You can put an iron curtain round yourself in a spiritual sense. You may be absolutely perfect within, in theory, at any rate, and be completely useless in the matter of evangelism. 'Let a man examine himself' [*1 Cor.* 11:28]. There are people who spend the whole of their time in safeguarding themselves and their doctrines and their activities, but in the end there is no activity in relation to the outside world. That is wrong – always. I repeat that the primary task of the church is that of evangelism.

Moving on from attitudes to methods, I would lay it down as a principle that we must always reduce our methods to the absolute minimum. That is a good rule, I think. We must never trust the methods. But let me put it in biblical terms. Take the Apostle Paul's words in 1 Cor. 9:22: 'I am made all things to all men, that I might by all means save some.' Now that is an apologia – the apostle is justifying his own evangelistic methods. He was being misunderstood and grievously persecuted by the legalists and the Judaizers and that is his answer.

So what does this mean for us? Well, I think it means this:

there must never be any variation in the *message*. The message is one and we must never change it in any sense. But I think that Paul teaches equally clearly that we must have a certain degree of elasticity in our methods. In 1 Corinthians 9:20–21 he tells us that when he deals with a Jew, he does so as with a Jew; with a Gentile, as with a Gentile; with a man who is under the law, as under the law; with a man who is not under the law, as without the law. 'Being not without law to God,' he says, 'but under the law to Christ' [1 Cor. 9:21]. So you must always speak to the people you are trying to reach, and deal with them, as they are, not as you would wish them to be.

Now, of course, every preacher wishes that every time he preached he had before him people who knew their Bibles from cover to cover, and had read all the theology, and were well versed in the Puritans. Here they are, they are ready for it! But it is seldom one gets a congregation like that, and if a preacher does not preach to the congregation that is in front of him, he had better go out of the pulpit. If I do not make my message clear to people as they are, I am a very bad preacher. I may say, 'But they ought not to be like that', but the moment I say that, I am being a bad preacher. It is my business to improve them, and if I do not start with them as they are, I will never help them. It is no use my giving a great exposition of the law to a people who know nothing about the law. I must teach them about the law first. That is exactly what the great apostle did, and you and I must do the same thing.

What do we know about some of these poor adolescents in this present age, young people who have never had a chance in life, many of them, kicked about from pillar to post by drunken parents and others, what do we know about them and their background? What right have we to postulate as to what these people should be like? No, our business is to deal with them as they are, and to try by all means to bring the knowledge of the Lord to them.

'Ah,' you say, 'but you're opening the door now to everything.'

I am not; I am controlling it by saying that the message does not vary. And I will add to that: the motive must always be constant. It must always be to bring those listening to a knowledge of salvation. And if you can make no contact at all with people unless you give them a cup of coffee, then I say in the name of God, give them many cups of coffee! What is your concern? Is it the purity of your church and your methods, or is it the salvation of the souls of men and women and boys and girls who are going to hell round and about you? As long as your motive is correct and pure it will govern your methods.

So I would say, you must never go in for change for the sake of change, that is worldly, but on the other hand, you must never say that all change is wrong or you will be with the Pharisees and the scribes. There must never be any levity. You must never allow your methods to contradict your message but how the giving of a cup of coffee contradicts the message passes my comprehension! Of course, if you are going to rely upon cups of coffee, then you are wrong again, because you are relying upon something you should not rely upon. It is only a means to an end. You rely upon the Word, and the Spirit upon the Word.

So there are extremes. It is not simple. You cannot lay down absolute rules and laws. It is easy to criticize people and their methods, but I say again, be very careful that you are not criticizing a work of God, something that God is prepared to honour even though you may think it is defective. We must never be guilty of rigidity, but neither must we ever be guilty of laxity. Christians who are rigid are very poor Christians; they are really legalists and probably suffering from the spirit of fear. They do not know much about the freedom and the liberty of the children of God.

Rigidity! Laxity! Both are wrong. Christians hold a balance in the middle. They know the truth; they know their motives; they know their own hearts; and they only employ methods to get a point of contact, to give an opportunity for the gospel. That is their only concern. And even there they must always keep watch to ensure that their methods never contradict their message. I suggest that you can never get closer to a definition than that. None of your 'ready reckoners' in the spiritual life! That is Pharisaism. This is a matter of the spirit. Let us watch our spirits and avoid the grave dangers at the two extremes.

So, then, we have explained, perhaps, more fully, and in a sense qualified, what I was saying in the last study. Because if we had left it only at that, it would have been an extreme emphasis and we must keep the two sides in balance. But now, having done that, let us come to the question of practice. 'Be not conformed to this world.' No longer thinking, but putting into practice. Yet, of course, thinking comes in all the time. The same general point has once more to be made here: we must avoid the extremes which will always lead us to miss the true biblical position. I am certain, as I say that, that I am being misunderstood and people are saying, 'Oh, he has become a compromiser, has he? I thought he was a man who held his views strongly; now he is saying a bit of this and a bit of that. There it is: common denominator, divide by two!' But I am saying the exact opposite. I am saying that you must hold two positions in tension, which is much more difficult; but that, I repeat, is the truly biblical position.

'Be not conformed to this world,' says Paul.

'All right,' says a man listening to me, 'I agree with that a hundred per cent, and therefore I'm going out of the world tonight to be a monk and enter a monastery. I'm finishing with the world. You cannot be a Christian in this world. I'm told here that I must not be conformed to it. How can a man be in business without being conformed to the world? How can a man be in a profession without being conformed to this world? No, no, there is only one thing to do: I'm getting out of it.' So he becomes a monk or a hermit.

Now this is what I call one of the wrong extremes, this violent reaction that says that the only way not to be conformed to the world is to go out of it. That was the whole grievous fallacy behind monasticism. It was a failure to understand the New Testament teaching. And, of course, this was the grand truth that was given to Martin Luther to see, and we need, many of us, to see the same thing at this present time.

But there is a second danger, which I would describe under the heading of legalism. 'Be not conformed to this world.' So the devil comes and he will get you right over to a legalistic position. Now this always appears to be the easy way, does it not? As I have said already, we all like to have rules and regulations. We always have a feeling that it is easier to be 'under the law' than 'under grace'. The law is cut and dried – one, two, three, four, five, six, seven rules – there they are, all numbered, and all you do is to look up the number. Perfectly simple! No trouble at all.

But that is not the position of the New Testament believers. They are not 'under law', but 'under grace', and they are being treated as fully grown adults. As the Apostle Paul says, in effect, 'While you were children and infants you needed a schoolmaster, somebody to look after you and to keep you in order; but you are no longer there, you have been taken out of that' [see *Gal.* 3:23–25]. That does not, of course, mean lawlessness, as I shall show you, but it does mean that you are not *under* law.

A modern illustration of the danger of legalism is the Amish people of North America. They are a subdivision of the Mennonites who began as a result of the preaching of Menno Simons, a Dutch Reformer of the early Protestant period. When many of the Protestants emigrated to America, his teaching also spread there. The Amish people of Pennsylvania live strictly according to their interpretation of our text – 'Be not conformed to this world' – and so anything which has arisen from modern society is looked upon as worldliness. They allow no electricity, no curtains, no photographs, no tractors, televisions or telephones. They wear very special clothing and only allow the use of a car if someone lives so far from the house where they hold their meetings that one is necessary – even then, the car must have no rubber tyres. Now you may laugh at them, but all this is something which is believed and practised by very honest people who are trying not to conform to this world.

I myself once knew a very godly man who told me that as a young man he had passed through a phase of legalism and the form it took in his case was that he felt it was wrong to do anything on Sunday which you could do the night before. So he used to put his boots on and tie them up on Saturday night and sleep in them. Again, you may laugh at this, and perhaps you are right. But all I want you to see is that the danger confronting some of us is not the danger of conformity to the world, but of swinging so violently against that in a spirit of fear, that we become sheer legalists which, remember, is equally bad and condemned in the New Testament in so many places.

The next danger, one which, again, we have already touched upon, is that of Pharisaism. There is not much difference between legalism and Pharisaism except that in the case of the Pharisee the sins are sins of the human spirit. The Mennonites, let me say this for them, are a humble people; I do not think I would describe these Amish Mennonites as Pharisees though I think they are badly instructed. Incidentally, they are also an interesting example of what the devil does with us. He will isolate one thing and make us concentrate on that, but we will not be equally clear on other things. Many of the Amish are tobacco growers and are doing very well indeed out of growing tobacco. They do not smoke it but they grow it and they make money out of it. This is the kind of thing that happens when the devil drives us to extremes and we have ceased to be biblical in our thinking. Where is there anything in the Scripture that condemns the use of electricity or the internal combustion engine? That is not biblical, that is prejudice and observance of a human tradition.

Now Pharisaism is different in the sense that it is mainly a matter of spiritual pride, or self-centredness and self-satisfaction. 'God, I thank thee, that I am not as other men are . . . or even as this publican' [*Luke* 18:11]. If that is your attitude to what you call worldliness, you are in as bad a position as the worldly Christian, quite as bad. And, of course, the other characteristic of the Pharisee, always, is censoriousness. The moment we become censorious we are hopelessly in transgression at this other extreme.

Then the fourth danger is that of the people who have not heeded this injunction at all. It is the danger of antinomianism, which, as we have seen, is the view that Christians do not need to obey moral laws, and I think there is a great deal of this at the present time. It is the opposite of the position taken by the poor Amish Mennonites and many others among us. This, again, is just a reaction. I have known Christians who are not concerned about their conduct at all. Their attitude is that once a man is saved, he is always saved, so it does not matter what he does. This view is always ready to raise its ugly head. If in any way you want to live a life that is as near as you can get to the world without actually sinning, you are revealing a worldly mind and outlook. It shows where your heart is and is condemned completely by Paul's injunction.

But perhaps the most subtle kind of antinomianism, and to me the most contemptible, is that which conforms to the world but uses as a pretext its concern about evangelism. So it teaches that women should wear make-up in order to make Christianity attractive to people who are not Christians. Oh, how subtle is the devil! It is a conforming to the world, it is a form of worldliness masquerading as a great desire to evangelize. I do not think the use of lipstick has ever been responsible for the salvation of a single soul. The world expects us to be different, my dear friends, and we must be very careful of these specious excuses suggested to us by the devil to allow us to do what we really want to do; that is the terrible thing.

What, then, are we to do? Once again, I cannot give you detailed instructions, I can only put principles before you. Here is the great overriding principle: 'Love not the world, neither the things that are in the world' [*1 John* 2:15]. Do not love them. If you have any love for the world as we have defined it, and 'the things of the world', you are already wrong.

Secondly, 'Abstain from all appearance of evil' [*1 Thess.* 5:22]. There are certain things that we all know are wrong, they are denounced in the Bible itself, so there must be no argument about this – we just must not do them; if we do, we are conforming to this world. Where it is plainly laid down that something is sinful, Christians must not even consider it; they reject it.

Thirdly, let us not be governed or moulded by the world. What do I mean by that? Well, to use the modern phraseology, if there is any desire in you to be 'with it', that is conforming to the world. I do not care what form it takes. Any desire to just 'be there', to be modern, up to date, and so on, is always of the devil. That is conformity to the world, whether it be in your appearance or in the articles that you write, or in anything else.

Then, fourthly, we must never be governed by the fashions of this world. Is there anything more ludicrous about the world than its fashions, its show and ostentation – the 'lust of the flesh, and the lust of the eyes, and the pride of life' [*1 John* 2:16]? That is the characteristic of the world – it is always a matter of show and ostentation. And look at the ridiculous extremes to which the world goes in its so-called fashions. Hairstyles, fashions for men as well as women, all swing from one extreme to another. We must never be conformed to this. Now let me be fair – I know it is difficult. People say, 'But I must buy what's in the shops.' I agree with you. Up to a certain point, one cannot help but conform. One is a helpless victim. All I am saying is that not only do you object to having to do that, but you do not want to. To put it another way, if ever you find you are governed by a spirit of fear and by public opinion, if you find yourself thinking, 'How will this affect me? Will it do so adversely?', then you really are conforming to the world.

'Then what are your rules?' asks someone. I cannot give you detailed rules, but let me put it like this: we must avoid all that; we must avoid all extremes. I would say to the Christian, never be aggressive in any sense. You can be aggressive even in your nonconformity to the world, but the Christian is never aggressive.

Or, again, never parade. Do not be part of any fashion parade, but do not parade on the opposite extreme, either. Never make a parade of yourself. It was the Pharisees who made 'broad their phylacteries' [*Matt.* 23:5]; and it was the Pharisees who always wanted to herald what they were doing so that the world would admire them. So if you are always announcing that you are not conforming to the world, then you are really conforming in a subtle way.

No, the way in which Christians live is always to be an expression of their new character; that is all they are concerned about. Christians know what they are doing and why they are doing it. There ought to be something almost instinctive about the Christian in this matter of not conforming to the world. I once saw something which has always struck me as being a perfect illustration of this. I knew a man who was converted out of a terrible life of drunkenness and many other even more terrible things. Now the great feature of this man was his extraordinary moustaches; they were an unusual length, and he told me that he had often fought over them. Another man, in a semi-drunken condition, would challenge him as to which of them had a wider span of moustaches and they would fight about it and many a time half kill one another.

Well, this man was converted, and I remember that a few

weeks after his conversion I was standing at the door at the close of a week-night service, saying goodnight to the congregation, when I saw this man coming towards me with no moustaches, and I was most annoyed. I felt sure that some busybody in the church had told him to shave them off. So when he came to me I said, 'Who told you to get rid of your moustaches?'

'Nobody,' he said.

'Now come along,' I said, 'don't you shield anybody. I don't like this sort of thing. I don't like these self-appointed detectives in the church. Tell me, who told you? I want to know because I want to correct that person.'

He said, 'Nobody told me to do it.'

'So why did you do it?' I asked.

He replied, 'I'll tell you; I did it this morning. I was getting up and I had a wash and as I was drying myself I happened to see myself in the mirror. I saw the moustaches and I said to myself, "Them things don't belong to a Christian!" So I got hold of scissors and I cut them off and shaved the rest.'

That is what I am talking about. The Christian has a feeling. He knows. There is something that tells him. There is a good text for this, is there not: 'Only let your conversation be as it becometh the gospel of Christ' [*Phil.* 1:27]. That is the test. Is it becoming? Does it fit in with, does it match, this glorious gospel that I profess to believe? And the Christian has this understanding instinctively within him, so he does not parade, he does not announce, he does not call his trumpeter, he just wants everything about himself to be in conformity with this great and glorious gospel.

The great characteristic of Christian men and women is always moderation. They are never at any extreme. In their dress, Christians are never showy, but, equally, they should never be dowdy either. For a Christian to dress in a dowdy manner is as bad as to dress in a showy manner, because if you do dress dowdily, you attract attention to yourself. Christians only want to attract people to the gospel. So I would say that Christians are always neat and tidy and that is something we can all be. They are not obtrusive or offensive in any sense at all. Christians are always inoffensive, as people who bear witness to Christ. Take, for instance, the question of alcoholic drink. There is a way of refusing it that does much more harm than good. But true Christians are courteous. They do not hold up a placard and announce their refusal. No, they speak quietly. People will look at a Christian and say, 'There's something different about that person.' So they have to ask what it is.

That is the way not to conform to the world. That is the way to bear your testimony to the Lord Jesus Christ and what He has done for you in His great and glorious salvation. I cannot get nearer a definition than that. That is the rule: 'Only let your conversation' – the whole of your life, demeanour, deportment, everything – 'be as it becometh the gospel of Christ.' You are not a worldling, but you are not a crank either – Christian cranks have always done more harm than good. Christians are men and women of moderation. They are like our blessed Lord Himself, who walked through this world often unrecognized, and yet there was always something. He could not be hidden, not because He made a show – 'He shall not cry, nor lift up, nor cause his voice to be heard in the street' [*Isa.* 42:2] – but His light would shine forth. That is the ambition of the Christian, and as long as we are governed by that we can be quite certain we shall not conform to this world.

Eight

*

> *I beseech you therefore, brethren, by the mercies of God, that ye present your bodies a living sacrifice, holy, acceptable unto God, which is your reasonable service. And be not conformed to this world: but be ye transformed by the renewing of your mind, that ye may prove what is that good, and acceptable, and perfect, will of God.*
>
> Romans 12:1–2

In these two verses, as we have already seen, the apostle gives us what is, in many ways, the most remarkable summary that is to be found anywhere in the New Testament of the Christian teaching concerning sanctification. It is the great theme in the New Testament, a theme that is applicable only to Christian people, to believers. The doctrine of sanctification has nothing to say to those who are not Christians, but it is vital for those who are. It means the kind of life we are to live because we are Christians, and here the apostle introduces it all in just two verses. We have considered the inducements, or the motives, which the apostle puts before us as he calls upon us to live this life: it is in the light of all we have been learning in this great Epistle; it is because of God's mercies to us.

So we are considering what we actually have to do in practice, and having seen what this means for us negatively, we come now to the positive: 'Be ye transformed by the renewing of your mind.' All these statements are important, but this really is one of the most crucial of all. Here the apostle tells us not only what we are to do, positively, he now also gives us the reason why we are not to be conformed to the world, and it is only as we understand this positive statement that we can see that it is inevitable that we must not be conformed. Paul thus provides us with the only real incentive to the practical living out of the Christian life. I do not hesitate to say that the whole secret of living the Christian life, the whole secret of understanding the biblical doctrine of sanctification, is found in these words: 'Be ye transformed by the renewing of your mind.'

So what does it mean? Well, I want to show you, first of all, that the apostle's doctrine is to be found in two words in this verse, namely, 'conformed' and 'transformed'. You see his contrast: Do not be *conformed* to this world; be ye *transformed*. Now we have been considering in detail what it means not to be conformed to the world and its ways, but now let us look at the meaning of this word 'conformed'. An excellent definition, given by the lexicographers, is: 'It is the act of an individual assuming an outward expression' – something he takes or puts on – 'that does not come from within him and which is not representative of his inner heart life.'

Now let me give you an example to show you what a good definition that is. The same root word is used in Philippians 2 with regard to our blessed Lord and Saviour and He demonstrates its meaning perfectly: 'Who, being in the form of God, thought it not robbery to be equal with God: but made himself of no reputation, and took upon him the form of a servant, and was made in the likeness of men: and being found in *fashion* as a man . . .' [*Phil.* 2:6-8]. In this account of the incarnation, we are told that the eternal Son of God was made in 'fashion' as a man. When our Lord appeared in this world as a man, it was not something that came from within Him, because what came from within Him was His eternal deity and Godhead. When you look at Him and see Him as the babe in the manger, or as the boy in the temple, or as the carpenter, you are not seeing an outward expression of what He really is, but something which He assumed. He took on this humanity; He was fashioned as a man in His incarnation.

Now in the Greek, this word 'fashion' is exactly the same word as the word we have here in the second verse of Romans 12, except that in Romans a prefix is added. Paul says: 'Never be in fashion with the world. Do not put on this outward appearance of belonging to it.'

Then, secondly, he says, 'But' – rather – 'be ye transformed.'
This means the act of a person changing his outward expression to a different one. It now comes from and *is* expressive of
his inner being. But here now the man is doing everything he
can with regard to his outward appearance to make it expressive of his inner being.

Again, let me give you an illustration which will help to
show you the exact meaning of this word 'transformed'. You
find it in Matthew chapter 17. The first two verses read: 'And
after six days Jesus taketh Peter, James, and John his brother,
and bringeth them up into an high mountain apart. And was
transfigured before them: and his face did shine as the sun, and
his raiment was white as the light.' The word 'transfigured' is
exactly the same word as the word translated here by 'transformed', and the idea is exactly the same. On the Mount of
Transfiguration our Lord now appeared in such a way, and in
such a form, as to give people some impression of His inner
nature and being. Down in the plains of life, before His
disciples and other people, though He was the eternal Son of
God, He appeared to be just a man. But Peter, and James, and
John looking at Him there on the Mount of Transfiguration
now saw something of the Godhead shining through; something of what He really was now became evident.

Another use of this same word is helpful; it is in 2
Corinthians 3:18: 'But we all, with open face beholding as in a
glass the glory of the Lord, are changed [transformed] into the
same image from glory to glory, even as by the Spirit of the
Lord.' Now that is exactly the same word, put in a slightly
different manner. But the idea is the same. Paul has just used
the illustration of Moses coming down from Mount Sinai after
receiving the Ten Commandments from God. When the
people saw Moses they ran to meet him, but suddenly they
stopped and were frightened. What frightened them? Oh,
Moses' face was shining! Because of his communion with
God he was beginning to reflect from his face something of
the glory of God. That is it. And the apostle says that that is
what is to happen to us as Christian people, that we are to go
on being transformed into the image of the Lord Jesus Christ.
Something of His glory is to be manifest in us, and it is through
us that He will glorify Himself among men and women.

So then, those are the two key words: 'Do not be conformed' and 'be transformed' and this is vital teaching. The apostle is telling us that when as Christians we live in this world in a worldly manner, we are like actors masquerading as something that we really are not. We are not giving expression to our true nature and being but are acting as if we were men and women of the world. We are putting on an expression which is not a true expression of what we are. We are involving ourselves in a contradiction.

'So,' Paul says in effect, 'instead of doing that, do the exact opposite. Let your true, real, inner nature now shine through. Let it be evident; let it be manifest. Let this happen to you, in its measure, which happened to our Lord on the Mount of Transfiguration. Let it be known that you have been created anew after His image. Let that be seen: "Be ye transformed." '

There is one further preliminary point. Does it strike you as odd that this is something which we are *commanded* to do? And yet this is the position. As Christians we are already changed. That is the regeneration; that is the rebirth. And yet the apostle tells us: 'Be not conformed . . but be ye transformed . . .' This is something over which people have often stumbled, but it is the characteristic New Testament way of teaching holiness or sanctification. I always like to put it like this. The apostle is really saying: 'Be what you are.' You have been transformed, so, because of that, transform yourself. In a sense, he is saying, 'If you, as a Christian, are living according to the mind and outlook of this world, you are being unnatural. So do not do that. Be natural. Let it be evident that you are a Christian. Throw the mask away, it doesn't belong to you any longer.'

There, then, is the great basis, and we must now consider how we are to carry out this exhortation. We are conscious that we are born again, that we are new creatures, how, therefore, are we to live the Christian life? Now the great practical exhortation, it seems to me, and this sounds quite mad to the world, is this: Do not start with your conduct.

'But,' says somebody, 'we are dealing with the whole question of conduct here.'

I agree. But Christianity deals with conduct by not starting with it. In other words, we must stop thinking about Christian living in terms of a mere modification of, or a mere improvement on, our former behaviour. It is not that. When you begin to consider how you are to live the Christian life, do not start immediately with the details of living. You will go wrong if you do. Start in the realm of the mind and of the outlook and of the understanding.

This is vital. I think I can say quite honestly that in my pastoral work there is nothing that I have had to say, in some shape or form, more frequently than just this very thing. People come to me over a particular sin or temptation that they have been fighting and say, 'What can I do about it?' And I invariably tell them, 'Forget all about that particular sin and temptation at first.' And they are amazed at that, but it is based on this teaching. In the Christian life you do not start with the particular problems. You start with the *whole* of the Christian life. This is a fundamental difference in approach and I venture to call it 'the differentia' of Christian teaching. It is the thing that separates Christian teaching with regard to conduct from every other type of moral teaching.

I remember reading once a comment which seemed to me to put it perfectly: 'Jesus demanded, not a reformation of behaviour, but a transformation of character.' If you believe in putting a text on your wall put up that! You see the difference? Moral systems are only concerned about behaviour and reformation of behaviour. That is their one interest. That is the one concern of the law of the land. It starts and ends with behaviour. But Christianity does not. Behaviour to the Christian is an end product and is not the primary concern. We are concerned with a transformation of character.

This is the whole secret of sanctification. People think that if only they can deal with a particular temptation and get rid of a particular sin, then all will be well. But it will not, of course, and the very fact that they think that, is absolute proof that it will not, because even if they do deal with that, something else will rise. They are starting in the wrong way and at the wrong end.

No, you must start by realizing who and what you are, the whole truth about yourself. You must not think of yourself as the person who does this or that wrong thing, but you must realize what you are as a Christian: 'Be ye transformed by the renewing of your mind.' The exhortation is: In the first instance, do not take up particular problems, and see what you can do about this, and then try to tackle that, so dealing with your life in a piecemeal manner. That is not Christianity, but morality. Get your thinking straight; get your whole outlook right. Start with the whole, then the parts will fit into position.

Now this is, to me, not only a vital but a very thrilling doctrine. It was something that the Apostle Paul brought out frequently in his writings. For instance, read again that section from the fourth chapter of his Epistle to the Ephesians, because there he sets it out in a fuller and perhaps greater way than here in Romans. Here he is only summarizing the whole teaching, but there he really does work it out, and it is the best commentary that you will ever find on this second verse of Romans 12. There in Ephesians 4, having again laid down the great doctrine, Paul stops and says, 'This I say therefore, and testify in the Lord' – what? – 'that ye henceforth walk not as other Gentiles walk, in the vanity of their mind.' 'Be not conformed to this world.'

Why do the others walk like that? Paul goes on, 'Having the understanding darkened, being alienated from the life of God through the ignorance that is in them, because of the blindness of their heart: who being past feeling have given themselves over unto lasciviousness, to work all uncleanness with greediness. But ye have not so learned Christ.' That is not what you have learned, says Paul; you have learned the exact opposite. 'If so be that ye have heard him, and have been taught by him, as the truth is in Jesus.' What then? 'That ye put off concerning the former conversation the old man, which is corrupt according to the deceitful lusts; and be renewed in the spirit of your mind.' He always starts with that. Then he goes on: 'And that ye put on the new man' – but you do not put on the new man until you have been 'renewed in the spirit of your mind'. Then you put on the new man – 'which after God is created in righteousness and true holiness' [*Eph.* 4:17–24].

There, first, is the great doctrine, the essential teaching. Then the apostle continues, in effect, 'All right, I want to help you. What does all this mean? Well, it means things like this: Wherefore putting away lying, speak every man truth with his neighbour . . . Be ye angry, and sin not: let not the sun go down upon your wrath: neither give place to the devil' [*Eph.* 4:25–27].

I do trust I am making this plain and clear to you. In Christianity you do not start with the particular, you start with the whole, whereas in every other type of thinking you start with the particular. So the whole approach to the problem is different, and it is because so many do not see this, that they get into a muddle and their lives end in failure.

You start, then, by dealing with your own mind. So if a man comes to me and says, 'I keep on falling into this selfsame sin, what can I do?', I never talk to him about that sin, though that is what he wants me to do. I talk to him about himself. I talk to him about his mind and his whole outlook. That is the only way in which Christianity gives us the victory. If you get your mind fixed on a particular problem, the devil fixes it still more, and you are already partly defeated because you are thinking so much about it. You must get right away from it and start in a different manner.

I could illustrate this principle to you in many different ways. I remember once hearing a man speak on 'Sabbath observance', and I have never forgotten the way he approached this subject. He had been asked to give this talk by a kind of committee within a denomination because the committee was concerned about the observance of the Lord's day. I remember very well how he began. He was absolutely scriptural, and was true to the teaching of the Apostle Paul in particular. He said, 'I always feel, when I approach a subject like this, that the first thing we have got to do is to put it into its family . . .' He meant that observance of the Lord's day is not something isolated, but is a part of a whole. So you do not start by immediately beginning to argue about Lord's day observance. You go away back, you put it into its context, into its setting, and then you will see it in proportion. And that is what you do with all the problems of the Christian life.

Or again, I have occasionally used an illustration like this: Think of these problems as hurdles. How do you jump over a hurdle? You do not walk up to the hurdle and try to elevate yourself over it. It cannot be done. If you want to get over that hurdle, you turn your back on it, and walk away from it as if you have forgotten all about it. Then, when you have gone a great distance – and the higher the hurdle, the longer will be your walk – you turn round, run for all you are worth, and vault over it. That is essentially the Christian teaching; you have this great background. So first you renew your mind.

And renewing means what it says – re-new. We once had a mind which we do not have any longer. The whole trouble with humanity is that it has lost its true mind, it has become insane. It needs to get back the mind it once had. The mind needs to be restored to a condition which has been lost. And this transformation by the renewing of the mind is a continuous process.

Here, again, is a very fascinating thought. In Ephesians, the apostle, you remember, puts it in terms of what he calls 'the spirit of the mind'. He says, 'Be renewed in the spirit of your mind' [*Eph.* 4:23]. That is an elaboration of his words here – 'by the renewing of your mind'. So why does he express it differently in Ephesians? This is a very important point because the mind, as such, is really just a neutral instrument. Take a man who is not a Christian, but then is converted. There is a sense in which he always has the same mind. A man who was rather dull and lacking in ability does not suddenly become a genius because he has become a Christian! Some people seem to think that he should, but they are wrong. Your faculties and powers are not changed when you are regenerate. You have the same instrument that you had before, the same mind in terms of the capacity to think and reason and be logical. That remains constant.

The Apostle Paul had the same mind exactly as he had as Saul of Tarsus. He had a very good mind as Saul of Tarsus; that is why he did better than anybody else in the examinations held by the Pharisees. He was always outstanding. He had a first-class brain – to call it 'brain' emphasizes the aspect of faculty or 'instrument'. So Paul is saying that what needs to be changed is not the apparatus, not the instrument, but 'the spirit of the mind'. There is something that even controls the mind, and that is what needs to be changed.

There are men and women in our world who are brilliant, who have wonderful brains – quick and alert. Yes, but they are using that ability to some base and unworthy end. That is one

of the tragedies of life today, is it not? You must not say that
these people who blaspheme and utter foul things on the
television are unintelligent. That is not their trouble. The
trouble with them is that they are almost devilishly clever.
The trouble is not in their minds, it is in the thing that controls
their minds. The thing that matters in a person is 'the *spirit* of
the mind', that essence, that ultimate power of control which
determines everything else. The interior principle of the mind
which directs all its processes is what must be renewed, not
the mind itself. It is the direction of the mind that needs to be
controlled and to be changed. And the apostle says that this is
the great key principle to Christian living. You must train your
minds to think correctly in the new way. You must take these
minds of yours that hitherto have been working in one
direction and redirect them.

The mind can be compared to a steam engine. There it is. It
has great power, and is standing on rails and facing in one
direction. Now what you must do, says the apostle, is to get
that engine on to one of those turntables that are found in
railway stations so that it is facing the opposite way.
Remember, it is precisely the same engine, with exactly the
same power, but it is now ready to go in a different direction.
Paul – the Saul of Tarsus, who persecuted the church with
such extraordinary ability, excelling everybody even in that –
now preached the gospel with the same energy and the same
ability and the same extraordinary manifestation of understanding.

And that renewal of the mind is the key, according to the
apostle, in this matter of living the Christian life. Let me
therefore sum it up in a number of propositions, which will
help, I trust, to fix this principle in our minds. Go back to the
original trouble with humanity. Why do we have to fight
against temptation and sin? The answer is, of course, the Fall.
What happened when man fell? Was it merely that Adam and
Eve disobeyed a particular commandment of God? Was it
merely that they committed one particular sin? Would to God
that it were!

But it was not. The real thing that happened there in the
Garden of Eden was a change in the mind and the spirit of
Adam and Eve. Until that point they had lived for God, to

enjoy Him and to obey His commandments; and all their thoughts of God were good and loving and obedient. But the devil came in and he did not merely praise that fruit and try to make it attractive. He did that, of course, but what he was really doing was insinuating into the spirit of their minds a new attitude towards God. 'Hath God said?' [*Gen.* 3:1]. God has said it in order to keep you down.

That is what happened; it was not the mere eating of the fruit. The real damage had been done before Adam and Eve began to eat it. The eating was simply the outward expression of the terrible change in their attitude to God and to themselves. They still had the same ability, but that which controlled the ability had now gone wrong. So you find a statement like this in Genesis 6:5 describing the people just before the flood: 'Every imagination of the thoughts of his heart was only evil continually.' That is man and woman as the result of the fall.

Now these words in Genesis 6:5 mean exactly what they say: 'The imagination of the thoughts of his heart', that is what needs to be renewed. Men and women have become carnal, fleshly, and that is the essence of their difficulty. There is only one thing that can deal with their conduct, and that is regeneration. Nothing else can touch it. That is why the people who talk in the name of Christianity of 'applying' Christian teaching to the problems of the world are missing the point. You cannot apply Christian teaching. A person who is not a Christian cannot live the Christian life because Christian living starts with 'the renewing of the mind'.

As we have seen, people who are not Christians are only interested in conduct and behaviour. Take a further example – take the pacifists. They say, 'Christ said, "Turn the other cheek."' They think that you can teach people who are not Christians to 'turn the other cheek'. But that is just what you cannot do. People have been trying to persuade the world to do this for centuries, that is the whole story of civilization, and it has always come to nothing. The idea that you can take Christian teaching and then get men and women to 'apply' it, to put it into practice, is, I think, a great denial of the Christian gospel.

No, the Christian gospel says, 'Ye must be born again' [*John*

3:7]. It is not what you do that is wrong, it is *you* who are wrong, and before you can do the right thing, you must be put right. That is Christianity. In the new birth we do not receive new faculties but a new disposition, a new heart. A new controlling principle is put into us, so that now we can use all these faculties and instruments in an entirely new manner. We start with a new way of thinking, and when we think in a new way, we will act in a new way. Thinking controls action: 'As he thinketh in his heart, so is he' [*Prov.* 23:7].

So my next proposition is that the appeal to the Christian is never to conform in a mechanical way to a certain pattern of behaviour. Never. There are people who misrepresent Christianity like that. They say, 'Now that you are converted, you do or do not do this, that and the other.' I think that is terribly wrong. To me, that is not Christianity, that is legalism, putting people back under a new kind of law. No, what you say to the new Christian is this: 'You are now a new man, a new woman, and, because of this, *therefore* . . .' You do not give out a list of rules and regulations, but you do say, 'Now remember what you are and who you are.' There is no sergeant major in the Christian life. Good behaviour is reasonable and intelligent. If you are following a particular code of behaviour, and do not quite know why, then this is the text for you: 'Be renewed in the spirit of your mind.' Do not live like that simply because other people do. You must know and understand why you are doing it.

In other words, in Christianity it is always the inward state that matters, the spirit of the mind, this transformation, this shining forth of the inner being. The conduct of Christian men and women is not something that they add on to their lives, it is not like putting on a suit. As we have seen, it is the outward expression of something that is within. This can be illustrated by something which we see at Christmastime. Before Christmas,[1] people buy their Christmas trees and on the branches they often hang silver or gold apples and pears. They tie this artificial fruit on to the tree with thin pieces of string or wire. The artificial is that which is put on to the tree. When you go into an orchard you also see apples and pears, but they are real,

---

[1] This sermon was preached on 26 November 1965.

they have grown from the inner life of the tree – now that is Christianity.

The difference between Christianity and morality is also the difference between true Christianity and hypocrisy. The hypocrite pretends and is not what he pretends; the true Christian truly is what he appears to be. So Christian conduct grows from the renewing of the mind. Now this does not merely mean a change of opinion, though that is included. It means much more. It means that a man or woman has seen the truth, and has been captivated and controlled by it. It means a total, instead of a particular, change. If my conduct has changed now that I am a Christian, it is not because I have introduced a partial change into my way of living but because *I* am different. It is because I am a new person in Christ Jesus.

Or, finally, the difference between Christians and the best moral people in the world who are not Christians, is not merely a difference of degree, but an essential difference. Good moral men and women may appear to be remarkably like Christians, at times they may even appear to be better, yet they are not; it is all on the surface. 'But God knoweth your hearts: for that which is highly esteemed among men is abomination in the sight of God' [*Luke* 16:15]. Christians, therefore, differ from moral people in the spirit of their minds. They differ in their hearts, in the centre of their lives. The Christian man or woman has a new perspective, a new point of view upon everything. 'Therefore if any man be in Christ, he is a new creature: old things are passed away; behold, all things are become new' [*2 Cor.* 5:17].

So in the area of conduct, is there one problem in particular that is worrying you above everything else at this moment? Well, here is the teaching of the apostle, this is his exhortation to you. Stop looking at it! Turn your back on it. Walk away from it. Go back. Go back into eternity. Go back into God's great purpose. Go back into man as originally created – go back as far as you can. Then turn round and you will be able to approach your problem in a way that will enable you to surmount it with ease.

That is the Christian way. 'Be ye transformed'! Remember this inner essence and then act by 'renewing the mind'. The Spirit is in you and He will prompt you. He will lead you. What

you must do is respond. So you must think about these things;
you must meditate on them and pray about them. That is the
'renewing of the mind'.

Nine

*

I beseech you therefore, brethren, by the mercies of God, that ye present your bodies a living sacrifice, holy, acceptable unto God, which is your reasonable service. And be not conformed to this world: but be ye transformed by the renewing of your mind, that ye may prove what is that good, and acceptable, and perfect, will of God.

Romans 12:1–2

We have seen that in the Christian life, everything must be considered in the light of our new position. I am so concerned about this because to me it is one of the most glorious aspects of the Christian faith and is certainly the key to successful Christian living. The Christian's attitude to behaviour is never negative. It is never small and it is never fearful. We do a very great disservice to our Lord and Master and to His way of life if we give that impression.

Of course, a false impression has often been given. The man of the world will tell you that that is why he is not a Christian. People say, 'But you Christians are so small and your life is so little and narrow.' And I am afraid that we have often given that impression; we have been fearful. We have misrepresented the gospel and have been a hindrance to people coming into the Christian life.

But the Christian approach should always be positive; it should always be big and always glorious. If we do not give the impression that it is a glorious thing to be a Christian and to live the Christian life, we have never understood this statement: 'Be ye transformed by the renewing of your mind.' What a possibility! What a wonderful way of looking at everything.

And there is no fear here because we are reminded at once of the great resources which are ours.

The Christian gospel is unique. It tells us: Be what you are; realize what you are; and proceed to show that you are what you are. Nowhere else in the world do we find such a message. And as we have seen, that is why we must always realize that no one can live the Christian life without being regenerate. Indeed, to tell anybody who is not a Christian to live the Christian life in any part or form is to teach heresy. It is the Pelagian heresy. Pelagius thought that you simply had to teach people the principles of Christian living for them to carry them out. That is false teaching which has been condemned, and always should be condemned, by the Christian church.

So I trust we are clear about this. The idea that all you have to do is to go to the statesmen of the world and tell them, 'Now this is what Christianity teaches, put it into practice', is a denial of the whole teaching of the New Testament. So when popes and others address the United Nations they should not appeal to them to put Christian principles into practice. They should tell them that they must be 'born again', because the people will never do it until they are, and apart from anything else, you are wasting your breath.

The main cause of the terribly confused state of the world is the foolish idea that men and women who have long since shed the Christian doctrine, can still hold on to the Christian ethic. It cannot be done. It is a sheer impossibility. That is what the apostle is saying. Each person needs this 'transformation', which, as we have shown, is comparable to the transfiguration of our Lord on the Mount of Transfiguration.

So Paul says that we must not be found conforming to the 'fashion' of this world. But how do we live in this transformed way? The whole point is, according to the apostle here, that this demands positive effort on our part. It is 'by the renewing of your mind', and especially 'by the spirit of your mind' [*Eph.* 4:23]. Now the Holy Spirit is in us as Christians, and He is always working in us, and what the apostle is telling us to do here is to listen to Him, to be guided by Him, and to put into practice what He tells us. Again, it is this two-sided teaching: 'Work out your own salvation with fear and trembling. For [because] it is God which worketh in you both to will and to do of his good pleasure' [*Phil.* 2:12–13]. Paul is really saying here: 'You have been born again, therefore renew your mind.'

What, then, does it mean in practice? Obviously, the first thing is that we must acquaint ourselves with the truth. Why were these epistles ever written? It was to help us to renew our minds. That is why Paul had to write Romans and that is why all the other epistles were written. We are not merely left with our experience and the activity of the Holy Spirit within us. He is the Spirit of truth and He caused these men to write the letters in order that we may be helped and taught. You cannot renew your mind unless you are acquainted with this Word. So being renewed means acquaintance with the truth as it is presented to us with all its argumentation in the New Testament.

Secondly, we must understand the truth that we read. We must read it and spend time in reading it, and we must struggle with it until we understand it. That is why we are considering this Epistle to the Romans like this, is it not? We are trying together to understand this teaching as the Spirit leads and guides us, and as we use our minds and understanding.

In addition, of course, it means that, having known what it is and having grasped it and understood it, we then constantly apply it. This demands an effort on our part, because, unfortunately, as the result of the fall and of sin, we have all become creatures of habit. We have been so accustomed to thinking in a certain way that we tend to go on in the same way, even after we have been born again. We do not automatically begin to think in the new way. We do, of course, in a fundamental sense and yet it involves a lot of training. You will find your mind slipping back into the old grooves. You have to pull it out, as it were, and direct it in the other way. That is what Paul means 'by the renewing of your mind'.

There, then, it is in general, but let me show you now what this renewal of the mind means in particular. Here I am, a regenerate man, very good. Now I have to think in an entirely new way; I must approach all the problems of my life in a new way. But how? Well, I must start by asking myself, 'What, after all, is the object of salvation?' As Christians we are converted people. We are regenerate. We have believed the truth. We rejoice in the doctrine of salvation; we rejoice to come to the Lord's table and partake of the bread and the wine. We 'shew the Lord's death till he come' [*1 Cor.* 11:26]. We believe these things. That is what makes us Christians and what we are as Christians.

But the danger is to stop at that, to say, 'Right, I'm saved now,' and then just to go on living a kind of life which really does not relate to that new birth. But the Christian man or woman must not do that but must say, 'Now, I must start asking questions. Why has all that happened? Why did the Lord Jesus Christ ever come into this world? Why did He die upon the cross and be buried and rise again?' And, as we study these epistles we discover there is only one answer to that and the apostle has set it before us, in a most wonderful manner, in chapter 5 of this great Epistle.

The ultimate objective in the incarnation and all that followed was the production of a new humanity. We were all 'in Adam', we are now to be 'in Christ'. He came in order to form this new humanity and He is the Head of the new race of people. The object of salvation, then, is not merely that we may be forgiven and not go to hell. The danger, I repeat, is to stop at that and to say, 'I have been saved from this, that and the other.' But we must learn to look at this positively. Christ is 'the firstborn among many brethren' [*Rom.* 8:29], He is 'bringing many sons unto glory' [*Heb.* 2:10]. It is by contemplating that, that Christians become renewed in their minds.

Take that great statement made by the apostle in Titus 2:11-15 where he puts it so clearly: 'For the grace of God that bringeth salvation hath appeared to all men' – why? – 'teaching us' – you see, salvation teaches us – 'that, denying ungodliness and worldly lusts, we should live soberly, righteously, and godly, in this present world; looking for that blessed hope, and the glorious appearing of the great God and our Saviour Jesus Christ; who gave himself for us' – what for? – 'that he might redeem us from all iniquity' – but here is the positive – 'and purify unto himself a peculiar [separate] people [for his own possession] zealous of good works. These things speak, and exhort, and rebuke with all authority.'

When we stop and ask ourselves: 'What is the ultimate object of salvation?' that is our answer. And then our whole attitude towards individual problems is already new and changed.

Let us go on. If the whole object of our Lord's coming and all that He did is the formation of a new humanity, then this, of necessity, essentially involves the fact that we should be transferred from one condition to another; and this is something that the New Testament writers glory in. Now there is no more wonderful statement of this than that made by this same apostle in the first chapter of his Epistle to the Colossians. 'Giving thanks unto the Father, which hath made us meet to be partakers of the inheritance of the saints in light: who hath delivered us from the power of darkness, and hath translated us into the kingdom of his dear Son' [*Col.* 1:12–13]. What a concept! That, again, is what he means here by renewing the mind: that you read a statement like that and take the trouble to understand it, and then proceed to work it out. You say to yourself, 'I am, ultimately, to be a partaker of the inheritance of the saints in light, but I can never be that without something happening to me. It is not merely that I am forgiven, that is not enough. I must be "translated" out of the kingdom of darkness, and transferred into the kingdom of His dear Son.'

And that is precisely what has happened to us, that is what it means to be a Christian. And it is because each of us does not have thoughts like this in the forefront of our mind and, indeed, controlling the whole of our outlook, that we fail and fall, that is why we grapple with little problems individually, as if we were still unconverted people. Here we are told how to approach the whole matter. We have been taken out of one kingdom and have been transferred into another.

Now this teaching is not by any means confined to the Apostle Paul. Peter puts this quite as plainly and clearly. 'But ye,' he says, 'are a chosen generation, a royal priesthood, an holy nation, a peculiar people; that ye should shew forth the praises' – excellencies, virtues – 'of him who hath called [brought] you out of darkness into his marvellous light: which in time past were not a people, but are now the people of God; which had not obtained mercy, but now have obtained mercy' [*1 Pet.* 2:9–11].

So this is how as Christians we face our lives in this world.

We do not say, 'Problem number one, problem number two, and now I must see what I can do,' and struggle against this in some negative and fearful manner. No, we go back and remind ourselves of where we are and of what has happened to us. We remind ourselves of the One 'Who gave himself for our sins, that he might deliver us from this present evil world' [*Gal.* 1:4].

Now to 'be renewed in your mind' means that you will not allow yourself to forget that; you go on reminding yourself of it. I put it like that because that is precisely how Peter puts it in. He is an old man, facing death, and in effect he tells the people: All your troubles are due to the fact that you have forgotten what you know. 'He that lacketh these things is blind, and cannot see afar off, and hath forgotten that he was purged from his old sins' [2 *Pet.* 1:9] – he knew it but has forgotten it. The 'renewing of your mind' means that you think so positively about these things that you will never be able to forget them again.

Peter goes on, 'Wherefore the rather, brethren, give diligence to make your calling and election sure.' He has already been saying to them, 'And beside this, giving all diligence, add to your faith [furnish out your faith with] virtue . . . brotherly kindness,' and so on [verses 5-7]. You must be active and positive, and in doing so you are renewing your mind. 'Give diligence to make your calling and election sure: for if you do these things, ye shall never fall: for so an entrance shall be ministered unto you abundantly into the everlasting kingdom.' Then: 'Wherefore I will not be negligent to put you always in remembrance of these things, though ye know them and be established in the present truth' [verses 10-12].

Now that is preaching! Do you get tired of hearing me saying the same things, my friends? Well, I am just doing what the Apostle Peter did. I am sure he was right and I am sure I am right! Our greatest trouble always is that we forget. Peter says it again in the next verse: 'Yea, I think it meet, as long as I am in this tabernacle, to stir you up by putting you in remembrance' [verse 13]. And I think this is the call that comes more than ever before to ministers today. Christian people are forgetting things they have known, and that is why we are in the present muddle and confusion; and the business of preaching is to go on reminding them.

Then Peter even says it once more. 'Knowing,' he says, 'that shortly I must put off this my tabernacle, even as our Lord Jesus Christ hath shewed me. Moreover I will endeavour that ye may be able after my decease to have these things always in remembrance' [verses 14–15]. He says, in effect, 'You were told these things. You believed them when you became Christians. But you are in trouble now. You are unhappy and failing. Why? Because you have forgotten! But you must not allow yourselves to forget – you must take yourselves in hand. I am stirring you up. I am going to make you do it. I am going to remind you of the things you know.' That is renewing the mind, becoming what you are, and realizing what you are.

Peter has already reminded his readers of what has happened: 'Whereby are given unto us exceeding great and precious promises: that by these ye might be partakers of the divine nature, having escaped the corruption that is in the world through lust' [2 *Pet.* 1:4]. 'You have got out of that corruption,' he says, 'well do not conform to it, then. Do not behave as if you were still in it.'

Or take again another wonderful statement of all this by the Apostle Paul at the end of Colossians 2. Having worked out his great argument about the cross up to verse 15, he says, 'Let no man therefore judge you in meat, or in drink, or in respect to an holyday, or of the new moon, or of the sabbath days.' Silly people – they were going back under the law. Though they had been emancipated, they were going back to those things. 'Which are,' he says, 'a shadow of things to come; but the body is of Christ. Let no man beguile you of your reward in a voluntary humility and worshipping of angels, intruding into those things which he hath not seen, vainly puffed up by his fleshly mind, and not holding the Head, from which all the body and joints and bands having nourishment ministered, and knit together, increaseth with the increase of God. Wherefore' – here it is – 'if ye be dead with Christ from the rudiments of the world, why, as though living in the world, are ye subject to ordinances . . .' [verses 16–20]. He says: What is the matter with you? You are muddled; renew your minds! 'Which things have indeed a shew of wisdom in will worship, and humility, and neglecting of the body; not in any honour to the satisfying of the flesh' [verse 23].

And, indeed, the Apostle Paul has had to say the same thing to the Corinthians: 'And I, brethren, could not speak unto you as unto spiritual, but as unto carnal, even as unto babes in Christ. I have fed you with milk, and not with meat: for hitherto ye were not able to bear it, neither yet now are ye able. For ye are yet carnal: for whereas there is among you envying, and strife, and divisions, are ye not carnal, and walk as men?' [*1 Cor.* 3:1–3]. You are born again but, he says, you are living as if you were not; you are thinking as if you were not; you are desiring as if you were not. You are contradicting yourselves.

And so the first thing we must realize is what we have been translated *from*; and then, positively, we must remind ourselves constantly of what we have been translated *to*: 'From the power of darkness . . . into the kingdom of his dear Son' [*Col.* 1:13]. But look at it in this tremendous statement in Philippians 3:20–21. Here is the positive aspect: 'For our conversation [our citizenship] is in heaven; from whence also we look for the Saviour, the Lord Jesus Christ: who shall change our vile body, that it may be fashioned like unto his glorious body, according to the working whereby he is able even to subdue all things unto himself.' The apostle is contrasting that with certain false teachers: 'For many walk, of whom I have told you often, and now tell you even weeping, that they are the enemies of the cross of Christ: whose end is destruction, whose God is their belly, and whose glory is in their shame, who mind [think about] earthly things' [verses 18–19]. But our conversation, our citizenship, the realm to which we belong, is not there, it is in heaven. We belong to the kingdom of God.

And, of course, the author of the Epistle to the Hebrews is saying exactly the same thing in that great eleventh chapter, where he puts up, one after another, the great heroes of the faith – Abel, Enoch, Noah, Abraham, Moses and all the others. What was their secret? It was that while they were in this world, they were looking 'for a city which hath foundations, whose builder and maker is God' [*Heb.* 11:10]. They realized that they were just passing through this world and that they belonged to that other city.

Now if you want to expound Scripture, use Scripture to do so and I am giving you, therefore, the biblical commentaries on this one phrase in Romans 12:2. One of the best expositions of this verse and of how it works out in detail and in practice is the fifth chapter of the second Epistle to the Corinthians. It is all summed up in one great statement in verse 17: 'Therefore if any man be in Christ, he is a new creature [a new creation]: old things are passed away; behold, all things are become new.' Here Paul is describing the new way of thinking. He says in effect, 'Because I am a new creature, a new creation, in a sense, nothing is as it was before; I see everything differently.' Here is one respect in which this is true: 'Wherefore henceforth know we no man after the flesh: yea, though we have known Christ after the flesh, yet now henceforth know we him no more' [verse 16]. This is a tremendous statement. Paul did not see himself as he used to. He saw himself once as a very fine man, a very godly, good man, pleasing God, a Pharisee, better than most other people, but now he says, 'This is a faithful saying, and worthy of all acceptation, that Christ Jesus came into the world to save sinners; of whom I am chief' [*1 Tim.* 1:15]. That is a new way of thinking, is it not?

The apostle not only saw himself in a different way, he saw others differently: 'no man after the flesh'. When Paul – Saul of Tarsus – used to look at other men the one thing he asked was, 'Is he a Jew or isn't he?' That was the controlling principle – Jews and non-Jews, people of God and 'dogs', with no good at all in them. But he did not think like that any longer; he had been renewed. And you and I, too, are to work this out. We are no longer to be governed by likes and dislikes and prejudices. We are renewed in our minds because of what has happened to us. And as the apostle delighted in the fact that he was the apostle to the Gentiles, as he had been boasting in chapter 11 of this great Epistle, so you and I must see everybody else in a new way. And this will solve many of the problems of our daily lives.

But the trouble is, is it not, that often, as Christians, though we are born again, we react as we used to react to people and to what they do and think and say. We must not do that. We must, for example, see them not so much as difficult people – if that is what they are – but, if they are not Christians, as slaves of Satan, and we must be sorry for them. Our Lord looked out upon the masses and saw them 'as sheep having no shepherd' [*Matt.* 9:36] and His heart was filled with compassion. And we must be like that. When we have this new way of thinking we do that, but we must make a positive effort. We must no longer just react instinctively to these people but must say to ourselves, 'Wait a minute, how do I look at all this?', and then remember that they are just the slaves of the devil; they still belong to the kingdom of darkness; they are 'not a people' [*1 Pet.* 2:10]. 'Wherefore henceforth know we no man after the flesh.'

This renewal of our minds not only changes our view of ourselves and other people, it changes our entire view of life in this world; and this is very important. We are in a unique relationship to this world. If our citizenship is in heaven, we are only 'strangers and pilgrims' here. That is how Peter puts it: 'Dearly beloved, I beseech you as strangers and pilgrims, abstain from fleshly lusts, which war against the soul' [*1 Pet.* 2:11]. And you and I must make ourselves think like this. We are in this world, but we are no longer of it. We are journeymen, we are sojourners, strangers and pilgrims – again, it is all put perfectly there in that mighty statement in the eleventh chapter of the Epistle to the Hebrews. The writer gives us these people's philosophy, as it were: 'These all died in faith, not having received the promises, but having seen them afar off, and were persuaded of them, and embraced them, and confessed that they were strangers and pilgrims on the earth' [*Heb.* 11:13].

Of course, that is the constant appeal of the New Testament. Paul writes to the Ephesians, 'This I say therefore, and testify in the Lord, that ye henceforth walk not as other Gentiles walk, in the vanity of their mind' [*Eph.* 4:17]. You cannot do that, you have not 'so learned Christ' [verse 20]. Do not go on living as if you were unchanged; you *are* changed. He brings it out again in the fifth chapter of that same Epistle: 'Be not ye therefore partakers with them. For ye were sometimes' – you were at one time, once upon a time – 'darkness, but now are ye light in the Lord' – well – 'walk as children of light: (for the fruit of the Spirit is in all goodness and righteousness and truth;) proving what is acceptable unto the Lord. And have no fellowship with the unfruitful works of darkness, but rather reprove them. For it is a shame even to speak of those things which are done of them in secret' [*Eph.* 5:7–12]. The world is not ashamed to speak of them in public any longer, is it? But you and I should be ashamed, and we must have nothing to do with it. 'But all things that are reproved are made manifest by the light . . . Wherefore he saith, Awake thou that sleepest, and arise from the dead, and Christ shall give thee light. See then that ye walk circumspectly, not as fools, but as wise, redeeming the time, because the days are evil. Wherefore be ye not unwise, but understanding what the will of the Lord is' [verses 13–17].

So the New Testament is full of this very argumentation, and I have often summed it up, as I have worked through this Epistle, in this way: You were, but you are no longer, thank God; now you *are*! That is exactly what Paul is saying here: 'Be not conformed to this world: but be ye transformed by the renewing of your mind.' You must realize that you belong to this 'chosen generation', this 'royal priesthood', this 'holy nation', this people who are to be a special possession for the Lord, 'who hath called you out of darkness into his marvellous light' [*1 Pet.* 2:9], that you may show forth what He has done and thus minister to His glory and to His praise.

Now to forget all this will simply lead to conformity to the world, or, to put it another way, if we do conform to the world, it just means that we have forgotten it all. It is a matter for the mind. The problem, I repeat, is one of thinking correctly. You know, says Peter, I am amazed at you: 'He that lacketh these things is blind, and cannot see afar off, and hath forgotten that he was purged from his old sins' [*2 Pet.* 1:9]. To conform to the world is not only to forget all these glorious things which we claim to believe, but it is also at the same time to contradict them, and we must never be guilty of that.

Then there is another great argument that is inevitable when you begin to think in this way. Here I am: I have been called out of the darkness and its kingdom and I have been translated into God's kingdom, and have been looking at myself functioning in this kingdom. But wait a minute, let us look ahead for a moment – let us consider what is awaiting us. Let us consider why God has done this to us. What is it for? Why has He given us the Spirit? Oh, it is in order to prepare us for that which is our destiny. The apostle has put this before us many, many times, has he not? There is a wonderful statement of it in the eighth chapter where he puts it like this: 'Moreover whom he did predestinate, them he also called: and whom he called, them he also justified: and whom he justified, them he also glorified' [verse 30]. 'Whom he did foreknow, he also did predestinate' – why?– 'to be conformed to the image of his Son, that he might be the firstborn among many brethren' [verse 29].

Now that is how we must think. We must say to ourselves day by day: 'I no longer belong to the darkness; I no longer belong to the "no people"; I am of the people of God; I am in His kingdom.' But what for? It is in order that I may be prepared for this glory which is coming. In other words, I do not live just from day to day, hand to mouth, allowing the world to influence me while I react to it. No, no, I have a total view. I realize that I am a pilgrim on the way to eternity, one of God's children going in the direction of home. I must keep my eye on that and walk in the light of that.

Was not that Moses' secret, according to the Epistle to the Hebrews? How did Moses do what he did? He did it, 'as seeing him who is invisible' [*Heb.* 11:27]. Why did he choose to 'suffer affliction with the people of God' rather than 'to enjoy the pleasures of sin for a season' [verse 25]? The answer is that, 'he had respect unto the recompence of the reward' [verse 26].

That is how the people of God live. They do not merely face one or other particular problem and ask, 'Shall I do it or shall I not?' and call upon the aid of psychology. Not at all! That is the world's approach. The people of God say, 'Who am I? What am I doing? Where am I going?' They have their eye on 'the recompence of the reward' [*Heb.* 11:25]. And if you have your eye on that, you will soon deal with your problems.

Our Lord Himself, according to the author of Hebrews, did that: 'Looking unto Jesus the author and finisher of our faith; who *for the joy that was set before him* endured the cross, despising the shame' [*Heb.* 12:2]. And, of course, the Apostle Paul has put all this before us in most eloquent language: 'I reckon that the sufferings of this present time are not worthy to be compared with the glory which shall be revealed to us.' That is it. He goes on, '. . . ourselves also, which have the firstfruits of the Spirit, even we ourselves groan within ourselves, waiting for the adoption, to wit, the redemption of our body' [*Rom.* 8:18, 23]. That is what we do.

The apostle uses the same argument exactly in 1 Corinthians 15:33-34: 'Be not deceived: evil communications corrupt good manners. Awake to righteousness, and sin not.' Why? Because we are going to rise and we are going to be like Him. This is the whole argument of 1 Corinthians 15. Ethics and the doctrine of the resurrection are inextricably mixed up. They belong together. I would remind you of that great statement at the end of Philippians 3. 'We look for the Saviour, the Lord Jesus Christ' – who shall come from heaven, and who, when He comes shall change this, the body of my humiliation – 'that it may be fashioned like unto his glorious body.' That is my destiny. That is where I am going. If I am a Christian, that is the truth about me. And the moment I keep these things in my mind so that they govern my thinking, my attitude to every particular problem is changed and all these other matters fall into position.

Finally, as long as you are governed by this new thinking, you will realize in a very acute manner that you have no time to waste. The time is short; eternity is coming. You had better start preparing yourself. As John says in his First Epistle: 'And now, little children, abide in him' – why? – 'that, when he shall appear, we may have confidence, and not be ashamed before him at his coming' [*1 John* 2:28]. What a terrible thing it would be if, when we saw Him as He is, the predominating feeling were to be shame! How terrible if, though we said we believed in Him and were grateful to Him for coming, we had lived 'according to this world'. We would see then what we had missed, how we had misunderstood it all, how unworthy we had been. We would be 'ashamed before him at his coming'.

No, no, let it not be that. Let us rather prepare for His return and go on then to what John says in the third chapter: 'Behold, what manner of love the Father hath bestowed upon us, that we should be called the sons of God: therefore the world knoweth us not because it knew him not' [*1 John* 3:1]. If the people of the world criticize you, thank them. They are telling you, in other words, that you belong to Him. They did not know Him and they do not know His people. 'Beloved, now are we the sons of God, and it doth not yet appear what we shall be; but we know that, when he shall appear, we shall be like him; for we shall see him as he is' [verse 2]. Then – 'And every man that hath this hope in him purifieth himself, even as he is pure' [verse 3]. It is inevitable logic. So you do not just start with the question of purification, you see yourself meeting Him and looking into His eyes, and you say, 'I must get on with this. I must purify myself, even as he is pure.' That is the motive.

Or again, as the Apostle Paul puts it in 2 Corinthians 5:10-11: 'For we must all appear before the judgment seat of Christ; that every one may receive the things done in his body, according to that he hath done whether it be good or bad. Knowing therefore the terror of the Lord, we persuade men.' That is it.

Or, as we are, after all, studying this great Epistle to the Romans, let us move on to chapter 13 where Paul, perhaps, at his most eloquent as regards this particular matter, writes, 'Love worketh no ill to his neighbour: therefore love is the fulfilling of the law. And that, knowing the time, that now it is high time to awake out of sleep' – why? – 'for now is our salvation nearer than when we believed' [*Rom.* 13:10-11]. Every day that passes means that we are a day nearer to His coming and the ultimate completion of salvation. In verse 14, Paul says, 'The night' – and it is night at this present time, is it not? 'The night' – the night of sin and evil, the night of the darkness of this world. But, thank God, we know that: 'The night is far spent, the day is at hand.' And as you see that, you apply this logic: 'Let us therefore cast off the works of darkness, and let us put on the armour of light. Let us walk honestly, as in the day; not in rioting, and drunkenness, not in chambering and wantonness, not in strife and envying. But put ye on the Lord Jesus Christ, and make not provision for the flesh, to fulfil the lusts thereof' [*Rom.* 13:12-14].

All these passages show what Paul's injunction means: 'Be ye transformed by the renewing of your mind.' You think in this way, you struggle, you strive to do everything you can to make yourself do that, and you never allow yourself to slip back into the old way of thinking. You are renewed in your mind, in the spirit of your mind, in the controlling principle of all your thinking and your entire outlook. This is the way in which the Christian faces the problem of how to live in a world such as this.

Ten

*

I beseech you therefore, brethren, by the mercies of God, that ye present your bodies a living sacrifice, holy, acceptable unto God, which is your reasonable service. And be not conformed to this world: but be ye transformed by the renewing of your mind, that ye may prove what is that good, and acceptable, and perfect, will of God.

Romans 12:1–2

We have now reached the stage at which we must consider the last phrase – '. . . that ye may prove what is that good, and acceptable, and perfect, will of God.' Paul, having shown us that the way of Christian living affects body, soul, and spirit – the whole person – ends here by telling us the real reason for presenting ourselves to God, the objective, which we should have in our minds. This is the ultimate motive for doing all he has been exhorting us to do. And he introduces this to us by the word 'that'. 'Be not conformed to this world: but be ye transformed by the renewing of your mind, *that* [in order that] . . .'

Now the authorities argue a good deal about this word 'that'. They say that it can be taken in two ways. It can indicate, as I have just suggested, the *object* of living in this way, the end to which it all leads; or it can be interpreted as the *result*: If you do all that, then you will 'prove what is that good, and acceptable, and perfect, will of God.' Well, I believe that the two ideas are both included in this word. The one quite inevitably leads to the other. Paul gives the reason why we should be living like this, and tells us that we can only arrive at that result by living in this way.

[127]

Here again, we are confronted by a vital statement introducing a most vital principle. The apostle has told us that what marks out Christians from everybody else is that they have new minds; that they no longer 'mind' earthly things, but spiritual things. They have a new way of thinking and a new approach to every problem, and we have been dealing with that. So far we have been looking at this in general, but now the apostle says that in particular this has to happen in one most important area and that is our understanding and appreciation of God's will with respect to ourselves. The ultimate object of the new mind is to enable us to understand and to appreciate the will of God in a way that was impossible before.

And that is the great subject that the apostle introduces to us here. Once more I am constrained to point out – and we can never point it out too frequently – that this is what differentiates Christianity from everything else. We must never take up the position of merely saying that the Christian teaching is better than everything else. No, what we say is that it is unique. It is not in series with anything else. It is not the chief or the highest or the best of the ethical systems. Its whole basis is different.

Here in this second half of Romans 12:2 we again see very clearly that Christian teaching is not only concerned about conduct. It is interested in that, of course, but only as conduct is an objective manifestation of an ultimate attitude. We saw that when we dealt with the words 'conformed' and 'transformed', but here it is again. This is where Dr Thomas Arnold, and the kind of religion that he introduced in Rugby School in the mid-nineteenth century, so violated Christian teaching. Those who teach that the Christian is just a good little gentleman are teaching morality; it has nothing to do with Christianity, and it is a contradiction of Paul's essential principle.

What, then, is the goal of Christian conduct? Well, it is not that I should be pleased with myself, nor that I should please others, nor that I should be above criticism or suspicion, nor that I should be a good citizen of my country. It is none of those things, though it includes them all. No, Christianity does not look at things from the human standpoint. The Christian is not interested in what people think or say but in what *God* says. The ultimate objective of the whole of the Christian life is to bring us into conformity with the will of God. We are once more reminded that this is always to be our view of salvation.

I suggest that many difficulties in the Christian church, even among evangelical people, are due to the fact that we have not always been careful to remember that ultimate objective and to emphasize it as we should. We must never view our salvation in a negative or partial manner; never. We are very liable to that. Some people seem to think that salvation is merely a question of forgiveness of sins. It starts with that, but to think of salvation solely in those terms is to miss this glorious emphasis that we have here and right through the New Testament.

Further, to think of salvation merely in terms of a very happy experience is not enough; many stop at that. 'Oh,' people say, 'I shall never forget that wonderful experience!' and they go on talking about it. Or they refer to a change in their lives. Someone says, 'Whereas I was miserable, now I'm happy. I used to get this trouble, but not any longer.' Experience! This wonderful change! Of course, that, too, is a vital part of Christianity, but the mere fact that you may be happy now, whereas you used to be miserable, or the fact that you have a new joy, is not the whole of Christian salvation, and it is very wrong indeed to think in those terms. It is still worse to think of Christianity merely in terms of deliverance from particular sins. It is that, but salvation does not stop there.

I have already referred to people who seem to think that all would be well with them if only they could stop doing one particular thing. But the apostle's statement is a terrible condemnation of such a view. That is a negative approach, and it reduces Christian salvation in its glory, to something small. Salvation is never small or negative. In these verses we are reminded that salvation is always positive; it is always great. What is the object of salvation? Is it merely to deliver me from hell? No, it is to make me conform to the will of God. I may not be guilty of certain sins, I may be highly moral, but I can still be utterly hopeless in the sight of God. You remember what our Lord said about the Pharisee: 'Ye are they which justify yourselves before men.' Highly moral! That is the ideal of the world and its systems. 'But,' He goes on to say, 'God knoweth your hearts: for that which is highly esteemed among men is abomination in the sight of God' [*Luke* 16:15].

And that is the trouble with the so-called 'good pagan', the 'moral person', the 'Christian agnostic', to use a term introduced by the late Lord Birkett and since borrowed by others. There is no such thing. People can behave well merely in terms of decency and good living, but Christian teaching is concerned about conformity to the will of God.

Now here, the apostle brings us up to that level, showing us the essential characteristic of this great teaching, and in a way this is what you may describe as the one big theme of the Bible; this is what the Bible is about. It tells us that we must get the right view of human beings and that all our troubles are due to the fact that we have the wrong view. The Bible tells us that man and woman were made in order that they might glorify God. That is especially why He made them in His own image and likeness [*Gen.* 1:26]. Man was meant to be the representative of God on earth; he was to be the lord of creation and he was meant also to be the companion of God. God made man for Himself in order that he might commune with Him and have fellowship with Him.

That is basic in the whole of the Bible and God has made it quite clear that men and women are therefore to live in a particular way. You find God's will, for instance, in the Ten Commandments. Or you can take the summary made by our Lord when He was asked which was the first and the chief commandment. He answered, 'Thou shalt love the Lord thy God with all thy heart, and with all thy soul, and with all thy mind, and with all thy strength: this is the first commandment. And the second is like, namely this, Thou shalt love thy neighbour as thyself' [*Mark* 12:30–31]. Now the men who asked that question had a great shock, of course. The scribes were interested in the details of the law, as moralists always are. But our Lord lifted the standard right up. He said, in effect, 'This is how man is meant to live, loving God with the whole of his being, in perfect conformity to God's will.'

There is another summary which is found frequently in the Old Testament and is quoted in the New. This summary is staggering. If you want to know what men and women are

meant to be like, here it is: 'Be ye holy; for I am holy' [*1 Pet.*
1:16]. That is the idea of the image and the likeness put in a
very practical manner. So we are not simply in the realm of,
'Shall I do this or mustn't I do that?' That is to reduce the
whole of this glorious gospel, the 'perfect law of liberty' [*James*
1:25] to a mere matter of rules and vetoes and prohibitions and
restraints. I get rid of all that because I am told that I am to be
holy because God is holy.

And that is the principle that the apostle teaches here in
Romans 12. That is the object of salvation: '. . . that ye may
prove what is that good, and acceptable, and perfect, will of
God.' We are meant for nothing less than that. As the apostle
puts it to Titus, 'Who gave himself for us, that he might
redeem us from all iniquity, and purify unto himself a peculiar
people, zealous of good works' [*Titus* 2:14]. Or, again, as the
Apostle Peter puts it: 'But ye are a chosen generation, a royal
priesthood, an holy nation, a peculiar people' – what for? – 'that
ye should shew forth the praises of him who hath called you
out of darkness into his marvellous light' [*1 Pet.* 2:9]. That is
how Christians are to live. They are to live in such a way that
people looking at them will glorify God. Our Lord summed
this up for us when He said, 'Let your light so shine before
men, that they may see your good works, and glorify your
Father which is in heaven' [*Matt.* 5:16].

So we are meant to live according to the will of God and to
rejoice in it. Here again we may quote the answer to the first
question in the famous *Shorter Catechism*: 'What is the chief
end of man?' Is it just not to go to hell, or not to get drunk, or
not to commit adultery? No! 'The chief end of man is to glorify
God, and to enjoy him for ever.'

And the apostle puts it in this most interesting way here. In
effect, he says, 'You must pay great attention to this renewing
of your mind because if you do not, you will never prove what
God's will is.' So he is really telling us that by nature men and
women do not prove what God's will is. Is that not their whole
trouble? The trouble is not that they commit particular sins
but that their whole attitude to God is entirely wrong. The
apostle reminded us of that in Romans 8:7 where he told us
that '. . . the carnal mind is enmity against God: for it is not
subject to the law of God, neither indeed can be.' Or, as he puts

it elsewhere, 'And you, that were sometime alienated and enemies in your mind by wicked works . . .' [*Col.* 1:21].

The apostle appeals to us. He says: The trouble is not merely that men and women are wrong in the whole of their thinking, they are particularly and exceptionally wrong in the whole of their thinking about God and about the will of God for them. It is only as they are saved and born again that they are given this new mind and outlook, and they must develop it as much as they can.

So there we are given the measure of the Fall of man and woman. What a terrible thing it was! It was not just a matter of eating a fruit. What really happened there was that their whole thinking about God and His holy will went wrong. As we have seen, the devil suggested it by saying: 'Hath God said?' [*Gen.* 3:1]. God said you must not touch that fruit, and He said that because He wants to keep you down.

The devil was querying the will of God, the righteousness, the goodness, the holiness, the acceptability of the will of God. The man and woman listened, and their whole view of the will of God has been wrong ever since. It is at this point that we see most acutely the devastating effect of the fall. Over and above all that it leads to in practice and in detailed behaviour, the most terrible thing of all is that it has led to a perverted view of the will of God. So that here the apostle is saying that you must pay great attention to this 'renewing of the mind' because only as you do this and co-operate with the work of the Spirit within you, will you come to 'prove what is that good, and acceptable, and perfect, will of God.'

Now you see how the apostle leads his argument up to this great climax? Take this word 'prove'. It means to test, to try, to examine, and ultimately to approve. So we can translate this phrase in different ways. We can say that it means, here is a way to test and thereby to understand and prove for ourselves. Or we can say that it means the power to distinguish between what pleases and displeases God so that the apostle is telling us that we should renew our minds in order that we may have a clarity of moral perception, a kind of tenderness of conscience.

Now that is the content of the word 'prove'. But in order to make this clear, let me give you some other examples of the use of this word. You find it, for instance, in Romans 2, verses

17 and 18. Paul is dealing here with the Jew. 'Behold, thou art called a Jew, and restest in the law, and makest thy boast of God. And knowest his will, and *approvest* the things that are more excellent, being instructed out of the law.'

Then there is another example in Ephesians 5 verses 8 and 10 where Paul says, 'For ye were sometimes darkness, but now are ye light in the Lord: walk as children of light . . . *proving* what is acceptable unto the Lord.' It is exactly the same idea. Then you also find this word in Philippians 1:9–10: 'And this I pray, that your love may abound yet more and more in knowledge and in all judgment; that ye may *approve* things that are excellent' – which somebody says should be translated, 'discriminate things that are different and so decide what is excellent and what is not excellent' – 'that ye may be sincere and without offence till the day of Christ.'

The apostle, therefore, is telling us that those who renew their minds, and obey the leading of the Spirit, will be able to discover certain things about the will of God. This is the most important thing that we can ever do and this is what the renewing of the mind as the result of our salvation enables us to do.

Now our Lord Himself once put this very clearly in John 7:16–17. People were questioning Him about His doctrine, and we are told, 'Jesus answered them, and said, My doctrine is not mine, but his that sent me. If any man will do his will, he shall know of the doctrine, whether it be of God, or whether I speak of myself.' He says, in effect, 'If you only do what I am telling you, then you will prove, you will know, whether my doctrine is only my own or whether it is, as I claim it to be, truly the doctrine of God.' But notice He says that you have got to do something about it. You cannot, as it were, look theoretically at the will of God and come to certain conclusions. You will never find out God's will in that way. You must put it into practice and then you will know.

And the apostle tells us here that if we renew our minds we will discover certain things about the will of God, and we will see that the great salvation in Christ has undone all the worst effects of the fall. First, when we think spiritually with renewed minds, study the Scriptures, and get hold of these doctrines we discover that the will of God is good – and that is a wonderful discovery. There is no greater proof of the fact that men and women have been converted – born again – than that they have changed their minds about the will of God. By nature, people always feel that God is against them and that His ways are bad for them; they dislike God's law. To quote Romans 8:7 again: 'Because the carnal mind is enmity against God: for it is not subject to the law of God, neither indeed can be.' The 'natural man' hates the law of God.

Of course, when people identify the law of God with their own little morality, they think they love it; but that is not the law of God. When they really know what the law of God is they hate it. That is why the bitterest opponents of the Christian faith have generally been Pharisees – good, moral, religious people. When Christ showed them what the law really meant they hated Him for it. Pharisees always hate it, and they always feel that God's law is against them. The old trick of the devil with Adam and Eve is repeated. When things go wrong, people instinctively ask: 'Why should God do this to me? What have I done that God should treat me like this?' That is a manifestation of this natural enmity. By nature people feel that God's will is bad, and they think they can live better lives without Him. They say they know what is best, and can run His world in an excellent manner.

People think that God's will is bad because they have a wrong view of themselves. They believe that they are animals, and therefore they want plenty of food and drink and sex, plenty of money, plenty of enjoyment. That is what they are glorying in, is it not? 'Isn't life wonderful?' they say. And all because they have such a deplorable view of themselves and think the will of God militates against their best interests.

'Surely' they say, 'you're not going to go all religious? You're not going to lose all the pleasures and happiness and fun of life? You're not going to take up that narrow way of living, surely not? It'll cramp your personality. You really should be expressing yourself. You're not going to allow yourself to be cramped like that, are you?'

Is not that the argument – that Christianity is something that fetters us, and has been the greatest hindrance to the development of the human race? People say things like that because their whole idea of men and women is wrong.

And another way in which they show that they have a wrong idea of humanity is that their one criterion, always, is 'happiness', but if people put happiness as their ultimate criterion they are bound to go astray. In the will of God, holiness is the criterion, not happiness. So men and women are wrong all along the line. They think that when they die that is the end of them. They do not see themselves as citizens of eternity, going on beyond death and the grave. Because of this wrong thinking they come to the conclusion that the will of God is bad and that God is against them. So, they say, people must emancipate themselves from the incubus of religion. They must get rid of these notions of God and morality and sin and all the teaching in the Bible. That is what they think and they have been putting their ideas into practice.

Now, as we have seen, the apostle tells us here that when our minds are renewed, and when we do everything we can to encourage that process of renewal, our whole attitude towards the will of God changes so that, far from regarding the will of God as bad, we come to see that it is good, we 'prove' that it is a good will. There is, of course, a powerful expression of this in Romans 8:28 where the apostle makes a great assertion: 'And we know' – here it is – 'that all things work together for good to them that love God, to them who are the called according to his purpose.' 'All things' – without any exception.

It is only a Christian who can talk like that; and nobody but a Christian ever does talk like that. But look at the way in which the psalmist in Psalm 119 had anticipated this and was able to say, 'Teach me good judgment and knowledge: for I have believed thy commandments. Before I was afflicted I went astray: but now have I kept thy word' [*Psa.* 119:66–67]. He is even able to rise to this height: 'It is good for me that I have been afflicted; that I might learn thy statutes' [verse 71]. Here is a man with understanding who in effect is saying, 'I now thank God that things went wrong with me, that I was in trouble, that I have been afflicted.' He thanks God for it. He says, 'The will of God is so good; I did not realize it at the time, but I do now.'

There is a great deal of this in the Bible. It is so wonderful that I do not apologize for giving you a number of quotations. Listen to Paul putting it in 2 Corinthians 1, starting at verse 8:

'For we would not, brethren, have you ignorant of our trouble which came to us in Asia, that we were pressed out of measure, above strength, insomuch that we despaired even of life.' Paul had obviously been desperately ill and had had many other problems in addition. 'But we had the sentence of death in ourselves, that we should not trust in ourselves, but in God which raiseth the dead: who delivered us from so great a death, and doth deliver: in whom we trust that he will yet deliver us' [verses 9–10]. This is the Christian. The will of God, says Paul, is always good. Even if I am at death's door, the will of God is still good. I do not always see it at that point but I know that it is and I am always able to say eventually: 'It was good for me that I have been afflicted' because 'all things work together for good to them that love God'.

Finally, there is a famous passage in the Epistle to the Hebrews which deals with this very matter. Writing to those people who were grumbling and complaining because they were being chastised and were having a difficult time, the writer says, 'And ye have forgotten the exhortation which speaketh unto you as unto children, My son, despise not thou the chastening of the Lord, nor faint when thou art rebuked of him: for whom the Lord loveth he chasteneth, and scourgeth every son whom he receiveth' [*Heb.* 12:5–6]. But this is the verse I want to emphasize: 'Now no chastening for the present seemeth to be joyous, but grievous: nevertheless afterward it yieldeth the peaceable fruit of righteousness unto them which are exercised thereby' [verse 11]. It is always for our good.

The writer also says in verse 9: 'Furthermore we have had fathers of our flesh which corrected us, and we gave them reverence: shall we not much rather be in subjection unto the Father of spirits, and live?' Abraham said, 'Shall not the Judge of all the earth do right?' [*Gen.* 18:25]. Of course He must, He can never do wrong. Because He is God, His will is always good, and it is always right. That is what you will prove; that is what you will discover. You will be revolutionized in your thinking of the Word of God in general and with respect to yourself in particular.

So God's will is good, and then Paul adds a second word: '. . . what is that good, and *acceptable*'. Now what is the meaning of this? Again, the learned commentators seem to be in trouble here. They say it cannot mean that human beings approve of the will of God, that is the sort of thing you must not say, so it can only mean something that God approves of. But I simply cannot bring myself to accept this meaning. It seems to me to be a tautology to say that the will of God is acceptable to God. Of course it is, because it is His will. I can understand the hesitation of Hodge and Haldane and their reluctance to say that this refers to man finding God's will acceptable. But I think the Bible teaches that and to me there is something rather wonderful about it.

Now it is not that I, in a pompous manner, say, 'I've come to the conclusion that God's way rather than man's way is right,' as if I were a judge sitting on the bench. Of course it is not that; that is verging on the blasphemous. But if you look at it from the experiential standpoint, I think there is a very deep meaning here. It is that men and women, having renewed their minds, not only find that God's will is good, they even begin to like it; they approve of it in the sense that they really desire it and rejoice in it. When the psalmist said, 'O how love I thy law!' [*Psa.* 119:97], he was expressing his approval. Surely, too, we find the same thought in Psalm 1, where it is put like this: 'Blessed is the man that walketh not in the counsel of the ungodly, nor standeth in the way of sinners, nor sitteth in the seat of the scornful. But his delight is in the law of the Lord' [*Psa.* 1:1–2]. He not only sees that it is good and right, he even delights in it.

In Romans 2:18, also, Paul expresses precisely the same idea: 'And knowest his will, and approvest the things that are more excellent.' And in the Gospels, too, there is teaching about this. We read, for instance, in John 3:33: 'He that hath received his testimony hath set to his seal that God is true.' Now that is an extraordinary statement. It is as if man is 'setting his seal' upon what God has said and done. That is what Hodge and Haldane are afraid to say, but I suggest to you that Scripture does say it, so that in a very odd way we can say that when men and women are converted and yield themselves to the will of God, they are giving their approval to it, or 'setting their seal' to it.

Or look at 2 Corinthians 1:19–20, where we find much the same thought, though not put quite so clearly. 'For the Son of

God, Jesus Christ, who was preached among you by us, even by me and Silvanus and Timotheus, was not yea and nay, but in him was yea. For all the promises of God in him are yea, and in him Amen, unto the glory of God by us.' We are putting our 'yea' to the yea that has been said once and for ever in the coming of the Son of God.

But let me give you a still stronger statement made by the Apostle John: 'Whosoever believeth that Jesus is the Christ is born of God: and every one that loveth him that begat loveth him also that is begotten of him. By this we know that we love the children of God, when we love God, and keep his commandments. For this is the love of God, that we keep his commandments: and his commandments are not grievous' [*I John* 5:1–3]. Now there it is. To the natural man or woman, the unregenerate, the commandments of God are grievous. They hate them, and find God a hard taskmaster. But, says John, to those who are born again, the commandments of God are not grievous. They are no longer against the grain, but are acceptable. Did not the poet have something like this in his mind when he wrote these words:

> *I was not ever thus, nor prayed that Thou*
> *Shouldst lead me on;*
> *I loved to choose and see my path; but now,*
> *Lead Thou me on!*
> *I loved the garish day, and, spite of fears,*
> *Pride ruled my will; remember not past years.*
>   John Henry Newman

'Pride ruled my will', and it was opposed to the will of God. But, he says, I am not like that now: that has gone; that was the old person.

Or take it as another has put it:

> *Teach me, O Lord, Thy holy way,*
> *And give me an obedient mind,*
> *That in Thy service I may find*
> *My soul's delight from day to day.*
>   William Tidd Matson

Renew your minds, says Paul, and you will not only find and prove that the will of God is good, you will find it highly acceptable – no longer grievous. You will love it. You will delight in it and you will want to know it and to carry it out more and more.

But ultimately you discover that God's will is *perfect*, and this, of course, is the climax. It is a perfect will because it is the will of God, but it is perfect in another sense, also, in that all it proposes with respect to us is perfect. What is God's plan for men and women? Perfection! God cannot plan anything less for us than that. God's will for us is not just that we should not go to hell, or that we should stop committing certain sins. No, no! He is bringing us to perfection's height; nothing less.

Now the apostle has already said this several times in this great Epistle. Take, for instance – and let this be your meditation – Romans 8:3–4: 'For what the law could not do, in that it was weak through the flesh, God sending his own Son in the likeness of sinful flesh, and for sin, condemned sin in the flesh' – why? – 'that the righteousness of the law might be fulfilled [filled to the full] in us, who walk not after the flesh, but after the Spirit.' Or take it again in the twenty-ninth verse of that eighth chapter: 'For whom he did foreknow, he also did predestinate' – what for? What has God predestinated for those of us whom he 'knew before the foundation of the world'? It is this and nothing less than this – 'to be conformed to the image of his Son', the spotless, sinless, perfect Son of God. The will of God for us does not stop short of this ultimate perfection which is perfect conformity to the image of his dear Son.

Or take that beautiful way in which the same apostle puts it in Ephesians 5 in connection with the relationship of husbands and wives, which he applies to the Lord's relationship to the church. 'Husbands, love your wives, even as Christ also loved the church, and gave himself for it' – what for? – 'that he might sanctify and cleanse it with the washing of water by the word, that he might present it to himself a glorious church, not having spot, or wrinkle, or any such thing; but that it should be holy and without blemish' [*Eph.* 5:25–27]. Perfect! This is His intent.

Our Lord had said the same thing: 'Be ye therefore perfect, even as your Father which is in heaven is perfect' [*Matt.* 5:48].

The will of God for us is perfection, so the apostle, in writing to the Colossians, says, 'I am made a minister,' and then, 'Christ in you, the hope of glory: whom we preach, warning every man, and teaching every man in all wisdom' – why? – 'that we may present every man perfect in Christ Jesus' [*Col.* 1:25, 27–28]. Nothing less than absolute perfection. Or again, he says in 1 Thessalonians 4:3, 'For this is the will of God, even your sanctification . . .' Entire sanctification. I am not discussing where that happens, but I am telling you that that is the ultimate objective. In 1 Thessalonians 5:23, Paul goes on to say: 'And the very God of peace sanctify you wholly [completely]; and I pray God your whole spirit and soul and body be preserved blameless unto the coming of our Lord Jesus Christ.'

Or take that glorious benediction in Hebrews 13:20-21: 'Now the God of peace, that brought again from the dead our Lord Jesus, that great shepherd of the sheep, through the blood of the everlasting covenant, make you perfect in every good work to do his will, working in you that which is wellpleasing in his sight, through Jesus Christ.' And Jude, in his little Epistle of just one chapter is not to be outdone! Listen to him! 'Now unto him that is able to keep you from falling, and to present you faultless before the presence of his glory with exceeding joy, to the only wise God our Saviour, be glory and majesty, dominion and power, both now and ever' [*Jude* 24–25].

We are marked for perfection, and so in Revelation 21:27 we are given a picture of heaven: 'And there shall in no wise enter into it anything that defileth, neither whatsoever worketh abomination, or maketh a lie: but that which are written in the Lamb's book of life.'

There is a city bright,
Closed are its gates to sin,
Naught that defileth,
Naught that defileth,
Shall ever enter in.
Mary Ann Sanderson Deck

That is the object; that is what it all means. Renew your minds, my friends. Give diligence to this. Do all you can to develop this new thinking, because as you do so, you will make these grand discoveries of the will of God, that it is always good, always right, always best for us and has our highest interests at heart. God is always perfect, and we will not find contentment until we have been restored, not only to the perfection that was in Adam, which he lost and which we have always lacked, but until we have found something even higher. We will discover that we will be 'partakers of the divine nature' [2 *Pet.* 1:4]; we will be like Him, 'without spot, or wrinkle, or any such thing' [*Eph.* 5:27].

Are you ready, then, to say something like this – and here is the test of whether you appreciate all I have been trying to say – are you ready to say:

> *Nearer, my God, to Thee,*
> *Nearer to Thee;*
> *E'en though it be a cross*
> *That raiseth me;*
> *Still all my song shall be,*
> *'Nearer, my God to Thee.*
> *Nearer to Thee.'*
> S. F. Adams and E. H. Bickersteth

Or:

> *Thy way, not mine, O Lord,*
> *However dark it be!*
> *Lead me by Thine own hand,*
> *Choose out the path for me.*
> Horatius Bonar

Beloved people, renew your minds: 'Be not conformed to this world: but be ye transformed by the renewing of your mind' in order that you may prove, concerning the will of God, that it is always good, always acceptable, always perfect.

Eleven

*

For I say, through the grace given unto me, to every man that is among you, not to think of himself more highly than he ought to think; but to think soberly, according as God hath dealt to every man the measure of faith.

Romans 12:3

As we begin our consideration of verse 3, it is wise to remind ourselves of the main divisions of this particular chapter, and, as we have seen, it is very simple to divide it into two sections.

The first section runs from the third verse to the eighth verse. Here the apostle gives us a picture of Christian men and women exercising their gifts in the church. In a way, it is inevitable that Paul should start there. Christians are people who come together – that is the church. They come together because they have been born again, because all the things that Paul has been expounding in the first eleven chapters are true of them. The first place you find a Christian, therefore, is in the church. Paul starts with the Christian living his life in the church.

In the second section, which runs from verse 9 to the end of the chapter, the apostle deals with Christians in their relationship to other people both in the church and in the world. Many have tried to divide chapter 12 up still further, but it seems to me that it just cannot be done, and you must be careful not to impose an artificial division. I would be content with saying that the chapter is the expression of the Christian character in daily life, not only in the realm of the church, but more

generally, and that Paul deals both with its general characteristics and with its particular manifestations.

So we must proceed to consider the first major section,
verses 3 to 8, where the apostle takes up the question of the
manifestation of the gifts of the Spirit in Christian believers in
the life of the church.

Now here the apostle deals with a subject that obviously
caused a great deal of trouble in the early church. I say that on
the basis that it is a subject with which he has to deal fairly
frequently in his epistles, and, as we have often reminded
ourselves, the epistles, in the main, were a response to problems
facing Christians. You must not conceive of this apostle, nor
any of the others, as literary men who just delighted in writing
and whose occupation was to write. They were much too busy
for that. I do not think they would have written at all had they
not had to write, and they generally had to write because of
circumstances that had arisen in the lives of the members of the
churches in different parts of the Roman Empire.

The subject of the manifestation of the gifts of the Spirit had
to be taken up on more than one occasion. Indeed, in many
ways it is the great theme of the First Epistle to the Corinthians. In that Epistle, this particular subject is considered
with the greatest thoroughness, particularly in chapters 8, 12,
13 and 14. But the problems that had arisen outstandingly in
the church at Corinth, had also arisen in the church at Rome
and in various other churches.

Truth is one; and whether the church be in Corinth or in
Rome, because Christianity is one, and because all Christians
are people who are born again of the Spirit, whatever their
nationality, or their background, or their culture, the same
kinds of problems will always arise. The New Testament gives
us abundant evidence of that. So the apostle deals here, in a
very condensed and almost summary way, with a problem that
he expands and deals with at greater length in 1 Corinthians.
Though in a briefer compass, the apostle's method of dealing
with the problem is identical here and in Corinthians; he even
uses the same illustration.

Now that is the sign of a good teacher, of course, but over
and above that, the apostle was a man who was inspired by the
Spirit, so when he was given the perfect illustration, he used it

and did not mind repeating it. It conveys the truth better than anything else, so he did not hesitate to employ it. We can say, therefore, that, in many ways, 1 Corinthians 12 is a commentary of this passage, or that this is a summary of 1 Corinthians 12.

So, let us analyse verses 3 to 8, and as we do so, we shall see at a glance that Paul is true to his own method. I have often commented on this; every man has his own idiom. Just as those who know anything about music, can tell you the composer even if they only hear a few bars, so with writers. They betray themselves by their style, and this is particularly true of this great apostle. He always wrote his letters in the same way; he had his characteristic method. Here, it is like this. First of all, he starts with himself; he uses himself as an illustration! 'I say, through the grace given unto me . . .' We will see in a moment why he does this. It is not because of any conceit or boastfulness, quite the reverse, as a matter of fact. He does it because this is essential wisdom. In a way, he takes the ground from beneath the feet of his readers by talking first of all of his own particular case.

Now in starting with himself, the apostle does two things. In a wonderful way, he asserts his authority and yet at the same time displays his humility. 'I say' – and here you might think that he is speaking as a kind of pope, but he is not. 'I say' – yes, but – 'through the grace given unto me' – and there is the perfect balance. He is, after all, an apostle, and he speaks with apostolic authority. But he is very careful to make it plain and clear that his authority is one which he has received. He wants to do these two things. He wants the Christians in Rome to listen to what he is saying, because he is speaking as an authoritative apostle; but at the same time he wants them to know that what is true of them is also, in principle, true of himself. And so he disarms all objections at the very beginning as he puts himself in with them. He is apart, and yet he is with them. He is a unique man, and yet as a Christian he is the same as everyone else. And you will find this almost everywhere in Paul's epistles. The great characteristic of his writing is the way in which he always combines these two elements. So that is how he now begins.

Having started with that personal note, Paul then lays down

two great principles which must always govern our thinking with regard to the exercise of the spiritual gifts. The two principles are clearly meant to lead us to the same conclusion. Their object is to destroy, at the very beginning, any tendency to self-assertion and to boasting. It is astounding that spiritual gifts have always been one of the greatest causes of these sins, with all the resulting quarrelling and tendency to division. Nothing so proves our essential sinfulness as the fact that we will even abuse the gifts, the highest gifts of God, appropriate them unto ourselves, and cause them to militate against the interests of the church.

Let me emphasize that we once more are looking at one of the ways in which Christian morality differs from all other views of morality and ethics. There have been moral systems outside Christianity. There have been, and there still are, people who are concerned about ethical conduct who are not Christians at all. And some people have, therefore, foolishly thought that there is no difference between Christianity and these other philosophical, ethical systems. Indeed, there is a popular teaching today which says, 'The pity is that Christianity has allowed these various miraculous accretions to come in. If only you could get rid of them, you would have a wonderful view of life to put to people and they would be ready to accept it. But unfortunately they have to swallow all this talk about the virgin birth and the incarnation and the miracles and the atoning sacrifice and the resurrection and so on.'

Now, quite apart from the historicity of Christianity, there is a feature of Christian teaching which marks it off from every other system that ever has been or is still in vogue today, and that is the insistence upon humility. If you take the great ethical teaching of Greek philosophy, you will always find that it tended to provoke conceit, not to say arrogance. The Greek philosophers were the people who *knew*. Some were known as gnostics; they were the elite, the thinkers, and they regarded everybody else as barbarians, as fools, as ignorant people whom they despised. They divided up the world, as the apostle has already reminded us in Romans 1:14 where he says, 'I am a debtor both to the Greek, and to the Barbarians; both to the wise, and to the unwise.'

[145]

So all these other systems always have the element of pride and self-satisfaction. The Greek philosopher thought he was such a good person because he took the trouble to think, and he had ability and understanding, and had studied the great teachers. So he put himself up on a pedestal. It is equally true today. Listen to some of the discussions on the television or radio. It always comes out, this touch of arrogance and conceit. 'We are the men who know, the wise!'

But what is emphasized here above everything else is the humility. The apostle puts himself in with the others, and they are all of them shown that any boasting or any appearance of self-satisfaction or any self-assertion is a negation of their position as Christians. Humility! Christianity brought something quite new into the world.

For instance, people have often asked, 'Why did the great apostle ever write that thirteenth chapter of the First Epistle to the Corinthians? Why did he say so much about love? Why did he not content himself with just saying that Christians must show love in their dealings with one another?' And there is only one answer. In the entire Greek language there was no word to express what is meant by the Christian notion of love. So the apostle had to say a whole series of things in explanation: 'Though I speak with the tongues of men and of angels . . .' Love is like this and is not like that.' He had to because there was no single word to be found to convey this idea. It was foreign to the whole of Greek thinking, and also to the whole of Roman thinking.

Modesty and humility were regarded by the best pagans as weakness; and, of course, that idea is still found everywhere in the world today. 'Believe in yourself', says the world. 'Trust yourself.' Self expression! Opposition to the gospel is generally expressed in those terms. I read in the paper that some great authorities in some conference have been making sweeping assertions to the effect that it is wrong to teach children the Bible because it will cramp them, and if you teach them the Christian way of life, it will interfere with their 'emotional stability'. The Christian teaching about sin, they say, is restricting, and all this teaching in the Bible about self-abnegation is bad for the psyche.

That has always been the attitude of people in the world.

They regard this glorious characteristic of humility as a weakness. That was true at the time of our Lord and the apostles, and it has remained true throughout the centuries. But here at once, in introducing his subject, the apostle reminds us of the necessity of humility. So, quite apart from the historical facts on which our faith is based, this great central characteristic is in itself a proof that we have something new, something unique, that has come into the world through our Lord and Saviour Jesus Christ.

What, then, are the principles that the apostle now lays down to bring us to the practice of humility? This is of vital importance because if we do not manifest humility, we are not carrying out what he has been saying in the first two verses. Furthermore, if we are not carrying that out, it means that all our knowledge, and the theological principles in the first eleven chapters, are of no value whatsoever to us; indeed, they may be doing us more harm than good because if we are proud of our knowledge, then the knowledge is of no value to us.

Here, then, are the principles. The first is that the Christian life is all of grace. 'I say, through the grace given unto me.' Paul repeats it, '. . . as God hath dealt to every man the measure of faith.' It is all of grace and of faith.

Now this is an argument which those of us who are familiar with the earlier part of Romans already know very well, because Paul has already dealt with it many times in establishing his great doctrine of justification by faith only. Take, for instance, chapter 3:27: 'Where is boasting then? It is excluded. By what law? of works? Nay: but by the law of faith.' There is no room for boasting in any part of the Christian life. The apostle's whole argument has been that you can never become a Christian because of what you are or because of what you have done. Never! It is in spite of what you are, in spite of what you have done. Salvation is by grace through faith. 'For by grace are ye saved through faith; and that not of yourselves: it is the gift of God: not of works, lest any man should boast' [*Eph.* 2:8–9]. No boasting!

Paul emphasizes this again in Romans 11:6. He says, 'And if by grace, then it is no more of works: otherwise grace is no more grace. But if it be of works, then is it no more grace:

otherwise work is no more work.' That has been his great point about our entry into the Christian life, and now here he is saying that this principle not only holds with regard to our entry but governs the whole of our Christian life. We do not merely start in this way, we continue like this; and if we do not continue, we have gone wrong and have lost connection with our point of origin. So his first principle is that our entire position is the result of grace and our whole activity is based upon it.

The second principle is to be found in verses 4 and 5, and this, again, is very familiar. 'For as we have many members in one body, and all members have not the same office: we, being many, are one body in Christ, and every one members one of another.' Paul here puts before us the famous picture, which he uses in so many of his epistles, of the church as 'the body of Christ'. The purpose of the illustration is precisely the same as that of the principle of grace that he has already laid down, but it is a wonderful illustration. The point of this analogy concerning the body is that the parts of the body are always parts of a whole, and that the parts have no sense or meaning except in their relationship to the other parts and all of them together to the whole and especially to the Head.

Then, having laid down his two principles, Paul goes on, in verses 6 to 8, to the application, and he gives us examples and illustrations of how the two principles now show themselves in operation. If we have the spiritual gift of prophecy, then we 'prophesy according to the proportion of faith'; if ministry or teaching, then, 'let us wait on our ministering: or he that teacheth, on teaching', and so on. These are but practical examples to show how these two great principles – which in themselves are illustrations of a yet more fundamental principle – reveal themselves in the life of the church with respect to the exercising of the spiritual gifts.

There, then, is our analysis of this first major section, and having looked at it like that in a general view, we must now produce the microscope and come to a more detailed exposition. The Bible is very logical and it is a good analogy to say you approach it as a scientist approaches an object to be studied. The scientist has a specimen in front of him on the table. Now he does not start with his microscope, but with the naked eye.

He looks at it and gets a general impression. Then, he comes to the individual portions and here he may have to bring in his microscope. Studying the Bible is a rational and scientific procedure. So we now come to our detailed exposition.

The first phrase that of necessity arrests our attention is this: 'I say, through the grace given unto me . . .' This, as I have shown you, is the key statement. I am sure we do not need to be reminded of what is meant by 'grace', and yet we cannot take any risks because the whole argument here depends upon its meaning. Grace is undeserved favour. It is kindness, blessing, something that comes altogether out of the heart of God, not in response to anything in us, but in spite of us and utterly undeserved.

But now, in particular, what does Paul mean by saying, 'I say, *through* the grace given unto me'? Is he referring here to the general grace that he had received as a Christian, the grace that brings the gift of faith, the grace that we all must have received before we could ever be Christians – does he mean that, or is he referring here to something more particular? I want to suggest to you that he means both, but particularly the second. He is, of course, referring to the grace that had made him a Christian, he who had been 'a blasphemer, and a persecutor, and injurious' [*1 Tim.* 1:13], he who had so hated Christ. Paul never got over that. The fact that he was a Christian at all was an amazing thing that could only be explained by the grace of God. But here, I think, the apostle has something more particular in mind: he is referring to the grace that had made him an apostle. He is asserting his apostleship.

Why do I emphasize this? Well, I think that the analogy of what Paul says elsewhere compels us to say that. It is something that he refers to so often. Let me give you some examples. Take his words in the very first chapter of this Epistle. In the first verse he says he is 'a servant of Jesus Christ, called to be an apostle', and then in verse 5 he adds, 'By whom we have received grace and apostleship [and, as we indicated at the time,[1] it is generally agreed that Paul means the grace of apostleship] for obedience to the faith among all nations, for his name.'

[1] See Romans: An Exposition of Chapter 1: The Gospel of God

Or later, in chapter 15 verse 15, Paul will say, 'Nevertheless, brethren, I have written the more boldly unto you in some sort, as putting you in mind, *because of the grace that is given to me of God.*' The context shows that Paul is referring to his calling to be an apostle. He continues: 'That I should be a minister of Jesus Christ to the Gentiles, ministering the gospel of God, that the offering up of the Gentiles might be acceptable, being sanctified by the Holy Ghost.' And then, the same point: 'I have therefore whereof I may glory through Jesus Christ in those things which pertain to God . . .' There very definitely we see 'the grace of apostleship', the *particular* grace that was given to Paul to enable him to function as the great apostle to the Gentiles.

There is a further remarkable example in 1 Corinthians. In the church at Corinth the Christians were tending to divide themselves up in a partisan manner. Some said, 'I am of Paul.' Others said, 'I am of Apollos.' A third group claimed, 'We are of Cephas,' while a fourth said, 'We are of Christ.' So the apostle had to deal with this and his argument is the same as that here in Romans 12:3: 'Who then is Paul, and who is Apollos, but ministers by whom ye believed, even as the Lord gave to every man? I have planted, Apollos watered; but God gave the increase. So then neither is he that planteth any thing, neither he that watereth; but God that giveth the increase. Now he that planteth and he that watereth are one: and every man shall receive his own reward according to his own labour. For we are labourers together with God: ye are God's husbandry, ye are God's building. According to the grace of God which is given unto me, as a wise masterbuilder, I have laid the foundation, and another buildeth thereon. But let every man take heed how he buildeth thereon' [*1 Cor.* 3:5–10].

Now here it is – 'According to the grace of God which is given unto me, I am a wise masterbuilder.' I am an apostle; I am a teacher; I am a planter of churches, and so on. It is quite clear there that the 'grace' to which Paul is referring is the grace that had made him an apostle.

But take what is, perhaps, one of the most moving statements of this grace that the apostle ever made: 'For I am the least of the apostles, that am not meet to be called an apostle, because I persecuted the church of God. But by the grace of

God I am what I am: and his grace which was bestowed upon me was not in vain; but I laboured more abundantly than they all: yet not I, but the grace of God which was with me' [*1 Cor.* 15:9–10]. Since here also, as in Romans 12:3, Paul is dealing with teaching, I argue that he is still making the same point. He is talking about the grace given to him that made him an apostle and a teacher, and he says that this is why they should listen to him.

Then the apostle repeats this in Galatians 1:15–16: 'But when it pleased God, who separated me from my mother's womb, and called me by his grace, to reveal his Son in me, that I might preach him among the heathen; immediately I conferred not with flesh and blood . . .' Again, Paul is referring not so much to his conversion as to his calling to be an apostle. He says it again in Ephesians 3:7–8 – and to me these are all very glorious statements which we can never afford to neglect – 'Whereof I was made a minister, according to the gift of the grace of God given unto me by the effectual working of his power. Unto me, who am less than the least of all saints, is this grace given, that I should preach among the Gentiles the unsearchable riches of Christ.' He is talking of the grace that called him and made him an apostle.

Finally, take that last, very personal example, which we have in 1 Timothy 1, where Paul talks of this grace in a particularly moving manner. He has been working out an argument and he winds it up by saying, 'According to the glorious gospel of the blessed God, which was committed to my trust. And I thank Christ Jesus our Lord, who hath enabled me, for that he counted me faithful, putting me into the ministry; who was before a blasphemer, and a persecutor, and injurious: but I obtained mercy, because I did it ignorantly in unbelief. And the grace of our Lord was exceeding abundant with faith and love which is in Christ Jesus. This is a faithful saying, and worthy of all acceptation, that Christ Jesus came into the world to save sinners; of whom I am chief. Howbeit for this cause I obtained mercy, that in me first Jesus Christ might shew forth all longsuffering, for a pattern to them which should hereafter believe on him to life everlasting' [*1 Tim.* 1:11–16].

I have produced that evidence because I am anxious to show

you that the apostle was very jealous, in the right sense of the word, on this particular point. It filled him with amazement, that he, of all men, should have been called to be an apostle. So Paul speaks now to the Romans and he asks them to listen to him because the grace of God has made him an apostle. And, of course, this grace not only calls a man, it equips him and enables him. Paul is really saying: I am asking you to listen to me because not only am I actually an apostle, but I have also received understanding in these matters. I have received wisdom; I have knowledge. As a result of His grace I have received certain gifts of the Spirit. I have discrimination; I am able to teach and I am able to explain and expound. I have been made an apostle in all these ways by the grace of God.

That is what Paul is saying, and it is a tremendous statement. But for the grace of God he would never have been an apostle at all; but for the grace of God he would never have been able to teach in the way that he did. It was God's grace that gave him this unusual insight, this special understanding, this peculiar faculty of discrimination which made Paul shine out so wonderfully among all the writers of the New Testament. Peter even pays him a tribute when he acknowledges that there are things in Paul's writing that even he found it difficult to understand [see 2 Pet. 3:16].

So it is the grace of God, says Paul, that has made him the man he is; it is not anything in him: 'I say to you, by the grace that has been given to me.' He is conveying to his fellow Christians that in and of himself he has nothing of which to boast. He is not saying, 'I, the great man Paul, am telling you; I, the brilliant pupil of Gamaliel am telling you; I, the giant intellect; I, the man who has studied as very few men have – listen to me.' It is not that. He is declaring, 'I have nothing but what I have first of all received, and my very office, my calling, my abilities, all I am and all I am doing, is solely the result of the grace of God. I have authority, but it is an authority that has been given to me and it has been given to me by the Lord Himself who said that He was going to make of me a minister, and a witness, and a teacher of the Gentiles.

That is what the apostle said in his testimony before Agrippa and Festus – you find the account in Acts 26. He was called, he was taken hold of, he was apprehended and he was appointed.

He was told what he was going to do and what Christ was going to do through him and in him, and it was He who equipped him with the abilities and the gifts he needed. And, of course, we remember how in the previous chapter of Romans, he has already told the Gentiles. 'For I speak to you Gentiles, inasmuch as I am the apostle of the Gentiles, I magnify mine office' [*Rom.* 11:13]

And all this is conveyed here in this phrase, 'through the grace given unto me'. This is very wonderful. Here again we see a perfect combination of the two characteristics already referred to. Here is a man who can say, on the one hand, 'Be ye followers of me' [1 *Cor.* 4:16; *Phil.* 3:17], and, 'Treat me as your example' [see 2 *Thess.* 3:9], and, 'Yet have ye not many fathers: for in Christ I have begotten you through the gospel' [1 *Cor.* 4:15] – I alone am your father. He can speak like that. Yet, on the other hand, when he does, there is never a touch of arrogance because he is always careful to add that he is what he is solely because of the grace of God. It is nothing in him. So, as we have seen, you get a curious paradox, this assertion of authority, and yet this humility. He is an exceptionally humble man because he is aware that he has nothing but that which he has received, and received freely and entirely as the result of the grace of God.

This is very important and significant. Let me illustrate what Paul is saying by what Peter says in his own way. Notice how he starts the fifth chapter of the First Epistle: 'The elders which are among you I exhort, who am also an elder, and a witness of the sufferings of Christ, and also a partaker of the glory that shall be revealed: feed the flock of God which is among you, taking the oversight thereof, not by constraint, but willingly; not for filthy lucre, but of a ready mind; neither as being lords over God's heritage, but being ensamples to the flock. And when the chief Shepherd shall appear, ye shall receive a crown of glory that fadeth not away' [1 *Pet.* 5:1–4]. That is Peter's way of saying exactly the same thing. 'I am Simon Peter,' he says in effect. 'I was with Him on the Mount of Transfiguration. There were only two others with me; even all the other apostles were not there. I am a very exceptional person.' And yet you notice the perfect balance: 'Neither as being lords over God's heritage, but being ensamples unto the flock.'

[153]

Now this is important for us because we are living in what is called an ecumenical age, when men are pressing us to become part of a great world church which will include the Roman Catholic Church. So we are facing the whole question of authority, which is one of the most urgent problems of the present time. Where does authority lie in the church? And the Roman Catholic answer is that the Pope is the authority. He speaks 'ex cathedra'. We are told he has the authority of Christ Himself.

But that is a complete denial of the apostle's teaching in this one phrase here in Romans 12:3. It is teaching which he gives everywhere else, and the Apostle Peter is equally careful to make the same point: 'not as lording it over God's heritage'. The minister of Christ is never to be addressed as, 'Your Lordship', or, 'My Lord'. But that, unfortunately, is what has happened in the church; that is what has gone wrong in the whole history of the church. It is that the church has departed from the New Testament concept of authority; it has forgotten this perfect blending of authority and humility, separateness, yet sameness: 'You are, I am. We are all in this together. Fundamentally we are the same.' Authority in the New Testament is always spiritual, never official. That seems to me the important principle here. It is not the office that matters, but the person. But with the church, as she has become, it is the office that matters; it is the office that makes the person.

There is no such thing as a hierarchy in the New Testament. There are divisions; I will have to emphasize that, as the apostle does. There are different offices, there are different callings, there are different gifts, but there is never this gradation leading up to some ultimate lord who is almost worshipped and who speaks with great authority. All that has come into the church from the world, from the state. It did not even begin at the time of Constantine; it had already been happening in the century before that.

There is no trace of worldly hierarchy in the first two centuries of the Christian era. At first we just read of presbyters and bishops, which were interchangeable terms, and deacons. But in the third century they began to divide up – a bishop, a presbyter, a deacon. After that we find not only a bishop but a kind of 'civic' bishop, a bishop in a town as distinct from a bishop in the country. Then there developed what was called a 'metropolitan', a man in a great capital who was even above the bishops of the cities. And eventually you had the man who was over the whole lot, the pope at Rome, a 'lord of lords', the one who was supreme.

That is what is meant by this notion of hierarchy, and all I am trying to show you is that it is something that is entirely remote from the New Testament and is, indeed, a blank contradiction of this essential teaching: 'I say, through the grace given unto me . . .' The apostles were not afraid to be humble. They had no need to dress themselves up, or to sit on so-called thrones, or to be removed as far away as possible from the people. No, they were always among the people. They were one with all other Christians. There was the common element that they never forgot. In the New Testament there is always a combination of authority and humility.

This is such an important matter that I felt I must place unusual emphasis upon it. As you think about the whole question of church unity – and it is being pressed upon us in all the denominations and in every conceivable kind of church – think about it in the light of the New Testament teaching. Ask questions: Where has the present system come from? Where do I find it in the New Testament? Can I find it there at all? The New Testament sheds great light on this subject. It is Paul, the greatest, perhaps, of all the apostles, who says, 'I am the least of the apostles, that am not meet to be called an apostle . . . but by the grace of God I am what I am' [*1 Cor.* 15:9–10]. As I speak to you and teach you, says Paul, I am not doing it as a man, I am not doing it merely as an official, but I am doing it through, by means of, as the result of, the grace that has been given unto me.

Twelve

*

> For I say, through the grace given unto me, to every man that is
> among you, not to think of himself more highly than he ought to
> think; but to think soberly, according as God hath dealt to every
> man the measure of faith. For as we have many members in one
> body, and all members have not the same office: so we, being
> many, are one body in Christ, and every one members one of
> another.
>
> Romans 12:3–5

We are dealing here, you remember, with the matter of
Christians exercising their gifts in the church. And, as we
have already indicated, the apostle takes up this matter here, as
he does elsewhere, because difficulties had obviously arisen
with regard to this question. Throughout the centuries, the
exercising of the gifts has been one of the causes of trouble in
the Christian church – hence Paul's teaching, for which we
should all be so profoundly grateful.

We have seen that the apostle starts to deal with this subject
by talking of the grace he has received. And then he goes on to
show that as this is true of him, it is true also of all the other
members of the church. His first principle is that all that we
have as Christians is the result of grace. Then his second
principle is the doctrine of the church as the body of Christ.

We have already begun to work this out. We have seen that
in the Christian church all authority is of grace; therefore there
is no hierarchy or reverence for status, calling a man, 'Your
Holiness', and so on. There is nothing like that in the New
Testament, and our object and ambition always should be to
have Christian churches which approximate as closely as is

possible to the New Testament pattern. So we need to be watchful about this because there is an extraordinary tendency in the Christian church to elevate offices so that through them men can be elevated. As spirituality goes down, offices go up along with ceremony and pomp and ritual.

You are familiar, for example, with what is called Anglo-Catholicism which began as the Oxford Movement in the 1830s with Cardinal Newman and Pusey and Keble and others like them. Now behind that movement lay the feeling that the church was not counting in the world as she should. How could authority be brought back to the church? And the answer given was that the Church of England had become too ordinary. The minister must therefore be elevated, and be called a priest. Then the priest must be elevated and set at one remove from the people, and he must be dressed up in vestments. And the communion table must be called the altar, and so on. All this was a substitute for spirituality, for spiritual power; it was a substitute for the grace of God.

But the Apostle Paul does not speak of his authority in terms of his office, but in terms of the grace that has put him into the office, the grace through which the revelation of the knowledge has come to him, and which has given him all his powers and faculties. In the New Testament we see an essential simplicity, an extraordinary contrast with what the Christian church has become throughout the centuries.

We are living in days when you and I have an opportunity, if we want to be biblical, of restoring again the primitive practice, the primitive idea, of the Christian church, and God grant that, even through a word like this in passing, some of us may be stimulated to think again along these lines. Do not start with what you see, start with the New Testament, and let us order all things according to this which we have as the sole authority in all matters of faith and conduct in the church, as well as in general.

Paul goes on to say that this grace is not only given to him, it is not only true of him. He says, 'I say, through the grace given unto me, *to every man* that is among you . . .' Here again is a most important point. Paul means every one, there are no exceptions. This is not to be true only of the officers of the church; it is to be equally true of all the members. The distinction between clergy and laity, which came in about the second century, is again a violation of New Testament teaching. There needs to be a distinction in the offices of the church, the apostles make that perfectly plain. But there must not be a rigid division between clergy and laity; that is not in Paul's teaching at all. All members of the church are in the same position. Some, because of the gifts given to them, are called upon to exercise certain functions which others are not called upon to undertake, but the principle of grace and the distribution of gifts is common to all. So we must learn to think of the church as a living community of people: each one has faith, each one has life from God, each one has a gift which has been given to him or her, and each one is to function in the total life of the church.

These points, too, are significant for us because more and more the idea has been creeping in that the vast majority of church members are really not meant to do anything but sit and listen, and the only people who function in the church are certain special people. Now let us be quite clear about this. You have often heard criticism of what is called 'a one-man ministry' and that criticism is perfectly right. I would argue that it is right that certain men be set apart for the work of preaching, but that does not mean that they alone function and nobody else does anything at all. That is not the picture we have of the New Testament church. The picture rather is given here – 'every man that is among you'. This is applicable to everybody, not only to preachers, pastors and teachers, but to every single member of the Christian church, as we shall see yet more clearly when we come on to the figure of the church as the body of Christ.

But now, at the end of the statement, we come to a most interesting and fascinating phrase: 'according as God hath dealt to every man the measure of faith'. Now this is clearly the crucial part of Paul's statement. Notice once more the emphasis on 'every man'. Every one! The word 'dealt' is not difficult – it means 'divided'. It is the idea of dealing out, doling out – as God has divided to every one the measure of faith.

But what is the meaning of this phrase 'the measure of faith'? It is important that we should be clear about it. What is the faith that the apostle is talking about here? There are some who try to dismiss it as just meaning justifying faith – the faith which brings us into the Christian life – the faith the apostle has been laying before us in the earlier part of the Epistle, for example, in chapter 3 verse 28:'Therefore we conclude that a man is justified by faith without the deeds of the law.' But obviously it cannot be that and for this good reason – justifying faith is the same in everybody. There is no such thing as a special or a particular justifying faith. The faith by which the Apostle Paul was justified is no different from the faith by which any one of us is justified. But here he is talking about 'the measure of faith' which immediately suggests a difference.

Then others have thought that Paul means here the faith which, in 1 Corinthians 12:9, is called 'the gift of faith'. In that passage, Paul is giving us a list of some of the gifts and he says, 'To another faith by the same Spirit'. He is talking there about a special gift of faith, and there are those who therefore think that here in Romans 12:3 he is referring to the same thing. But again, we can easily demonstrate to you that he is not doing that. In 1 Corinthians 12:9 Paul is writing to people who are Christians, all of whom have been justified by faith, and he says that some have been given 'the gift of faith by the same Spirit'. By that he means the particular kind of faith that is exemplified in men like George Müller, and Hudson Taylor who founded the China Inland Mission [now the Overseas Missionary Fellowship]. Not everybody receives that gift, but it was 'divided', or 'dealt' to George Müller. As a result, he was able to pray with confidence and assurance, and amazing things happened – we can read about them in his story. Now here in Romans 12 that is obviously not what is meant because that special gift of faith is only given to some people, whereas here the apostle's emphasis is that a 'measure of faith' is given to every Christian.

What, then, does the apostle mean? Well, I come to the conclusion that the best explanation is that Paul is saying, 'according as God hath dealt to every man some gift through faith'. Every one of us has some particular gift through the channel of faith. I believe that Paul's words in 1 Corinthians 12:4: – 'Now there are diversities of gifts, but the same Spirit' – say the same thing. The Spirit gives these gifts. He is the one Spirit but there is a great diversity in the gifts that are given.

But perhaps the best exposition of this phrase is in Ephesians 4:7 – it is interesting to notice that the apostle constantly has to say these same things to different churches. There, in Ephesians 4, he has been emphasizing the great principle of unity. In verse 4 he begins, 'There is one body, and one Spirit, even as ye are called in one hope of your calling; one Lord, one faith, one baptism, one God and Father of all, who is above all, and through all, and in you all' – then – 'But unto every one of us is given grace according to the measure of the gift of Christ.' That expresses very clearly what Paul is saying here in Romans 12:3.

We receive grace, the apostle says in Ephesians 4:7, and then he goes on to talk about functions: 'Wherefore he saith, When he ascended up on high, he led captivity captive, and gave gifts unto men . . . And he gave some, apostles; and some, prophets; and some, evangelists; and some, pastors and teachers; for the perfecting of the saints . . .' [verses 8, 11–12]. But here is the point: the grace is given, 'according to the measure of the gift of Christ'. He has ascended up on high, He has sent the Holy Spirit, and, through the Spirit, He now distributes these gifts to the members of the church. And it is He who decides the particular 'measure' or the particular 'gift', or you can even say, the particular 'grace' that is given to each one. 'And to every one of us is given grace according to the measure of the gift of Christ.' Any gift we may have is the gift that comes to us from the Lord Jesus Christ through the Spirit, through our faith.

Here we are, every one of us, in the church, and Paul says, 'God hath dealt to every man [every one of us] the [or a] measure of faith.' This is a very important point and the first thing we must keep clearly in our minds is that here, and in 1 Corinthians 12, which, as I said, is a commentary on Romans 12:3, Paul is not referring to natural gifts. Of course, we are given natural gifts, and when we become Christians and receive the Holy Spirit, our natural gifts are sharpened and heightened, but that is not what Paul is talking about here. Here he is saying that we are given something new, something we did not have before, not a natural, but a spiritual gift, the kind of gift that is given only to the Christian. It is not something that we have by nature. By faith, we can improve this kind of gift and increase it, but we can never create it or produce it. The whole emphasis is upon this: 'as God hath dealt to everyone'. The very essence of Paul's teaching is that all these varying gifts are given to us by the grace of God; He deals them out.

Now faith itself, of course, is a gift: 'By grace are ye saved through faith; and that not of yourselves: it is the gift of God' [*Eph.* 2:8]. So at no point can we claim that it is what *we* have done that determines our Christian life. The apostle makes it very clear here that no one has a particular gift because of his or her faith. But sometimes people tend to teach that kind of thing. They say, 'Now, of course, if you have great faith you are likely to get such and such a gift.' But that is the wrong way round. It is not our faith that determines the gifts we receive. It is God who measures and distributes these gifts He determines the amount given to every person. That is the whole point of this teaching.

In other words, here we see again, the sovereignty of the Holy Spirit. That is the great emphasis of 1 Corinthians 12. It is the sovereignty of the Giver, the Controller, the Holy Spirit, who distributes to every man severally as He wills [see *1 Cor.*12:11]. That is what the apostle is saying here and we must never lose sight of it.

But then let us go on to remind ourselves, also, that while it is He who gives all the gifts, every one of us receives a gift. The gifts vary in character, they vary in kind and in importance. So that we end by drawing the deduction that we are not all meant to be the same, and we are not all meant to function in the same manner. In the church we are not all meant to be doing the same things. This is implicit in the teaching here: 'God hath dealt to every man the measure of faith.' A particular gift has been given to every single one of us. It is not the same in each case; we are not postage stamps and we must not desire to do the same thing. The emphasis is upon the sovereignty of the Giver and the diversity of the gifts. Here, you see, is the basic doctrine.

So what happens in the light of that? Well, says the apostle, that determines how we think of ourselves. Now trouble arises because of what men and women think of themselves. Quarrels, disputes, jealousies, envies and wranglings are all the result of people's wrong and conceited opinions of

[161]

themselves. Look at the state of the world, look at the state of society – torn, divided, factions, jealousies, envy. Look at the politicians, ready to cut one another's throats at any moment, members of the same party pretending to a loyalty that is a sham. They even reveal their duplicity more and more openly; no one can trust another. 'Uneasy lies the head that wears the crown.' There are others watching, waiting, and they will pounce. That is true, too, in all the learned professions – the medical profession, the legal profession – envy and jealousy run through them all.

So the apostle is concerned to tell each person 'not to think of himself more highly than he ought to think; but to think soberly' – why? 'according as [because] God hath dealt to every man the measure of faith'. If you grasp the principle that all the gifts come from Him, that it is He and He alone who decides what gifts everybody is to have, and that they are to be different, then you will immediately be able to control your thinking about yourself.

How, then, should you think of yourself? Well, let us pursue what Paul says. He makes a most interesting statement. He says that, as a result, none of us should have 'high thoughts' of ourselves – that is what Paul's word actually means – 'not to think of himself more highly'. The apostle says, 'Don't go in for hyper-thinking concerning yourself.' 'Hyper' is always wrong. It means excess, something that is too high. 'Now,' says the apostle, 'don't be high-minded. Don't think more of yourself than you ought to think.'

Then Paul goes on – he is so careful and so concerned about this – the Christian must not 'think of himself more highly *than he ought to think'*. So how ought a man to think about himself? Paul's answer is that we should think about ourselves as it behoves us to think about ourselves. Another translation might be: 'Do not be high-minded above that which you ought to be minded about yourself.' Paul constantly uses this word 'think' – 'not to *think* of himself more highly than he ought to *think*; but to *think* soberly.' This takes us back, does it not, to the second verse: 'Be not conformed to this world: but be ye transformed by the renewing of your mind.' We reveal that we are truly Christian when we begin to show this renewed mind in our thinking about ourselves.

[162]

But what does Paul mean when he says, '. . . but think *soberly*'? This is a very interesting word. 'Soberly' must not be thought of primarily in terms of not being drunk, although that definitely does come in. The Greek word used by the apostle means 'to be in one's right mind'. The trouble with those conceited people who think too highly of themselves is that they are lacking in balance. To use a colloquialism, they are 'not all there', they are too up in the air, they do not realize where they are. It is a form of insanity. Of course, drunkenness illustrates the same thing. A man who takes too much drink knocks out his higher centres, his judgment, and his sense of balance, and becomes a man capable of doing anything. He will fight anybody; he can give a final opinion on anything; there is nothing he cannot do! What is the matter with him? Well, he is certainly not sober minded! He is acting in an insane manner; he is not thinking as a man ought to think.

So the apostle is telling us here that we ought to think of ourselves in a rational manner. In other words, we are not to be governed any longer by our impulses, by our desires and instincts. We have a 'new mind', a mind which has been renewed, and he is now giving us a picture and an understanding of what this means in the church. Instead of asserting our rights and putting ourselves forward, and claiming this and that for ourselves, we stop and say, 'Who am I? What am I? What entitles me to boast? What do I deserve?' And the moment we ask those questions, we are beginning to act in a sober manner; we are really beginning to think. We are not being governed by something else, a kind of passion, we are collected and calm; we are really facing the facts.

The apostle constantly has to say this. He has put it all perfectly in one verse: 'Who maketh thee to differ from another? and what hast thou that thou didst not receive? now if thou didst receive it, why dost thou glory, as if thou hadst not received it?' (*1 Cor.* 4:7). That is exactly what he is saying here in Romans 12:3. 'Wait a moment,' he says in effect, 'you are about to assert yourself. You say, "Look at the gift I've got! Look at me!" And then you despise the other man, or he, perhaps, with his smaller gift, is jealous of you. Stop! Think for a moment. Think soberly. Think rationally. Come to yourself. Be saved. What makes you differ from another? Do you decide the difference? Have you decided the genes which went into you? Or, in the spiritual realm, have you chosen the gifts that you possess? "What hast thou that thou didst not receive?" ' And the logic is inevitable: 'Now if thou didst receive it, why dost thou glory, as if thou hadst not received it?'

In other words, Paul is telling us that we are all to be like our Lord. Look at Him, the Son of God, the One in whom 'dwelleth all the fulness of the Godhead bodily' [*Col.* 2:9], and yet the One who says, 'I have not spoken of myself; but the Father which sent me, he gave me a commandment, what I should say' [*John* 12:49]; 'I do nothing of myself; but as my Father hath taught me, I speak these things' [*John* 8:28]. That is what He is always saying. And again, He says, 'Take my yoke upon you, and learn of me; for I am meek and lowly in heart' [*Matt.* 11:29]. This, our Lord says, is how you are to function.

And here in Romans 12 the apostle is simply pressing that teaching upon us. We are to remember that our Lord said also, 'Without me ye can do nothing' [*John* 15:5]. We are to remember that He looked at those disciples who had been with Him for three years, who had seen His miracles, who had seen Him dying and buried, who had seen Him alive after His resurrection, who were aware of all the facts – it was to them He said, 'Tarry ye in the city of Jerusalem, until ye be endued with power from on high' [*Luke* 24:49]. Without the gift of that power even they with their knowledge, the first eye-witnesses, could not be true witnesses to Him and to His great salvation. It is what was given that enabled them. There is a hymn which seems to me to sum it up very well:

> *And every virtue we possess,*
> *And every conquest won,*
> *And every thought of holiness,*
> *Are His alone.*
>
> H. Auber

Do not think too highly of yourselves; do not think above what you ought to think; think 'soberly', think in a sane, rational manner.

We can, therefore, put it like this. The first thing we must do is learn to look at these gifts in the right way. We must not look at them subjectively or in terms of ourselves. That is always the fatal mistake. The moment we begin to look at the gifts like that, we go astray. We must look at them objectively, indeed, I would almost venture to go so far as to say that we should always look at these gifts in an impersonal manner.

What do I mean? I mean that the gifts are not ours and therefore they are nothing about which we should boast. We have not produced them; we have not generated them; they are not a reward for anything that we are. He, with His master strategy, has determined to give these gifts, 'dividing to every man severally as he wills'. So they are entirely His and therefore we can go on to say – and this is most important – that we must never overestimate any gift.

There is a great tendency to do this. The Christians in Corinth were in confusion because they were overestimating the gift of tongues. And people have had too high an opinion of many other gifts. Preaching has been overestimated many and many a time, and this has led to grievous trouble. Towards the end of the Victorian era, for example, there was undoubtedly a worshipping of preachers and we are still reaping some of the results of that. Preachers were almost idolized. This is no longer the case, and that is a good thing; but there remains the danger of overestimating the importance of gifts, certain gifts in particular.

It is equally important to emphasize that we should be on guard against the opposite danger: never underestimate the importance of any gift. This, again, is very common. There are people who have said, 'Oh, I'm a nobody in the church, my little gift, you know, I don't really count.' He says, 'I cannot speak, I cannot teach, therefore what I do is unimportant.' It is a lie! Such an attitude seems very humble but it is quite wrong. He has no right to say that! He is despising the gift which has been given to him by the Holy Spirit. The whole point and purpose of this teaching – and we will see it still more clearly when we come on to the analogy of the church as the body of Christ – is that nothing is unimportant; everything is important. So we must not overestimate some gifts and we must not underestimate others, neither with respect to ourselves or anybody else. To overestimate, to be puffed up, is bad; to despise another is equally bad.

[165]

The way to be right on this is to get the right view of the gifts, to understand that they are not natural, they are not human, that they are all given. This ensures the right balance so that you will never be boastful, and at the same time will never indulge in mock-modesty.

I remember a man addressing a meeting who thought that he was giving a word of encouragement to the ordinary members of the church. He was using an illustration of a building and he said that in a building certain great stones are placed at the corners – the cornerstones – and after that other great slabs of stones are built up. Then the builder generally sends men along with wheelbarrows who pour loads of small stones in the gaps between the great stones. And this preacher waxed so eloquent on this that in the end he had worked himself up to saying that, really, what mattered was not the great big cornerstones and stone slabs but the little stones that filled in the gaps.

Now that was just folly. The preacher was exaggerating the importance of the small stones. His desire was to take a little out of the boastfulness of the big stones and that was quite all right. But he went so far as to reverse the teaching and to give the impression that the only people who really did matter in the church were the people about whom nobody knew anything at all. He was virtually dismissing the apostles and the Reformers and the great leaders of the church throughout the centuries. That is just nonsense and is not scriptural teaching. You would never have a building at all if you did not have the big stones; but it is equally true to say that the little ones *are* necessary to fill in the gaps.

The point is that we must not look at the gifts in this personal way. That is fatal. We must not compare and contrast the gifts in a competitive sense. We must realize the truth that we have nothing but that which we have received. We can go further and say that we deserve to receive nothing, and so we should end by saying to ourselves, 'What a privilege it is to be in the church at all, what a privilege to have any gift whatsoever, it does not matter what it is! The amazing thing is that He has ever looked upon us in His grace and has called us and has put us here, and has dispensed some gift to us according to the measure of faith.'

There, then, is Paul's first principle in dealing with this matter. Work it out for yourselves in terms of your whole conception of the Christian church and you will see how important it is. Shall I ask you a question? What is the gift you have been given? And how is it functioning in your life?

Thirteen

*

> For I say, through the grace given unto me, to every man that is
> among you, not to think of himself more highly than he ought to
> think; but to think soberly, according as God hath dealt to every
> man the measure of faith. For as we have many members in one
> body, and all members have not the same office: so we, being
> many, are one body in Christ, and every one members one of
> another.
>
> Romans 12:3–5

Paul's first principle in these verses, you remember, is that
everything is of grace, and now we come to look at his second
principle which, in a way, enforces the first. This is that the
church is the body of Christ, and the apostle presents it both as
a doctrine and as an illustration. In verse 4, he works out the
points that he feels are essential to his argument in terms of
what is true of our physical bodies. Then, in the fifth verse, he
applies these points.

The doctrine of the body is most important, as Paul shows
here, both for practical reasons and as a part of our whole
understanding of the New Testament doctrine of the nature
of the Christian church. As I have been reminding you,
difficulties arose in many of the early Christian churches
largely because the believers had never understood the real
nature of the church, and the apostle had to be constantly
teaching them. For instance, in 1 Corinthians the apostle
deals with this doctrine not only specifically in chapter 12,
but also in the whole Epistle up to the practicalities in the
last chapter. He starts off in the first chapter by saying that he
hears that there are divisions among the Christians with

some saying, 'I am of Paul'; others saying, 'I am of Apollos'; others, 'I am of Cephas'; others, 'I am of Christ'. He asks, 'Is Christ divided?'

Exactly the same failure is seen here in Romans. When there are troubles over the exercise of gifts, it means not only that people have not understood the truth concerning the gifts *per se*, but that beyond this they are defective in their understanding of the church. Now this, of course, is of unusual importance at a time like the present when there is much talk about the unity of the church, and it is right that this doctrine should be considered. Our Lord prayed in His high-priestly prayer, 'That all may be one' [*John* 17:21], even as He and the Father are one, and a Christian who does not believe in the unity of the church is a most unworthy Christian. You cannot be a Christian without desiring that unity with the whole of your being. But before you begin to talk about amalgamating denominations, you should ask, 'What is the Christian church?' And much of the confusion that exists at the present time is solely due to the fact that people are by-passing this most important question. And, indeed, that raises a yet more fundamental question: 'If a church is a gathering of Christians, what is a Christian?' So you see the all-importance and the immediate relevance of this great subject?

Now here the apostle is concerned primarily about the use of the gifts, but he says that you cannot understand that unless you first understand the nature of the church; and his way of explaining this doctrine is to say that the church is the body of Christ.

Paul has other comparisons also. He sometimes compares the church to a great empire. Writing to the Gentiles, he says, 'Ye are no more strangers and foreigners, but fellowcitizens with the saints' [*Eph.* 2:19]. This was an obvious comparison for him to use. He was a Roman citizen in the Roman Empire; and what was more natural than to point out that the church in some respects is similar to a great empire? She has her central authority and government, but, as in an empire, her citizens are scattered in different parts of the world.

Again, the apostle compares the church to a great building erected upon its foundation. Or he compares the church to a family. He says not only that we have become fellowcitizens with the saints, but are 'of the household of God' [*Eph.* 2:19]. And then he also sometimes compares the church to a bride. What the bridegroom is to the bride, our Lord is to the church. No one analogy is perfect, and Paul has to use a multiplicity of analogies to illustrate this great doctrine.

But I think you will agree with me, particularly as you read Paul's epistles, that of all his illustrations the one which he obviously felt was, in many ways, the best, is the church as the body of Christ. He uses it in 1 Corinthians 12:12–27, and also at the end of Ephesians 1, especially in verses 22 and 23. The same idea is repeated once more in Ephesians 4:15–16 where he talks about '. . . the head, even Christ: from whom the whole body fitly joined together and compacted by that which every joint supplieth, according to the effectual working in the measure of every part, maketh increase of the body unto the edifying of itself in love', and the analogy is implicit in other statements also. So clearly this is a most important subject. In effect, the apostle says, 'If you want to understand the nature of the church, a very good way of doing so is to consider the nature, or the character of the human body, the physical frame.'

Let us start, then, by looking at what the apostle teaches us here in the fourth verse about the nature of the body. As I have reminded you, fortunately he has worked it out for us in 1 Corinthians 12, and we will interpret what he says here in the light of his more detailed and elaborate teaching there. Now the body has a head, where the brain is to be found within the skull. From the brain come out all the various nerves, and forces of control, and the directing power. And Paul's fundamental analogy is that what the head and brain are to the rest of the body, the Lord Jesus Christ is to the Christian church. He is the Head, out of whom and through whom the whole body is compacted in the way indicated in Ephesians 1 and 4.

There are most important lessons to be learned in this statement concerning the physical body. Paul says: If you are to be right about the exercise of these gifts that you have received in the church, if you are to avoid overestimating yourself and underestimating others, if you are to avoid jealousy and envy and all these feelings that cause so much division, if you are to avoid falling into the error into which the Corinthians fell over the question of spiritual gifts, then the best thing to do is to understand something about the essential constitution of the human body, and to realize that, in so many respects, it is the truth concerning the nature of the Christian church.

So let me put this teaching in terms of a number of principles. The first is that the body is an organic unity – 'As we have many members in one body.' A body is not just a collection or an aggregate of independent parts loosely attached together. The body does not consist of a number of fingers which are stuck on to a hand, and then a hand stuck on to an arm and an arm stuck on to a shoulder and so on. The unity of the body is not like the unity of a train. You think of a train with an engine and a number of trucks attached to it by couplings, but that is not the analogy at all. In the body, you have a vital relationship, an organic unity, which means that there is a living connection between the parts. It is not a kind of soldering or tying on but an inner unity, as Paul suggests in such a wonderful way in Ephesians 4:16. This, remember, was written nineteen hundred years ago but Paul has extraordinary insight, the accuracy of which is confirmed today by the study of human anatomy. The unity, you see, is provided by the blood system, the vascular system and the nervous system, and that is the basis of this organic unity. You have your heart with its main blood vessels coming out of it. They go along and they divide, and keep on dividing until you get the small capillaries, but it is all part of one system; it is one vascular system. And the same is true of the nerves, with the multiplicity of minute tendrils and divisions. All of them can ultimately be traced right away back to the nerve centres in the brain or in the spinal cord.

Now this is not a lecture on anatomy! But the apostle is using an anatomical illustration, and he has the whole principle here. This is the very point he is making: 'Many members but one body'. The one body is not a collection of many members; the body is more important than the parts. Indeed, we could go further and say that this organic unity comes into being and is a fact because of the way in which the body develops. Where have your fingers come from? Have these fingers been developed independently and then been made to coalesce with the arms?

No, that is not at all how it happened. The whole of one's body was originally just one cell. That cell was fertilized and then began to develop and to divide. It sent out proliferations. A little root formed the right arm, another one went to form the left, others the head, the trunk and the legs. All these individual parts have come out of an original unity, so they have been in organic connection with the central parts from the very beginning. That is the simple truth about the human body, and the apostle's teaching is that it is exactly the same with regard to the Christian church.

It is because this truth is so frequently forgotten that the church gets into such terrible error. Let me, then, just draw it out to this extent before we go any further. Because of this organic, vital, living unity that characterizes the Christian church, you must never think that you put yourself, or anyone else, into the church, into this relationship. You cannot do that. A man or woman can join a church but that does not mean that they have become a part of the body of Christ. There is a statement at the end of the second chapter of Acts which puts this right once and for ever: '*The Lord* added to the church daily such as should be [as were being] saved.' It is He alone who can add to the church.

Now you can add people to statistics; that is not difficult at all. And the Christian church is far too often treated as though it is like the train I mentioned, rather than the body – people think they can make these odd additions. But that is not right, and the whole idea that you achieve unity by adding denomination to denomination is not the way to get the unity that the Bible talks about. It is the Lord alone who can create this, 'the unity of the Spirit, in the bond of peace', as Paul puts it again in Ephesians 4 [verse 3]. It is 'the Lord' who adds to this body. As 1 Corinthians 12:13 expresses it so well: 'For by one Spirit are we all baptized into one body.' We do not do it, it is something that is done to us. It is the Spirit alone who can perform this operation. It is such a vital operation – a living, a life-relationship – that no human being can ever do it. You do not solder people on to the Christian church. If they are not in a vital, organic relationship to the Head and the other parts, they are not a part of the Christian church at all.

Then, further, Paul goes on to show that there is a great variety in the parts. 'We have many members in one body, and all members have not the same office.' Now this is obvious, is it not, about our human bodies. The body is one, but look at the variation in the different parts – hands, feet, eyes, ears and so on. Then there are the sub-divisions of the parts; they are all different with differing functions. But the thing that Paul emphasizes is that we must realize this variety. There are some people who seem to think that every church member should be identical with every other, and, indeed, there are some teachings that tend to produce that kind of person, but it is a violation of Paul's teaching. As the individual members of the body are not the same and were never meant to be, so all Christians are not meant to be the same. They are not meant to be the same in their temperament, in their abilities, or in the way they do things. The great thing about the body is that you have a variety in unity, or a unity expressed in a variety.

If you find a number of Christian people who all seem to be doing the same thing in the same way – I mean by that that they almost get to look like one another, they walk like one another, and they speak with the same sort of accent and use the same phrases – then I would say that you are entitled to deduce that you are not looking at the work of the Holy Spirit. I am not saying that they are not Christians, but I am saying that another influence has come in which is false to the spirit of Christ.

You see, we are in the flesh and the cults always tend to produce a standard type; it is their characteristic. But it is never the characteristic of God's work. There is always variety in God's work. You find the same in creation. No two flowers are identical, no two persons are identical; in fact, our two eyes are not identical and the two sides of our faces do not measure exactly the same. That is true of nature and of the body: it is equally true of the church. A situation that produces postage-stamp Christians is wrong; it is not true; it violates the essential doctrine concerning the nature of the Christian church.

Now you will all know the kind of thing I mean. All too

often I have seen people when they first become Christians – obviously born-again Christians – and then have met them again in a year or two only to find that they have conformed to a pattern. For instance, I knew a very forceful minister who never said 'Amen', but always, 'A-men', and I used to watch how his followers gradually adopted the same habit. They all always said 'A-men' in exactly the same way. Well, my dear friends, I am deliberately giving you this ridiculous example so you may see how wrong this is. It is not only true of church members. At one time there was a well-known preacher in South Wales who was a very eloquent man but did not know how to use his voice properly. As a result, he kept losing his voice, and had to have long holidays. At last he discovered the secret of preaching without losing his voice, and that was to speak with a nasal intonation, and he began to do that and solved his problem. He also had a tuft of hair that tended to come down over his right eyebrow and when preaching he would toss it back periodically. Before long he had produced a whole school of young preachers who spoke with a nasal accent and tossed their hair back repeatedly! That is carnal and entirely foreign to New Testament teaching. The spiritual teaching concerning the nature of the Christian church is unity expressed through variety.

That, of course, leads to the third great principle, which is that the different parts clearly have different functions; all members do not have the same office. The apostle works that out in detail for us in 1 Corinthians 12. The functions of the eye and the hand are obviously different; the feet and the ears again have different tasks and so do all the other parts of the body. They also differ in their degrees of power and importance. The apostle talks about the 'comely parts' and the 'uncomely', 'less honourable' parts which we tend to despise [verses 23–24]. But the point which Paul is making is that each one has a different, and important, function.

Now people tend to forget this, and that is the cause of the envying and the despising and the wrong view of ourselves and of one another. We want to be this and we want to be that. It is a very real problem, and if you do not know something about this in your personal experience, then I fail to understand you, because the devil will always tempt a spiritual person along this line. We all want to be doing certain things and it is difficult for us to reconcile ourselves to doing something else.

I mean something like this. There are many people who are prepared to go to foreign lands, to the Far East or Africa or somewhere else, and are ready to perform menial tasks, tasks of charity and of love, for the sake of the Lord and the gospel. They are prepared to go to the ends of the earth, but they are not prepared to carry out the same works of love in this country, though they are often needed. There is a glamour about foreign work and so our carnal nature wants to be doing that. Sometimes I have had to point out to young men that all Christians are not meant to be preachers. But there are people who obviously have that impression. It is amazing how frequently one has to say this. A certain type of person is converted and immediately his first thought is that he must come out of his current profession because all Christians should be doing full-time Christian work. But we are not all meant to be doing this. Christians are also called to function in society in many different areas of work.

This was one of the grand discoveries that Martin Luther made at the time of the Protestant Reformation – that you could be as good a Christian sweeping a floor as you could be in a monastery or a nunnery. The failure to understand this is due to the failure to realize this principle concerning the working of the physical body, which is such a perfect analogy of the working of the Christian church.

But, fourthly, not only must we get rid of the notion that we are all to be doing the same thing – as the apostle puts it, 'If the whole body were an eye, where were the hearing? If the whole were hearing, where were the smelling?' [*1 Cor.* 12:17] – but Paul goes even further and says that each function of every single part in the body is not only important, it is essential to the working of the whole body.

Now the function is not only important in and of itself, it is also of importance with regard to the other parts, indeed, it is important for the whole of the body. You realize when you think of the human body – as the apostle suggests so plainly – that some parts of our body are 'less comely'. We do not talk about them in public and we do not write about them – that is the Christian and the decent practice. But because you do not speak of them, you must not say that they are of no use, of no value. Of course they are, we could not live without them. Every single member has a function which is not merely important, but is essential to the working of the entire body, and if that particular member were not there, the body would not only be abnormal, it would be incapable of functioning as it should. So work that out for yourselves in terms of the Christian church. There is no such thing as a non-essential Christian – no church member is unimportant. Each one of us has a function which is of vital importance to the whole.

The fifth principle is that no function, therefore, of the body is independent of the others, or independent of the head. Not one of the members of the body can exist on its own; it only has meaning as it is related to the others, and as they all together are related to the head.

Now the moment you realize this, you realize that the body works harmoniously when all the particular parts and portions fulfil their function and this happens when, and only when, they are called upon to take part in the total action of the body for specific purposes. They must not act alone; they must never act independently. They are a part of the whole and they only act when they are moved by the whole body. This is the central point that the apostle is stressing here and is pressing home. People tend to think of their gift as *their* gift, something in isolation, and they forget everybody else. 'This is what I've got,' they think and they are anxious to display their gift. In Corinth all the Christians were wanting to speak in tongues and all, perhaps, were wanting to do it at the same time. That is the very thing which Paul has to correct and he does it in terms of this analogy of the body.

Let me illustrate this in medical terms. The moment any part of my body begins to act on its own, independently of me, or independently of the other parts of my body, it means that I am ill. The best illustration that I can think of is the illustration of a person suffering from an attack of epilepsy when different parts of the body are in convulsions. The person does not want the parts of his body to move in this way, that is the essence of the disease. Some irritation somewhere is making the limbs do things without the person willing it or desiring it. That is a diseased condition.

Or take a yet simpler example: Have you noticed people who have what are called 'tics', perhaps a twitching of certain muscles of the face or of the eye? That is not something voluntary. The people do not want that to happen, it happens in spite of them. It is a sign of an abnormal, not to say a diseased condition. The moment the individual parts of the body begin to act on their own, independently of the rest of the body, and not in the way they are supposed to act, you are face to face with a diseased condition.

If you read the history of the Christian church, you will see that condition illustrated time without number. That was the essence of the trouble with the church at Corinth. You can, if you like, describe the church at Corinth as a church in convulsions; and there are similar churches today. One man is supposed to be preaching from the pulpit but others begin to shout or to sing. So the apostle says, 'Let all things be done decently, and in order' [*1 Cor.* 14:40]. 'God is not the author of confusion, but of peace' [*1 Cor.* 14:33]. The situation was that these people were beginning to act on their own, and were not functioning as parts of the body. Such independent actions always lead to a diseased condition and to confusion and to chaos.

So, then, principle number six is that each particular function contributes to the whole. The body is always meant to act as a whole and each part is involved in that total action. Let me show you what I mean. Take the speaking which you can see and hear me doing at the moment. What makes this possible? It is, of course, the harmonious working of all the parts of my body. I once defined health as that state and condition in which a man forgets that he has a body. You are really healthy when you forget about your health and when you forget that you have a body. Everything is working so well that you are not aware of it. The moment your attention is directed to a particular part, it is probable that there is something wrong there.

The functioning of the whole body is made possible because each part is behaving in the way that it is meant to behave. I cannot perform any action without the whole of my body being involved. For instance, my mind is engaged as I speak to you, but my will is engaged too. I am choosing to speak; yes, but though I may have a good mind, and I may have worked out a good message, if my heart were not functioning properly I would not be able to speak. This means that my heart also is involved. And my circulation must be all right; my muscles and my nerves must be all right; my limbs must be all right; nay, more, my digestive organs must be all right! 'But,' you say, 'does a man preach with his stomach?' Of course not! But if his stomach is diseased he will not preach as well as if it were not.

You see, all these parts of man, they all come into the act of preaching. If there is anything wrong at any point, it will affect my preaching. That is because the body is a whole, a unit. Every single function is of vital importance, and every single function contributes to the functioning of the whole. In other words, the body is the glorious thing it is because of this extraordinary balance, this cohesion, this inter-relationship, this harmony; and that is the condition of the body when it is functioning correctly, as it should. And that is how the church should be.

Then the seventh principle is that the great thing we must all remember is that every single function, every single member, every single part or portion of the body, therefore, must always be subject to and subordinate to, the will and the control of the head. We find an illustration of this in the Book of Acts: 'Now when they had gone throughout Phrygia and the region of Galatia, and were forbidden of the Holy Ghost to preach the word in Asia' – they wanted to travel to Asia and they were on the verge of going in, as parts of the body of Christ, they were beginning to move – 'and were forbidden of the Holy Ghost to preach the word in Asia. After they were come to Mysia, they assayed to go into Bithynia: but the Spirit suffered them not' [*Acts* 16:6–7]. They were going to act on their own, but were prevented by the Spirit. In the same way, we must realize that we all are to be subordinate to the Head. We do not decide when to move; we do not decide what to do. He does that.

And so the last principle is that failure in any one part always affects the whole body – and this is where understanding this doctrine becomes desperately serious. You say, 'I don't count in the church. I'm an unimportant member.' That is already wrong. As I have been showing you, there is no unimportant part of the human physical frame and there is no such thing as an unimportant church member. But you are still more wrong in that you have forgotten that, because of the organic unity, your condition affects the whole. Paul says in 1 Corinthians 12:26, 'And whether one member suffer, all the members suffer with it . . .'; and the other side of that is, 'or one member be honoured, all the members rejoice with it.'

As we have seen, in the physical body there is an organic unity. Consequently, if there is trouble in any one part of the body the whole body will suffer. Take, for instance, a man who suddenly gets an infection in the tip of his little finger. 'Trivial', you say. 'It's the tip of the little finger, what does it matter what happens there?' But it does matter. If you get an acute infection in your little finger, you will soon have a headache. You will soon be running a temperature; you will be sweating; you will not be able to think; you may become delirious. There was only trouble in the tip of the little finger, yes, but remember, the blood that passes through that finger goes right round your body. Get poison there and the whole system will be poisoned. That is the teaching and you see how important it is.

So the truth you and I must hold in the forefront of our minds, and concentrate on, is not the importance of our particular places or positions or functions, but the fact that whatever our positions, they are given us by God and are essential to the working of the whole. And, above all, we must be careful to remember that whatever we are, and however unimportant we may appear to be to others in the church, because we are in it and because we are a part of this body, our supreme duty is to make sure that we are always healthy. I must make sure that there is no spiritual disease in me, because if there is disease in me and I suffer, the whole body will suffer. The Head is also involved in the suffering. So the New Testament is not so much concerned with what our function may be as with our sanctification, our holiness, our health.

How often do you see in the newspaper a heading to this effect: 'Sunday school teacher charged with so-and-so'. Then you read the story and you find that this man, this poor man who is in court, had been a Sunday school teacher perhaps twenty or thirty years ago. He had not been a Sunday school teacher for years but that is what has been picked out, and the whole church comes into disrepute. That can be true of every one of us. Because of the organic unity, what happens to any one part involves the whole.

So the call to us is not to think at all about the particular function that is allotted to us. By that I mean that we should never think of it in terms of its importance or its unimportance. Instead, we should say, 'By the grace of God I am what I am' [*1 Cor.* 15:10]. The position is a gift to me, it is not of my choosing or of my making. He has put me there. I am vital; I am as much a part of the body as the most exalted or the most glamorous. I am in the same body as they are and I have a function which is, ultimately, as essential as theirs. The functions differ in degree and in importance, but not in their ultimate value.

There should never, therefore, be pride; there should never be envy; there should never be despising. We must discover what we are and what gift is given to us. We are not all meant to do or to be the same, but in this glorious variety and variation we reveal the unity, the wonder of it all, the church as the body of Christ. And when we think of ourselves as individuals, we must think about only one thing and that is that we should always be totally, completely, spiritually healthy in His service. We should never be the cause of hindrance. Take again my illustration from the human body. You tend to think glibly, 'The stomach has got nothing to do with preaching.' Well, all I say is, make sure that the stomach is not diseased, make sure that it is not causing indigestion, because then it will certainly affect the preaching.

Be ready, be always at His service, so that whenever He acts or moves there is no hindrance, no lack, no restraint, no obstacle, no blockage anywhere. Make sure that every part is ready. And then, He acts and He does His mighty and amazing work, and His name is made glorious in the earth.

May God give us understanding of this and the grace to apply it to our own case and position as 'members severally, and together, of the body of Christ'.

Fourteen

*

*For as we have many members in one body, and all members
have not the same office: so we, being many, are one body in
Christ, and every one members one of another.*

Romans 12:4-5

The word 'so' in the fifth verse reminds us immediately that
the apostle is applying the illustration which he has been using
in verse 4 to the state and condition and nature of the church.
That is his whole object. He is dealing with life in the realm of
the church and with some of the difficulties that arise,
especially in connection with the use of the varying gifts
which God in His grace has given to us as His people.

So we come now to see how Paul uses his illustration. This
fifth verse is most important because it is the verse which,
perhaps more clearly than any other in this particular Epistle,
gives us an understanding of the apostle's doctrine of the
church. He gives us this doctrine in greater length in other
places but, in this Epistle, this is a crucial verse.

Now we are living in an age in which Christians talk more
about church unity than they have for many centuries. Since
the Reformation there has been comparatively little talk about
the unity of the church. That was a great division, and it led to
further subdivisions, so it is not at all surprising that little
attention has been paid to this doctrine. And, for the reasons
which I shall put before you, I think we must all plead guilty in
this respect, and plead guilty on behalf of many of our
forefathers.

But today the position is very different indeed, and the whole question of unity is constantly referred to. One section of the church holds a conference or council to promote it, another does the same, and they are all talking about it. So it is unusually important that we should understand something of the teaching of the great apostle on this vital subject, and here we have it, in a summary. Now I have often had occasion to say, in dealing with this Epistle to the Romans, that we must always remember that we have here a summary of doctrine, and our business is to expand the summary, to draw out the doctrine. That is the function of teaching, and of preaching, and that is what we must now do.

Paul says, 'So we, being many, are one body in Christ, and every one members one of another.' But look at the content of that! Let us realize some of the things that he tells us about the church and particularly about the unity of the church. That is what Paul is concerned about. He is very afraid that in some way the church may be torn apart or marred by a false view of the gifts that are given to particular people in the church. Let us therefore consider Paul's teaching about this unity.

The first proposition is that the church is the body of Christ. 'We, being many, are one body in Christ.' Here is the New Testament teaching about the nature of the church, and it means something like this: the church is not a human institution but a spiritual society, a supernatural society. Now when you look at the whole history of the church, you find that this has obviously been forgotten. The very identification of the church and the state is at once a complete denial of this fact and so is the view that everybody in a parish is a Christian. No, here is something 'in Christ', something, therefore, which is not natural. It is not material, not physical, and not human. It is super-human and super-natural; it is a spiritual society.

So as members of the church we are not merely people who believe certain things, even about our Lord; we are not merely people who believe His teaching. You can do all that and not be a member of the church. Of course, if you regard the church as a human society or institution, then you can join it as you can join any other club or organization. But if we accept the fundamental proposition that the church is a spiritual body, a spiritual society, then we must emphasize that merely to believe things about Him does not mean that we are truly members of the church and parts of His body.

I put it like this because there is a common idea abroad that what makes a man or woman a Christian and a member of the church is being interested in the teaching of Jesus Christ – 'Jesus', as people who think like this generally call Him – and being concerned to apply the teaching of Jesus to their own lives and to the lives of other people. They may also believe that obedience to the teachings of Christ is the best way of running a state or of putting an end to war, and so on.

Now while that may be all right up to a point, that alone is not sufficient because, by definition, a member of the Christian church, in the New Testament sense, is someone who is in a vital, living relationship to the Lord Jesus Christ. The whole analogy of the body proves that. As we have seen, the point of the apostle's illustration in verse 4 is that a body consists of many parts all controlled by the head and the great nervous system that starts from the head.

And the same point is made when Paul comes to apply the illustration: 'We, being many, are one body in Christ.' Sometimes he refers to the church as 'Christ', as in 1 Corinthians 12:12 – 'so also is Christ', meaning the church. So the basic New Testament definition of the church is that she is the body of Christ. He is the Head, she is the body, and we, as individual members, are parts of this body. And that, at once, emphasizes the fact that it is a vital and a living relationship. He dwells in the church. His life and fulness are in the church and He functions in and through her.

Now in the opening of the Acts of the Apostles Luke reminds us of that. He says, 'The former treatise have I made, O Theophilus, of all that Jesus began both to do and teach.' Then Luke goes on to tell us about what the church did, but it is Jesus who is doing it through the church. She is, in other words, His body. This, of course, is quite basic and fundamental to any thoughts about the church. Before we begin to talk about amalgamation, we really should start by asking the question: What is a church? What is *the* church? And, I repeat, the point at which we must of necessity start is that she is a spiritual society, a spiritual body.

Then I go on to lay down a second proposition, which follows from the analogy: the church is one – 'We, being many, are one body in Christ.' Here is the direct teaching about the unity of the church, and Paul could not have employed that analogy of the body if this were not of necessity true. A body has only one head, and one head has only one body. You cannot have one head with a multiplicity of bodies; that would be a monstrosity. There are many parts and functions but there is only one body. And the apostle is saying that all true believers are members of this one and only body, which is, alone, the true church, the church militant and the church triumphant. Or, if you prefer it, the church visible, and the church invisible. There are those who have belonged to the church on earth who have gone on to glory, but they are still part of this body. The church will ultimately consist of all who have ever been true believers throughout all the centuries – Old Testament as well as New.

So there is to be no discussion, therefore, about this question of the unity of the church. It is something that is inevitable. But I am concerned to emphasize that the teaching is that this is a unity which should be visible, and here comes the message to all of us. There is a danger, perhaps, that some of us, as we talk about the ecumenical movement, may give the impression that we do not believe in the unity of the church. But as we have seen, if you do not believe in that, it means you do not accept the New Testament teaching about the church. Our Lord made that perfectly plain, did He not, in His great high-priestly prayer in which He prays for unity. We read that He prayed, 'That they all may be one; as thou, Father, art in me, and I in thee, that they also may be one in us: that the world may believe that thou hast sent me' [*John* 17:21]. In other words, one of the purposes of this unity is that the church may evangelize the world: 'That the world may believe that thou hast sent me'.

Now in talking about 'the oneness and the unity of the invisible and the visible church', or, 'the church triumphant and the church militant', we must be very careful that we do not fall into a trap. Very often true Christian people, evangelical people, have been content to say something like this: 'The visible church is, of course, divided up, but the invisible church is not.' They draw a distinction, which is quite right, between the visible and the invisible, a distinction which is true of the church on earth. There are many people who, while claiming to be members of the church, deny everything in the gospel that we regard as essential. Nevertheless, they are members of the church visible.

So we say, 'Ah, yes, but are we members of the church invisible? That's what really matters. We don't know who belongs to the church invisible, but God does, and all who belong to the invisible church are one. That's the unity,' we say, 'which He is speaking about.' And then we tend to go on to say this: 'It doesn't matter about the visible church; let it be divided up as much as you like. Let the true Christians remain in apostate denominations. It doesn't make any difference to the true, the invisible church.'

But I suggest to you that that is very wrong, not only in the light of John 17 and the statements in the high-priestly prayer of which I have just reminded you, but also in the light of Romans 12:5, and, indeed, in the light of all the appeals about visible unity which are found in the New Testament. It is the duty of Christian people not only to believe in the unity but to make the unity visible, and we are sinning if we do not believe in the unity of the church, and in the visible unity of the true church. We must not fall back on that argument about the invisible church. It is always our duty to be doing our utmost to achieve the visible unity of God's people here on earth. If we do not, we are dismissing our Lord's last petition in His high-priestly prayer.

Now why am I making such a point of this? Well, for one reason only. While there are people who talk about the unity that we do not believe in – which I shall deal with in a moment – it is imperative that as Evangelicals we should not only be concerned about unity among believers, but, because we believe the Scriptures, we should be more concerned about it than anybody else. And I believe that we have a unique opportunity in this respect at this present time when people are talking about being ready 'to throw everything into the melting-pot'. Are we ready to do that? Should not all believers come together and make their unity, which is fundamentally spiritual, visible also, and thereby bring glory to His name, and be the means under His hand of evangelizing a gainsaying world?

I think this comes as a challenge to us and I am presenting it like that to you. Are you as an Evangelical content to be divided from other Evangelicals? Are you who are true believers content not to be in a living, visible, fellowship with all other true believers? Have we a right, especially at a time like this, to allow secondary, third-rate, tenth-rate matters – often of sheer tradition and accident of birth – to divide us who claim to believe the same truth, who claim to be living members of the living body of Christ? That is what is involved here, and I believe it comes to us with a special urgency in these years through which we are passing.

So then, the church is one: 'We, being many, are one body.' Paul does not say 'many bodies' but 'one body'; we are 'many' only in the sense that we have differing gifts and different functions. And we must emphasize that this unity of the church is not something to be argued about, but something to be stated as of necessity true in the light of the illustration, quite apart from the explicit teaching.

Then I go on to say, as my third proposition, that the unity is a spiritual unity. And this, I think you will see, again follows of necessity. Look at the various illustrations that are used. Take our Lord's words in John 15: 'I am the vine, ye are the branches' [verse 5]. That is the nature of the union. The church is, as has often been said, an organism, not an organization. But, having started in purity as an organism, by degrees the church became an organization; and you can read the story of how this came about. Of course, it proceeded at a gallop when Constantine decided to become a Christian, and bring in the Roman Empire with him. As a result of that, the whole organization of Rome was transferred to the church and has continued to be part of the church. Although throughout the centuries there has been a great battle about this organization, many people today think of the church purely in terms of an organization run by men and women. But that is utterly remote from everything that is found in the New Testament itself.

So we must point out that just as the body is not a collection of parts – and here I am applying the illustration which we analysed in detail in the previous study – so a church cannot achieve unity merely by forming a coalition or by gathering together the different parts. We are being told today that the different sections, the different parts, must come together in order to provide a 'united front'. Now political parties can do that, and in a time of war they generally do. They decide, for the time being, and for a given purpose, to form a coalition. But, as we have seen, this is not what we have here. The body is not a collection of parts; there is an essential unity, and the members are parts of that.

Neither can unity be achieved by ignoring or suppressing certain things. The tendency today, in what is called the ecumenical movement, is to take the different sections of the church and then say, 'Now, what modification has this one got to make?' Or we say, 'That one must make a concession also. The pope must have his wings clipped a bit and his power somewhat curtailed: that is the modification in the Church of Rome. The Church of England must also make her modification and the Free Churches theirs.' So people gather together to consider the accommodations, and then they hope that they can coalesce their churches into one. They get their coalition by ignoring and by suppressing certain ideas for the sake of a common front. We saw this during the Second World War when we had a coalition government, and in the First World War. It is only possible on the grounds that the parties making the coalition do not deal with party politics for the time being. They do not cease to believe the principles they stand for, but they say that for the time being they will not consider them because they have a common enemy. And there are people who approach the whole question of church unity with that mentality, but it is the negation of the spiritual unity that we have here.

So let me put it like this to you: the unity that the apostle speaks of is a unity that can never be produced by human beings – never! 'So we, being many, are one body in Christ, and every one members one of another.' This, again, is something that follows of necessity from the illustration of the body. As we have seen, the human body starts with one cell, which becomes impregnated and grows and develops. The proliferations come out and form neck and arms and feet and trunk and so on. And it is exactly the same with the church. This is something supernatural; it is miraculous; it is the divine 'something'. And so the illustration proves to us that men and women can never produce this unity, and, of course, the Bible never exhorts us to. What Paul does exhort us to do, is to *maintain* the unity – which is entirely different. He does not tell us to produce it but to keep going what is already there. 'Endeavouring,' he says in Ephesians 4:3, 'Endeavouring to keep the unity of the Spirit in the bond of peace.' That is not creating it, but keeping it in existence. It is God who brings it into being.

Let me put it like this. I think it is very important to realize that unity in the church is not something in and of itself; it is simply the result of something else. Go back to the illustration of the body. The unity of the body is not something that you can, as it were, abstract from the body and consider as something that exists in and of itself, and then try to produce. The essential beginning, the original life, spreads outwards; it is part of the very being of the body. It must never be considered, therefore, in isolation.

And that, I feel, is the trouble with so much of this modern talk about unity. It is always talked about as something in and of itself; but there is no such thing. That is why it is so difficult to define unity. Let me use another illustration. Take a flower. A flower is one; it is a whole, a unity. But if you try to analyse that unity by pulling off the petals and the stamens and so on, at the end, you have no flower, there is nothing there. And it is exactly like that with respect to the church.

But let us put it positively. The unity of the church is the result only of the creative work of the Holy Spirit. This is the absolutely essential principle. This is how the church ever came into being. This is the only way in which we ever become parts of the body of Christ. What does the Holy Spirit do? Well, the first thing, of course, is to give us a new birth. No one can be a member of the church unless they are 'born again' [*John* 3:3], 'born of the Spirit' [*John* 3:5]. This is absolutely fundamental. You may be born British but it does not make you a Christian. You may be born the child of Christian parents but that does not make you a Christian. 'If any man have not the Spirit of Christ,' says Paul in Romans 8:9, 'he is none of his.' And though men and women may be very good and moral and excellent members of a visible church, it does not mean that they are members of the body of Christ. This is something spiritual; it is something, therefore, that can be produced by the Holy Spirit alone, and that is His first great action. He takes hold of us one by one and deals with us, and this great act of re-creation takes place.

Then, as 1 Corinthians 12:13 puts it, the Spirit baptizes us into the body of Christ. 'For by one Spirit are we all baptized into one body, whether we be Jews or Gentiles, whether we be bond or free; and have been all made to drink into one Spirit.' This is an action which, again, the Holy Spirit alone can work. It is not the baptism with the Spirit but the Spirit baptizing us, whom He has first of all made regenerate, into the body of Christ. Unfortunately there is confusion today about that. It is the Lord Jesus Christ who baptizes with the Spirit. But here we are told of an action of the Spirit baptizing us into the body of Christ and making us members of that body. He alone can do that. We cannot do it ourselves and we cannot do it to others. Being a Christian, being a member of the body of Christ means that we are 'partakers of the divine nature' [2 *Pet.* 1:4]. That is why I am emphasizing that the church is not a human institution. It is supernatural; it is divine; it is spiritual in its very essence.

This means that His life is in all the members. 'So we, being many, are one body in Christ.' The analogy explains it, it is stated explicitly in other places. He is the Head and all the fulness comes from Him. And this is the point: you cannot be a member of the body of Christ without His life and energy and all that He is in His fulness, coming down to you. It is in you of necessity; it follows because you are a member of His body.

Now at this point let me throw out a problem for you to consider. Do you not think that this has something to tell us about children being members of a church? There are those who have held the view that the church consists of true believers in the Lord Jesus Christ with their children, and that baptized children are members of the church. Many sections of the church believe this teaching, but it seems to me that we must be careful when we say something like that, for this reason. You are saying that because that child has been baptized, he or she has become a member of the church. But the church is the body of Christ and anyone who is a member in the body of Christ has the life and the fulness of Christ in them in exactly the same way as it is in their parents who are believers. So if the children are members as the result of baptism, they are receivers of the divine life. Therefore, because they have not been able to believe, because they are unconscious babies, you are teaching baptismal regeneration.

I think that these questions must be considered anew. We have been content to drift on and to repeat what has been said by those who have lived before us. But is it not essential that we, as Evangelicals, should re-examine all these matters afresh in the light of the teaching of the Scriptures? I therefore raise that problem for your consideration. Of course, a child can believe on the Lord Jesus Christ – but not an unconscious infant. I suggest that true members of the body of Christ are those who are 'born again', and that is only those who have faith in Him and can give expression to that.

So we need to consider once more the relationship of children to the church. I do not want to go into that now, but if anybody wants to use the argument of 1 Corinthians 7, I suggest that it teaches no more than that the children of believing parents have a right to come to the meetings of the church, and that they therefore have advantages which other children have not. But it does not mean that they are born again. It does not mean that they are members of the church, the body of Christ. So, again, the analogy compels us to think of that. If we are members of the church, we are members of Christ.

There is one other matter which, again, is most important. This unity, this true spiritual unity, which is the characteristic of the church and of the members of the church, is a unity of the whole person – and I want to emphasize in particular that it is a unity that includes the mind.

Here, again, we come to a most crucial matter in the present debate. You are familiar with the slogan, 'Doctrine divides'. Indeed, unity and doctrine are being put up as enemies or as opposites, and we are told that if you are going to start talking about doctrine, about teaching, you will never get unity. The result is that when people talk about unity, they are really talking about some vague, general spirit of friendliness, 'a brotherliness', as they put it, and it is this general spirit, they say, that will lead us to true unity.

And then, of course, they have to go on to say that you can only get that as the result of a suppression of thought and a discounting of doctrine. This, I think, is one of the great problems facing all of us as evangelical Christians at the present time, because some Evangelicals are now talking like this. They say, 'Doctrine doesn't matter. What matters is that so and so has the Spirit.' It is being said that men and women may receive the Spirit in all His fulness and continue as Roman Catholics, believing in transubstantiation and in all the magic of the Mass, and the sacramental views of the Roman Catholic Church. What people believe is not import-ant; what matters is that they have the Spirit within them.

Such talk is becoming quite common at the present time. People are saying that you can have true unity in spite of profound disagreement concerning vital and essential doc-trines. But I want to put it to you that again this is a complete denial of the teaching of this one verse, Romans 12:5, even without going any further. You cannot have unity unless it includes unity of mind and of thinking. The illustration makes that impossible. Christ is the Head of the body, which is the church, and, says the Apostle Paul to the Corinthians, 'We have the mind of Christ' [*1 Cor.* 2:16]. So we all have the mind of Christ – we must have. Everybody who is a true member of the church is a member of Christ and a part of the body of Christ, and it is the one mind of Christ that controls the whole.

Not only that. The Spirit who produces this unity is the Holy Spirit, who is also called 'the Spirit of truth' [*John* 14:17; 15:26; 16:13]. He is contrasted with the spirit of error, and our Lord said about Him, 'He will guide you into all truth' [*John* 16:13]. So it is essential that this unity should be a unity of mind and not a vague unity of spirit.

Or take it like this: if we believe in the Holy Spirit, we must believe in the devil and in evil spirits. That is why we call the Holy Spirit the *holy* Spirit – to show that He is the eternal antithesis of the others. We are told in the Scriptures, and we know in experience, that there are other spirits. They are clever and subtle, and their head, the devil, can transform himself into 'an angel of light' [*2 Cor.* 11:14]. So how do I know that the spirit that is speaking to me is the Holy Spirit and not some other spirit; how do I determine it?

And there is only one answer: only by using my mind. That is why John puts it like this: 'Beloved, believe not every spirit, but try the spirits whether they are of God: because many false prophets are gone out into the world' [*1 John* 4:1]. And in 1 Thessalonians 5 you find the same teaching: 'Prove all things; hold fast that which is good' [verse 21]. How can you prove unless you use your mind? A teaching which says that you must not think and that unity does not involve the mind, is a denial of the illustration of the body, and a denial of explicit biblical teaching. No, the mind is involved, and the New Testament makes this abundantly clear.

Look at this teaching in this one Epistle, this great Epistle to the Romans. Here is the apostle in chapter 12 dealing with the question of the unity of the body; but notice, he has already written eleven chapters before he comes to that. What has he been dealing with in the eleven chapters? Doctrine! Teaching! This profound, essential teaching without which a person is not a Christian at all. In other words, Paul cannot deal with the question of unity until he has expounded his great doctrine. And it is exactly the same in all the other Epistles. That is how the 'therefore' comes in: 'I beseech you therefore, brethren.' The doctrine is a vital, an essential part of the unity.

But let me give you some supporting evidence. In Acts 2:42, in the description of the early church, we see this principle in action: 'They continued stedfastly' – first – 'in the apostles' doctrine [teaching]' – then – 'and fellowship, and in breaking of bread, and in prayer.' You do not start with fellowship, you must start with doctrine. There is no fellowship apart from the doctrine. The order is absolutely vital.

Now notice that it is not *our* doctrine; it is not the theology of the theologians. It is *the apostles' teaching*. That is the basis, and there is no unity apart from that. The church is built 'upon the foundation of the apostles and prophets' [*Eph.* 2:20]. It is their teaching that constitutes the very foundation.

Or look at the beginning of Ephesians 4. That is where Paul talks about 'endeavouring to keep the unity of the Spirit in the bond of peace' (verse 3). And he continues: 'There is . . . one

Lord, one faith, one baptism' [verses 4–5]. And then Paul goes on to show how there are different offices in the church in order to instruct Christians in this knowledge and to build them up together that they may come eventually to 'the measure of the stature of the fulness of Christ', in perfection [verse 13]. And Jude talks about 'the faith which was once delivered unto the saints' [verse 3]. The faith! The teaching! There is only one teaching, and it has been delivered once and for ever.

Notice, too, how careful the Apostle Paul always is to point out that his teaching is exactly the same as the teaching of all the other apostles. He had come late into this truth, he had been a persecutor, but he wants to show that it is the same doctrine, so he writes to the Galatians, 'I marvel that ye are so soon removed from him that called you into the grace of Christ unto another gospel: which is not another; but there be some that trouble you, and would pervert the gospel of Christ.' Then he goes on to say, 'As we said before, so say I now again, if any man preach any other gospel unto you than that which ye have received, let him be accursed' [*Gal.* 1:6–7, 9]. You will never get anything stronger than that.

Then listen to Paul in the second chapter of Galatians. He says, 'And I went up [to Jerusalem] by revelation, and communicated unto them that gospel which I preach among the Gentiles, but privately to them which were of reputation, lest by any means I should run, or had run, in vain' [verse 2]. And in 1 Corinthians 15 he makes this same great point. He emphasizes that the gospel which he preached was exactly the same as the message preached by all the other apostles: 'Therefore whether it were I or they, so we preach, and so ye believed.' They were all preaching exactly the same message. And in the early verses of that fifteenth chapter of Corinthians Paul reminds the Corinthians of what the message is.

Men and women only become Christians as they believe in the truth concerning the Lord Jesus Christ. There are people who say, 'Oh no, you believe in the Lord Jesus Christ, not in the truth about Him.' But who is He? What has He done? Why should I believe in Him? You cannot separate these things. And, indeed, the apostle himself puts it quite plainly in 1 Timothy 2 where he tells us to pray for all sorts of people and then writes, 'For this is good and acceptable in the sight of God our Saviour; who will have all men to be saved, and to come unto the knowledge of the truth' [verse 4]. And the truth is this: 'There is one God, and one mediator between God and men, the man Christ Jesus; who gave himself a ransom for all, to be testified in due time' [verses 5-6]. That is what makes people Christians: they have come to the knowledge of the truth; their minds are engaged. Those who are members of the body of Christ all have this mind, this understanding. It is the great argument of the whole of 1 Corinthians 2. and, indeed, in 1 Corinthians 12:3, Paul says – and this is very important – 'I give you to understand, that no man speaking by the Spirit of God calleth Jesus accursed: and that no man can say that Jesus is Lord' – and that is not merely saying it but believing it, saying it from the heart – 'but by the Holy Ghost.' And all who are members of this body say that. They do not say that Jesus is only a man, a great man, a good man, a religious teacher, no, they assert that He is the Son of God incarnate and they believe all that follows from that.

And so I come to my last point. It is only this understanding, and the inclusion of the mind, that keeps us together in the unity. It is a vital part of the unity. It is the only thing that preserves it – you will never preserve unity unless your mind is engaged. As Paul thanks God for the Christians in Philippi, he says, 'Even as it is meet for me to think this of you all, because I have you in my heart; inasmuch as both in my bonds, and in the defence and confirmation of the gospel, ye all are partakers of my grace . . . And this I pray, that your love' – not sentimental love – 'may abound yet more and more in knowledge and in all judgment' [*Phil.* 1:7, 9]. And then at the end of the chapter, in verse 27, he says, 'Only let your conversation be as it becometh the gospel of Christ: that whether I come and see you, or else be absent, I may hear of your affairs, that ye stand fast in one spirit, with one mind striving together for the faith of the gospel.'

He says the same thing again in Colossians chapter 2. He prays for the Christians at Laodicea, 'That their hearts might be comforted, being knit together in love, and unto all riches of the full assurance of understanding, to the acknowledgement of the mystery of God, and of the Father, and of Christ . . . For though I be absent in the flesh, yet am I with you in the spirit, joying and beholding your order' – they are like soldiers standing in rank; they are all standing 'in order' as Paul puts it – 'and the stedfastness of your faith in Christ . . . Rooted and built up in him, and stablished in the faith, as ye have been taught, abounding therein with thanksgiving. Beware lest any man spoil you through philosophy and vain deceit, after the tradition of men, after the rudiments of the world, and not after Christ' [*Col.* 2:2, 5, 7, 8]. And so it is in all Paul's epistles.

My last quotation is from 2 Thessalonians 2:15: 'Therefore, brethren, stand fast, and hold the traditions which ye have been taught, whether by word, or our epistle.' You cannot maintain the unity without the mind being engaged; error and heresy divide, they are the cause of confusion. And they belong to the realm of the mind.

I therefore conclude that nothing is more dangerous, more unscriptural, than to put unity, and understanding and comprehension of the gospel as opposites, to put up doctrine and unity as antitheses. No, the unity is unity in the faith, in the doctrine, in the understanding. It is a unity of mind as well as a unity of heart and a unity in the realm of the spirit, speaking generally. These things are vitally important. The world is full of other voices, but here is the teaching of Scripture and it follows inevitably from the illustration of the church as the body of Christ.

Fifteen

*

So we, being many, are one body in Christ, and every one members one of another. Having then gifts differing according to the grace that is given to us, whether prophecy, let us prophesy according to the proportion of faith.

Romans 12:5–6

'Having then gifts differing according to the grace that is given to us.' That phrase sums up the argument that the apostle has been putting before us in verses 4 and 5 and we have seen that Paul's teaching concerning the church as the body of Christ is a very profound doctrine. I have tried to show its relevance to all the talk about church unity and have shown that you cannot begin to talk about unity until you are clear in your mind as to what the church is. So we saw that unity is a spiritual, visible unity which can only be brought about by the Holy Spirit Himself. It is a unity which includes the mind and doctrine and it is a unity which includes the Head and the Head governs all the rest.

The next thing I would say about this unity is that it is living and functioning. This, of course, follows directly from the statement that it is an organic unity; not organizational but organic. The church, as we have said, is an organism, not an organization, and therefore I deduce that the unity is living and active. A body is meant to be active. That is what it is for. It is the means by which a person operates and expresses himself.

So here again we must draw the distinction between a body and a machine. The working of a machine is mechanical, while the working of the human body is physiological; and there is

[197]

all the difference in the world between mechanics and physiology. Physiology is the study of the working of a living organism, which is quite different from engineering or the study of machinery. A machine is dead. You can do many things with it, but you can never make it come alive, even with these new computers which, people say, can think. But they do not. You put information in, and you pull a lever and you get your result. That is not thought. The great difference between a machine and a body is the living, vital, active element which is of the very essence of a body.

Now, as the body of Christ, the church is obviously meant to do the work for which it was brought into being. This is true of our human bodies. We have been given them in order that we may function and express ourselves, and the body is most appropriate for the functioning of a human being. That is why each of us has a body, and not a machine, and this is equally true of the church. The church expresses a living and an active unity.

How does she do this? What are her functions? What was she created for? The New Testament itself gives many answers to those questions. Take that great statement which is made by the Apostle Paul in 1 Timothy 3. 'The church,' he says, 'is the pillar and ground of the truth' [1 Tim. 3:15]. It is said, and I believe that this is right, that Paul means by this that the church is a sort of pedestal on which a great notice-board is held up before the world. That is one of her primary functions, if not the primary function. The first task, the first business of the church, is to preach the gospel, to make known the good news of salvation. If preachers are heralds of this good news, then so is the whole church. The preacher is not apart from the church, but is a part of it.

Or, as Peter put it to those early Christians to whom he was writing: 'But ye are a chosen generation, a royal priesthood, an holy nation, a peculiar people' – what for? – 'that ye should shew forth the praises of him who hath called you out of darkness into his marvellous light' [1 Pet. 2:9]. It is the same idea.

So it is through the church as the body of Christ, this living organism, that God makes known the truth concerning Himself and His great salvation. Some of the early church fathers sometimes used to say that the business of the church is to 'bring children to the birth.' Some of you may be surprised that I say that because the Roman Catholic Church has been so fond of calling herself 'the Mother'. But John Calvin used exactly the same term and we must not allow them to misappropriate it. There is a sense in which we are all born of the church. That does not mean that the church, in a theological sense, is essential to our salvation, but that it is through the church and by the church that we are born. There is no question about this. It is she who engages in the activity that leads to our birth. It is not her activity, it is God's, as I shall show you, but this is God's chosen way of doing it. So there is a sense in which the church is our mother, as Paul puts it in Galatians 4:26, 'But Jerusalem which is above is free, which is *the mother of us all*'. The church was created in order that she might function in that way.

Now I emphasize this because if the church is not active in this way, she is failing. I do not care how orthodox a church may be, if she is not acting she is failing. The body is not a dead mechanism, it is an active organism. You can have a perfect machine with every screw in position, every wheel in place, but if nothing happens, it is no use. And if the church is not active, it means that there is something wrong with her; she is diseased.

The characteristic of the body is that the various organs and parts are always working, enabling the whole body to keep functioning. A man who spends his time lying in bed doing nothing is doing violence to his body. He was never made, he was never given a body, in order to lie in bed or lounge on a couch all day. No, the body is meant to be active.

And this is something which, I think, should come as a challenge to all of us – that if we are not manifesting the activity for which the body was created, there is something wrong with us and we must not rest on our orthodoxy or anything else. A dead church is a contradiction in terms, and a church can be orthodox and dead. A dead church is a church that is not heralding the gospel, a church in which nobody has come to birth as the result of her witness. Such a church is not functioning as she was meant to.

But let me hasten to add that you must keep a balance, and

that is where this analogy of the body is so important and, at the same time, so fascinating. Though the church is meant to be active and living, I must again emphasize that the activity of the church is the Head's activity. It is not hers. Take this analogy again. What the body is to me, to my brain, to my personality, the church is to Christ. He is the Head of the church, which is His body.

It is the head that controls everything: this is where movement is initiated, this is where everything starts. So the fundamental proposition is that the activity of the church is the activity of the Lord Jesus Christ and not merely the activity of the church herself. And, therefore, this analogy teaches us that one of our dangers is to try to act on our own and independently of Him. There are always extremes here: the people who do nothing and the people who try to do what they cannot do, who try to act on their own and independently of Him.

Now the history of the church abundantly proves the danger of independent activity. I believe this is one of the great lessons we all need at this present time. Let me illustrate what I mean. The church can never organize a revival – never! Oh, how often have people tried to do this! But it cannot be done. No matter how hard you try, you will never organize a revival. You can organize activities, but I am talking of a true revival, a movement of the Spirit, the vital activity of the whole church when men and women are converted by the thousand, struck down, perhaps, even before they get to the meeting. All that is characteristic of a true spiritual revival and it can never be organized, men and women can never produce it and neither can the church.

Furthermore, as I have already said under another heading but must include here also, the church can never add to her true membership – though so often she makes the attempt. I remember a few years ago reading an address which was delivered by the moderator of one of the denominations. In his address he put a programme before his denomination and got the people to pledge themselves to it, and they went back from the assembly in great enthusiasm. He said, 'Let us decide together to add to the church, in the next eighteen months, fifty thousand members.' Now the man was speaking in all seriousness, but he was speaking in an utterly unscriptural manner. He was viewing the church as if she were a business organization. Businesses can decide to send people out with leaflets, and call from door to door and knock to get fresh customers. You can add to the number of your customers by those sorts of methods and this is done frequently. This moderator thought that the church could do that, but, poor man, he discovered that she could not.

Of course, I repeat, you may well add to the numbers on your church roll, though you cannot even do that at the present time – and thank God for that – because all these methods fail. Patently, they should never be attempted. If the church consists only of those who are born again, you cannot sit down and say you are going to add a given number during the next year. To make the attempt is indicative of a failure to understand the doctrine of the true nature of the church. And the analogy itself compels us to say this because it is the Head who gives the orders, it is He who moves; it is He who controls the gifts and everything else.

So there is this danger of activism, of busy-ness, of failing to remember the nature of the church and to think of her in organizational or mechanical terms. Activism! That, I suppose, is the commoner of the two besetting sins of the church.

Then a third danger is 'hypochondriasis'. Let me explain. We have just considered the danger of activism. It is possible to be so busy that you have no time to think about your health at all, and that almost invariably ends in backsliding. If you live on your activities, you will not only go wrong in your belief, you will go wrong, eventually, in your spiritual life. It is like living on alcohol or stimulants. They will carry you so far, but in the end you will collapse. I am not sure but that we are not witnessing something of that at the moment, and, if I may venture on a prophecy, I think we shall witness it still more in the next few years. We shall see a collapse, when people have reached the stage of exhaustion. They have been so active that there is no energy left at all.

But then, as I say, the other extreme is hypochondriasis. This means that you are so busy studying your own health that you have no time to do anything at all. You sit there, feeling your pulse, taking your temperature and testing yourself in various

[201]

ways. This becomes a full-time occupation, and you become so worried about your health that you cannot think of anything else. You cannot go to work because there you would have to be doing things, and if you are compelled to do things, then you do not have time to take these various tests. Hypochondriasis!

And there are people who are always worrying about their spiritual life, and worrying about the minutiae of belief, so concerned about correctness that they have no time for anything else. They are constantly turning in upon themselves and watching themselves – spiritual valetudinarians, spiritual hypochondriacs.

But somebody may say, 'What should be the true position?' What are we meant to do as the body of Christ? He makes only two demands of us, and the analogy of the body proves this. We are called to be spiritually healthy, and we are called to be ready and responsive. We must concentrate upon being ready, and upon being spiritually fit, so that when He gives the slightest indication, we are immediately obedient. When there is no blockage, no paralysis and no hindrance, then we have fulfilled what He really demands of us. It is not to act apart from Him or instead of Him, neither is it to be doing nothing, in a morbid preoccupation with the 'mumps and measles' of our souls, as Charles Lamb called them. It is, rather, to be in such communion with Him that health follows naturally, health, which is sanctification, growing in the faith, reading the Scriptures, praying, doing the things which are a part of this spiritual exercise. We must do all that and, above all, we must keep ourselves in a condition of responsiveness.

One of the best ways of testing our sanctification is to determine our sensitivity to the will of the Lord. We should be men and women who know Him so well that we are able to interpret immediately any of His desires or His behests. Consider an obvious illustration. In the old days, the servant whom the king prized above everybody else was the man who was sensitive to his master, and always kept his eye on him. The king did not have to shout at him or command him or threaten him. Just a word, a slight movement, a look, was enough. The servant understood at once. He was always ready to carry out his master's every whim and every desire. That was the perfect servant.

You and I are meant to be like that, and if we only concentrated more on Him and sought to develop this responsiveness, this sensitivity to His desires, then I think the church would experience an activity that she has not known for many a long day. We would then experience life-giving activity coming down from the Head, and not this excitable, mechanical activity which we tend to produce. That is what the church is for as the body of Christ.

Then the last point under this particular heading is this: it follows that the activity of the church will always be in conformity with the thinking and the mind of the Head. Here is a tremendous principle which I think we can say has been neglected by every single major section of the Christian church. According to the analogy, the activities of the body are meant to be conformable to, and consistent with, the person who is functioning through the body. So we are not meant to behave like animals or like machines but like human beings. Our activities, the activities of our bodies, are to be essentially consistent with what makes human beings human. In the same way, all the activities of the church ought to be in accord with the fact that she is the body of the Lord Jesus Christ. He Himself said to Pilate, 'My kingdom is not of this world: if my kingdom were of this world, then would my servants fight' [*John* 18:36].

On another occasion our Lord said, 'Even the Son of man came not to be ministered unto, but to minister, and to give his life a ransom for many' [*Mark* 10:45]. He said, 'The kings of the Gentiles exercise lordship over them . . . But ye shall not be so: but he that is greatest among you, let him be as the younger; and he that is chief, as he that doth serve. For whether is greater, he that sitteth at meat, or he that serveth? is not he that sitteth at meat? but I am among you as he that serveth' [*Luke* 22:25-27]. And, of course, He said these things to His disciples and others in order that they might have a clear notion of His kingdom which now takes the form of the church.

But this truth has been violated many, many times. There have been eras when the Christian church has made people confess that they were Christians at the point of the sword, and yet thought that they were carrying out His will. They said, 'It's good for a person to be a Christian, but here are people who don't want to be Christians, so we'll compel them to confess the Lord Jesus Christ.' But that activity is a complete denial of this principle. It is the exact opposite of what our Lord has always done. He is the antithesis of that.

But can we not go further? By now I think that everybody would more or less recognize that for the Christian church to start a war or to take part in it – I do not mean as citizens of a nation but specifically for the purpose of spreading the gospel – is also a complete denial of this doctrine. But is not any alliance between the state and the church an equal violation of this principle? And yet not only did the Roman Catholic Church fall into that error, but Luther perpetuated it, and, indeed, so did John Calvin, not in exactly the same way as Luther, but equally definitely. Ulrich Zwingli in Zurich did the same – he actually died on the field of battle. But, in any case, he said that it was the business of the state, the ruler, to enforce true religion. Calvin, too, said that it was a part of the function of the state to preserve religious practice and to punish those who did not conform.

And, of course, in this country also the same was true of the Church of England, and of John Knox in the Church of Scotland. Of course, we understand how the Reformers, with so much to do, did not have time to do everything, or to consider all these questions. They were concerned about one great thing, the great central matter of the doctrine of salvation. So they perpetuated these views on church and state, and it led to untold misery. But the point I am establishing is that all this is quite wrong in theory. The church does not belong to the kingdoms of this world: 'My kingdom is not of this world.' The church is a spiritual body, a spiritual society, and any desire for such a relationship violates that principle.

But I want to take the argument even a step further. Surely the attempt to maintain the life of the church by means of social entertainment, is an equal violation of the principle that the activities of the church should conform to the Head? And this, of course, has been the great sin of the church, especially during the last hundred years. All these things are so important today. I believe that we are living at the end of an era and I am one of those who thanks God for that. Let us get back to the New Testament and start afresh.

The argument for social entertainments was this. In 1859 Darwin wrote his book, *On the Origin of Species*, and this led to an attack on the faith. Not only that, industry was spreading, towns were prospering and growing and people were receiving a better education. 'Now the danger is,' said the church leaders, 'that we shall lose these people; how can we hold them? They don't seem to like our prayer meetings; they don't like too much preaching; they don't like relating spiritual experiences and conferring together about these matters – so we must do less of that or we shall lose them. On the other hand, they do like other things. They like dancing, card-playing, games and so on. They like lectures on literature. Why not give them all this, and thereby we shall hold them?'

But surely this, also, is a violation of the whole principle that the activity of the body has to be consistent with and to conform to the mind of the Head, and he came into the world not to do things like that, not to interest us, but 'to seek and to save that which was lost' [*Luke* 19:10]. He came to give a new birth; He came to form a spiritual kingdom, 'not of this world'. He is concerned about our souls, our relationship to God. He does not say that there is anything wrong with the body as such. He does not say that people should not play football or any games they like, but organizing games is not the function of the church. The task of the church, in a sense, is not to hold people but to save people and build them up in our most holy faith. And the moment she compromises that, she is merely revealing that she has misunderstood this principle.

Now if you try to maintain the organization, to maintain the appearance of the church, in ways that are inconsistent with the principle, you will find that you have only a temporary success, and the history of the twentieth century is proving that abundantly. At the beginning of this century ideas about what was called 'the institutional church' were in great vogue, but you do not hear much about that now. They were a complete failure. And people who are only held in the church by those other activities are not being held by the living truth, and eventually they will tire of the entertainments and activities and will have nothing at all. No, the church must realize that she is the body of Christ, in a living relationship to the Head, and see that all her activities must be consistent with Him.

Now there is the great principle. Whatever the specific decisions, as to the principle itself, there is no question at all. And, of course, this has been demonstrated abundantly throughout the running centuries. We see the church trying to bolster herself up by various worldly means, but they all fail, and she goes down almost to the point of extinction and the scoffers begin to think that she is finally finished, but then suddenly God arises. He moves the whole body and there is a mighty revival and people are brought in, truly converted, and we see living fellowships – people praying, talking together about Christian teaching, building one another up in the faith, and really interested in the things of the Spirit, in other words, a true church instead of an organization or a social gathering.

All this follows from the principle we have been studying, and that is Paul's argument in 1 Corinthians 13:1: 'Though I speak with the tongues of men and of angels, and have not charity, I am become as sounding brass, or a tinkling cymbal.' Now a brass band can collect a crowd and it will keep the crowd together for a certain length of time. A man who is just a good speaker will collect a crowd and provide entertainment, but there is no church there. He will get a following, but that is not the business of a preacher. It is not the preacher's job to attract people; the only thing that he can be from that outward standpoint is 'sounding brass', or 'a tinkling cymbal', and of no value. He may indulge in the heroics that the apostle speaks of – 'though I give my body to be burned' – but it is of no value. And, of course, it will attract temporary attention. It will call a crowd together and for a while they will perpetuate the memory of this man but is there a church there? That is the question.

And likewise with knowledge. With knowledge you can interest certain types of people, and they will find what is said tremendously interesting and pleasing and fascinating, but if there is no life there, there is no church and whatever has started will eventually vanish into thin air. For a very long time now, the church has failed to see the need for conformity with the Head, and we are living in an age when we are seeing the outworking of this failure. In spite of all that the church has done in this twentieth century in terms of organization, look at the present position. It really does not work; it cannot work. The church cannot keep going on her own self-initiated activities. Her activity must always be in conformity to, and with the thinking, the mind, the spirit of the Head Himself.

And so it comes to pass – and it is one of the most glorious things about the life of the church and being in the church – that here we really are not dependent upon numbers; we are dependent upon the Scriptures. 'Where two or three are gathered together in my name' [*Matt.* 18:20], then He is there. The power of the Spirit, in this vital, living, real sense, working through one person can do more in a minute than thousands can do in a hundred years. And that is precisely what the whole of church history demonstrates so clearly. Is it not time we came back to this? Here it is: 'We, being many, are one body in Christ, and every one members one of another.'

My last point about the character of this unity is that it is a unity in which we are always aware of our one-ness and of our inter-dependence: not only are we members of Him, but 'members one of another'. Now here are some of the subsidiary principles that come under that general heading. This oneness is made up of many who are different: 'So we, being many, are one body.' You see the variety? Later, we shall be drawing certain deductions from that as to how we are to regard our gifts, and how we are to exercise them, but let me mention it in general at this point. This is the glory of the church – 'many' constituting unity, the one. And the one consists of a perfect adaptation of the many to one another.

Secondly, therefore, we should always think of the whole more than of the parts. That is difficult, is it not, but the analogy compels it. Here the apostle is warning the Christians in Rome: Now, he says, if you start thinking of yourselves and of the parts and the function of the parts, you will go astray.

That was the whole error of the church at Corinth. That is schism, says Paul, and the way to counteract it is to realize that the whole is more important than the parts, and that we should always be thinking of the whole. Let us work that out a bit more. What, after all, is the central and most essential glory of the human body? Is it not the balance and the harmony of the varying parts? How different they are! How refined is the eye, how crude, in a sense and by contrast, is the foot, and so on. If I took you through the various organs of the body you would find that not only are they all different, but they differ in a very striking manner. And yet the marvellous thing about the body is that the different parts are all in balance and all work in harmony together.

Furthermore, we should realize that the individual part has no real meaning in and of itself. Now that is a pretty extreme statement, but it is right. An isolated finger is really unthinkable, is it not? It is ridiculous. Think of a finger just on its own, with nothing else! It is useless; there is no point in it. Moreover, the part cannot function by itself, in isolation. I have already indicated, in working out the truth about the body, that if a part does try to do that, or does so for some reason, then it means disease; it is an abnormality. But I am talking here about true functioning, and the body has been so made and so constructed, so organized by God who made it, that the parts cannot function without the Head. But neither can they function without one another. There is an extraordinary inter-dependence – 'members one of another'.

At this point, work out for yourselves, as I would beg you to do, the analogy of the body, not only in terms of anatomy but still more of physiology. Physiology concerns the working of the body; not merely a knowledge of the parts but of how they function. And if you do that, you will find that every part is dependent upon every other part; they all interact and they all help one another.

The next point, therefore, is that the value of any particular part is that it contributes to the functioning and the activity of the whole and is of benefit to the whole. In other words, the action of my finger is not something in and of itself. If I merely waggle it, it is a purposeless action, or if it is not purposeless, it is ridiculous. The object of every action is to accomplish something that I want to see accomplished. I beckon with my finger to call your attention, for example.

So, finally, as parts of the body of Christ, we must be content with our lot, our position, our gift, our activity in the body, whatever it may chance to be. Now we arrive at that, do we not, by an inevitable logic. If it is the whole that matters, not the parts, and if each part is thus inter-dependent upon all the others, as well as upon the Head, and if its own individual action has no real value except in its relationship to the whole, and if the parts are essential to the harmonious functioning of the whole, then I end by saying that I must be content with my part – the part I am in – with my lot.

To start with, I do not determine my part, and I have no right to be there at all. It is all of His grace that I am in the body – that ought to be enough for me. But over and above that, I say to myself, 'Surely, what matters is His functioning, not mine?' I do not ask, 'Do I find what I'm doing wonderful?' It is the whole body that matters, and I am only of interest and of value as I am given the privilege of playing a part in that. I do not care, therefore, what I do – I do it, and, in a sense, I am vital to it; I am essential to it. That is the way in which we evaluate the importance of what we are and of what we are privileged to do.

In the church, therefore, as Christian people and as active members of the body of Christ, our main interest should never be in what we are doing, but in what He is doing; our activity is only a part of that. The analogy of the body, I think, puts this perfectly.

But perhaps I am presuming too much upon your knowledge of physiology! So let us try a military analogy. The business of the soldier in the army is, ultimately, to be concerned about the whole – what the fight is about, why his country is involved, and so on. He is not there to do exploits himself; he is not there to make a name for himself. The man who wants to cut a great figure or to do something dramatic is probably a greater danger than a help, more useful to the enemy than to his own side. No, he should be concerned about the whole campaign, the whole thing. He does not direct that. All he has to do is to be ready, so that when the command comes down to him, he can act immediately.

That is what I am trying to say, and as you work these things out and consider them in your own life and in your relationship to the church, as you look at them in the history of the church throughout the centuries, you will see quite clearly that most of the difficulties and the disappointments and the heartaches, and, above all, the failure of the church, are mainly due to the failure to understand this essential teaching that 'we, being many, are one body in Christ, and every one members one of another'.

You may say that you are not important. But you are! That part next to you is more important, perhaps, but he cannot go on without you and he is dependent upon you, and he will suffer if you are not in a fit condition to do your part. So all of us are vital, all of us are essential, all of us have a great privilege, and the way to avoid problems and disasters is always to be thinking of the whole body and especially of the Head. Then you will always be looking at Him, keeping your eye on Him, ready, sensitive, responsive, so that when He initiates an action, it is carried out. That is the great New Testament doctrine of the Christian church and her unity and functioning.

Sixteen

*

Having then gifts differing according to the grace that is given to us, whether prophecy, let us prophesy according to the proportion of faith.

Romans 12:6

We come now to the practical application and outworking of the principle that the apostle has been laying down. It is most important that we should carry in our minds exactly what the apostle is setting out to do here. Having laid down his great doctrine in the first eleven chapters, he now comes to the practicalities and the living of the Christian life, and he tells us that the great overriding principle we must bear in mind is that we hand ourselves over completely to God – 'Present your bodies a living sacrifice . . . which is your reasonable service' [verse 1]. We must not be 'conformed to this world,' but we must be 'transformed', especially in the renewing of the mind, that we may prove 'what is that good, and acceptable, and perfect, will of God' [verse 2]. That is the great general principle. We renounce the self-life, which is the worldly life, and we begin to think of ourselves and all we do in terms of the new relationship that is in Christ Jesus [verse 3]. Then Paul puts that negatively by saying that this means that every one of us should 'not think of himself more highly than he ought to think; but to think soberly, according as God hath dealt to every man the measure of faith' [verse 3].

Then Paul goes on to his great illustration of the body. The church is the body of Christ, and therefore we should always think of ourselves not as isolated individuals, but as parts of

[211]

this great body [verses 4-5]. Then, having laid down that principle, Paul says, in effect, 'Now let me illustrate what I mean.' So he takes up some of the particular gifts, and shows us how we should exercise them. Paul always does this. Every man has his method and here is the Pauline method to perfection. You would have thought that his teaching was perfectly plain already, but he is not satisfied: 'Having then' – 'Having therefore' – 'gifts differing according to the grace that is given us . . .' In other words, he there sums up what he has given us as a statement in verse 3 and as an illustration in verses 4 and 5.

Let me say, once more, that the whole essence of the art of teaching is repetition. Paul never takes anything for granted. He always goes on: 'Having then gifts differing according to the grace that is given to us' – well, if it happens to be prophecy, then this: 'let us prophesy'; or if it is a question of ministry, then that: 'let us wait on our ministering', and so on.

In view of this, we must start now with the apostle's summary of the doctrine, and this is very important. It is most interesting to me, as I observe and read what is happening round and about us at the present time, and listen to people talking, how so many of the difficulties, and most of the confusion – if not, indeed, all of it – arises from the fact that people will speak and write in terms of their prejudices rather than of the plain teaching of Scripture. It is almost incredible to see how they can put in print – with the Scripture there before them – a mere manifestation of their own prejudice. I recently read an example of this, in which a man writing about 'speaking in tongues' actually says, with 1 Corinthians 14 in front of him, that the people who spoke in tongues in Corinth were obviously the more emotional and less intelligent types – this, though the Apostle Paul says, 'I thank my God, I speak with tongues more than ye all' [1 Cor. 14:18]. The Apostle Paul, therefore, becomes just an emotional, unintelligent type! So thank God that we have the Scriptures before us, and thank God that the apostle goes on repeating these things: 'Having then gifts differing according to the grace that is given to us.'

What does this tell us? The first principle is that any gift we have received is always according to the grace that is given to us. Let us remind ourselves again of this; the apostle repeats it so I must also. The gifts that he is talking about here are not our natural gifts. We all are born with certain natural gifts which differ tremendously. But Paul is dealing here with the special spiritual gifts given to us as members of the church and which are meant to be exercised in the body for the benefit of the whole church, and through the church to those who are outside. Therefore these gifts are only given to those who belong to the body; in other words, they are only given to those who are born again and not to anybody else. I am not saying that they are given to all members of the visible church, but to those who are truly Christian, the people who are members of the body of Christ.

The apostle says this in 1 Corinthians 12:11: 'But all these' – he has described the varying gifts – 'all these worketh that one and the selfsame Spirit, dividing to every man severally as he will.' So it is He who decides which gift to give to each person. That is a categorical statement. And that is the teaching of the whole of 1 Corinthians 12. Paul says, 'There are diversities of gifts, but the same Spirit. And there are differences of administrations, but the same Lord. And there are diversities of operations, but it is the same God which worketh all in all' [*1 Cor.* 12:4–6]. And then, specifically, in the eleventh verse, it is He who divides 'to every man severally as he will'. Now that, to me, is the crucial statement; it is the great overruling, overarching principle of 1 Corinthians 12, 13 and 14; and if we do not start with this and are not clear about it, we are bound to go astray somewhere in our understanding of the spiritual gifts.

But there is a problem here and it is our business to face problems. Whether we can solve them is another matter, but at any rate we must not evade them. In 1 Corinthians 12:11 we have the categorical statement that he 'divides' or 'dispenses' the gifts, and here in Romans 12:3, we are told that, 'God *hath dealt* to every man the measure of faith.' All these words bring out the point that it is God the Holy Spirit who decides the particular gift He will give to each particular Christian. He is the Lord, and the lordship of the Spirit is the great truth that is emphasized. But here is the problem. Have you noticed the last verse in 1 Corinthians 12 or the first verse of 1 Corinthians 14? 'But covet earnestly,' Paul says, 'the best gifts: and yet shew I unto you a more excellent way.' And in 1 Corinthians 14:1: 'Follow after charity, and desire spiritual gifts, but rather that ye may prophesy.' So the problem is that on the one hand we are told that it is the Spirit who decides, but on the other hand we are told to 'covet earnestly the best gifts' – incidentally, the translators should have used the same translation for 'desire' and 'covet' in 1 Corinthians 14:1 and 1 Corinthians 12:31 respectively, as they both translate the same Greek word. If it is the Spirit who decides what to give to each Christian, how, then, can we be told to 'covet earnestly'?

The way to reconcile this apparent contradiction is first of all to be quite clear as to what the apostle is saying in 1 Corinthians 12:31. The Authorized [King James] Version reads thus: 'Covet earnestly the best gifts: and yet shew I unto you a more excellent way.' Unfortunately that is a wrong translation, but what is so interesting is that the inaccuracy of the translation is not confined to the old version. The New English Bible is even worse: 'And now I will show you the best way of all.' I have also looked up the other translations, the Revised Version and Revised Standard Version, and all of them have made the same mistake.

The mistake is to introduce the idea of a comparative, which leads to an entirely false interpretation and exegesis of the statement. In evangelical and other circles at the present time we are told that the apostle teaches here that you should not be bothering about the gifts but should go in for the graces. It is suggested that Paul is saying, 'The mistake you are making at Corinth is that you are interested in the gifts, while you should be interested in His love. Why don't you go in for love? This is the more excellent way.' And people give that interpretation very largely because of a wrong translation of the phrase 'more excellent way'.

Now quite apart from the exact translation – which I am coming to in a moment – Paul cannot possibly mean what that interpretation tells us, for this reason: if the apostle is telling us not to be concerned at all about gifts but only to seek the grace of love, why does he start his statement by saying, 'Covet earnestly the best gifts'? And, again, having given his great hymn or poem of love in the thirteenth chapter, back he comes to it again in the first verse of the fourteenth chapter: 'Follow after charity' – certainly! – 'and [as well] desire spiritual gifts.' In other words, he is not brushing the gifts aside and saying the one thing to seek is love.

More or less the whole of the thirteenth chapter is mis-interpreted in the same way. It is maintained that Paul here says quite plainly and clearly that the various gifts are going to pass away – 'Charity never faileth: but whether there be prophecies, they shall fail; whether there be tongues, they shall cease' [verse 8]. But those who make this interpretation are not always so careful to say, '. . . whether there be knowl-edge, it shall vanish away' [verse 8]!

The argument, therefore, is that the apostle is teaching that the gifts were only temporary, and that once we had the New Testament Scriptures the gifts would no longer be necessary. So there have never been such gifts since the end of the apostolic age, and it is very wrong to seek for them and to look for them at any other time, and particularly not now. But as we have seen, what Paul says about tongues and prophecies, he also says about knowledge! So to be consistent, you have to say that since we have had the Scriptures, knowledge has passed away. The whole thing is wrong, of course. The apostle is contrasting what is true of the church while she is still on earth, and what will be true of us all as members of the church when ultimately we are glorified, when 'I shall know, even as also I am known' [verse 12].

Is it not almost inconceivable that people should put gifts and love up as opposites and say that the gift of love puts the others out of court and that Paul is telling us not to consider them? That is not interpretation, it is prejudice. Because there are difficulties about this whole doctrine of gifts, the issue is evaded with the claim that the apostle does not believe in the gifts at all, but tells us to go in this better way of love.

Now by merely looking at the Scriptures we should have been saved from that error, but unfortunately the translation is also wrong. There is no comparative in the original statement. It was very interesting to me, in looking this up, to find that the man who deals with this translation in the best and clearest manner is none other than the great Charles Hodge. This is interesting because Hodge, as many of you know, held the view that these gifts really did end at the time of the apostles; and I have already dissented from that view. But he was an honest expositor and translator and he has to say quite plainly and clearly that there is no comparative at all, nothing in the original Greek about 'more excellent'. Paul is not saying that one thing is more excellent than another. This, says Charles Hodge, is the right translation: 'Yet shew I unto you a way according to excellence'. That is what the apostle actually wrote. He will show them 'an excellent way', or 'a way of excellence'.

And then Hodge goes on to point out very rightly – and it seems to me that it is the only possible true explanation of this whole statement – that the apostle is saying, 'I will show you the way *par excellence* to obtain these better gifts.' That, I think, gives us the key to the understanding of this passage, and it fits in with 1 Corinthians 14:1: 'Follow after charity.' If you put charity first and then 'desire the spiritual gifts', you will receive them in the right proportion and you will never abuse them.

So we might put it like this: The apostle says in 1 Corinthians 12:31, 'Seek the better gifts.' He is very concerned about that and he goes on with it in the fourteenth chapter. Some gifts are better than others and the trouble in Corinth was that they were not seeking these superior gifts. So Paul makes it quite plain that, in his opinion at any rate, they were putting first what should not be put first, something which he invariably puts last, namely, 'tongues'. 'Seek the better gifts', he says, 'and, moreover, I will show you an excellent way to do that.' That is the meaning of 1 Corinthians 12:31. So, far from saying that they must not go in for gifts at all, nor seek them, the apostle is telling them to 'covet them earnestly'. But, he says, the way to do that is to covet them earnestly in terms of love, otherwise even these gifts will be useless. Then he goes on to say, 'Though I speak with the tongues of men and of angels, and have not charity [this love], I am become as sounding brass, or a tinkling cymbal . . . and though I have the gift of prophecy . . . and though I have all faith . . . and have not charity, I am nothing.'

This is a most important point, but it still leaves us with our problem. We have got rid of this completely false exegesis which thinks it can solve the problem so simply by saying that even Paul in his day was against exercising and seeking gifts, so how much more should this be true of us. But we are still left with the problem of reconciling the statement that the gifts are dispensed according to the will of the Spirit with the exhortation to 'covet earnestly the best gifts'.

What, then, do we make of this? Now the word 'covet' is very strong. It means 'to desire intensely' – so, I say again, how anybody can say that the Apostle Paul discouraged people from seeking gifts, passes my comprehension. He goes out of his way to use one of the strongest words he could have ever found – 'intense desire'! And he repeats it in 1 Corinthians 14:1: Do all you can, he says, in terms of desiring at any rate, to obtain these gifts.

Now, once more, Charles Hodge helps us to arrive at the right solution to our problem. And he does it by using a comparison. You ask: How do you reconcile those two things?

Well, he says, let me give you another problem: How do you reconcile two further things – that salvation is the sovereign gift of God, and yet the Scriptures exhort us to seek salvation? 'Strive to enter in at the strait gate' [*Luke* 13:24]. Seek it for all you are worth. How do you reconcile those two? It is the same dilemma, and the same principle is involved: the sovereign Giver, and yet the intense desire on the part of the receiver. And Hodge shows that there is certainly no essential contradiction between the two. Paul is saying that it is right for us and we should all, indeed, have within us a desire to be of value and of service in the body of Christ. That is right and good, as long as it is always within the terms of the doctrine of the church as the body of Christ, with its unity, its one-ness, and the principle of love.

In other words, we should all of us, as Christian people, be filled with a burning desire to see the success of the kingdom of God in this visible form of the church. We should all be most anxious for that success, and do all we can to further it and to be of service and of use. You should not be lazy in the church, and you should not say, 'Let somebody else do the work, I'm only going to get the benefits. I never study, I never think, I never pray, I leave it all to the preacher or somebody else.' That is all wrong; you should be keenly anxious to play as great a part as you can in the life and the functioning of the church, but in your coveting you must never transgress the doctrine of the church as the body of Christ, for if you do, your desire becomes a false ambition, and that is always wrong. Not only that, your longing must never transgress the law of love. You must not be anxious to function in the church in order that you may be important. That is self-love, which is all wrong. That is the 'puffing up' that Paul talks about, and it makes you despise others and become impatient with them.

As long as the coveting is governed by those two considerations, it is always right. And so Paul lays down his teaching, which is: 'Covet earnestly the best gifts [the better gifts].' First, what are they? Well, he tells us that in 1 Corinthians 14 where he says that the better gifts are those that profit the body. I am hoping to put this before you a little more clearly later, but let me put it like this now. Take the comparison that the apostle works out in 1 Corinthians 14 between 'tongues' and 'prophecy'. He tells us to desire prophecy – 'Follow after charity, and desire spiritual gifts, but rather that ye may prophesy' [*1 Cor.* 14:1]. Why? Because prophecy is the gift that is most profitable for the church. You see how consistent Paul is? Think of the whole question, he says, not in terms of your personal enjoyment, but in terms of the benefit to and the edification of the church. That is what makes one gift 'better' than another. Gifts are not better in any other sense. That is the sense in which, in these chapters, Paul uses the comparative.

Secondly, the best way of coveting the better gifts is to 'follow after love' – to make certain that you are filled with a spirit of love. If you want to function in the church in terms of the better gifts, concentrate first of all on love; be a person who is filled with love. Paul says that the man or woman who is filled with love is the one who can be most safely trusted with the better gifts. Those who are not filled with love will misuse them for themselves and their own aggrandizement and self-glorification. If you really want the better gifts, says Paul, go in for love, then you will get the best gifts because God will be able to trust you with them. And as they are then used in this wonderful spirit of love, they will be of inestimable value to the life and the growth of the whole of the church. That is the second principle.

The third principle is that while you covet earnestly the better gifts, you must always be content with the gift that is given you. It is all right to covet the better, but if you are not given it, do not sulk, do not grumble, do not complain, do not be like the man who was given one talent and hid it in a napkin. That man said, 'I've only been given one gift, what's the use of one? He's a hard master!' And so he did nothing with his talent. That is what our Lord condemned and the apostle is inculcating the same principle.

So if you find that you have not been given any of the 'best gifts', but only, as it were, some very ordinary gift, one of the 'less comely parts' that Paul talks about, then do not grumble and grouse and say, 'I'm not being dealt with fairly.' That is to violate the law of love and is altogether wrong. You have forgotten the whole doctrine of the church as the body of Christ. No, 'covet the best', but if it is His will that you have one of the others, say, 'Thank God that I am in the body at all; thank God that He deigns to use me in any way.' Say with the psalmist, 'I had rather be a doorkeeper in the house of my God, than to dwell in the tents of wickedness' [*Psa.* 84:10]. That is the principle.

There, then, it seems to me, is the way in which we reconcile these two statements. There is nothing wrong in your having an intense and earnest desire, on condition that you are right in those three respects: the doctrine of the body, the doctrine of love, and the doctrine that we are to be content with whatever place or portion we are given. It is all to His glory and to His praise.

Now that being the doctrine, let us draw a few deductions from it, and these are the ones that I think are rather important at the present time. First, you must never talk about 'claiming a gift'; there is no such thing. Why not? Because, if it is a question of claiming a gift, we would all want, and we would all have, the same gift. No, you may 'earnestly desire', with its three qualifications, but you cannot go beyond that. To talk about 'claiming' is a contradiction of His sovereignty as the Giver.

Secondly, Christians are clearly not all meant to have any one gift. The whole teaching of these three chapters shows us that that is not and cannot be the case. The apostle has put it in terms of his own illustration of the body when he says, 'The body is not one member, but many. If the foot shall say, Because I am not the hand, I am not of the body; is it therefore not of the body . . . If the whole body were an eye, where were the hearing? If the whole were hearing, where were the smelling? But now hath God set the members every one of them in the body, as it hath pleased him. And if they were all one member, where were the body?' [*1 Cor.* 12:14–15, 17–19]. He is here dealing with the question of spiritual gifts, remember. So obviously Christians are not all meant to have any one particular gift.

Listen again: 'Are all apostles? are all prophets? are all teachers? are all workers of miracles? Have all the gifts of healing? do all speak with tongues? do all interpret?' [*1 Cor.* 12:29–30]. Could anything be plainer? And yet there are people who say that all Christians who are baptized with the Holy Spirit should have one particular gift – that of tongues. Paul makes it perfectly clear that the people in the church at Corinth did not all have this one gift. They did not all speak with tongues. And yet people say that we should. It is unscriptural and wrong to put one thing in the centre and make it everything. It indicates a loss of balance, and a falling away from the scriptural position.

My third deduction is that it is not in the province of any person to give a spiritual gift to another. That is the province and the prerogative of the Holy Spirit. The Apostle Paul could not give to other people the gift of speaking in tongues. I can prove that to you from 1 Corinthians 14: 5 where he says, 'I would that ye all spake with tongues.' 'I *would*'! But he could not. He said in effect, 'It would be quite pleasing in my sight if you all did speak in tongues; and I am still more anxious that you should all prophesy.' Great apostle that he was, Paul nevertheless did not have it in his power to give any gift to others.

I feel from what I am reading at the present time, and from what I am told, that my fourth deduction is still more urgently needed. In the light of this teaching, this doctrine, you and I must never do anything in any way to try to produce this gift either in ourselves or in anybody else. It is the gift of the Holy Spirit. We can desire, but we cannot produce, we cannot help in any way at all. It is the Spirit who dispenses 'to every man severally as he will' [*1 Cor.* 12:11]. But sometimes you will be asked after a meeting, 'Are you coveting the gift of speaking in tongues? Very well, we can help you.' Then you will be invited to come to another room, to an after-meeting, and there you will be told what to do.

It has actually been put in print. This is the kind of thing you may read or hear: 'Now then, the first thing you must do is surrender your jaw. Relax it and surrender your tongue. Then utter any sound that comes to you and go on repeating it.' In other words, you are told to start this off, and when you have surrendered your jaw and your tongue and have begun uttering sounds, you will probably find that it will come and you will speak in tongues.

Now this is what I am concerned about. Not only is there no such teaching in the New Testament, but I solemnly and seriously suggest to you that it is entirely contrary to the teaching of the New Testament. Look at the apostles in that room on the morning of the day of Pentecost. Did they surrender their jaws and tongues? Did they utter odd sounds? Of course not, the thing is ridiculous; they knew nothing about it. They found themselves speaking in tongues. There is not a word of instruction anywhere in the New Testament telling people what to do in order to get the gift. The most we are to do is 'desire', 'covet earnestly', with the proviso I have given. Nothing beyond that. This is a *gift*, my friend. You cannot help the Spirit. He does not need it, and if it is something that He gives, it is even wrong to attempt to help Him. He decides, not you. You do not say, 'I'm going to have the gift of tongues.' And no one else can say, 'I'll help you to get it.' They cannot! To me, such teaching comes very near to blasphemy.

I say again, it is the Spirit alone who decides which gift to give, and it is the Spirit alone who can give the gift. And if you start trying to help, you come near to sinning in a very serious manner against the blessed Holy Spirit Himself. Moreover, you are exposing yourself, first, to psychological influences, and, second, you are opening the door to other strange, eerie or occult influences, which are ever ready and waiting to pounce and bring the work of the Holy Spirit into disrepute among us.

Now I am not suggesting that people who speak in tongues

as a result of this kind of procedure are all demon-possessed, but I am seriously suggesting that some of them may be, and that others are undoubtedly the victims of a psychological process.

This is a most important matter, especially at the present time when there is a new interest in these things. I am one of those who believes that the baptism with the Holy Spirit is something distinct and separate from regeneration, and I am deeply concerned lest that great doctrine should get into disrepute because of muddled, unscriptural teaching with regard to speaking in tongues. No, no! Throughout the centuries there have been men baptized with the Holy Spirit – men like Whitefield, the Wesleys, Moody and Finney and the rest – and not one ever spoke in tongues. They never tried to. They never tried to surrender their jaws and to utter sounds. It is all wrong; it is unscriptural, and it is historically wrong.

So my next general principle, therefore, is that we are all given some particular gift. As we have already seen, every member of the body has his or her gift and place and function. It seems clear that some have more than one gift; it is obvious that the Apostle Paul had. If you take the list he gives in 1 Corinthians 12, it becomes very clear that he had several of the gifts. He spoke in tongues: he thanks God that he spoke in tongues more than all of them. He worked miracles – he had the gift of healing. So you may have more than one gift, but what is important is that we all realize that each and every one of us has a particular gift as a member of the body of Christ.

The next thing that Paul emphasizes is that the gifts differ: 'Gifts differing according to the grace that is given to us'. This was something that had caused the Christians in Corinth to go astray, as I have been showing you. They had forgotten this 'differing'; they all wanted to be the same and, in particular, they all wanted to speak in tongues. That was their error and we, too, must understand that gifts differ from Christian to Christian.

Oh, how often, in my pastoral experience, have I had to deal with this problem! There are many Christians who can confirm the point I am making because they have passed through this misunderstanding themselves. We have already considered this problem, but I must return to it. When an intelligent young man is converted I can almost predict that he will very soon be assuming that he is meant to be a preacher. Or he may feel that he must go into full-time work. He says, 'It's no use my going on any longer as a school-teacher or in business or anything else, every Christian must be in full-time service.' But, as we said earlier, there is no such teaching in the Scripture! To assume that is to deny the analogy of the body. We are not all meant to be preachers; we are not all meant to be full-time Christian workers or foreign missionaries.

Now this really has been most grievous. The teaching that has been so prevalent has been this: 'The need is the call.' So in a missionary gathering pressure is exerted in that way. People are told, 'Now, you need not wait and bother to ask yourself questions, here is the need, the need in Africa, the need in Asia, the need in South America. There is an appalling need. And the need is the call.' But that is completely unscriptural. If that is the case, then everybody should respond. But they are not meant to; they cannot! You must have certain gifts before you can possibly respond to such a call. To say that the need is the call is to show an ignorance of the New Testament doctrine concerning the call. When God calls a man or woman to a particular task, He gives them the ability to do the work; He always gives them the gifts they need.

There is a statement in the Old Testament that puts this in a particularly memorable and graphic manner. It was spoken by David when he was an outlaw, on the run from King Saul. We are told in 1 Samuel 30 that while David and his men were away, some of the Amalekites sacked the town of Ziklag where David had been living. They carried away the wives of the men and their children and possessions. David came back and determined to do something about this, so he collected six hundred men, and chased after these Amalekites. But after they had gone a certain distance, two hundred of David's men became quite exhausted and could not go any further, so David said to them, 'You stay here and look after the supplies while I and the other four hundred go on and fight.' And they went on and attacked the Amalekites and recovered everything.

Then we read: 'And David took all the flocks and the herds, which they drave before those other cattle, and said, This is David's spoil.' Then: 'And David came to the two hundred men, which were so faint that they could not follow David, whom they had made also to abide at the brook Besor: and they went forth to meet David, and to meet the people that were with him: and when David came near to the people, he saluted them. Then answered all the wicked men and men of Belial, of those that went with David, and said, Because they went not with us, we will not give them ought of the spoil that we have recovered, save to every man his wife and his children, that they may lead them away, and depart' [*1 Sam.* 30:20–22].

And this is the immortal statement made by David in response: 'Then said David, Ye shall not do so, my brethren, with that which the Lord hath given us, who hath preserved us, and delivered the company that came against us into our hand. For who will hearken unto you in this matter? but as his part is that goeth down to the battle, so shall his part be that tarrieth by the stuff: they shall part alike. And it was so from that day forward, that he made it a statute and an ordinance for Israel unto this day' [*1 Sam.* 30:23–25].

I am now going to say something that may shock you! Do you as a Christian feel a bit ashamed of yourself because you are not a foreign missionary? Do you feel that you are less a member of the body of Christ because you are not on the foreign field, or because you are not in the whole-time ministry as I am? If you do, you are very wrong. It is a failure to understand this doctrine of the church as the body of Christ. We are all in it together. One person is in the front line, the other is watching the stock at home, but the one who is watching at home is as essential and as vital as the one in the front line, and, as David lays down, they must be equal sharers.

And that principle is carried on into the New Testament. What is important is that you are a member of the body of Christ, and that you have your gift and exercise it wholly to the glory of God, whatever it may be. You are a part of the whole enterprise and you will get your reward. Just the same as the one who is in the front line, you will hear the words: 'Well, done, thou good and faithful servant' [*Matt.* 25:21]. Those who look after the goods at home, those who are faithful in their ministry in the home church, are acting according to the gift given to them by the Spirit just as much as the men and women who have gone overseas and may be suffering the hardships of the front line.

Do you feel that I am discouraging people from going into foreign mission work? I am not. What I am saying is that no one should go to the foreign mission field or into the ministry, without being absolutely certain of God's call. No one must respond simply because there is a need. It is God who calls, whatever the task, whatever the position. He decides, He calls, and He and He alone equips for the work. And it is because this principle has been so often forgotten and denied in practice, as a result of carnal zeal and enthusiasm, that it is true to say – and this I believe is statistically correct – that of all the people in the United States of America in recent years who have volunteered for overseas missionary work in terms of 'the need is the call', two out of every three have never gone back after their first furlough. They served for one period only and realized during that time that they had never been called. They should never have been there and if they had been obeying the teaching of Scripture, they would never have gone. He decides; He calls; He equips.

Seventeen

*

Having then gifts differing according to the grace that is given to us, whether prophecy, let us prophesy according to the proportion of faith.

Romans 12:6

We have already begun to consider the first part of this verse and we have emphasized the point that all these gifts are given by God. We have seen, too, that Paul is not talking about natural gifts here, but about spiritual gifts. I believe that sometimes the spiritual gift may, as it were, be superimposed upon a natural gift, but it remains a spiritual gift. Some of the spiritual gifts, however, are distinct and separate and do not seem to have much relationship at all to the natural gifts.

So we now continue with our study of spiritual gifts and we turn to a point that is often asked: 'Are you doing something purely academic here? Are you talking about the gifts simply because you are expounding the Epistle to the Romans? Of course, it is of interest for us to know something about what the early church was like, but that has nothing to do with us; all that finished with the apostolic age. Has it any real relevance or application to us at this present time?'

Now that is an important question. I have already touched on it, in passing, but now I want to take it up in a little more detail. We have considered the argument, which is sometimes based upon the teaching of 1 Corinthians 13, which says that the apostle is teaching that we must not be concerned about the gifts because they are all to pass away. Those who hold this view go on to say that at the end of the apostolic period all these gifts ceased because now that we have the Scriptures they no longer apply. Well, in our last study I tried to give you a hurried exposition of 1 Corinthians 13 on that point, so I leave it at that.

But let us look at it in this way. You notice the list of the gifts that the apostle gives us here: '. . . whether prophecy, let us prophesy according to the proportion of faith; or ministry, let us wait on our ministering: or he that teacheth, on teaching; or he that exhorteth, on exhortation: he that giveth, let him do it with simplicity; he that ruleth, with diligence; he that sheweth mercy, with cheerfulness' [*Rom.* 12:6–8]. Now I think you will all have to agree that whatever you may think of the gift of prophecy, all the others are clearly gifts that have continued in the church ever since apostolic times and are in evidence at the present time. I find it is almost laughable that people should say that they do not see any evidence of the gifts today. It means, of course, that they are only thinking of speaking in tongues or of prophecy or of miracles. They do not realize that all these others are equally gifts – the apostle does not seem to draw any distinction, but puts them all into the same category. We are entitled, therefore, to argue that if some of these gifts have been in evidence throughout the history of the church and still are, then why not all of them? It is a fair question, and is part of the answer to those who say that the gifts finished with the apostles.

Another important argument is that if you feel that there is not much evidence of the working of the gifts in the church in these days, then the explanation may be the low state of spirituality of the church. One of the greatest dangers, it always seems to me, is to interpret the Scriptures in the light of our experience, instead of testing our experience by the teaching of Scripture. So often that happens at the present time. People lay down as the norm what they have and what they are familiar with, and they test everything by that. But we should rather ask: What is the New Testament picture of the church? How do we come out when tested by that standard? And, I repeat, the result may well be that the absence of the manifestation of gifts is due solely to the low state of spirituality in the church. We know that that is true because Scripture itself teaches that. If a church backslides, or falls from the truth, or limits the truth of

God, then she will lose her power; and, of course, the history of the church throughout the centuries demonstrates very clearly that this has frequently happened.

Let us be very careful, therefore, lest we be found to be 'wresting the Scriptures' simply in an attempt to bolster up our prejudices, or justify our own low state of spirituality. That is what the apostle means in 1 Thessalonians 5:19 when he says, 'Quench not the Spirit.' You lay it down to start with that certain things do not happen, cannot happen, or are not meant to happen, and then, of course, you will find they do not happen. But your argument has gone in a circle and you have been altogether wrong. That is one of the most common ways of quenching the Spirit.

So I go on to a fourth point, and this is still more pertinent. We are involved here in the whole question of the doctrine of the sovereignty of the Holy Spirit, and we must be very careful not to limit the work of the Spirit. This doctrine is taught us here: '. . . according as God hath dealt to every man the measure of faith.' It is *God* who has dealt it. We emphasized that when we were considering the third verse. Here it is again in the sixth verse: 'Having then gifts' – the fact that they are called 'gifts' should always remind us that they are His sovereign prerogative – 'gifts differing according to the grace that is given to us . . .' The sovereignty of the Spirit! And we may deduce that it may be the will of the Spirit, at times, that none of the gifts should be given or be strikingly apparent. It is for Him to decide and we must therefore be very careful as we approach this subject.

There are certainly many evidences in the Scriptures that God, for His own great purposes, seems at times to withhold certain influences from the church and from the individual. He does it sometimes to teach us and to humble us and to do many other things, or, if we misuse His gifts, He is likely to withdraw them. Unless, therefore, you have absolute proof, or a statement which is specifically explicit, that the gifts were only meant to be temporary and at a given point were to be withdrawn, be very careful that, as you lay down your rules, you are not quenching the Spirit. You may, at the same time, be fighting against the whole teaching concerning the sovereignty of the Spirit in His dispensation of these gifts.

[228]

But then I want to make a suggestion. Is there not clear evidence in the passages that deal with these gifts – and it is evidence that is supported, as I shall show you, by the history of the church, especially in times of revival – that we can divide up the gifts into two main groups? There are what one may call *regular* gifts and there are *unusual* gifts. Now I was tempted to use the classification 'ordinary' and 'extraordinary', but I did not because one does not like to use the word 'ordinary'. By 'regular' I mean that they are constantly or normally in evidence, apart from days of backsliding and of quenching of the Spirit.

Now here, in Romans 12, the majority of the gifts referred to, excluding the gift of prophecy, certainly seem to come under the heading of what I am calling 'regular' gifts. In the list in 1 Corinthians 12, 'miracles' and 'healings', may be called the exceptional, the unusual; and then the more ordinary are wisdom, understanding, helps and governance.

Or let me put it to you like this. In the church – and thank God that this is in evidence at the present time – you see the gift of faith. But there are occasions when you see the gift of faith in a most unusual and exceptional degree. There are many Christian people who have the gift of faith. Of course, as we have already seen, the gift of faith mentioned in 1 Corinthians 12 is not saving faith because every Christian has that. You cannot be a Christian at all if you do not have faith to believe the message – that is faith unto salvation. But not all Christians have what is called there 'the gift of faith', though many have it in a mild or in a regular degree.

But then you suddenly come across people in whom this faith is manifest in a marked or in an unusual way. There are obvious examples of this. Think of a man like George Müller of Bristol. If you do not know the story, then you should familiarize yourself with it, and you will find that there is something for people to answer who say that all the gifts finished when the New Testament came into being! How do you explain a man like George Müller of Bristol and the faith which he had? Read the marvellous story of how that man had sufficient faith to put up buildings without a halfpenny and took in all those orphans. When there was a shortage of money, he never issued a report or an appeal. He responded with naked faith. There are amazing stories of his faith. Once, when he was on a voyage across the Atlantic to attend a meeting in America, the ship suddenly became fog-bound. But George Müller began to pray and the fog dispersed in a most exceptional manner.

You find similar examples of great faith in the life of Hudson Taylor, who founded the China Inland Mission, now the Overseas Missionary Fellowship. And there have been other people in the history of the church who, beyond any question, have been given a very definite gift either of faith or of healing – it is sometimes difficult to tell which they had. Now here we are in the realm of well-attested facts. We must be very careful lest we become guilty of quenching the Spirit because we have laid it down that the giving of gifts ended with the apostles. There was a man called John Welsh who was as Reformed and Calvinistic as his father-in-law John Knox. It was said of him – and there is good evidence for this in a book which was written by an equally Reformed and Calvinistic writer – that when he lived in the South of France, he was used to raise a woman from the dead. Now you have to face facts. Be careful lest, in your neat and tidy arrangement of truth, you be found fighting against God. We need to be very humble in these matters.

Or take the gift of prophecy: let us use this as an illustration. Take John Welsh again, or another great minister in Scotland, Alexander Peden. If you read the lives of those men you will find that they were able to make exact prophecies of events that were going to happen in Scotland – and which did happen. So we must be very careful not to quench the Spirit, but not only that, we must not be guilty of contradicting men whom we regard as heroes.

But, to put it more generally, take a time of revival, that is, an outpouring of the Spirit of God. I do not mean an evangelistic campaign, but a revival. Men cannot produce revivals and they cannot organize them. There is much confusion about this. Unfortunately, our friends in America tend to confuse the two and announce that a revival will be held when they mean an evangelistic campaign. But I am talking about a visitation of the Spirit of God, the sort of thing that you can read of in the writing of Jonathan Edwards. In the town of Northampton, Massachusetts, from 1740 to 1742, and, indeed, before that, in

1734, there was an outpouring of the Spirit of God in a most amazing manner. And there have been many such events in the long history of the Christian church.

Now when there is a true revival like that, there is always a manifestation of some of the gifts; sometimes one, sometimes others. One gift that is always given in an exceptional way at such a time is the gift of preaching and teaching. You will also find the gift of prophecy, that is, the foretelling of events which subsequently take place. And the gift of discerning of spirits is also often given. I could tell you many well-attested stories to illustrate this; some of them are almost incredible. I could tell you how men, filled with the Spirit of God, have been able to detect the working of evil spirits in a meeting.

All I am trying to show is that we must be very careful lest we even become people who deny historical facts. But, above all, it is terribly dangerous to lay down our own rules. We are concerned with a truth that is limitless and endless. 'I know in part,' says the apostle (*1 Cor.* 13:12). So let us always remember that and let us all be ready to be surprised and amazed.

History demonstrates the point that I am trying to make. There are periods in the church when you almost feel that there is no manifestation at all of any of the gifts. Then revival suddenly comes and you see them demonstrated in a most unusual manner. So I feel it comes to this: the fact that you cannot be a Christian at all without having the Spirit of God in you means that each one of us who is a Christian has a spiritual gift. But then the baptism with the Spirit heightens those gifts and perhaps adds to them. That, it seems to me, is the way in which you reconcile the teaching of Scripture with both the history of the church and its condition at the present time. It is all in the sovereign power of the Spirit, and it is He who decides what to give.

I have talked to you about revivals and there have been many revivals in the history of the church when there has been no speaking in tongues. Do not forget that. There have been instances of individuals baptized with the Holy Spirit with no evidence at all of speaking in tongues. We have seen that there are two errors here, and we must be careful we do not fall into either of them. One is to dispute whether such people have therefore ever been baptized with the Spirit; and the other is to say that there is no such thing as a unique baptism with the Spirit apart from regeneration, and that even if there is, there can be no gifts. We need to be careful and to be scriptural on all sides.

I say again that my position is that I believe in the baptism of the Holy Spirit as a separate, distinct, unique experience. It may be accompanied by remarkable gifts; it may simply manifest the 'regular' gifts in a heightened degree. It is not for us to say that none of these things can happen. Anything is possible in the sovereignty of the Spirit.

So I am equally opposed to the people who make the rules on the one side, and to those who make the rules on the other; those who say that none of this can happen now that the apostolic era has ended, and those who say all Christians *must* speak in tongues. Both groups are putting forward man-made and equally unscriptural rules. We do not decide these things. Our business, our duty is to be open always to His gracious influences and to what He may decide to do. We cannot predict this. And in the long history of the church we see His sovereignty being demonstrated. He confounds all our man-made rules and systems and regulations. Thank God that He does, for then the glory must always be His and His alone.

And so I leave the subject at that, and now take up a very practical issue. People have often asked me: 'In the light of this teaching, how do you know what your particular gift is?' I know this is troubling many people at the present time and it is not an easy question to answer. The headings of the answer, as I see it, will be something like this: everyone has some natural gifts; there is no such thing as a person entirely devoid of every gift. So if we all have natural gifts, how do we know what our natural gift is? I think that is an equally fair question. And the answer, in both cases, is surely this: the gift will manifest itself, and as long as we are functioning as we should, it does not really matter whether or not we know what our gift is.

Let me illustrate what I mean. Take people who have a natural gift of singing. How do they know that they have it? Well, the answer is that they just find themselves singing. They do not sit down and say in a kind of vacuum, 'Now I wonder what my gift is? I wonder whether I have got the singing gift?' No, it is because they have the gift that they find themselves singing, and it is so with all these other natural gifts.

So I would say to all who tend to be worried about this matter of the spiritual gifts that it is wrong for you to worry in this way. All you and I must do is seek to know Him, and submit ourselves to Him. We must tell Him that we do not care what we do, nor what we are, as long as we are His and are functioning as He wants us to. You do that, and I suggest to you that you will soon know what your gift is.

Sometimes He has to persuade us as to our gift; we may even fight against it. But it does not matter. In His sovereign power He will make the gift manifest itself and probably any who are troubled about this are already exercising the gift without knowing that they are doing so. I do not think that that is a bad thing. It is preferable to boasting about gifts and parading them. It is more consistent with the humility and the meekness of the Christian man or woman.

But we also have another test at this point and one which is very valuable. This is that other people can bear witness to the gift you have, and it is one of the duties of the Christian church as a whole to do this. In other words, discerning our gift is not left entirely to us. The church is involved, because a gift is always for the sake of the whole body. And so, throughout her long history, the church has been able to do two things. She has been able, on the one hand, to question claims which people make as to certain gifts which they think they have; and, on the other hand, she has been able to indicate to people who are not aware of them, that they have certain gifts.

So we find instructions in the Pastoral Epistles to choose certain men as 'elders' and as 'deacons', and we are told to look for certain qualifications. You do not appoint a man to teach unless he is 'apt to teach'. You do not call a man to be a preacher if he cannot speak. There is an extraordinary common sense in the Bible, is there not? You are to look for certain qualities and for manifestations of the gifts – and the list of the characteristics are given in 1 Timothy 3 and in Titus.

Here, therefore, we have great encouragement in this matter of discovering what our particular gift is. Not only will you find that it is revealing itself, but the church will be able to help you. People sometimes think that they have a gift, but the church does not always agree, and it is important, as we have already seen, that the one who claims the gift should be ready to listen to the church. Any man who has been a pastor for any length of time will know exactly what I am talking about. I have had men who have come to see me to tell me that they have been called of God to be preachers. Am I claiming that I have the gift of discrimination or of wisdom? Well, to the glory of God, I have been able to advise such brethren, as gently and as patiently and as quietly as I can, to examine the matter again to make sure. Why? Well, it was evident to me that they were lacking in certain of the basic, essential gifts needed by preachers, and I am happy to say that afterwards – I think almost without exception – these men have come to me and have thanked me.

Mark you, at the time, some of them did not like it and they felt that I was against them. I think of one man in particular, a most sincere and honest man, who had had a marvellous conversion, and was quite sure that he was called to preach. But I was quite sure that he was not. He did not have the mental capacity, the knowledge, or the ability, even to learn, leave alone to teach others, and without these no one can qualify for the position of a pastor, preacher and teacher. However, I was away from my church for a Sunday and a visiting minister, who was a very pleasant man, came to preach. So this young friend of mine, of course, approached the visiting minister and told him about his call. The visitor, being a nice person, and not knowing the man, encouraged him for all he was worth. The poor young man, therefore, was convinced that I was against him, but later he came to see differently.

Now it is important for all of us to listen to the voice of the church on these matters. And it works both ways, because, thank God, we have had other men who have been humble and perhaps guilty of fearfulness, who have not been aware of their gifts. The church has often had to encourage such men, and has had to open their eyes to their gifts, and to convince them. Some of the greatest preachers that the world has ever known have trembled at the thought of preaching. They have done their utmost not to, and have almost had to be pushed into the pulpit: you can read their biographies. That was, in a sense, true of the great George Whitefield. Then the church has had to show a man that he has been given a gift of preaching, and it is his duty to put it into operation.

Those, then, are the general matters which seem to me to introduce this subject which the apostle is putting before us here. He goes on: 'Having then gifts differing according to the grace that is given to us, whether prophecy, let us prophesy according to the proportion of faith.' Now at this point we can only define what is meant by the term 'prophecy', which is the first gift Paul deals with, and with which he illustrates his general principles. What is this gift of 'prophecy'? Here, again, is a subject which can be very difficult but I think that the difficulty very often arises because people have relied on their own ideas and prejudices instead of on the Scriptures.

Let me tell you what prophecy does not mean. It does not merely mean that a man has a gift of expounding the Old Testament prophecies. There have been people who have taught that. They say, 'Prophecy means the gift and capacity to expound the writings of the prophets as they are recorded in the Old Testament.' It may amaze you to hear that that was the interpretation given by John Calvin and Martin Luther. But more recently commentators of almost every school of thought have generally agreed that that interpretation is entirely wrong. It does not fit in with what the New Testament tells us about prophecy.

Why did Luther and Calvin teach that, do you think? I do not know, and it is always dangerous to impute motives to people. But I wonder sometimes whether it was because of some of the things that were happening at that time among the Anabaptists. The Anabaptists claimed that they had been given various New Testament gifts, that the gifts had all been revived in them, and both Luther and Calvin were very opposed to the Anabaptists. That may have influenced them. Whether it did or not, does not matter. What is clear is that that is a totally inadequate explanation of what is meant by the gift of prophecy.

Others have confined prophecy to foretelling the future. Now prophecy does sometimes include prediction, but it is not only that. Indeed, you can have prophecy without any foretelling of the future at all. Others have said that it is a gift or a capacity which certain people have to discover the truth and the facts about others, about their condition and what they are to do. Again, I would say that that may happen at times, and be a part of prophecy, but to confine prophecy to that is certainly entirely wrong. And there are others who restrict their definition of prophecy solely to a knowledge of the will of God in certain particular respects. Again, that may be included, but prophecy must not be confined to that.

What, then, is the gift of prophecy? Well, I would define it as a direct inspiration of the Holy Spirit. What for? Its purpose is to give a word from God, or the word of God, to the church. Now there is a very good definition of prophecy in 1 Corinthians 14:3. In verses 1 and 2 we read: 'Follow after charity, and desire spiritual gifts, but rather that ye may prophesy. For he that speaketh in an unknown tongue speaketh not unto men, but unto God: for no man understandeth him; howbeit in the spirit he speaketh mysteries.' Then verse 3 continues, 'But he that prophesieth speaketh unto men to edification, and exhortation, and comfort.' The same point is made in verse 31 of that chapter: 'For ye may all prophesy one by one, that all may learn, and all may be comforted.'

That is the content of prophecy. It has been defined like this – and I feel it is rather a good definition – prophecy is 'the inspired delivery of warning, exhortation, instruction, judging, and making manifest the secrets of the heart'. Someone who makes a prophecy has been given this gift of passing on, as it were, a word from God to the church and to individuals in the church.

But perhaps the best way of reaching a definition is to ask: What is the difference between prophecy on the one hand and preaching and teaching on the other? Because there is a difference. And I would say that the difference can be put in one word – immediacy. And this means that a word is given to people and comes to them.

Now preaching and teaching are not like that. A preacher and a teacher is a man who takes time to study; he takes time to think, to prepare; he arranges his material and gives it order and system. A preacher and a teacher should not enter into a pulpit without any preparation, and trust to the inspiration of the moment. That is not preaching and teaching, but that is prophecy. Prophecy is something that is given to someone immediately and directly. Let me give you my proof for saying this. In 1 Corinthians 14:29 we read: 'Let the prophets speak two or three, and let the other judge.' Then in verse 30: 'If any thing be revealed to another that sitteth by, let the first hold his peace.' You can picture the meeting. Here is a prophet speaking a prophecy, but a word is revealed to someone sitting by him. That is it; that is prophecy. It is a direct revelation.

Now a difficulty arises in this way: a preacher and a teacher may also be a prophet. I have no doubt at all about this. I say it again to the glory of God, I think I know just a little about this. I think I know something of what it is to be preaching or teaching, and suddenly to find myself prophesying. I am aware that my words are not what I prepared, but have been given at that moment, and with clarity and force and directness. I am speaking, and am listening to myself, as it were, because it is not me. The prophecy may come in the middle of a sermon, or a teaching, but it is differentiated from teaching and preaching by this immediacy, this sense that God is revealing a message.

In my next study I shall go on to show you how this has to be safeguarded. When I talk about 'revelation', I am using the apostle's term: 'If any thing be revealed to another' [*1 Cor.* 14:30]. But do not think that this means revelation in the sense that the writers of the Scriptures were given revelation. It does not mean that. It simply means that you are saying things that are not the result of your thought and meditation and preparation, but are just stating what has been shown you, given to you to say. That is prophecy in its essence.

That there is a distinction between prophecy, and preaching and teaching, can be proved quite clearly from Acts 21:9 and 1 Corinthians 11:5. Writing about Philip the Evangelist, Luke says, 'And that same man had four daughters, virgins, which did prophesy.' And in 1 Corinthians 11 we are told, 'But every woman that prayeth or prophesieth with her head uncovered dishonoureth her head: for that is even all one as if she were shaven.' Now those two verses alone prove that women can prophesy; but the Scripture also tells us that it is not permitted to a woman to preach or teach. This is why it is important to be clear in our minds about the difference between prophesying on the one hand, and preaching and teaching on the other. A message may come to a woman, but that does not make her a preacher or a teacher.

We have some idea, therefore, as to what is meant by prophecy, but as we go on to consider what Paul says next about it, and as we look at how it is to be done, we will be helped to understand more clearly what prophecy itself really is.

Eighteen

*

Having then gifts differing according to the grace that is given to us, whether prophecy, let us prophesy according to the proportion of faith.

Romans 12:6

We have seen that prophecy is essentially a revelation, not in the sense of being equal to Scripture, but in the sense that a particular truth is laid upon the mind of a believer by the Holy Spirit in order that he or she may communicate it to the members of the church. As we saw in 1 Corinthians 14:3, prophecy has a specific object: 'He that prophesieth speaketh unto men to edification, and exhortation, and comfort.' That is the function and business of prophecy. But what we are particularly concerned about now is this statement here in Romans 12:6. If we have been given the gift of prophecy, says the apostle, 'Let us prophesy according to the proportion of faith.'

Two main interpretations of these words have been put forward. The first suggestion is that they mean, 'Let us prophesy according to the proportion of *our own* faith' – which means that we must be sincere. The danger with all these gifts, as we have seen, is that one tends to overdo them, if one may use such an expression, in order to exaggerate one's own importance. So this interpretation would have the apostle saying here, 'If a man has the gift of prophecy, then let him prophesy in a manner that is sincere; let him never go beyond what is revealed to him.'

You see, the devil comes and tempts such a man to say

something striking and remarkable which will bring credit to
him and exalt him in the opinion of others. His danger is
either to add to what has been given him in order to be
spectacular, or to withhold something that has been given to
him because he thinks that it will not be popular, causing
people to dislike it and therefore to dislike him. These are the
dangers that confront someone who has this gift of prophecy,
and the apostle's solution to the problem is, therefore, to say,
'Do it according to your own faith, the proportion of your
own faith. You will know when you are going beyond what
you have been given, and when you are holding something
back. Don't do either. Be honest. Let what you know to be
right in terms of the faith that you have, govern you and
control you.'

Now that is the subjective interpretation of this statement
which somebody has summed up very well like this: 'Let him
prophesy according to the strength, clearness, fervour, and
other qualities of the faith bestowed upon him.' You do not
allow self or the flesh to come in; you are quite honest; you just
deliver the message as it has been given to you, and in no way
do you add to or subtract from it.

The second interpretation takes a more objective view of
this statement about the way in which those who have the gift
of prophecy are to prophesy. Incidentally, I would like to raise a
point that may be troubling someone. It is possible to have the
gift of prophecy without being a prophet. In the New Testament there are these orders – apostles, prophets, evangelists.
The prophets were a very special group of people to whom
revelation was given in a manner only secondary to the
apostles themselves, and they spoke with great authority.
This gift of prophecy is not that. We are not dealing here with
an order within the church. We are dealing, rather, with a gift
which was much more common and more widespread than the
exceptional calling to the body or order of people who were
given the name 'prophets'. As there were not many apostles, so
there were not many prophets in the early church, but the *gift*
of prophecy was obviously much more widespread.

So the second interpretation would translate the statement
like this: 'Let us prophesy according to the proportion of *the*
faith'. Or, to give still another translation: '. . . whether

prophecy, let us prophesy according to the analogy of the faith' – 'the faith', something objective.

In the New Testament you find references to 'the faith', meaning the body of truth that has been delivered to God's people. There is a perfect example in the third verse of the Epistle of Jude. 'Beloved,' Jude says, 'when I gave all diligence to write unto you of the common salvation, it was needful for me to write unto you, and exhort you that ye should earnestly contend for *the faith* which was once delivered unto the saints.' And you will find that expression in many places in the New Testament.

So this second interpretation means that the inspired utterance must always conform to the body of teaching and doctrine that has been given by God to the church through the apostles and prophets and that one who is giving a prophecy, must never add to the revealed body of truth, nor, again, subtract from it. Every prophecy that is uttered, it says, must always be tested in terms of this 'faith' that has been given to us. And this is very important.

For myself, I am very ready to accept both expositions. I think both are right. The one who utters the prophecy must obviously be sincere. But I think there is the further element – that the prophecy should always be tested by 'the faith'. What are my grounds for saying that? Well, we have a specific statement by the apostle himself in 1 Corinthians 14:29 where Paul says, 'Let the prophets speak two or three, and let the other judge' – let the other be testing what is said. As the prophets are speaking, as they are making their utterances, these utterances must be tested, and the only way in which you can test them, of course, is by 'the faith'. Or take the way in which this same apostle puts it in 1 Thessalonians 5:19–21. He says: 'Quench not the Spirit. Despise not prophesyings. Prove all things [test them]; hold fast that which is good.' That is the context. You must test these utterances, and you test them, obviously, only by this faith that has been given to the church: the whole body of truth.

This, of course, is something that is of necessity true. All truth is given by the Holy Spirit and it is therefore self-consistent; it will never contradict itself. He is not going to say one thing on one occasion and deny it on another. There are certain characteristics of truth that come from the Spirit, and therefore every utterance given to the church through the apostles and prophets is to be tested by this truth. There is a very good example in 1 Corinthians 12:3 where Paul says, 'Wherefore I give you to understand, that no man speaking by the Spirit of God calleth Jesus accursed.' He cannot do that. So if ever you hear a man who claims to be under the inspiration of the Holy Spirit saying that 'Jesus is accursed', you can know that he is not speaking from the Holy Spirit.

Our Lord Himself said that the Spirit was given in order to glorify Him; so if a man does not glorify Him, but speaks against Him, he cannot possibly be speaking by the Spirit of God. But, Paul says, conversely, 'No man can say that Jesus is the Lord, but by the Holy Ghost' [*1 Cor.* 12:3]. Now, when he says there, 'No man can say that Jesus is the Lord,' he does not just mean uttering the words, anybody can *say* that. Paul means really saying it from the heart, believing it and rejoicing in it. No one can do that except by the Holy Spirit.

Or let John interpret this principle. In 1 John 4:1-3 we read: 'Beloved, believe not every spirit, but try the spirits whether they are of God: because many false prophets are gone out into the world. Hereby know ye the Spirit of God: Every spirit that confesseth that Jesus Christ is come in the flesh is of God: And every spirit that confesseth not that Jesus Christ is come in the flesh is not of God: and this is that spirit of antichrist, whereof ye have heard that it should come; and even now already is it in the world.' So as these people are uttering these prophecies, as we are told in 1 Corinthians 14:29, the others have to judge, they have to test the words. You do not accept a prophecy unquestioningly.

And, of course, you find the same thing in other epistles. In Galatians 1:8, for instance, Paul says, 'But though we, or an angel from heaven, preach any other gospel unto you than that which we have preached unto you, let him be accursed'! There were people going round claiming to be preachers of the gospel, but Paul says that the Christians were not to listen to them because it was a false gospel, another gospel, which was not a gospel. He was always exhorting people to judge and to evaluate and to test these things.

Indeed, John, again, reminds his readers, 'Ye have an unction from the Holy One, and ye know all things [*1 John* 2:20], and by 'all things,' he means, 'all these things'. Again, in verse 27, he says, 'But the anointing which ye have received of him abideth in you, and ye need not that any man teach you: but as the same anointing teacheth you of all things, and is truth, and is no lie, and even as it hath taught you, ye shall abide in him.' Now this is what is meant by Paul's injunction: Let us prophesy according to the proportion of the faith.

Everything must be tested, therefore, and we only accept it on condition that it fits into the pattern of truth that has already been given. In the days of the early church, before the New Testament canon had been formed, and before, indeed, any of these books had been written, this was how the first believers obeyed this command: they had heard the teaching – they would not have been members of the church but for that – they had subscribed to it and they knew what it was, and that, together with the unction and anointing of the Spirit who was in them and on them, enabled them to test what claimed to be a prophecy uttered under the inspiration of the Holy Spirit.

This is a very important matter at this present time, particularly in the light of two things. The first is the Ecumenical Movement and the statements that are made by leaders of churches in the name of Christ. We must test them. The second reason is a certain new interest in the gifts of the Spirit. This requires careful testing at all times. There were people in the early church, as we have seen from the quotations I have given you, who went astray in this respect because they had forgotten that the prophecy must always be 'according to the proportion of the faith'. They had forgotten about the importance of careful testing.

Paul's phrase in Romans 12:6 is the basis of what we call systematic theology, it is the great justification for it. Indeed, it calls us to have a systematic theology. Systematic theology is something like this: you read your Bible and see that it is full of doctrines, particular doctrines, from beginning to end. All the great doctrines of the faith are taught somewhere or other in the Scriptures. Now the student of systematic theology studies these doctrines in systematic order. You can start, as many do, with the doctrine of Scripture itself, or you can start, as I personally would always do, with the great doctrine of God Himself.

In the Scriptures we find the doctrine of the triune God, the doctrine of man, the doctrine of the fall, the great doctrine of redemption in all its parts and portions, including the doctrine of the church, and the Spirit in the believer, and sanctification. And, eventually, we end with glorification, and the final state of perfection when everything shall be complete. Now systematic theology sets all those doctrines out in order. So you can interpret Romans 12:6 in this way: anyone who is given the gift of prophecy must make quite sure that each prophecy is in accordance with the teaching of systematic theology.

You notice what I am saying? I have defined systematic theology as putting in order the doctrines that are to be found in the Scriptures. But sometimes theologians have not stopped at that. They have added their own speculations, or they have started using their own logic, and they have pressed things a little bit further than is warranted in Scripture. I am not defending that. That is always a danger and it is very difficult to safeguard yourself against that danger. Anyone who utters a prophecy in the church must be certain, says the apostle, that it in no way contravenes, that it in no way fails to fit into, this systematic statement of the truth – it is not so much the systematic statement, but the truth itself that must not be contradicted. That is what the apostle is emphasizing.

Now you can see what an important matter this is. It governs not only prophetic utterance, but also applies equally to exposition – what I am doing now – and to preaching. A man should always preach 'according to the proportion of faith', and he should always teach accordingly. There have been great troubles in the church, and sometimes even tragedies, because men have not always done this.

We should always compare Scripture with Scripture. That is where people who do not believe in theology tend to go astray. They come to a statement and they get out their lexicons and arrive at an interpretation in terms of particular meanings of words. But then later on, somewhere else in Scripture, the same statement appears and the context demands a different meaning to the one they have given. Anyone will see there is a contradiction. They should never allow that to happen. If only they had been careful in the first instance to check their interpretation or exposition by the whole statement of doctrine, they would never fall into that error. That is where people who rely overmuch on lexicons and upon concordances for the interpretation of Scripture, instead of on the systematic body of doctrine, invariably get into trouble. Their method may sound very biblical, but it is not.

In other words, what we should all be doing – and particularly those of us who are called to preach and teach – is this: we should read our Bibles right through, and as we read we will see the great body of doctrine laid out. So we get that into our minds, and then, when we come back to a particular verse, all that doctrine will help us to interpret it. A particular verse must never be interpreted in such a way that it does not fit in to the whole body of truth.

Now let me show you how important all this is at the present time. Any teaching which tends to speak a little disparagingly about doctrine or about theology or teaching is wrong. The apostle says that prophecy must be uttered 'according to the proportion of faith', and if you dismiss and deride the only standard by which you can apply that test, you are contradicting Paul's direct command.

The danger is that people say, 'Ah yes, men of intelligence can interpret the Scriptures and can read theology and doctrine and so on, and be learned in the Word of God, but here is direct inspiration and we are going to listen to this direct inspiration. We don't care what your doctrine says.' That was the whole trouble with the Quakers – it is exactly where they went astray. George Fox, the founder of Quakerism, very rightly saw the danger of a dry-as-dust theology, or a kind of intellectual belief of truth, which has no power or value for life. Furthermore, he was undoubtedly a man who was baptized with the Holy Spirit, and he himself kept the balance, more or less, while he was alive, though even Fox, at times, tended to say things which were a bit loose. But many of his followers fell into serious error. They went so far as to say that they did not care what the Bible said because they had been given a direct word. They put this 'inner light', this direct illumination, before the Scriptures; they put it against the

Scriptures and in a sense said that you do not need your Scriptures because you can get God's word directly.

And, of course, this teaching has reappeared in many forms. I remember once listening to a preacher who had dabbled a good deal in mysticism, and his great phrase to us was always, 'Get into yourself!' That was his way of expressing the Quaker 'inner light'. He was saying, 'Be still and begin to listen, and God will speak to you.' The 'inner light'; the direct illumination and inspiration.

So while I accept that the gift of prophecy is one of the gifts that may be given to anybody in the church at any time, we must not set this over against the Scriptures. The same Spirit who gives the prophecy gave the Scriptures, and He gave the Scriptures to the 'apostles and prophets' largely in order that we might be enabled to 'prove and to test the spirits'. If you deride Scripture and doctrine, you will have nothing with which to test the spirits, and there are evil spirits who can appear as 'angels of light' [2 *Cor.* 11:14], and delude, were it possible, even the very elect. So it is very wrong and dangerous to put prophecy over against Scripture. It is even worse to put it above the Scripture – nothing can be more dangerous.

Or let me put it in a second way. There are those who say that people may be given the gift of prophecy, and other gifts, and may be baptized with the Holy Spirit and given these gifts, without it making any difference to their doctrine. This is being said rather freely at the present time. We are told that bishops, even cardinals, I believe, in the Roman Catholic Church, have recently been baptized with the Spirit and are speaking in tongues and so on. But then, if you say, 'Does this mean, therefore, that they no longer believe in the assumption of Mary and the immaculate conception? Do they no longer believe in transubstantiation and all those other additions which are not scriptural at all and which, indeed, are contrary to Scripture? Do they therefore renounce these errors of Roman Catholicism?' The answer we are given is, 'Not at all; it does not make any difference. They may still hold these grievous errors. The great thing is that they are now speaking in tongues, or prophesying.'

This is where things become very dangerous. Surely when men and women are baptized with the Holy Spirit, they have an understanding of the truth and begin to apply it. Their prophecy will be 'according to the proportion of faith', and they will immediately have to face their whole doctrinal position. If you could tell me about Roman Catholic bishops and cardinals who, as the result of the baptism of the Spirit, have tried to reform the Roman Catholic Church and have consequently been turned out or have decided to leave, then I would whole-heartedly accept the genuineness of their experience. But what I cannot accept is that this can have happened to them and yet they still go on preaching and teaching the same old errors. No, to accept that is to discount doctrine, and the moment you do that, you cannot test whether your prophecy is according to the proportion of faith.

Let me give you a third deduction which we draw from this most important clause. It is that since the time of the apostles there has never been any new truth. 'The faith which was once and for ever delivered to the saints,' wrote Jude [verse 3]. The truth was given to the apostles and prophets. The church, says the apostle, 'is built upon the foundation of the apostles and prophets' [*Eph.* 2:20], and you cannot add to the foundation. You build upon the foundation, you do not add to it. In other words, we believe that the whole truth is here in the Scriptures. Here, therefore, is the only test we have, and the only standard whereby we judge anything that claims to be revelation or truth from God.

And, once more, this is where we convict the Roman Catholic Church. I am not here to preach against the Roman Catholic Church, I am only illustrating the point that the apostle is making. Here we see a Church that has added so much to the teaching of the New Testament. In the New Testament you never find the Roman Catholic doctrine on Mary. There is no suggestion here that she is a 'co-redemptrix'. Nor can you find the immaculate conception or transubstan-tiation. They are not here, and Catholics do not even say that they are. They say, 'No, this has been revealed to us since then.' So they are contravening this statement that truth has been delivered once and for ever to the saints.

My fourth deduction is that we must always be very careful, therefore, not to base our teaching and our preaching upon a prophetic utterance. Prophetic utterance is only of value as it directs attention to the faith that has already been given. It brings out some particular aspect or facet of the faith and emphasizes it, because it may be needed supremely at that present time; but prophetic utterance never lays down doctrine, and our doctrine must never be shaped or decided by a prophecy.

Let me give you one example. This was one of the issues that tended to cause a great deal of trouble in connection with the movement associated with a man called Edward Irving, round about 1830 and a few years following. He and his followers claimed that the gifts of the early church – speaking in tongues and, particularly, prophetic utterances – had been restored to them and this undoubtedly happened. But the teaching about the secret rapture of the saints came in for the first time in 1831, in that circle, and it came in directly as the result of a prophetic utterance.

The great S. P. Tregelles is my authority for this statement and I will quote his words to you. He says, 'I am not aware that there was any definite teaching that there should be a secret rapture of the church at a secret coming until this was given forth as an utterance in Mr Irving's church from what was then received as being the voice of the Spirit. But whether anyone ever asserted such a thing or not, it was from the supposed revelation that the modern doctrine and the modern phraseology respecting it arose.'

You see, here is a teaching that was quite new, and today most people are ready to agree that the doctrine of the secret rapture should be rejected. The prophecy was given in a conference held at a place called Powerscourt in 1830. Irving and his followers used to hold prophetic conferences and at those conferences Tregelles was often present, together with Benjamin Newton and J. N. Darby. They soon broke from one another, I know, but in 1830 there they were, and they heard this teaching for the first time and they all accepted it. Why? Because it was a prophetic utterance and they did not take the trouble to test it, 'according to the proportion of faith', as they should have done. So we should always be extremely careful that we do not teach doctrines simply because they have come to us in a prophetic utterance.

My fifth deduction is also most important today, especially

in the light of past history. Prophetic utterances must be tested with unusual care when they involve the actions of others, and when they involve the actions of the whole church. Now in a prophetic utterance a message is often given telling somebody else to do something, or sometimes telling the man speaking, or, indeed, the whole church to do something. There is great danger here. It has sometimes happened that a prophetic utterance has been received as an authentic word from God, and for that reason has been acted upon, with near tragic results.

I give you one illustration. Again at the time of Edward Irving, there was a very learned man, a barrister called Robert Baxter, who lived in Doncaster. He was taken up with this teaching, and claimed that he had been given revelations, generally, poor man, about himself. There was never a more honest man. He was very able and he sincerely desired God's best. But he really believed that the Spirit had told him to leave his wife and children and give up his career. Thank God, before he actually took this step, he came to see how wrong it was. Here, you see, was a prophetic utterance that blankly contradicted Scripture. Scripture does not tell a man to cut these natural ties. It tells us the exact opposite, in fact. But because it appeared to be a message from the Holy Spirit, Baxter was ready to act on it, as, indeed, he was on another occasion when he felt that he was called upon to go to a certain court one afternoon and make an utterance there. Again, he fortunately did not go, and later he came to see that he had been suffering from a delusion. But let me quote to you from an excellent modern book on the history of Pentecostalism in this country. It is by a well-known and able Pentecostal writer, Mr Donald Gee. In his book, he says: 'The enthusiasm of novelty that attends the first experience of such spiritual gifts as prophecy, tongues, or interpretation of tongues, tends to unbalance the believer's perspective for a time, especially if he is not well rooted and grounded in the Scriptures of truth beforehand. This proneness to undue emphasis upon messages has been a constant danger amongst newcomers into the Pentecostal revival, and, strangely enough, the highly educated fall as readily victims as the unlearned and ignorant. The thing can be innocent and simple enough, so long as the use of such spiritual gifts does not take on the directive character in private or church affairs. That is where trouble begins.'

Now there is a man writing from a long experience of the Pentecostal movement, and his words reinforce the warning that we get from the history of Irvingism.

Then, finally, let me put to you what I regard as a further most important point, something that we neglect only at our great peril. There is, surely, a principle to be discovered here in this whole matter of the exercise of the gifts, and it is a principle that seems to me to govern the exercise of any gift and of all the gifts. It is put here for us in this one phrase: '. . . prophecy, let us prophesy according to the proportion of faith.' This is a marvellous thing to consider. In these matters there is a blending of the supernatural and the natural, the divine and the human, and we get into trouble when we fail to realize that both are present, and both should always be present. There is God's part in this and there is our part, and that is where we see that we are dealing with something which the Scripture calls a mystery, or a marvel, something that the natural person does not understand at all. He probably thinks we are all mad in studying Scripture like this; he cannot follow it; he does not recognize anything outside his own comprehension. But we are in the realm of the spiritual.

What are the rules? Well, I suggest to you that the rules are these. The first thing that is emphasized here is that these things are always 'given'. My warrant for saying this is 1 Corinthians 14:30 where Paul is dealing with the prophets. In verse 29 he says, 'Let the prophets speak two or three, and let the other judge.' Now listen to this: 'If any thing be revealed to another that sitteth by, let the first hold his peace.' That is the principle: it is given. Here are the people in the church and someone is giving a prophetic utterance, but a message is now given to another who is 'sitting by'. So I deduce that a prophetic utterance is not self-initiated; it is not something that we can give whenever we want to.

This is supported by 1 Corinthians 14:18, which, it seems to me, is the only conceivable interpretation of this verse in Romans. In 1 Corinthians 14:18 the apostle says, 'I thank my God, I speak with tongues more than ye all,' and the word 'more', as the authorities point out, is an adverb and means 'more frequently'. So Paul is saying, 'I thank my God, I speak with tongues more frequently that ye all.' Now if speaking in tongues is something that people can do whenever they like, then I see no point whatsoever in that statement of the apostle because all he is saying is that he decides to speak in tongues more frequently than anybody else. But if he means that he finds himself taken up by the Spirit and speaking in tongues, if it is a kind of spiritual ecstasy into which he has been lifted – not something that he has decided to do, but something that has been given – then there is point in his claiming that he knows more about it, and does it more frequently than anybody else. And this applies to all the gifts, every one of them. It applies to miracles and healings and tongues and prophecy – they are always given, always initiated by the Spirit.

Is this not something that should be obvious to us? Look at it in the Book of Acts. The apostles had the gift of miracles; does that mean that an apostle could work a miracle whenever he liked? Obviously not. No, they were given a special commission. Peter and John, going up to the temple, see the man at the Beautiful Gate and they fix him with their eyes. There is a commission here. And you find exactly the same thing with the Apostle Paul at Lystra in Acts 14:9.

But have you ever noticed that not only in the case of miracles and healings and things like that is a gift 'given', but even in speech. This is most important and interesting. We must never forget this given element. Take, for instance, Acts 4:8. Peter and John are on trial before the Sanhedrin in Jerusalem, and the rulers say to them, 'By what power, or by what name, have ye done this?' Then we read: 'Peter, filled with the Holy Ghost, said unto them . . .' He had been filled with the Spirit on the day of Pentecost, but here he is filled again. What does it mean? Well, it means that he was given another special enduement. He did not do anything himself, it was done to him. He was filled with the Spirit in order that he might choose the right words. It was the Spirit who came upon him again in a special manner in order to enable him to do this particular task.

And, of course, you find the same thing further on in Acts 4: 'When they had prayed, the place was shaken where they were assembled together; and they were all filled with the Holy

Ghost, and they spake the word of God with boldness' [verse 31]. You also find the same thing in chapter 5:12-16: 'By the hands of the apostles were many signs and wonders wrought among the people.' There was an unusual profusion of miracles after the death of Ananias and Sapphira in order to impress this great truth upon the multitude of people, and, 'They brought forth the sick into the streets, and laid them on beds and couches, that at the least the shadow of Peter passing by might overshadow some of them.' And we are told, 'There came also a multitude out of the cities round about unto Jerusalem, bringing sick folks, and them which were vexed with unclean spirits: and they were healed every one.'

In Acts 19 also we read that 'God wrought special miracles by the hands of Paul' [verse 11]. 'Special'; 'unusual'. It is always given – a special occasion, a special enduement of power. *You* do not do these things; *you* do not just say, 'I'm going to work a miracle now,' or, 'I'm going to speak in tongues now,' or, 'I'm going to prophesy.' You cannot do it. They are all given and they are all controlled by the Spirit Himself.

Sometimes I think that one of the most wonderful statements on this subject, one which clinches this matter, is given by the Apostle John in the first chapter of the Book of Revelation, in verse 10. John is introducing his book and he puts it like this: 'I John, who also am your brother, and companion in tribulation, and in the kingdom and patience of Jesus Christ, was in the isle that is called Patmos, for the word of God, and for the testimony of Jesus Christ' [verse 9]. Then in verse 10: 'I was in the Spirit on the Lord's day, and heard behind me a great voice, as of a trumpet.' What does he mean by saying, 'I was in the Spirit on the Lord's day'? Was he not always in the Spirit? Was he not a man who had been baptized with the Holy Spirit on the day of Pentecost and filled again many times over, as the Book of Acts tells us?

Now the Authorized Version is not quite accurate here. A better translation is this: 'I became in the Spirit on the Lord's day.' The Spirit was always in John but he 'became in the Spirit'; which means that he was taken up into the Spirit. He was given a special experience by the Spirit. He was lifted up into this realm, and there he began to see things. And that, I suggest to you, is the great controlling principle with all these gifts; this propensity is given to certain people, one gift to one, a different gift to another.

Yes, but you cannot use a gift whenever you like! That is where I am in trouble with so much I am hearing at the present time; that is where I feel that delusion tends to come in, leave alone something worse. When a man tells me, 'I can do this whenever I like,' I feel that, as I understand the words, 'the proportion of faith', there is something wrong in what he is telling me, for here this given element must always be stressed. There is the first principle.

The second I just mention. Though the use of a gift cannot be initiated, it can be stopped. It can be controlled. In 1 Corinthians 14:27 we read that the people are told to speak in tongues, 'by two, or at the most by three, and that by course', and only two or three in one meeting are to use the gift of prophetic utterance [verse 29]. The apostle makes this quite plain. Now if you can lay down that only two or three are to speak in tongues or prophesy, and many are stimulated or are feeling the impulse, it is obvious that they are in control. Moreover, Paul says, 'If anything be revealed to another that sitteth by, let the first hold his peace' [verse 30]. This other man sitting by indicates that he has received a message, so the first, seeing that, sits down and the second man gets up.

Then there are other statements which are still more specific. In 1 Corinthians 14:32, we read: 'And the spirits of the prophets are subject to the prophets'; and in verse 33: 'For God is not the author of confusion, but of peace, as in all churches of the saints.' Where there is confusion and disorder it is not the Holy Spirit, except in the most exceptional circumstances, and even then the confusion is caused by the weakness of the flesh. There should be no confusion. Indeed, the chapter ends with Paul's exhortation, 'Wherefore, brethren, covet to prophesy, and forbid not to speak with tongues. Let all things be done decently and in order.'

In other words, though the gifts are given, though they are the activity of the Spirit in power, there is no loss of self-control. This is the mystery; this is the paradox of it all. That is the difference between this and hysteria where there is loss of control. And when there is loss of control, and people cannot obey these clear and distinct injunctions, it is not 'according to the proportion of faith'. This, then, is the marvel which confronts us. We cannot start it, but we can control it. We see the divine and the human; the supernatural and the natural. God has so ordered these things that there is perfect harmony. God is never the author of confusion. He is always the author of peace.

Nineteen

*

Having then gifts differing according to the grace that is given to us, whether prophecy, let us prophesy according to the proportion of faith; or ministry, let us wait on our ministering: or he that teacheth, on teaching; or he that exhorteth, on exhortation: he that giveth, let him do it with simplicity; he that ruleth, with diligence; he that sheweth mercy, with cheerfulness.

Romans 12:6–8

We are dealing here, let me remind you, with the apostle's application of the teaching that he has been laying down with regard to the exercise of the gifts given to us, as members of the body of Christ, by the Holy Spirit. Paul has laid down the principles as to how the gifts should be used, and now he takes up some practical examples in order to make his teaching abundantly clear. We have been dealing with the first illustration, that of prophecy, and we have seen that he lays down certain very important principles concerning the use of gifts in general.

Now the apostle does not say that he has given a complete list of all the gifts. If you look at 1 Corinthians 12, you will find that other gifts are mentioned there. In Romans 12, the apostle is not setting out to deal with the doctrine of the gifts but rather with just this one special aspect, namely, how they should be used. And he is especially concerned to show us that they must not be abused and so bring trouble into the life of the church. That is why he puts it all under the heading of the doctrine of the church as the body of Christ.

So we must go on reminding ourselves of Paul's purpose here, particularly, perhaps, as we come to a series of illustrations which he puts before us in a kind of staccato manner. His point is the importance of our using the particular gift that has been given to us and concentrating on that and keeping to that. That is the great principle but it is almost obscured by the words that have been added by the Authorized translators at this point. Very often these translators added words to the original simply in order to make it easier for us to understand the teaching, and in the vast majority of cases this is a great help. In many Bibles, these additional words are generally put in italics in order that we may know that they are the additions of the translators and not a translation of the original. A Bible which does not do this is a poor version in that respect. But here the Authorized translators really have almost made it more difficult for us to understand Paul's meaning. At the beginning of verse 7 they have added the words 'let us wait' and 'our'. Then in verse 8 the words 'let him do it' are not in the original. It would be better if these words had not been added because the staccato style of the original helps, I think, to bring out the meaning.

Now at this point I think the Revised Standard Version is a good translation. This reads like this: 'If service, in our serving; he who teaches, in his teaching; he who exhorts, in his exhortation; he who contributes, in liberality' – and so on. Even there the translators have added just a little; the original is still more staccato.

So why do I think that this helps? Well, in this way – that what the apostle is saying is this: If this is your gift, do it. If it is prophecy, prophesy according to the proportion of faith; ministry, on ministering; teaching, on teaching; exhortation, on exhortation. Whatever the gift that has been given to you, exercise that gift; let that be your concern; let that be your desire, and never desire to go outside it.

It is the business of each person to use his or her gift and to exercise it to the full and to the glory of God, and to the benefit of the church. That is what Paul is saying – that is the whole object of this passage. Whatever your gift may be, concentrate on that. Do not cast coveting eyes, or critical eyes, on the other person's gift, and do not persuade yourself that you are gifted to do something else. Let us all function according to the gift we have been given, according to the particular member of the body that we happen to be.

The apostle brings that out in his very form of words, but also by showing us the variety of the gifts. Sometimes the shade of difference between the gifts is rather a fine one. But there are these shades of difference, and his point is that it does not matter how fine the difference, you must keep to the gift you have been given. It may be very similar to another, but do not imagine that because you have this, you can do the other also. We see clearly from experience, and still more clearly from the history of the church, that great trouble has often been caused in the church because people have not been careful to observe this teaching. They must remember that it is the Spirit who dispenses the gifts; it is God that 'hath dealt to every man the measure of faith'.

That, then, is the big principle, the point that Paul is anxious to bring out through the medium of his illustrations. He has said it already, but the illustrations help to drive it home. He has dealt with prophecy; now he goes on to 'ministry': 'or ministry, on ministering'. This is a very interesting term. There are those who feel that Paul has put this here in order to talk about ministry in general, any form of ministry. But there is no point in saying that because he is simply giving us illustrations. Here, ministry has the more confined meaning of 'service', or 'ordinary management'.

A term is used in the list of 1 Corinthians 12 which helps us at this point. Verse 28 reads like this: 'And God hath set some in the church, first apostles, secondarily prophets, thirdly teachers, after that miracles, then gifts of healings, helps . . .' Now I think that the word 'helps' stands for the same thing as the gift of ministry which Paul is dealing with here. It means the general business of the church; not the particular functions of the preacher and the teacher and so on, but taking part in the general administrative work of the church of God.

A little help is given us in 2 Timothy 4:11 in the words that Paul uses with regard to Mark – John Mark, at times one of his travelling companions. Paul says, 'Only Luke is with me. Take Mark, and bring him with thee: for he is profitable to me for the ministry.' In other words, Mark was very helpful to him. There is, inevitably, a certain amount of business in connection with the life and functioning of the Christian church. For example, we have a church building, and we have it in order that people may come and listen to the gospel. Now a building does not look after itself, it has to be looked after in various ways. There are also other essential matters of organization and of business which have to be transacted in connection with the functioning of the life of any church.

In the early church, that need arose at once, as you can see when you read Acts. A problem occurred over certain widows and others who had become members of the church. They were in financial and other difficulties so something had to be done to help them; and when the members of the church in Jerusalem pooled all their possessions and money, there was a fund that had to be handled. Now somebody had to do that. We are told in Acts 6:4 that the apostles felt that they could not undertake this because they had to give themselves to prayer and the preaching of the word. So they said that somebody else must be appointed. That is the kind of thing to which I am referring.

Obviously, the business side of the church should be kept down to a minimum; the less that is done the better. And, of course, there are people who do the exact opposite, and that has been a curse, especially in the twentieth century. There are people who are never happy unless they are thinking of a new committee or some sub-committee or some additional organization. Now that is remote from the Bible, but there is an essential minimum that cannot be avoided. And some people are given a gift by the Spirit to do this work. It is a gift that shows itself in many ways: in business tact, for example, and in administrative ability. It is a very special gift and in Paul's list it comes immediately after the gift of prophecy. Here, at once, the apostle is making an important point. People tend to look at the gift of prophecy and think it is wonderful and they tend to despise other gifts. But here, immediately after prophesy, comes ministering.

Again, how often in the history of the church we have seen the importance of this gift. A man may be a very good, even a great, preacher but he may be a thoroughly bad businessman. He may, indeed, be a man who has to be looked after, even in his own preaching work. There have been many such men. So it is so foolish to compare and to contrast these gifts in order to say that some are of less importance. We must realize that they are all gifts which are given by the Spirit to different persons.

Included under this heading of 'ministry' are the general duties carried out by deacons. Now here I do not think the apostle was thinking in terms of the order, the office, of deacons – I hope to deal with that later, God willing. Here he is dealing with the gift, the ability; not so much the setting of a man apart, as recognizing the people who are endowed with this gift. Paul is saying: 'If you have been given the gift of being able to handle these practical, external matters in connection with the life of the church, then exercise that gift for all you are worth.' That is why the translators put in the words, 'Let us wait on our ministering'. That is your gift, so exercise it. Do not think that you are a teacher or a preacher or any one of these other things but use the gift you have been given. Give thanks to God that you are in the church, and that you have been given such a gift, and realize that it is as essential to the harmonious working of the body of Christ as is any other gift. Use this gift to the glory of God.

I do not want to stay with this, but I have often taken occasion to tell men who act as sidesmen or ushers in this church how grateful I am to them, and not only sidesmen but all others who help in ministering. It is a great thing for a preacher and a pastor to feel that he is free to concentrate on the work that he has been especially called to do, and that he is relieved from troubles and worries and anxieties. I have often told the sidesmen, for instance, how important they are. They are the first people whom visitors to the church meet. So if they do not do their ministering as they should, then an impression may be made upon visitors which will render it very difficult for the message of the preacher to get through to them. That is the sort of thing that Paul is talking about. The Holy Spirit enables men to act as sidesmen in a manner that is conducive to the harmonious working of the whole life of the church, the spread of the gospel, and the extension of the kingdom of God.

The next gift is teaching: 'he that teacheth, on teaching'. In the original it is more or less this: 'Teaching; teaching', that is, 'If this is your gift, do it, and do not try to be doing something else.' So now, teaching. This is an important matter. You notice that here, as everywhere else in the New Testament, teaching is differentiated from prophecy, and it is also differentiated, as we shall see, from exhortation. Now it is important that we should notice these things. Later, I will try to show the significance, but for now, let me give you some examples of how these gifts are always put separately. Take Acts 13:1: 'Now there were in the church at Antioch certain prophets and teachers.' There is a difference between these two, between the gift of prophecy and the gift of teaching. Or in 1 Corinthians 12:28: 'God hath set some in the church, first apostles, secondarily prophets, thirdly teachers.'

We find exactly the same in Ephesians 4:11: 'And he gave some, apostles; and some, prophets; and some, evangelists; and some, pastors and teachers.' Do not worry about the other terms at the moment, but just notice that Paul always differentiates like that between the gift of prophecy and the gift of teaching. And here Paul is saying: If you have the gift of prophecy, concentrate on that; if you have the gift of teaching, concentrate on that. Do not try to concentrate on prophecy, but on the gift that you have been given.

So what is the difference? Well, I think it comes out in what we said in the last lecture about prophecy. Prophecy always has the element of direct and immediate inspiration. The verse that we dealt with in 1 Corinthians 14 brings that out very clearly: 'If any thing be revealed to another that sitteth by . . .' [verse 30]. Prophecy is unpremeditated, unprepared; the revelation is given. But that is not the case with teaching. Teaching is quite different; it is something that results from preparation.

Take, for instance, the apostle's words to Timothy in 2 Timothy 2:2. 'And the things that thou hast heard of me among many witnesses, the same commit thou to faithful men, who shall be able to teach others also.' This is the characteristic of the teacher. Teachers do not teach as the result of a direct inspiration but as the result of having been taught, of having been given the knowledge and the information which they now pass on to others.

I can elaborate that and take it a step further. The teacher, far from being someone who receives the direct inspiration and message, is not only able to teach because of having been taught by others, but is exhorted to study and read. Take 1 Timothy 4:14–16: 'Neglect not the gift that is in thee, which was given thee by prophecy, with the laying on of the hands of the presbytery. Meditate upon these things; give thyself wholly to them; that thy profiting may appear to all. Take heed unto thyself, and unto the doctrine; continue in them: for in doing this thou shalt both save thyself, and them that hear thee.'

There, you see, Timothy is being exhorted to 'study' and to prepare himself, as best he can, for this great task of teaching. And a teacher who does not study and read and think and meditate and ponder and arrange is failing completely to carry out the injunction of this seventh verse of Romans 12. There is another statement of the same thing in 2 Timothy 2:15: 'Study to shew thyself approved unto God, a workman that needeth not to be ashamed, rightly dividing the word of truth.'

So the teacher is obviously in an entirely different category from someone who has the gift of prophecy. Those who are given the gift of teaching have the ability not only to read but also to understand and to assimilate what is read. But still more important, the teacher has the gift of imparting to others what has thus been gained – that is the essence of the gift of the teacher. Now this is a very important distinction. We have all probably known men who are great readers and can be described as great scholars, but sometimes they are hopeless teachers. They know it all, they have read it all, they have wonderful memories, but they simply cannot impart their knowledge.

I once had to sit and listen to a lecturer who was an outstanding authority in his field. He was the late Sir Bernard Spilsbury, who for many years had been the Home Office expert called upon in connection with crime. No man knew medical legal matters with such great thoroughness as Sir Bernard Spilsbury. But I think all who ever heard him lecture would agree with me when I say that he was probably the world's worst lecturer. He had a vast knowledge, not only of medical legal matters, but on pathology in general. But he was a bad teacher because he gave out this vast knowledge without any light or shade, without any variation in his emphasis. Important things were uttered in exactly the same way as the comparatively unimportant ones, vital matters and mere details came out in a monotone.

Now that was thoroughly bad teaching. The man was an expert at his own particular work, but he could not help any of us to become similar experts. You must have encountered similar people, in the church, and in other places. They may be able to write well but they cannot communicate their knowledge in spoken words. They can instruct you through their books, but they cannot teach you through lecturing or through speech.

Now, as I said, the gift we are talking about is this particular gift of being able to transmit what you know to others, but not as an evangelist. The teacher's task is to build up believers and establish them in the faith. Teaching is a very real gift, and the apostle is saying: If you have been given the gift of teaching, then act as a teacher; keep yourself to that. That is the gift you have been given; so use it.

The next gift is the gift of exhortation. 'Or if your gift is exhortation,' says Paul, 'then concentrate on that: He that exhorteth, on exhortation.' Now exhortation is obviously different from prophecy and from teaching. Are you not fascinated by these wonderful distinctions of meaning? You know, apart from the glory of the truth that we are considering, from the mere standpoint of the exercise of the intellect, there is nothing in the world that is comparable to Scripture.

What is the difference between teaching and exhortation? I do not think there is much difficulty about this. Teaching appeals primarily to the mind. It is meant to communicate knowledge, and if it does not, it is failing. But exhortation deals more with the heart and with the will. That is the essential difference between the two. In a sense, the exhortation comes after the teaching. You first give the knowledge; you present the truth. Then exhortation is that which drives it home. I am one of those who believe that every sermon should end in exhortation or application. When you exhort you encourage, rebuke, rouse, stimulate, call for application, call to prayer – almost anything. Exhortation is concerned with taking the truth that has been taught and applying it to the Christian life in its various aspects.

Now this, again, is a special gift. I emphasize the fineness of the distinction because men have got into great trouble when they have not been able to differentiate between teaching and exhortation. A notable example comes to my mind. There was a famous preacher in Scotland called James Fraser of Brea who was a very learned man and a very good teacher, a man who built up his people in their most holy faith. A minister in a neighbouring parish, who was not a teacher, had the gift of exhortation, and this caused great trouble to Fraser because the man, who did not compare with Fraser from the standpoint of ability and of understanding, appeared, on the surface, to be a more successful minister.

What do I mean by this? Well, this man would get results from his preaching. The fact was that people came and talked to him about their souls. In those days there were no appeals to people to come forward at the end of a service, but anyone under conviction would go to the minister, and this happened very frequently in the other man's ministry. And what was so tantalizing and troubling to poor, good Fraser of Brea was that his own people, to whom he had preached for years and who admired him greatly, would go to this other church for some reason or another, perhaps on a Sunday night, and would come back having had a true experience of conversion. He was upset, I think, simply because he was not careful to draw the distinction between teaching and exhortation. This is where there is difficulty, at times, on both sides, and the world, of course, and the church, tend to aggravate it.

Thomas Shepard, a seventeenth-century Puritan in New England, was a very similar type to Fraser of Brea. On one occasion, when he was ill and could not preach, he had to spend his time in bed, but his wife went to hear the minister from some neighbouring church who was taking his place. So there was poor Thomas Shepard in the depth of depression, and, as Alexander Whyte puts it in his lecture on Thomas Shepard, the foolish woman went home and simply sang the praises of this voluble preacher. He had no depth and no teaching ability but he had an element of entertainment in his ministry, and as she went on, glorying in this man and the wonderful time they had had, she was driving her poor depressed husband into still further depths of depression and a feeling of utter hopelessness as a minister of God.

But it was all due to the failure to draw this distinction. We must keep this in our minds, and also remember that none of the gifts are self-generated. So if a man is given the gift of teaching, then let him exercise that. The other man has the gift of exhortation and it may appear on the surface, to him and to others, to be more spectacular and more useful, but it is not; he has received the gift in exactly the same way. And very often it is the case, of course, that the exhorters could do nothing at all were it not that they had been preceded by teachers. Exhorters often just skim the cream from the surface; the milk has been placed there by the faithful teachers. These other men come along and cream off the surface, for which they get great publicity and praise. All right, there should be no comparisons here. Their heads should not be turned; the others should not be depressed; both gifts are given by God.

I sometimes think that perhaps the greatest example of someone with the gift of exhortation that I have ever encountered in my reading was a man called Howell Harris. Generally speaking, Harris did not have a prepared sermon. He did not take a text and analyse it and then present its teaching and apply it. When he spoke, he addressed the conscience directly. Of course, there was an element of teaching in his sermons but essentially he was an exhorter who spoke to the heart and the will, and did so with tremendous effect. At first that was almost all he did, but as he went on, he saw the need of more study and more doctrine.

Another interesting thing is that the early Methodist Fathers – especially the Calvinistic Methodist Fathers in Wales and those who belonged to them in England, Whitefield and others, and later the Countess of Huntingdon – appointed men who were called 'exhorters' to function in the societies that came into being as the result of that great revival. They were called 'exhorters' because it was felt that they had not got the gift of teaching but they could exhort. Now it is very important for us to remember that this is a special gift. Here were men who were not equipped from the standpoint of the mind, nor did they have the ability to read and to grasp truth and to report it to others, but they exercised a very profound ministry in speaking directly to the conscience and to the heart and to the will, and they were greatly used of God.

So the apostle is saying here that if your gift is that of exhortation, then remember that it is that. Do not imagine that the gift of exhortation makes you a teacher. As we have seen, much unhappiness has been caused because men do not realize this. Sometimes evangelists try to teach, and it is rather pathetic to observe the results. I once knew a man in the ministry, who, in my opinion, should never have been called as a minister. He was obviously an exhorter, and a remarkable one, but he became a minister of a church, though he could not teach nor do other things that a teacher and preacher should do.

I also knew another man who, as a young man during the 1904-5 revival in Wales, became an outstanding leader among the young people in a whole area. He had a wonderful gift of exhortation which he had received in the baptism of the Holy Spirit that came in that revival. (This is what a revival means; it is a baptism with the Spirit, an outpouring of the Spirit.) But the tragedy was that because he had this gift, he thought, and so did everybody else, that he should 'enter the ministry', as the term goes, and become a preacher and a pastor. So he went to college and came out absolutely dead with regard to any usefulness in the church. And he remained dead because he was trying to do something that he had not been gifted to do. He ceased to act as an exhorter – that, of course, he would now regard with disdain – and had tried to become a teacher and a preacher. But he could do neither. So by failing to draw this vital distinction, not only do the men themselves go wrong, but the whole church. It pushes exhorters into the full work of the ministry, which they are not capable of exercising because they have not been given the gift.

Paul's next gift is this: 'He that giveth, let him do it with simplicity.' The original is, 'He that giveth, with simplicity.' What does this 'giving' mean? I do not think it means the official distribution of a benevolent fund belonging to the church. I believe this is something personal. It refers to men and women who happen to be in a position in which they can give to others and can help others who are in need. They can give from their superabundance. And again, the apostle says to them that this is a gift. There are people who have money but they do not have the gift of giving. It is a special gift as much as

[265]

all these other gifts, and the apostle tells the people with this gift to concentrate on that. This is a most important point. Do we realize that giving is a gift given by the Spirit?

Furthermore, the apostle says that the giving must be done 'with simplicity'. The best commentary on this is the words of our Lord Himself in the middle of the Sermon on the Mount: 'Take heed that ye do not your alms before men, to be seen of them: otherwise ye have no reward of your Father which is in heaven. Therefore when thou doest thine alms, do not sound a trumpet before thee, as the hypocrites do in the synagogues and in the streets, that they may have glory of men. Verily I say unto you, They have their reward. But when thou doest alms, let not thy left hand know what thy right hand doeth: that thine alms may be in secret: and thy Father which seeth in secret himself shall reward thee openly' [*Matt.* 6:1–4]. 'He that giveth, with simplicity.' Do not appoint a trumpeter; 'Let not thy left hand know what thy right hand doeth'.

Oh, what a subtle thing this is! 'Simplicity' means single-ness of eye, purity of motive. Do not give to enhance yourself in any shape or form. Give for the glory of the Lord, for the benefit of the church and your fellow members. Illustrations come to my mind. I have known certain men in the ministry who have attracted great publicity to themselves over this matter of giving. I remember very well a small town where there were two ministers, one a Presbyterian, and one a Baptist. The Presbyterian minister was a very gifted man, a spectacular kind of person, almost eccentric, who attracted attention to everything that he did; and his supporters and others were always praising him. On one occasion, there was a great story that went round of how this man was riding one day on his bicycle and passed a poor tramp who was in rags. He got off his bicycle immediately and gave this poor tramp his overcoat, and went on riding. This was the Presbyterian.

But I remember the comment of certain wise people in that neighbourhood. They said, 'Yes, everything he does always becomes well-known. But,' they added, 'that poor old man, the Baptist minister, has not only given his overcoat, but his coat and vest and trousers many times over and nobody ever knows he has done it.' 'Let it be done with simplicity.' You may say,

'Of course, the first man had not made it known himself.' But the question one often wants to ask of this kind of person is, 'How has it become known?'

I remember once reading in a paper a paragraph about a well-known minister here in London. The paragraph said that an extraordinary rumour had gone round that he had taken to drink. Actually, he had not taken to drink, but in his large and great heart he had heard that the wife of a publican living in a public house not far away from his home was not well, and with great graciousness and charity he was just turning in every day to ask how she was. But how did it get into the newspaper? Is not this issue subtle? Why should these generous acts always be known in certain instances but never heard of in others which may be still more notable? Oh, how subtle the devil is! And how subtle we are! The apostle says: If the gift you have been given is the gift of giving, do it with simplicity. 'Let not thy left hand know what thy right hand doeth.' Do not worry about the publicity; keep your eye on God and on His glory.

And then, '. . . he that ruleth'. Here is something that is again very helpfully illustrated for us in 1 Corinthians 12 where the apostle says, 'God hath set some in the church, first apostles, secondarily prophets, thirdly teachers, after that miracles, then gifts of healings, helps, *governments*' [verse 28]. This means exercising rule or presiding in any shape or form in the church. This is the task of taking care of the brethren and it has now been allotted to elders in particular.

The apostle is not dealing with this in terms of an office, I think that comes later, but he is concerned here only with the gift. In 1 Timothy 3, on the subject of offices in the church, Paul refers to this office like this: 'If a man know not how to rule his own house, how shall he take care of the church of God?' That is it. That is ruling; that is government. You find it again in a well-known statement in Hebrews 13:7: 'Remember them which have the rule over you, who have spoken unto you the word of God: whose faith follow, considering the end of their conversation.' The writer is again dealing with this as a general gift, as also in 1 Timothy 5:17: 'Let the elders that rule well be counted worthy of double honour, especially they who labour in word and doctrine.' There were elders, there were

[267]

governors, there were rulers, who ruled but were not able to 'labour in the word and doctrine.'

Now that is what Paul means here by ruling. Some people were able to exercise government in the church, but they had not been given the gift of teaching and of preaching. We see this also in 1 Thessalonians 5:12–13: 'And we beseech you, brethren, to know them which labour among you, and are over you in the Lord, and admonish you; and to esteem them very highly in love for their work's sake. And be at peace among yourselves.' And, again, in Acts 20:28 we are told the same thing about the elders of the church at Ephesus. These elders watch over the church, they watch over the interests, spiritual and external, of the members of the church, and Paul says to them, 'If you have had the gift of ruling, do it with diligence; do it with earnestness; do it with zeal.' You must put your back into this work and you must continue at it, realizing that this is your gift, and you must keep yourself to it.

Peter puts this very well in 1 Peter 5:2–4. He is addressing the elders and says he is an elder himself: 'Feed the flock of God which is among you, taking the oversight thereof, not by constraint, but willingly; not for filthy lucre, but of a ready mind; neither as being lords over God's heritage, but being ensamples to the flock. And when the chief Shepherd shall appear, ye shall receive a crown of glory that fadeth not away.' That is it: 'He that ruleth, with diligence'.

And, lastly, 'he that showeth mercy'. Showing mercy means attending to the suffering and to the distressed, and this, too, is a special gift. It is the gift of being able to minister to, and to help, those who are in trouble, who are ill or suffering in other ways. It seems to me that Phoebe, referred to in Romans 16:1, is an illustration of someone who showed mercy. It is clear that women exercised this particular gift. You find it again in 1 Timothy 5:10. Paul is dealing there with widows and says a widow must be, 'Well reported of for good works; if she have brought up children, if she have lodged strangers, if she have washed the saints' feet, if she have relieved the afflicted, if she have diligently followed every good work.' All that is included in the gift of showing mercy.

And Paul says here in Romans 12 that if this is our gift, then, 'do it with cheerfulness'.

Is that, again, not interesting? Does it strike you at first as being rather strange? What does Paul mean? The commentators all point out that the word 'cheerfulness' is a translation of a Greek word from which we get our word 'hilarity' – 'do it with hilarity'. But I do not think that is a good translation. Paul means 'cheerfully'. Do not show mercy in a legalistic manner. What a terrible thing it is to see people doing a work of charity, a work of mercy, in a mechanical manner. That is the way to tell the difference between nurse and nurse, and doctor and doctor, is it not? Some may do their work quite properly but the way in which it is done makes such a difference. A cheerful doctor, a cheerful nurse, have a right manner; they are not, as it were, proud of themselves. How hopeless it is if they do their work merely mechanically or as a matter of duty. It is said about doctors, is it not, that sometimes the man himself does much more good than his medicine. And it is quite true! We are not machines, we are not animals, and this cheerfulness of disposition, this happy frame of mind helps us; it cheers us; it lessens pain; it makes us feel better.

The apostle is saying that if you have been given the gift of showing mercy, then let yourself go, as it were, as you exercise it. Do it with a whole heart, brightly, happily. Do not say, 'I would like to be a teacher, but I've only been allotted this task.' If you show mercy in the right way, you may do much more good than many sermons. The history of the church is full of examples and illustrations of that.

So we have gone through the list, and the point the apostle makes right through is this: Whatever your gift may be, exercise it with all your might. This is your gift. It is wonderful; it is valuable; it is essential. Do not be looking at others in any shape or form, look only to the Lord; look to the benefit of all the members together of the one body of which you also are a part.

Twenty

*

> *Having then gifts differing according to the grace that is given to us, whether prophecy, let us prophesy according to the proportion of faith; or ministry, let us wait on our ministering: or he that teacheth, on teaching; or he that exhorteth, on exhortation: he that giveth, let him do it with simplicity; he that ruleth, with diligence; he that sheweth mercy, with cheerfulness.*
>
> Romans 12:6–8

We have looked at the list that the apostle puts here of the gifts that are given to the members of the Christian church. We have looked at them one by one and have underlined and emphasized the main teaching concerning them as we find it in the New Testament.

We must confine ourselves to the particular emphases that the apostle presses upon us here, but we may indulge ourselves, perhaps, to the extent that we may explain that there are other gifts in addition to these. So when you read Romans 12 it is good also to consult 1 Corinthians 12, in order that you may have a fuller understanding of this matter. Indeed, we can go so far as to say that the list in 1 Corinthians 12 is not complete either; for there are varying gifts, and I feel constrained to mention one.

The background in which I, personally, was brought up, was one in which the expression 'the gift of prayer' was often used, and I am quite sure that it is an accurate term. Throughout the years, I have noticed and have been very impressed by the fact that certain men are given this particular gift of prayer – I am referring, of course, to public prayer – and I would not hesitate to say that it is a distinct and separate gift. I mention this in order to try to show yet more clearly the wonderful character of the church, particularly from the standpoint of the gifts that are 'dealt', as Paul puts it in the third verse here, or as they are dispensed by the Holy Spirit.

Let me give you one illustration of what I mean. I remember very well something that happened many years ago in a church to which I had been invited for a centenary celebration. The day before, I had preached twice somewhere else, then had travelled, and had arrived at this church and had preached in the morning. In the afternoon I had listened to a number of people giving a historical account of the church, after which I joined large numbers of visiting preachers and others for tea. The result was that I began to feel very tired, but I still had to preach in the evening, and I remember asking to be excused, and I went and slept. However, when I woke up, I found that everybody had gone out of the house into the evening service and I was alone, and so I rushed to the chapel.

Now this is what I want to tell you – I remember entering the chapel and walking forward. I could see in the pulpit a man whom I had never seen before and about whom I knew nothing The congregation were finishing the first hymn, so I sat down and began to listen to this man reading the Scriptures, for which he had an unusual gift. After the second hymn, he began to pray and it was something I shall never forget as long as I live. I have described how tired I was; I have no doubt but that I was on the verge of exhaustion – there is a difference between tiredness and exhaustion, and this was exhaustion. But I remember distinctly how, after this man had been praying for a very short time, I was completely revived. I do not think I have ever heard a man pray in public as that man prayed that evening. It is very difficult to describe these things, but it was true prayer in the Spirit, and as he was praying, I was physically restored and revived and was able to enter that pulpit full of vigour, perhaps more than I had ever known in my life before, and it was entirely due to this man's prayer.

I remember commenting about it afterwards to the minister with whom I was staying that night. 'Oh yes,' he said, 'haven't you heard him before?'

I said, 'No, I've never even seen him before.'

And the minister told me a story of how, about twelve years

before, a great Association had been held in that selfsame place. The last day had been taken up by preaching services in the morning, afternoon and evening with two preachers at each session. All the best preachers in that denomination in Wales had been invited to preach there on this great occasion. 'But,' said the minister to me, 'you know, when it was all over, and for many, many months afterwards, what the people were talking about was not the preaching of the great preachers, but the prayer offered by the same man who offered prayer at tonight's service.'

That is what I mean by a gift of prayer. The man was a minister, but he was not, apparently, a very good preacher; his gift was this astonishing gift of prayer. I know without any doubt that it is very real – but do not ask me to define it. I have known many people like that man. I knew people who, it seemed to me, received this gift of prayer in the Welsh Revival of 1904 to 1905. In their baptism of the Spirit they were given this gift, and though many of them afterwards became very ordinary Christians, if they took part in a public prayer meeting they were transformed, and it was amazing to listen to them praying. I often found it difficult to reconcile such prayers with such people, and can only say that it must have been due to this particular gift of prayer, or gift in prayer. I have no doubt whatsoever that it is something which is definite and distinct.

We must be careful not to put a limit to the gifts that the Spirit may choose in His sovereign will and power to give to any of us. Remember, again, that in 1 Corinthians 12 the apostle is primarily concerned not to write a disquisition on gifts but to control excesses and to deal with the doctrine in terms of the great truth of the church as the body of Christ, and the unity of the body.

Let me also underline something which I have said, I think, more than once, but I understand that some people still have not quite grasped it. I am not saying, and the Scriptures do not teach, that it is a case of 'one person one gift'. One man or woman may have several gifts. I think I indicated that it is clear that the Apostle Paul had several of these gifts; that should be expected, and it is still possible.

Having dealt with that, let us now turn to a subject I was

hinting at in the last lecture. There are two or three questions that we must consider in the light of this particular teaching that is before us. The first – and people are very concerned about this – is: 'How are these gifts given to us?' Or, to put it the other way round: 'How do we receive any of these gifts?'

This is an interesting and important matter and in some ways a rather difficult one. Do these gifts come to us directly, immediately, or do they come to us indirectly, mediated through somebody else, and by the laying on of hands? You cannot evade that question because it is raised in the New Testament itself, and in the subsequent history of the church it became a matter of interest many times and is certainly of interest to a large number of people at the present time. So what is the answer? As I have said, it is a difficult question, and it seems to me that the only answer we can give is that the same is true of the receiving of the gifts as is true of the receiving of the Holy Spirit Himself in the baptism of the Spirit.

Now the Book of Acts teaches us quite plainly that the baptism of the Spirit may take place in both ways. The Holy Spirit came upon the apostles and the others in the upper room on the day of Pentecost directly, immediately; nobody had laid hands on them. The Holy Spirit fell upon them as they were there together in that room praying. And the same thing happened in the case of Cornelius [*Acts* 10:44].While Peter was still speaking, the Holy Spirit fell upon Cornelius and his household.

But when Peter and John went down to Samaria after the preaching of Philip, they laid their hands upon the believers who then received the Holy Spirit [*Acts* 8:17]. In the case of the Apostle Paul himself, Ananias first laid his hands on him [*Acts* 9:17]. And in Ephesus, the people who had been baptized with John's baptism only were baptized with the Holy Spirit after they had been baptized in the name of the Lord Jesus and after the apostle had laid his hands upon them [*Acts* 19:3–6].

Since the baptism of the Spirit occurred both directly, and through the laying on of hands, I would argue that the same is undoubtedly true with regard to the gifts also. It is clear in the Book of Acts that this gift of laying on of hands was a gift that was possessed by the apostles, but it was not confined to them because it was through Ananias, who was not an apostle, that Saul of Tarsus himself was filled with the Holy Spirit [*Acts* 9:17].

There are other questions which arise in this connection in the New Testament. What is the meaning of the term 'laying on of hands' in Hebrews 6:2? The author says, 'Leaving therefore the principles of the doctrine of Christ, let us go on unto perfection; not laying again the foundation of repentance from dead works, and of faith toward God, the doctrine of baptisms, and of *laying on of hands*' [verses 1–2]. Well, it does seem to me that we must grant that this is probably a reference to what, as we have just seen, is taught in the Book of the Acts of the Apostles – that there was a laying on of hands through which action the Spirit came, in this particular form, upon believers.

Furthermore, the subsequent history of the church seems to establish that point quite definitely, because that was the custom which continued afterwards and, indeed, it is the origin of what is called 'confirmation' as it is still practised in the Anglican Church, in the Lutheran Church and in various other Churches. After baptism, whether it was a short or a long interval does not matter, hands were laid upon new believers in order that they might receive the Holy Spirit.

Then there are other references which are of interest. The Apostle Paul says to Timothy, 'Neglect not the gift that is in thee, which was given thee by prophecy, with the laying on of the hands of the presbytery'[*1 Tim.* 4:14]. And then take, with that, Paul's words to Timothy in 2 Timothy 1:6: 'Wherefore I put thee in remembrance that thou stir up the gift of God, which is in thee by the putting on of my hands.' Now I would argue that in his letters to Timothy the apostle is referring to Timothy's ordination for the work of an evangelist, which was the special office for which Timothy had been set apart. But here we are not considering quite the same thing.

Of course, the New Testament teaches that an office involves a gift. That is why, in 1 Corinthians 12 and in Ephesians 4, under this heading of the spiritual gifts, we find the offices mentioned as well as the particular abilities. That, of course, is because the people appointed to offices are those who already have the gifts, so that one moves naturally from the gifts to the offices in which the gifts are exercised.

As we look at the question of how the gifts come to us, I would say that we must be careful not to be too dogmatic and we must not confine the Holy Spirit's working to one way or to the other. As the baptism of the Spirit may come directly, immediately, or through the intermediary of another person and the laying on of hands, so with regard to the gifts. I would say that both are possibilities.

The only qualification I add is that the subsequent history of the church seems to indicate that the common experience is that the gifts come directly and immediately rather than through the mediation of the laying on of hands. I am not excluding the second, but I do say that it is rare. Therefore, if you hear, as you may well do at the present time, a great deal about this 'laying on of hands', as if that were the universal method, then remember that that teaching is not only un-scriptural, but is not consistent with what seems to be very definitely and clearly the experience of the church ever since these early days. I do not at all think this should make us stumble. You would expect that men like the apostles should be given unusual gifts and endowments, and there is no doubt at all but that one of their gifts was the gift of being able to impart the Spirit with accompanying gifts to other people.

That is one problem that seems to arise from the teaching here in these verses in Romans 12, but they also raise another question, and I feel constrained to put this before you also. What light does this teaching here cast upon the life of the early church? Now I will show you why I think this is a most important question. If you read this passage intelligently and spiritually you should immediately say, 'What was the early church like?' Paul is here addressing the church. He is laying down his doctrine that 'we being many, are one body in Christ, and every one members one of another. Having therefore gifts differing according to the grace that is given to us, whether prophecy . . .' and so on. He is showing the Christians in Rome how they ought to conduct themselves in the church, and that, at once, tells us something about the life of the early church.

But what does it tell us about it? Well, it obviously tells us at once that the life of the early church was the life of a functioning body. The church was clearly, in practice, a body, and the various parts and members of the body were functioning. The apostle takes that for granted. He says, in effect, 'I know that in your church there at Rome are some who have this gift of prophecy; there are others who have the gift of ministry; others the gift of teaching; others the gift of exhortation; others this gift of giving; others of ruling; others of showing mercy.'

In 1 Corinthians 12:13–14, particularly verse 14, you find exactly the same thing. In Paul's teaching on how to control the life of the church you see at once that the church was a body, with the various members of the body playing their part. That was its outstanding characteristic. For instance, the apostle says in 1 Corinthians 14:26, 'How is it then, brethren? when ye come together, every one of you hath a psalm, hath a doctrine, hath a tongue, hath a revelation, hath an interpretation. Let all things be done unto edifying.'

Now I call attention to this because if Paul is incidentally giving us a description of the daily, regular life of the early church, then the question that we ask is this: How have things become as they are today? Take these verses 6, 7 and 8 in Romans 12, or take 1 Corinthians 14 – is that a picture of the functioning of the church today? And this becomes important for us in this way. Are you going to say: 'Oh no, of course that has nothing to do with us; that was the early church before we got the Scriptures'? But if you begin to say that, you will find that very little of the New Testament applies to us today. You will have to keep on saying about most of it, 'Ah yes, but that was the early church.' How do you decide when the words were meant only for the early church, and when for now? No, that is about the worst form of dispensationalism that one can ever be guilty of – yet there is a great deal of this teaching at the present time. I think, therefore, that this is one of the most urgent matters confronting us.

Let me put it to you like this. Here we are in this age which is called the ecumenical age and everybody is talking about the church. That is a very good thing; we all ought to be talking about the church. It has perhaps been one of the greatest defects of evangelicalism in particular that we have not talked sufficiently about the church. We have been individualistic, and we have been almost solely evangelistic, and there has been no talk about the church. And that is obviously quite wrong, because you cannot read the New Testament without seeing that the doctrine of the church is in the very forefront the whole time. So it is our duty to talk about it.

All this is right, but on one condition – we must do it in a scriptural manner. And here, it seems to me, there is a heaven-sent opportunity for us all at the present time. We must say, 'Yes, we must be right in our ideas as to the nature of the Christian church, and as to her functioning, but,' we go on, 'there is only one way of being right, and that is to go back to the New Testament itself.' And these verses in Romans force us to do that.

But it is here that the danger to which I have referred comes in. It is that some of us want to say, 'But all this has nothing to do with us, that was only the early church.' So we rule it all out and we start our thinking at the Reformation or perhaps even in the following century when the Westminster Confession was drawn up, and we are governed in our whole thinking by that. We just start there; we want to go back to that but not further back. But that seems to be not only wrong, but completely unscriptural. We are to go back to the New Testament itself, and we have no right to lay down any definition unless it is strictly in accord with the teaching of the New Testament.

Well, we are confronted by this issue here in Romans 12 where the apostle is writing to the church at Rome and telling them how they are to function. So let me try, therefore, to give you a picture of the early church as we find it in the New Testament. It is clear that the apostles held a very special position. At the end of Ephesians 2, the apostle Paul says that the apostles and prophets are the very foundation of the church. That is obvious; I do not think we need stay with it. They were clearly in a very special position because our Lord had chosen them and had given them the message, and He had not only given them power but infallibility. Since they were infallible in their teaching, their words are the basis and the foundation of the church.

It is equally clear that the evangelists in the New Testament do not correspond to what we think of when we use the term 'evangelist' today. The evangelist in the New Testament – Timothy, for instance, and Titus, Philip, and people like that –

was a man who acted as a deputy of the apostles. The evangelists of the New Testament were sent out by the apostles as
their representatives and the apostles delegated power to them
to perform particular functions. If you read the epistles to
Timothy and Titus you will see exactly what I mean. The
evangelists had great authority and great power, but it was all
delegated; they were not apostles but they deputized for them.

So we read of 'apostles, prophets, evangelists'. They come in
that order and always before the teachers. And these were all,
we must surely agree, special men in a category entirely on
their own. Clearly, special offices were raised up in order to
found the Christian church. And as they belong to the
foundation, they are not repeated. You do not repeat the
foundation, you build on it. You repeat the individual stones
in the building as it goes up, but you cannot repeat a
foundation, that is once and for all. 'Built upon the foundation
of the apostles and prophets', says Paul, and the word 'apostles'
includes the evangelists since they were the apostles' deputies.

Nevertheless, it is quite clear that, though the apostles,
prophets and evangelists had a unique work to perform, the
great characteristic of the life of the early church was the
participation of all the members. As we have seen, the great
analogy of the church as the body of Christ, which the apostle
repeats so frequently in his different epistles, inevitably carries
that notion. It was not that the apostles and prophets and
evangelists did things while everybody else just sat and
listened. No, no, every member was active and participated in
the life of the church.

But having said that, we must also say this. It is equally clear
that other offices began to appear. Acts chapter 6 reminds us of
how the office of a deacon first came in: 'And in those days,
when the number of the disciples was multiplied, there arose a
murmuring of the Grecians against the Hebrews, because their
widows were neglected in the daily ministration. Then the
twelve called the multitude of the disciples unto them, and
said, It is not reason that we should leave the word of God, and
serve tables. Wherefore, brethren, look ye out among you seven
men of honest report, full of the Holy Ghost and wisdom,
whom we may appoint over this business' [*Acts* 6:1–3].

Now that is how it happened. It was because the multiplicity of converts had raised a problem. They were living a kind of common life, and were forced by sheer necessity to introduce a division of labour and to assign particular duties to certain people. That is how the office of deacon arose, clearly under the leadership of the Holy Spirit. There is this extraordinary element about it. On the one hand, it looks like an improvisation, yet, on the other hand, when you remember the character of the early church, 'filled with the Holy Spirit' (this expression keeps on being repeated), you can see that the improvisation, if you want to use such a term, was suggested by the Holy Spirit Himself.

Then, in addition to deacons, another office also appeared. This was the office of what is called a 'presbyter', that is an 'elder', or 'overseer'. I want to point out that these are alternative names or designations for the same function or office. The word 'presbyter' means primarily somebody who is old; 'elder' means exactly the same thing, but 'overseer' does not carry so much the connotation of age as of function.

Now there is very little doubt, it seems to me, and most authorities are agreed about this, that the office of presbyter, elder or overseer, which was adopted by the early church under the leadership of the Holy Spirit, was a continuation of the way in which the worship and life of the synagogues had been ordered. The Jews used to meet in their synagogues Sabbath by Sabbath. There was an order in the worship, as we see when we read of our Lord that he returned to His home town of Nazareth and on the Sabbath went, 'as His custom was', to the synagogue, and was handed the scroll to read [*Luke* 4:16–17]. In each synagogue there were 'elders', senior men, men of ability, who had been selected to be the leaders, and from their number one was generally appointed to be a kind of presiding officer who supervised the service.

Now such elders came into being in the early church, and their function was primarily to rule and govern, but, as we have seen, some had, in addition, the special gift of teaching – they were 'apt to teach', as we are told in the Pastoral Epistles. They were a particular order of people who were there for the management of the life of the church, and one of their functions was to teach and to instruct and to build up, in our most holy faith.

Now as far as the New Testament teaching is concerned, leaving out the apostles, prophets and evangelists, there were only two offices and they were the presbyter/overseer and the deacon. But how were these men chosen? Well, it is very interesting, again, to notice what we are told about this. In Acts 20:28, when the apostle is addressing the elders of the church at Ephesus who have come down to bid him farewell on his journey to Jerusalem, he says, 'Take heed therefore unto yourselves, and to all the flock, over which the Holy Ghost hath made you overseers, to feed the church of God, which he hath purchased with his own blood.'

So the first answer must always be: They were chosen by the Holy Spirit. It is the Holy Spirit who is the prime mover in this matter. But having said that – and you must always say that and start with it – the next thing that is perfectly clear is that it was the church herself under the leading and the guidance of the Holy Spirit who chose these people. We read in Acts 6:3 that the apostles said, 'Wherefore, brethren, look ye out among you seven men of honest report, full of the Holy Ghost and wisdom, whom we may appoint over this business.' The choice was made by the church, and it is very important, especially at this present time, that this should be emphasized.

Almost every day of the week, we read, not only in religious papers but also in the secular press, talk about 'one church' – one church in every country – a territorial church, an all-inclusive, comprehensive church, in every country. That is the aim: one church only in England, another in Scotland. They are to be in communion with each other but territorially distinct. And there is always this additional comment – 'Of course, the united church will be episcopal in its government.' It will be governed, it is said, by bishops.

Now that is why I am putting all this before you. Here, in Acts, we are reminded that the choice was made by the people, by the church. Indeed, you read a most extraordinary statement in Acts 13:1–3: 'Now there were in the church that was at Antioch certain prophets and teachers; as Barnabas, and Simeon . . . As they ministered to the Lord, and fasted, the Holy Ghost said, Separate me Barnabas and Saul for the work whereunto I have called them. And when they had fasted and prayed' – that is the church, remember – 'and laid their hands on them, they sent them away.' The church exercised this choice.

But there is still one other step in this, and that is an action which was taken by the apostles. Take, for instance, Acts 14:23. We read here about Paul and Barnabas concluding a journey: '*And when they had ordained them elders in every church*, and had prayed with fasting, they commended them to the Lord, on whom they believed.' It is quite clear that this was an action taken by Paul and Barnabas – *they* ordained the elders.

'What is the point of all this?' asks someone. I will tell you! This is one of the great arguments of the Roman Catholic Church and the Church of England for saying that only a bishop can ordain a man to be an elder. So it is a very important question for us. Are you quite happy to go into a comprehensive church which is episcopally governed? Are you prepared to say that unless a man has been ordained by a bishop, he is not fit to administer the communion service or to baptize?

So, Christian people, you must not say, you cannot say, that this has nothing to do with you. It has everything to do with you! I am trying to show you that in the New Testament it was the members of the church who did these things; and there have been forefathers of ours who have been content to die rather than give up the right of the individual church member in this matter. So that is why all this is so important.

This verse in Acts 13 says quite clearly, does it not, that it was Paul and Barnabas who ordained these men, undoubtedly by laying their hands upon them, but it does not say that it was Barnabas and Paul who chose them. No, I think the principle is laid down for all time in Acts 6.3–6. There was the instruction: 'Wherefore, brethren, look ye out among you seven men of honest report, full of the Holy Ghost and wisdom, whom we may appoint over this business.' Then we read: 'And the saying pleased the whole multitude: and they [the multitude] chose Stephen . . . and Philip, and Prochorus, and Nicanor, and Timon, and Parmenas, and Nicolas a proselyte of Antioch: whom they [the members of the church] set before the apostles: and when they had prayed, they [the apostles] laid their hands on them.'

Now that seems to me to be the order, and it is perfectly

plain and clear that the choice was made by the members of the church, that they set these men apart and then the 'official act of ordination' was done by the apostles. And you will find in the Pastoral Epistles that it was also done by the evangelists acting as the delegates or the representatives of the apostles. That is why in 1 Timothy 3 the Apostle Paul reminds Timothy of the sort of men whom he, as the delegate and representative of the apostle, must ordain to particular offices in the church.

Not only that, we find something further. As the years passed there was a development in the ordering of the life of the church. From a simple beginning when there was just a gathering of people who had believed and who were baptized with the Holy Spirit and had received the gifts, the element of order became necessary. And as you follow this along you find that it became more and more so. There is a suggestion in the New Testament that among the elders one or another was appointed to preside. There were a number of elders but one (who might be changed from time to time), was given the position of presiding.

What is the evidence for this? Well, look at what happened, for instance, in the Council of Jerusalem, which is recorded in Acts 15. There we are told that James, the brother of our Lord, presided over the conference. Now this, in a way, was common sense, but it was clearly the leading of the Holy Spirit, for James was able to say, 'It seemed good to the Holy Ghost, and to us' [verse 28]. I believe that is the background to the meaning of the statement in James 3:1: 'My brethren, be not many masters.' They all wanted to be leading and presiding, as it were, at the same time. But in order to conduct all things 'decently and in order', as Paul puts it at the end of 1 Corinthians 14, they had to decide among themselves who was to be put into the position of presiding or ruling elder.

But while all this is true, it is equally true to say that this was only for the ordering of the life of the church. That is why Peter is so careful to tell the elders to carry out their work, 'Neither as being lords over God's heritage, but being ensamples to the flock' [1 Pet. 5:3]. They did not suddenly become great and unique people, different from everybody else. No, not even the apostles. The common life of the church was always to be preserved. So that the Apostle Paul, as we have seen in the very first chapter of this Epistle, says, 'I long to see you, that I may impart unto you some spiritual gift, to the end that ye may be established; that is,' he hastens to add, 'that I may be comforted together with you by the mutual faith both of you and me' [*Rom.* 1:11–12]. He was an apostle, yet he was one of them. It was to be an exchange – 'the mutual faith both of you and me'.

The whole problem, in other words, is this: How do you combine freedom and order? How do you combine liberty and discipline? And that is the way in which the Holy Spirit led the early church in this matter.

So I would sum it up like this. The picture we have of the early church is of a body of people who believed the gospel, who were filled with the Holy Spirit and who received gifts. They were an active body and they actively manifested the gifts. There was order, certainly, and control, but the great thing was the life that was in all the parts. It had to be controlled because of excesses, but the control did not mean that the members were silent and that only one man, or a number of men, were doing things. No, no; it was a pneumatic church, a pneumatic body, with the life of the Spirit showing itself in varying ways in each member so that everyone took part in the life of the church.

These churches were individual churches – the church in Corinth, the church in Laodicea, Ephesus, and so on – and they were clearly independent in their government. But they were not independent in their life; they were all interested in one another and they wanted to help one another. If they found that there was a variation in the teaching, they met together and discussed it.

So there were these units springing up over the Roman Empire and I have tried to describe their life to you. What I am emphasizing is that there was life in every member, and it was meant to show itself in the life of the church. In addition, there was order, and discipline. Everything was to be done 'decently and in order'. But if that is the picture given of the Christian church in the New Testament, then I ask again: Where have we come from? Where has the church as we know her today come from? Can you justify what has happened to the church? And what should we be doing about it?

Christian Conduct

All these things were written for us, and for our guidance in this our day and generation, and our conduct in the life of the church will be judged according to the New Testament standard.

Twenty-one

*

Having then gifts differing according to the grace that is given to us, whether prophecy, let us prophesy according to the proportion of faith; or ministry, let us wait on our ministering: or he that teacheth, on teaching; or he that exhorteth, on exhortation: he that giveth, let him do it with simplicity; he that ruleth, with diligence; he that sheweth mercy, with cheerfulness.

Romans 12:6–8

We have agreed that the church, at the present time, each local church, does not seem to conform, speaking generally, to the picture that we are given in the New Testament, especially here in Romans 12.

That is important in and of itself. If we say that we believe the Scriptures to be the Word of God and our sole and infallible guide in all matters of faith and conduct, then we should believe that the church should always conform to the picture and the pattern which we have of her in the New Testament. Therefore, any variation in that, or any departure from it, should be of concern to us.

But there are two very special reasons why we should pay great attention to this subject today. One is the Ecumenical Movement, and we have said that a failure to emphasize the need for unity, and, even more, the failure to be concerned about the doctrine of the nature of the church, have, perhaps, been the besetting sins of those of us who are evangelical. We have gone in for movements and we have not been very interested in the church. We have been charged with that, and I think we ought to be honest enough to admit that there is a great deal of truth in the charge. Evangelical people are to be found among all the denominations and they seem quite happy about that, as long as they can come together for certain interdenominational activities. But to be content with that is to ignore the whole doctrine of the nature of the Christian church.

The second reason why we should not neglect the doctrine of the church, is that there is a great deal of new interest in what is called the manifestation of the gifts of the Holy Spirit in the life of the church. This, again, is something that a paragraph like this in Romans 12 obviously compels us to consider. So we have been doing this and we have seen that the main picture of the early church is one of pneumatic life. It was a living body, thrilling with life, a life that manifested itself in various ways, sometimes, even, in excesses, because children tend to run to excesses. But the excesses of children are better than the inactivity of death. This is a great picture of life, with some outstanding ministries.

As I have shown, it is quite clear also that, as time passed, two offices emerged, those of elders and deacons. And those are the only two offices that are recognized and described plainly and clearly in the New Testament. But as the life of the church went on, there was a further development. It seems quite clear, from Acts chapter 15, that gradually a system began to develop among the elders in which one man was chosen to preside over the discussions of the church and over the handling of its affairs.

So the picture we find in the New Testament is that the church – and this is the fascinating thing to me about it – is a perfect blending of freedom and order, of discipline and liberty; the life and the activity of the Spirit and yet everything, as Paul puts it, done 'decently and in order'. There were a number of such churches in different parts of the world: the church of God which is in Rome, the church of God which is in Corinth, and those in various other places. We read of Antioch and the church there, and in the Book of Acts reference is made to the churches of Galatia.

Each church functioned within itself, it was an independent church, ruling itself. But the churches were not independent in the sense that they were not interested in all the other churches. They had had the same experience, they believed the same things, they had the same blessed hope, and naturally, therefore, they were interested in all such people everywhere. Not only that, they were visited from time to time by the apostles. Paul and others went on missionary journeys and on their journeys they would also visit the churches that had already come into existence, and they would send people like Titus and Timothy to visit them, too. So they were all kept in touch with one another in that way.

Yet it is perfectly clear that each church was independent, and I think this is one of the important subjects for us to consider at this present time in view of the ideas of church organization that are to be found round and about us. I suggest that in the New Testament there is no evidence at all that anybody outside a particular church had a right to interfere in its affairs, still less to dominate them.

Now here is the principle which we must consider. No group of churches could control the life of an individual church nor is there any suggestion that particular officials had any legislative and controlling power. There is no vestige of a hint that the state had any power over the life of the church. The churches had nothing to do with the state. Indeed, some believers were even misunderstanding that fact and had to be reminded, as we shall see in the thirteenth chapter of Romans, that, after all, though they were members of the church, they were still citizens of the state and must submit to the ruling of the state in matters that applied to it. But not in the church. The state had no jurisdiction whatsoever over the local church. Indeed, I am suggesting that nothing had jurisdiction over the local church – no group of churches, no body of ecclesiastics, no one man at the top had authoritative, legislative control over the life of the church.

But someone may say – and it is the old familiar argument – that surely Acts 15 contradicts what I have been saying. All who believe in any form of Presbyterianism, for instance, are very fond of quoting that chapter. It is the only bit of evidence they have, so they are bound to quote it. And they would argue that we see there a typical Presbyterian picture; a council, a kind of general assembly, meets at Jerusalem, with a moderator, James. Having considered the matter, they arrive at a decision, and issue their edict, which is then carried out.

Considerable significance is attached to a word that is used in Acts 16:4. We are told, that Paul and Silas set off on their journey, and that Timothy joined the company. And then, 'As they went through the cities, they delivered them *the decrees* for to keep, that were ordained of the apostles and elders which were at Jerusalem.' Now great weight is put upon that word 'decrees', which, it is said, savours of legal enactments. That is the main argument for what is called Presbyterianism, which really means that chosen elders from a group of churches in an area meet together in council and, having elected their own moderator, then have authority and power over the life of the local church.

So how do we answer that? Well, it seems to me that this is a perfect example of the tendency always to argue backwards from a present position. In other words, if you take the statements as you have them in Acts 15, you are not entitled to come to any such conclusion. What happened in Acts 15, we are told, is that some of the apostles were down in the church at Antioch, and while they were there, certain men came from Judaea and taught the brethren in the church at Antioch. They said, 'Except ye be circumcised after the manner of Moses, ye cannot be saved.' They maintained that they had come down from Jerusalem with the authority of the church and the apostles there to preach and to teach that it was not enough for people to say they believed the gospel. In addition, they must be circumcised as Moses had taught. Indeed – and they made it quite plain – the law had to be kept. So an argument arose.

We are told, 'Paul and Barnabas had no small dissension and disputation with them' [verse 2]. But the church in her wisdom decided that it was no use going on like this, just arguing and wrangling. They said that the right course of action was to send Paul and Barnabas, and certain other people, up to Jerusalem to speak to the apostles and elders about this problem.

Now that is what happened. So you do not have here an ecumenical council, some great general council of the church. This is not a picture of some central authoritative body which can call together delegates from all the churches and decide and enact and determine what is to happen in all the churches. No, what you have here is a consultation between two

churches, and the initiative, it is most important to notice, did
not come from the church in Jerusalem or from the apostles,
but from the church at Antioch. They sent representatives and
asked to be received and to enter into a consultation with the
church in Jerusalem.

They went to Jerusalem because the men who had been
teaching the false doctrine said that they had been sent down
from Jerusalem. The trouble had originated in Jerusalem, so
naturally the members of the church at Antioch wanted to go
to the fountainhead. In any case, the church at Jerusalem was
the first, the mother church, so naturally she was held in great
respect and everybody else paid great attention to what was
believed in Jerusalem. Generally, too, the apostles were there;
they went on their journeys but they always went back there.
Historically, Jerusalem was a kind of headquarters. So naturally the people in Antioch were very anxious to know what
was really taught there. Had some new idea come into the
teaching of the church at Jerusalem, the mother church? They
wanted to be sure.

So there is no suggestion here at all of a central machinery, of
a supreme court of the church. And there are other factors
which make this doubly certain. You notice that Paul and
Barnabas did not go up to consult the apostles and elders only;
they went up to consult the whole church at Jerusalem. We
read in verse 4: 'And when they were come to Jerusalem, they
were received of the church, and of the apostles and elders, and
they declared all things that God had done with them.' And in
verse 12: 'Then all the multitude kept silent.' So it was not
something like a conference of cardinals, or a conference of
bishops, which takes place from time to time in the Vatican or
at Lambeth, or even a gathering of church leaders, as takes
place in Free Church circles. We are told: *'All the multitude'*.
The church was present. 'All the multitude kept silence,
and gave audience to Barnabas and Paul, declaring what
miracles and wonders God had wrought among the Gentiles
by them.'

But it is the twenty-second verse that really is crucial: 'Then
pleased it the apostles and elders with the whole church, to
send chosen men of their own company to Antioch with Paul
and Barnabas.' And verse 23 carries this point on: 'And they

wrote letters by them after this manner; The apostles and elders and brethren send greetings unto the brethren which are of the Gentiles in Antioch and Syria and Cilicia.' In other words, it is quite clear that there is nothing at all here which in any way is comparable with the idea of a general assembly of elders or presbyters, making enactments and determining the whole life of all the churches.

'But,' you may say, 'what about the word decrees in the fourth verse of the sixteenth chapter?'

But that is simply, of course, to base an argument upon a particular translation of the Authorized [King James] Version. If you turn up that word, you will find that it may also be translated 'decision' and there is no doubt but that a decision was taken. The believers considered this matter and discussed it together and they did so very prayerfully, because you notice James was able to make this remarkable statement – and oh, that the Christian church had always remembered this; may we all be given grace to remember it at the present time! – 'It seemed good to the Holy Ghost, and to us' [verse 28].

That is it! They were given a unanimity. They were all in the Spirit and they were praying for His guidance, and I personally have no doubt at all but that James was speaking under the inspiration of the Spirit. He was not merely speaking as a chairman. He had no unusual executive powers as a president. He was simply appointed to take the chair in order that the discussion might be orderly, but he did not speak *ex cathedra*, with everything he said being regarded as infallible. Not at all! He was one among the others and he spoke the voice of the Spirit and of the apostles and elders and the members of the church who were present together. And together they arrived, therefore, at this decision.

It was a temporary decision for a temporary problem. What exactly was to be done with these Gentile converts? Had they to keep various parts of the law or not? And you notice the wisdom that was given to arrive at a temporary answer until the problem should disappear, which it did. So it is wrong to elevate this into some great enactment. But that is what happened in the subsequent history of the Christian church, and I have taken you through the evidence in order that I may demonstrate my contention that the New Testament provides no basis for any claims for executive authority and power over the local church outside the local church itself.

So, then, if that is the picture of the church in the New Testament – every church autonomous, independent, with nobody being able to impose any decisions upon it from the outside, whether other churches or the state – then I repeat that the question that obviously arises in our minds is, if that is so, where has the church, as we know her, come from? How have we ever arrived at the present position?

We should all know something about these things because we will all have to take decisions in the coming years, whatever Church we belong to. And it is our duty as Christians always to decide according to Scripture and not prejudice. We must not say, 'I was brought up a Roman Catholic, and I am going to defend this.' Or, 'I was brought up a Presbyterian or a Congregationalist, or a Baptist, or a member of the Brethren.' If you are simply defending the system you happen to be born into, then you are not behaving in a scriptural manner. We must have scriptural reasons for what we say. We have a new and a marvellous opportunity of doing this, and I urge upon you the importance of considering these matters, and of preparing your mind for the great responsibility that devolves upon you at a time like this.

So, then, what happened? How has the New Testament church become what we know today? Is there any connection between then and now? Yes, there is, and the process can be traced in the history of the church. The real difficulty arose over the whole question of discipline, especially in the matter of doctrine. While the apostles were alive, everything was referred to them because they were the apostles, these unique men. 'The church is built upon the foundation of the apostles and prophets' [*Eph.* 2:20]. They did these rounds of the churches, and everything could be referred to them, and we have seen that that was the course taken by the church at Antioch.

But then the apostles died, and the question arose almost immediately: How do you exercise discipline? Men set themselves up as teachers and they began to preach things that were wrong – heresies. What could be done about them? That is how the difficulties arose. And the modern situation came into being because it was felt that there must be some authoritative way of resolving problems. So the early church had to grapple with this great problem, and, remember, they were men and women in the flesh as we are, prone to error, ever ready to insinuate a little human wisdom, perhaps, instead of adhering to the primitive pattern. It is very natural, and all very understandable, but the question for us is: Was it right?

This is what actually happened. I have laid stress upon the fact that it obviously became necessary to appoint one of the elders to preside, to act as chairman, if you like. Now if the man chosen to preside happened to have a particularly strong personality, or was an unusually able and gifted man, quite unconsciously his authority and power tended to become greater and greater. This happened in a number of cases. And, in addition to that, the members of the church themselves might well feel, and indeed did feel, that there must be some sort of a ruling, and that everybody must submit to this ruling. So they would agree that where there was a difference of opinion the president should be allowed to decide. You can see how the change came about. The president was only one of the elders and no more. But he had been put into a position of authority and in these ways and for these reasons, authority and power were increasingly added to him.

By the middle of the second century, men in the position of presidents or chairmen were regarded as a separate order of officers in the church. Gradually, the very name was changed, and they began to be called 'bishops'. Now in the New Testament, as I have indicated, 'bishop', 'elder' and 'overseer' are alternative terms for the same person – we see this in Philippians 1:1. But now this word 'bishop' began to be isolated and applied only to the presiding elder. And soon there was a separate order of bishops. Instead of only elders and deacons, there were now bishops, elders and deacons.

So that is how the three-tiered system developed. The bishop, the overseer, was at the top, then came the elders, and then the deacons. But once you start along that line you cannot stop. At first there was a bishop in each church – I am not just saying what I think, this is sheer history. Obviously he was the presiding elder and he became the bishop. Sometimes there would be more than one bishop in a church and they took the chair in a kind of rota. However, the important point is that having started with this new office, as the problems increased, so did the power of the bishop.

The next development came when it was felt that the bishop of a town church was abler and more important than the bishop of a country church. People have always thought that there is some peculiar merit about a town, and that people in towns are more intelligent than people in the country, a complete fallacy, of course. And so it began to be said that the opinion of the bishop in the town was better than that of the bishop in the country. And this went on to such an extent that when there was a gathering of bishops, the one who always presided was the bishop from the town. And so developed what is now called a diocesan bishop, a bishop over a number of others, and he often had a great territory under his rule.

Then, of course, the next step followed. As a town is more important than a village, so a county town is more important than an ordinary town, and a capital is more important than a county town. And so we find the rise of the metropolitan bishop. Here was a man who was a bishop over a whole country. He was more important than the bishops in the towns, who were more important than the bishops in the villages, and in the country districts. There were a number of these metropolitan bishops: one in Rome, another in Corinth, another in Antioch, and another in Alexandria in Egypt.

It was illogical to stop there, was it not? Who decided between the metropolitans? Well, obviously, you must have one who was supreme – and there was your pope. And that is exactly how it happened. And, let me remind you, all this was brought about by the need for discipline, especially in the matter of belief. The church felt that to solve problems you must have someone who spoke with authority, and this authority became greater and greater, so that, at the end, what the pope in Rome said was true; he spoke infallibly, *ex cathedra*. This definition had not yet been made, but that is what came to be believed and practised. There was a great fight over this, and it lasted for many centuries – I am giving you a bird's-eye view of it all.

But there is one other major factor that I must mention.

About the year 325 the then Roman emperor, whose name was Constantine, decided for purely political reasons (I think we must all agree) to become a Christian. I could give you the political reasons but I shall not do so because it would only confuse the point I am trying to emphasize. He felt it was the right and obvious thing to do – it paid him to do it. Leaders change. Roman emperors used to persecute the Christians, but Christians became so powerful and there were so many divisions among the followers of the pagan gods, that this astute man Constantine conceived the idea that, after all, if he only put these Christian people first and became one of them himself, it would solve many problems for him; and indeed it did.

And so the Roman Empire came into the Christian church and as a result something else happened which one could almost have prophesied. Here was an opportunity of really controlling all the churches! The Roman Empire, you remember, was a very highly organized state. The centre of government was at Rome and at Rome was the head of all, the emperor. Then, coming down from him, were the proconsuls and consuls, and the governors like Pontius Pilate, and so on. You started with this one great head and the offices went down and down in ever-increasing numbers to the local level; but it was all governed from the head.

So, first in the church there were bishops and elders and deacons, with a development among bishops into local, diocesan, metropolitan, and pope. But now, after the Roman Empire became officially Christian, all kinds of other offices developed. You may have wondered where deans came from and archdeacons and rural deans and prebendaries and all these other offices that you know of in connection with the church. Well, they really all came in with the Roman Empire. The church simply borrowed the governmental procedures of the Roman Empire. And the result of all this was, of course, that, with everything determined from above downwards, the local church completely lost her power – and there you have your typical Roman Catholic system. No longer does the church have authority to appoint her own officers; it is taken right out of her hands. No one, except a bishop, can ordain anybody, and the same is true of confirmation. That was what gradually developed, and you see how far removed it is from the New Testament picture.

Then came the Protestant Reformation and the great thing that happened there was that God opened men's eyes to see the truth about the way of salvation, and they saw that with great clarity. Now let us be fair to the Reformers. It is very difficult for any man or any body of men in any age to do everything. They saw this big thing, that people were being held in darkness. The Reformers wanted to have liberty to preach the gospel, the true way of salvation, and Luther and the rest did that. But they did not deal with the whole life and organization of the church in a corresponding manner.

Luther carried over much more from Rome than Calvin and the other Reformers in Switzerland and other places. He was concerned about one great doctrine – justification by faith only – and he had to fight for that. He was troubled by the rise of the Anabaptists who appeared to him to be jeopardizing everything because they were going to annoy all the authorities. Do not forget that for fifteen centuries the state had been ruling the church with an iron government, and everything was under the control of the prince and the ruler and the emperor. So I am not criticizing the Reformers, I am simply explaining them, and explaining what they failed to do.

And, of course, here in England, Anglicanism took over practically the whole Roman Catholic system of church government – all the various offices. They dropped the pope – Henry VIII saw to that! Instead of the pope being right at the top, it was Henry VIII, and territorial and national interests took the place of the international aspect of the church. Otherwise there was no change. All the various offices and the church government continued as before.

John Calvin was the father of Presbyterianism. But as I have tried to show you, he also did not go back to the New Testament pattern. Again, let us be fair, these men again were up against the problem of discipline. They felt that order must be maintained, and the appearance of some 'wild sects' as some of them were, tended to harden the thinking of the Reformers. They felt that there must be a system which could maintain law and order.

But quite soon the people who became known as Independents began to appear. They protested that the Reformers were not following the New Testament pattern but instead were perpetuating much that had come in wrongly through the centuries. They had reformed the doctrine in the matter of teaching and the way of salvation, but why had they not been equally radical with regard to the nature of the church? And so towards the end of the sixteenth and still more in the seventeenth century you had the rise of Independency in its various forms, whether Congregationalist or Baptist does not matter from this standpoint. And since then, of course, there have been various other developments.

So there is a picture of how the church, as we know her, came into being. And I suggest to you that we have arrived at a point now when we really must reconsider all these things. Men set themselves up; men, who may be used as evangelists, turn themselves into 'movements' and they quite often impose themselves upon churches. We must admit that the position today has become chaotic, and you cannot see this in the New Testament. The New Testament is always interested in *churches*, not in movements or organizations; it is always churches. But we are in a terrible confusion, and I suggest that we must avail ourselves of the opportunity that is given to us today to go back to the New Testament and try to see how our church may be restored to a condition more like that described in these three verses in Romans 12.

Let me put it, then, very bluntly and very simply like this: I think I have shown you that you cannot find a pope in the New Testament, nor many of these other offices. Nor can you find a hierarchical system like the one today that tyrannizes the local church. But let us be quite honest: Can you find what is sometimes called 'the one-man ministry' in the New Testament? Frankly, I cannot find it there. Yet this is always taken for granted and it has developed more and more, has it not? One man does everything – the preaching and the teaching and a good deal of the organizing and everything else. Everybody else just sits down and listens and looks on. One-man ministry! Not the variety of gifts that we read of in Romans 12: 'Having then gifts differing according to the grace that is given unto us . . .', let all of us exercise them. That seems to have gone.

So we must start afresh. We must be concerned about one thing only, and that is that we really do conform to the New Testament pattern. This is important because if we really do pray and long for the blessing of the Holy Spirit upon us, we must honour His Word; we must conform to the pattern that He has so plainly indicated. I feel that we must reform ourselves if we really are genuine in our seeking for and longing for revival.

'Well, then,' asks someone, 'you have shown us how we have departed, all of us, in a sense, from the New Testament; so what must we do?'

Many solutions have been tried. The Quakers of the seventeenth century tried a solution. George Fox used to revile the churches, 'the steeple houses', as he called them. He was violent about them, I know, but he objected to the division of Christian people into clergy and laity; and I for one am ready to say he was absolutely right on that point. But he went too far in that he did not recognize any offices at all. He further felt that all men or women who are Christians and have the Spirit in them have gifts, and should surely have liberty to express those gifts. But he was refused that liberty, not only by the Church of England, but even by the Nonconformist churches who had come to believe in this 'one-man system'. He protested against this, and in that sense his protest was right. That led the Quakers to develop their own kind of meeting, where nobody is appointed to preach, and nobody has prepared a sermon, but you sit down and wait until you are moved by the Spirit, and then you speak.

But I think that it must be admitted by now that the answer provided by the Quakers has not proved to be the solution. Also I think I can prove from the New Testament that it could not be a success because it does not conform to the pattern which we have been seeing in the New Testament.

Others have attempted the same thing. I have often commended from this pulpit the commentary on the Epistle to the Romans by Robert Haldane. Now Haldane had a brother, James Alexander Haldane, a greater preacher than Robert, and a man who had a remarkable ministry in Edinburgh, but he ruined it completely because after studying the New Testament, he felt that he must stop preaching as he had been doing. (He had been doing almost everything in his church.) He felt that there should be a more general meeting where anybody could get up and speak. He would do this in the Sunday morning service, for instance. But it came to nothing and he wrecked a great church. I suggest that he, again, was not being scriptural in that he failed to notice that there is a division in the gifts – some have one gift, and some another, with some called to preach and to teach in a special way.

Then, of course, there is the so-called Brethren movement – the Plymouth Brethren, as they are sometimes called, a movement that began with J. N. Darby and others. They were facing this exact problem, and all honour to them for not evading it. This was the issue that brought them into being. They said, 'What we are familiar with is not the New Testament practice and we must go back to that.' Again, I suggest that, while most of them were right, they went too far and failed to recognize certain distinctions and divisions of labour. And it is interesting to notice that by now many of them – and I believe this is particularly true in the United States of America – have come to believe that certain men should be set apart, entirely and whole-time, as preachers and teachers. They have not done away with the expression of the gifts in various other meetings, but they have come to see this need and in a sense this is a criticism of what they did at the very beginning.

Then there is the story of Edward Irving and the so-called Apostolic Church, the Catholic Apostolic Church, which he started in London, has a great deal to teach us. Like James Alexander Haldane, Irving also stopped preaching as he had always done as a Presbyterian, but, alas, his new church ended in tragedy.

Since then, there have been other attempts and efforts. There is a church known at the present time as the Apostolic Church which claims to have apostles and prophets among its members. Again, we could easily show that this is not scriptural. And, last of all, at the present time, there is what is called the charismatic movement, which, again, has arisen out of a reconsideration of the doctrine of the church and the gifts, and to that extent, of course, it is right.

But – so that we may bring this to some kind of conclusion –

what would I suggest, what would I indicate, as being the true way? In the light of the scriptural teaching and the history which I have put before you, the history of how things went wrong, the history of the experiments and the endeavours to restore the New Testament pattern, I suggest that the great lesson, surely, is the need to beware of the danger of swinging from one extreme right over to the other. There is one extreme, ending up with the pope and his absolute authority, but the danger is to react by going right to the other extreme where there is no order at all, no church membership, no offices, no preachers or teachers or pastors.

What is the true way? Surely, we are called to come back to the New Testament pattern. We must recognize that some are given the special gift of preaching and teaching; others are given the gift of being pastors. Some people have the gift of government; and there are various other gifts of expression and of exhortation. Towards the end of Acts 15, there is an interesting word which is very germane to this whole consideration. In verse 32 we are told that Judas and Silas, who had been sent to Jerusalem with Paul and Barnabas, 'being prophets also themselves, exhorted the brethren with many words, and confirmed them'. Then in verse 35 we are told this: 'Paul also and Barnabas continued in Antioch, teaching and preaching the word of the Lord, with many others also.' That is it. In the church there are a number of men who are given the gift of teaching, they are 'apt to teach', and they can preach.

So we must reconsider this. It is not a case of 'one man only'. If others have the gift, they must be given the opportunity of exercising it. But this must not be done in a disorderly, haphazard manner. No, there must be order and a system. You can maintain all your liberty in other meetings of the church, you can give opportunities for the exercise of all the gifts that the Holy Spirit has given to us severally, and one by one. I believe that the Methodist Awakening of two hundred years ago in both its branches, both Calvinist and Arminian, came very near to what I would regard as the scriptural position. In their class and other meetings, opportunities were given to men and women to talk not only of their experiences, but to give a word of exhortation, to offer an interpretation of a Scripture, and so on. I believe there must be an opportunity in the life of the church for all to give expression to the gift that God has given them.

But clearly there will always be, and must be, public services led by men who have been obviously gifted and have been set apart to preach and to teach. And so the whole body of the church can be edified, and also, at the same time, a word can be addressed to those who are outside. So many times, it seems to me, the experiment has gone wrong because of a failure to remember that one does not have a church meeting, as it were, in full view of the public. Church meetings should take place within the body of the church. But when you are addressing the public, you put forth the men who have obviously been gifted by the Spirit to expound the Word and to preach the gospel of salvation.

Now all that, it seems to me, comes out of verses 6, 7 and 8 in Romans 12. There we see a picture of the church, and we ask: Why are we so different? We must get back to the New Testament pattern, and we must pray to the Holy Spirit to enlighten the eyes of our understanding, to open the Scriptures to us and, above all, to deal with our spirits and our prejudices so that we shall not merely be defending some inherited position, but shall be always open to the guidance of the Spirit and follow Him as He leads us back to this pattern, which He Himself has revealed to us in the New Testament Scriptures. May God hear us in this respect and guide us, to His own glory.

Twenty-two

*

Having then gifts differing according to the grace that is given to us, whether prophecy, let us prophesy according to the proportion of faith; or ministry, let us wait on our ministering: or he that teacheth, on teaching; or he that exhorteth, on exhortation: he that giveth, let him do it with simplicity; he that ruleth, with diligence; he that sheweth mercy, with cheerfulness.

Romans 12:6–8

Our consideration of these verses in Romans and our brief historical review and survey of the story of the church has been undertaken against a background of much talk about church unity. Our object has been to make sure that the only unity that we are interested in is one which reproduces the pattern found in the New Testament. We must examine every proposal, every attempt at unity in the light of this teaching. It is no use just starting with things as they are and modifying them a little bit here and there – the Roman Catholic Church with a little modification, the Church of England with a little modification, and so on, until we get one great church which will still maintain most of the characteristics of all the different sections that are being amalgamated

That is not the way in which we view these things. We say that we must look at everything in the light of the New Testament teaching; and as people are interested in unity, we Evangelicals of all people ought to be interested in it. The church is to be one and she is to be seen to be one, and surely the call that comes to us is to manifest the type of unity that you read of in the New Testament and to assert that that, and that alone, is the Christian church rather than some counter-feit produced by men.

But still we are left with one further problem, or, rather, a further aspect of this same matter. The church, as we have known her, is not only different from the New Testament church in her order, and in her government, but there is also, surely, a great difference between her way of conducting worship, and the New Testament way of expressing worship. Here, in these verses, we are given a picture, a little cameo, of the kind of thing that happened in the early church. I have also reminded you several times of the similar passage in 1 Corinthians 14 where the apostle says, in verse 26: 'How is it then, brethren? when ye come together, every one of you hath a psalm, hath a doctrine, hath a tongue, hath a revelation, hath an interpretation. Let all things be done unto edifying.' Ephesians 5:19 again gives us a picture of the church: 'Speaking to yourselves in psalms and hymns and spiritual songs, singing and making melody in your heart to the Lord.' Such pictures give us an insight into the type of worship that was character-istic of the early church.

So, once more, if we are intelligent readers of our Scriptures, we must obviously ask ourselves: Does our worship corre-spond to those pictures, and if not, why not? And how have we moved from what we find there to what we are familiar with today? I do want to stress the all-importance of asking these questions. Evangelical people, it seems to me, have so often gone in for a type of Bible study or Bible reading, whatever they may call it, which has been most defective. We have been content with a kind of letter knowledge of the Scriptures, and we have not always tried to look at the doctrine, to dig it out, and to see its relevance to us.

The worship of the early church surely demands our atten-tion because it has much to say to us. Today there is an increasing tendency towards what is described as a liturgical style of worship with vestments, as they are called, and all the accompanying trappings and paraphernalia. Now this is taking place, I think, in most sections of the Christian church. I have been observing, during the last thirty or forty years, an increasing tendency to modify the worship in what are called the Free Churches by introducing set prayers and responses and formal services at the communion table, and in baptism, and so on. The Free Churches have imitated what they have seen in the Anglican Church, and the Anglican Church in turn, as I shall show you, took most of its liturgy from the Roman Catholic Church. In recent times great impetus has come from all that is to be seen on the television, and all that is reported in the papers.

That is the position, so we must ask: Where is that form of worship to be found in the New Testament? How does that compare, for instance, with what we see in these three verses in Romans 12? In other words, it seems to me that, at the present time, a dispute which has often taken place in the church, is in an acute form once more. There is a major division between what are sometimes called 'religions of authority' and 'religions of the Spirit'. Or, if you prefer, there is a vital difference between the Catholic type of worship and the truly Protestant type of worship. There is all the difference in the world between a worship that is mainly dependent upon ceremony and ritual, and a simple type of worship which exalts the freedom of the Spirit.

Now if you feel inclined to ask, 'What has this to do with me?', then all I say is that you do not know your New Testament. It has everything to do with you. If you really believe that the New Testament is the Word of God you must really be concerned about worship, and, whether you like it or not, as I have already reminded you, you will be compelled to take decisions on these very matters. If you do not see the trend to Rome, then I am afraid you must be blind. It is moving forward, and moving very rapidly. The proposal to have one church in this country – and that is the proposal – tells us that the church is to be episcopal in its government and liturgical in its form of worship; and most people are very happy to accept that. The ultimate objective is to have one great world church including the Church of Rome, or, rather, the Church of Rome including all the others. And so you will be committed to a liturgical type of worship.

So the question is: Do you want that? Do you believe in that? Do you regard that as right? And it is a question that is raised for us by these three verses because here we have a picture of the worship of the New Testament church. So a further

[303]

question is: Is this a vital issue or is it only a matter of taste? So often throughout the years I have heard people say – and have been sickened by it – 'The language of the litany is so beautiful. Cranmer was a master at language and used a kind of liturgical language; and the prayers are so beautiful.' That is an argument that one hears frequently among Free Church people as well as among Anglicans.

The question I ask is this: Is our form of worship to be decided by tradition or is the New Testament to be our standard? Now we must not approach this question merely in terms of prejudices – that is always wrong. We must not say we object to these things because we have not been brought up in that tradition. And the others must not say, 'This is right because this is our tradition.' All of us are called upon to re-examine everything in the light of the New Testament itself. To us nothing matters except the question: Is it right? And we discover whether or not it is right by coming to the bar of the New Testament Scripture. Is it in accord with that?

Now at this point there is an important matter of principle that I must put before you. You will know that at the time of the Protestant Reformation, those godly men who were raised up at that time in general agreed that the New Testament is the ultimate and the only source of authority. But they tended to differ among themselves at one most important point, and it was this: In what sense is the New Testament teaching binding? And here a division emerged between Martin Luther and John Calvin, and not only between those two great men, but also between two sections of the church in this country.

Martin Luther taught that Scripture is an absolute authority on all matters of doctrine with respect to salvation, but that with regard to understanding church government or forms of worship, New Testament teaching is not binding. He said that it is allowed to the wisdom of the church to produce a form of worship and, indeed, a form of church government. But Calvin took a very different view. He said that the Scriptures are not only binding in matters like the doctrine of salvation, they are equally binding and are to be our only rule, with regard to church government and also to forms of worship.

Now as far as Britain was concerned, the Church of England followed Luther. The Church of England has always taught that while the Scriptures are binding in the matter of the doctrine of salvation, they are not binding in the matters of church government and of worship. But another group of believers arose in this country who ultimately became known as Puritans, and from among the Puritans a group whom we may describe as 'the radical Puritans' followed the teaching of Calvin. So we see here two bodies of people, all believing in the infallibility of the Scripture and its unique inspiration, who came to different conclusions with regard to church government and forms of worship.

I have laid that down for your guidance because I am most anxious that we should look at this whole situation in a dispassionate manner. We must not be governed by prejudice and likes and dislikes; we must really make a great effort to arrive at a truly reasonable opinion in the light of the teaching of the Scripture and in the light of what has happened in the history of the church.

So, let us go to the Scriptures first. Have we any teaching by our blessed Lord Himself with regard to this question? Does our Lord Himself prescribe read or recited prayers? Did He teach that we were always to offer our worship in the same language and in the same words as people do who use the same prayer book every Sunday? Can anything be proved or established in terms of the teaching of our Lord and Saviour?

The example, of course, put forward by those who believe in a liturgical form of worship is the Lord's Prayer. They point out that our Lord said to His disciples: 'When ye pray, say . . .' [*Luke* 11:2] 'Here He is,' they say, 'composing a prayer that He intends them to repeat.' And so in compiling their prayer books and repeating these prayers Sunday by Sunday they say they are simply doing what our Lord and Master Himself first taught the church.

Obviously this must be examined; it is the only real bit of evidence that they can produce. How do we deal with this argument? Now this has been dealt with many times; it was answered by many of the leading Puritans, men like Dr John Owen and others, and I will show you the arguments which they have always brought forward and which seem to me to be inevitable from a study of Scripture. What was our Lord doing when He told His disciples, 'When ye pray, say . . .'?

Well, the Lord's Prayer should surely be regarded as a model prayer. Our Lord was not saying that we should repeat this prayer mechanically every time we pray. If we look up Luke 11:1–2 we read that the disciples came to Him and said, 'Lord, teach us to pray, as John also taught his disciples.' They were in difficulties about praying. We are not surprised at that; we have all known the same difficulty. Prayer can be very hard. So they asked their question, and our Lord replied, 'When ye pray, say . . .' Surely what He meant was: This is the kind of manner or style in which you should pray.

In other words, you always start with adoration: 'Our Father which art in heaven, Hallowed be thy name . . .' You do not start with your petitions and your desires, but you must always worship God. Our Lord was instructing his followers on the great principles of prayer; and the first is that we must always recollect and realize that we are approaching the almighty and everlasting God. Before everything else, we must offer our adoration and worship. We must desire the coming of His kingdom, and we must long for His will to be done, 'as in heaven, so in earth', and so on. And it is only then that we come to the personal petitions and desires.

So our Lord was saying, 'in this manner', 'in this kind of way'. He was not composing a prayer for His disciples which they could simply recite mechanically or even repeat in the spirit. He was concerned about laying down the principles, the general ideas, for the ordering of their prayers. That is the first answer to the argument that would base the use of liturgies and litanies on our Lord's giving of the Lord's Prayer.

But, secondly, the account which is given in the sixth chapter of Matthew's Gospel surely indicates quite clearly that our Lord was dealing there with private rather than public worship. He talks about going into our room, shutting the door and praying in secret, and says, 'And thy Father which seeth in secret shall reward thee openly' [*Matt.* 6:6]. And that seems to me to be a very powerful argument.

Thirdly, Owen points out – and I think there is a good deal to be said for this – that in any case, even if our Lord were dictating a prayer for His disciples to repeat, He was actually speaking under the Old Testament dispensation. It was all before His death; it was all before Pentecost. And as you do find a kind of ritual and ceremonial in the Old Testament, then our Lord was just showing how they should be praying in their position at that time. I think that can be pressed too far, but as far as it goes there is some point in what Owen says.

But – and this is surely the final argument and a conclusive one – even if we grant that our Lord dictated that prayer and intended that we should repeat it word for word, as so many of us, indeed, tend to do in our services – granting all that, how does that justify repeating set prayers Sunday by Sunday? The Lord's Prayer, after all, was uttered by the Lord Himself, whereas the prayers that are used in the prayer books are the compositions of men from different centuries, different traditions, and so on. So that even if you could justify the reciting of the Lord's Prayer, it surely does not entitle you to go any further and say that all prayers should be prayers that are composed, written and printed, and are to be read and repeated Sunday by Sunday.

That, then, is the only evidence that can be even remotely adduced from the teaching of our Lord and Saviour. But what about the apostles? Now here I think everybody is agreed that there is no evidence whatsoever, either from the practice or the teaching of the apostles, that they believed in formal, set prayers. They did not repeat prayers, but their prayers varied according to their circumstances. They did not have prepared prayers which they taught the people; they never gave any instructions to the people to repeat particular prayers. All this, in itself, of course, is in many ways the most significant argument of all.

There, then, is the evidence as far as the New Testament is concerned. What about the subsequent history of the church? What about the early centuries? Now this is extremely interesting. There is no evidence in the first three centuries that anything remotely approaching a prayer book was used. The first-century Christians did not have liturgical services. These made their first appearance in the fourth century, and there seems very good evidence that it was at a place that is familiar to us, a place called Antioch.

Let me read to you some evidence out of the writings of the great Father in the church, Tertullian, who lived round about AD 200. This is how he described the form of worship with

[307]

which he was familiar. He says, 'They pray looking towards heaven; not like the idolaters who looked on their idols and images; not embracing altars or images as did the heathen; not as they who repeat their prayers after their priests or sacrifices, but pouring out our prayers conceived in our breasts.'

That is very important, is it not, and very significant? Tertullian contrasts what the pagans did who 'repeat their prayers after their priests or sacrifices'. In contradistinction to that, he talks of Christians 'pouring out our prayers conceived in our breasts', which, I suggest, is in entire conformity with the teaching of the New Testament itself.

And then another quotation from Tertullian. Talking about someone being received into the Christian church, he says: 'After the believer who is joined unto us is thus washed, we bring him in to those who are called "Brethren", thither where they are gathered together for to make their prayers and supplications for themselves and him who is newly illumin-nated.' What sort of prayers are these? 'These prayers and supplications,' he adds, 'the President of the Assembly [notice the term] poureth out according to his ability.' He does not read set prayers, but he pours out his prayers 'according to his ability'. And Tertullian says, 'He doth this work at large.' In other words, he continues long in his work of offering praises unto God and in the name of Jesus Christ. But the relevant phrase is, 'he poureth out according to his ability', and the ability varies from case to case, from man to man in this matter of pouring out prayers from the heart.

So how did set prayers come in, in the fourth century? Well, this form of worship came in very gradually. It came in first at Antioch, then it began to appear in other places, but the Christians did not all have the same prayers. Some were composed by a man in Antioch, another man in another place would compose others, and eventually this began to happen in the church in Rome. But she was far from being the first.

However, when that great event took place to which we have referred, when the Emperor Constantine and the Roman Empire came into the church, they then, of course, took over everything. And as they took over the government of the church, they did exactly the same with forms of worship. They standardized everything, laying it down that the same prayers had to be offered everywhere. This in itself shows that at first they were not. There was a liturgy in Antioch, a different liturgy in Alexandria, and so on. But Rome put an end to that. Everybody everywhere had to offer the same prayers. And they had to be in the same language, so they had to be in Latin. Of course, that has been modified now, and it is an interesting concession, but the principle still remains.

And at the same time, Rome not only standardized the prayers, but also began to introduce various other innovations – vestments, for example, these robes to be worn by men called 'priests'. They borrowed most of this ritual from pagan mystery religions. There is no question about this: it is not my theory. That was the policy. The church leaders picked out what they regarded as the best from the pagan religions. This was what the people had been accustomed to. In all pagan religions there always had been, as there still is, a good deal of dressing up and ceremony. So the church leaders took over all that and said that they had 'baptized' these things into the Christian church. They pointed out that under the Old Testament dispensation Aaron had been clothed with various elaborate garments and so had the priests, and in this way they introduced all these vestments, which are still being worn.

So if this is how the wearing of vestments and liturgical worship came into the church, the question is: Why did anyone ever think of doing all this? Why did it begin in Antioch? Now we really must consider this very carefully. There were two main reasons – I am trying to put the argument for liturgies as fairly as I can. I do not want to give the impression that this was only done at someone's whim. There were what were regarded as two very powerful arguments.

The first was that very often the ministers, the priests, whatever they were called, were rather ignorant and not capable of offering prayers. Because they were often men who were badly educated they found themselves in difficulties. So they welcomed the provision of prayers.

But, secondly, and this was still more important, there was always the danger – as we saw earlier in the matter of church government – of heretical teaching. Because of this, men with heretical views who were in positions of leadership were very careful when they preached, as they knew they were being watched, and their tendency was to introduce their heresies into their prayers. Prayers are sometimes sermons and not prayers. We are probably all a bit guilty of this at times and it is something we must always watch. Now some of these heretical teachers quite deliberately introduced wrong teaching through the medium of their public prayers, and as long as every man had freedom to pray extempore prayers, nothing could be done about it.

But, as we have seen, the Roman Church, like the Roman Empire, was always keen on discipline and she always wanted to standardize everything. And, of course, let us agree, this problem of discipline is important and something has to be done about heretics. So after the Roman Empire became Christian, it was decided that the only way to deal with heresy was to prescribe the prayers, to set them down and to say that these, and these alone, were the prayers that were to be offered. And in this way it was hoped that true worship could be preserved and the danger of heretical teaching coming through the medium of prayers excluded. If, then, we want to be generous, we can grant that the motive was a good one.

Yes, but that led eventually to the full Roman system, with all the ritual and the ceremonial – greatly elaborated, of course, over the question of the Lord's Supper and baptism. And then the question of other sacraments was raised, and there was a corresponding liturgy, and statements were developed for each one. It became a vast organization, in a sense, with its complicated liturgy. That was the typical procedure of the Roman Catholic Church right through the Middle Ages. All the worship was conducted by the priests, and the people were away in the distance somewhere, often not understanding a word of what was being said. But that did not matter, it was what the priests did that mattered, and the people were remote, taking no part, except for some occasional responses which were indicated in the liturgy.

That, then, brings us up to the time of the Protestant Reformation. This again, surely, should be of great interest to all of us from every standpoint. It is important to know why the traditions in which we have been brought up are as they are, but it is still more important, I repeat, to know what we should be thinking and saying and doing at this present time of change and transition. What happened at the Reformation? Again, it is very interesting to observe that Luther took over most of what had been done by Rome. Of course, he corrected the things he had come to see were quite wrong, but he was primarily concerned about the great doctrine of justification by faith only. As we have seen, he believed that the New Testament teaching was not binding for church government or forms of worship. So he took over most of the Roman Catholic type of worship.

Now Calvin is interesting in this matter, and he is often misunderstood at this point. Many of us in Britain, and particularly those who are interested in Puritan teaching, tend to think that Calvin's views were the same as those of the Puritans. But they were not, not at all! Calvin believed in having a liturgy and he believed in set prayers, though he allowed more liberty for extempore prayer than the Roman Catholic Church had ever done, and, indeed more than the Church of England did. This is just a fact of history. Be careful in your arguments, lest you use the name of Calvin wrongly. There is a sense in which it can be argued that the Church of England, in the matter of worship, is nearer to Calvin than some of the Puritans were.

When you come to England, you come to the name of Thomas Cranmer, the man who composed the Church of England Prayer Book, and he did more or less what Luther had done in Germany. He did not do away with liturgy and a prayer book, but took the idea over and, again, he rid it of all the errors of Roman Catholicism. So he composed those prayers which – let us admit very readily – are masterpieces from the literary standpoint. We are not concerned about that. We can grant that they are masterpieces, and that he had an unusual facility in the matter of producing written prayers.

But the important thing to ask is this: Why did Cranmer do it? Why did he decide to have a prayer book and to perpetuate the Roman Catholic type of worship? And again we must be fair and recognize that this man, and those who were with him, were men of their age. Not only that, they were men who were confronted by certain very special problems – it is always our duty as honest thinkers to take in the circumstances in which men were placed when they came to their decisions, lest we judge them unfairly – and the biggest of the problems facing Cranmer was the problem of ignorant clergy. They had been, most of them, brought up as Roman Catholics, and they were ignorant of the Scriptures. Many were also devoid of any spiritual experience. They had changed over to Protestantism in a spirit of fear, out of expediency, and for the various other reasons which such people have for changing sides. So they changed in the time of Henry VIII and then went back to Roman Catholicism in Mary's time and then back again in the time of Elizabeth. Many similar men did much the same thing in the time of Oliver Cromwell and the Commonwealth and in the Restoration. Vicars of Bray, changing according to the political climate!

So Cranmer was confronted by such people, but apart from their spiritual state they were actually ignorant, and one of his arguments was that they must be provided with prayers. They could not pray themselves, and if their congregations were therefore to be helped in any way, then he must provide these ministers with prayers which they could read in their services with the people.

In addition to that, and this again is a most important point, try to conceive the situation – fifteen centuries of Roman Catholicism! The system was in the very blood and bones of the people. They had never heard of anything else or thought of anything else. Suddenly comes this explosion, the Protestant Reformation. Now the leaders of Protestantism in England had come to believe the great doctrine of justification by faith only. But the people did not see it as clearly, and one of the arguments that Cranmer used was this: he said in effect, 'If we are now not only going to change our doctrine of salvation, but the whole form of worship as well, then we will lose everybody and we will lose everything. The thing that matters,' he said, 'is that they should be right on the doctrine of salvation – justification by faith only. Styles of worship are indifferent and we can afford to go on with the existing form of worship until we have truly educated the people.'

Now I think there is something to be said for that argument. As a temporary device, a temporary expedient, surely, there is not only a great deal to be said for it, I suggest that there is a New Testament justification for it in something that was done by the apostles and elders. Earlier we were discussing what happened at the Council of Jerusalem, as it is recorded in Acts 15, and you remember the decision reached at that conference? There had been a very real problem because the Gentiles were coming in to the church and the Judaizers were saying that they must all be circumcised and go right back under the law. 'No,' said this Council in its wisdom, led by the Holy Spirit. 'It seemed good to the Holy Ghost, and to us, to lay upon you no greater burden than these necessary things; that ye abstain from meats offered to idols, and from blood, and from things strangled, and from fornication' [*Acts* 15:29]. They laid that down as a principle.

Now that no longer applies to us. We do not abstain from blood in that sense. That was a decision for a period of transition in order to avoid a clash. They said: We will make it perfectly clear to the Gentiles that they do not have to come back under the law, but in order to make it easier for Jewish and Gentile Christians to live together, we will appeal to the Gentiles to abstain from these particular things for the time being. And it was only for the time being.

So I am suggesting that Cranmer and others were partly motivated by the same sort of argument. 'Here are the people so accustomed to this form of worship – well, let us not offend them unnecessarily, let us be clear about our great doctrine of salvation but let us make this concession: Go on using your liturgy, get rid of the Roman Catholic accretions and errors and make it a pure and true liturgy. That is a good temporary measure.' And I am prepared to grant that as a temporary measure it was justifiable.

Now try to put your mind back into that sixteenth century with all those difficulties. These men were confronted by the ignorant populace, deeply prejudiced, who said, 'It has always been done like this!' Do you not say things like that sometimes? I hear that argument very frequently, not only from Anglicans but from Baptists and Methodists and others. People were like that then, and we must recognize it and meet it. There is nothing wrong in principle in resorting to a temporary expedient or measure when the problem does not concern a vital, essential truth. It is a right principle, for the sake of brotherhood and friendship and the true unity of the Spirit, to make the kind of appeal and concession that was made by the Council of Jerusalem. That is an argument for the Prayer Book in the reign of Queen Elizabeth, and still more in the reign of Henry VIII when it was first produced, and then in the reign of Edward VI. But I suggest that that is the most that can be said for it. And it does not justify the perpetuation of that form of worship for ever and ever.

So that was the argument of people like Cranmer. But immediately there arose these other people whom I have described as 'radical Puritans' and they objected to the Prayer Book from the very beginning. They said, 'It may be expedient, but, surely, we must be governed in these matters by the teaching of the New Testament itself. Can we stop at only changing our view of the doctrine of salvation? Surely the New Testament teaches us also about the form of government in the church, and about the form of worship and we must be consistent. We must carry the Reformation right through.' And the fight began at once. If you have ever read of that great man John Hooper, Bishop of Gloucester, you will know that he was one of the leaders in all this, and many others came after him. They claimed that they were just going back to the New Testament, and they said that everything that had been added on quite unjustifiably, chiefly by the Church at Rome, must be undone and discarded.

Then you come to the next century, to the great conference held in Westminster Abbey, the famous Assembly of Divines, called in 1643. At that time there was confusion in this country, partly political but very largely also religious, concerning not only bishops, but the whole issue of a form of worship. The bishops were enforcing the use of the Prayer Book; every other form of worship was prohibited. So with the political agitation, and the problem of the war, the English Civil War, that was being waged, it was decided that an Assembly of Divines should be called. It was held in Westminster Abbey in London, and produced the Westminster Confession of Faith, and with it a Directory of Public Worship.

Now here is a very interesting matter in this whole connection. The majority view among the men at the conference was that of the Church of Scotland, which was Presbyterian. It is not always realized that though the Church of Scotland owed so much to John Calvin, it departed from his teaching on the issue of church worship. Members of this conference felt that there was need for ministers to be helped and guided, but they did not agree with Calvin that there should be a stated liturgy and formal prayers. What they said was this: In this Directory we give you the subjects about which you should pray, a general idea with regard to what you should pray for, and how you should pray, but we do not give you the words.

In other words, they did precisely what I suggested in my interpretation of the use of the Lord's Prayer given by our Lord Himself: When you pray, this is the way in which you should proceed. You start with worship and adoration and then go on. You must have order in your prayers; you must not just jump about from petition to petition. So the Directory was concerned simply to introduce an element of order. It gave an indication of subjects in general but it certainly did not prescribe exact words nor give an instruction that these words, and no others, should be prayed and offered as petitions Sunday by Sunday, world without end.

Then the end of my historical review brings me to the events of 1662 when two thousand men were ejected out of their livings in the Church of England. The argument was mainly over this one matter of church worship and was not primarily a matter of doctrine. The Act of Uniformity laid it down that all ministers must use the Prayer Book which was produced at that time, slightly modifying the previous one. That was the whole issue. Now people like Richard Baxter and others, who were among those ejected, had no objection to a liturgy. In fact, Richard Baxter believed in having a liturgy. But what he objected to was that it should be compulsory. He objected to the ruling that made use of the Prayer Book a condition of being a minister in the Church of England, and forbade the offering of extempore prayers. It was this whole element of compulsion that was the crux in 1662.

We must look at this matter further in our next study, when I hope to consider the principles that should govern us in our thinking on this subject. We must get out of the attitude that says, 'Ah, they're beautiful prayers! Isn't the language perfect?', or some similar prejudice often based on ignorance on the one hand, or sheer thoughtlessness on the other. I suggest to you that there are certain very vital principles here. It is not enough just to react to certain things with violence and abhorrence – though I am in great sympathy with such a reaction, if I may say so! No, we must have solid, scriptural grounds for saying – if this is what we do say – that Prayer Book worship is not our understanding of how the worship of Christian people in the church of God should be conducted. We must be able to show from the Scriptures the reasons why we long to see a restoration of New Testament patterns of worship and why we are prepared to commit ourselves to do everything we can to work for that.

May God bless us in the meantime, and enable us to consider these matters in a spirit of humility and of prayer in the light of the teaching of the Scriptures.

Closing prayer

O Lord our God, we come unto Thee and we are amazed more than ever that there is a Christian church at all. We see ourselves, and we see other men and women in this age and in other ages. O God, we thank Thee that what we do see clearly, above all else, is that the church is Thine and that she would have perished long ago were this not true. Lord, we thank Thee for Thy great patience and longsuffering with us, and now again we yield and submit ourselves unto Thee and the Word of Thy grace, praying that Thou wouldest control us by it and lead us by it and ever give us a single eye to Thy glory and to Thy praise. Hear us, O Lord, as we come in the name of Thy dear Son, our blessed Lord and Saviour. Amen.

Twenty-three

*

> *Having then gifts differing according to the grace that is given to us, whether prophecy, let us prophesy according to the proportion of faith; or ministry, let us wait on our ministering: or he that teacheth, on teaching; or he that exhorteth, on exhortation: he that giveth, let him do it with simplicity; he that ruleth, with diligence; he that sheweth mercy, with cheerfulness.*
>
> Romans 12:6–8

We have agreed that when we read a passage like Romans 12:6–8, it behoves us to examine ourselves to see whether or not we conform to it. The church should always be doing that; the church should always be 'under the Word' and should be always reforming herself according to it. There is no doubt that many of the great troubles that have afflicted the life of the Christian church have been due to the fact that she has forgotten to do that. The danger is always that we just go on thoughtlessly continuing patterns which we have been accustomed to, or in which we have been brought up.

Now for Christian people that is always wrong. It is unintelligent, apart from anything else, and it is certainly not spiritual. It is the kind of attitude our Lord was condemning in the woman of Samaria, as we see from her story in John 4. If you cannot establish that your tradition is scriptural, then it is wrong to continue in it. In any case, we should always be ready to examine ourselves and the whole of our Christian life according to God's Word because whether we like it or not, we are all involved in present-day movements towards church unity and we must all take some kind of decision.

Then there is, as we have seen, the tendency in all the

churches to turn more and more to liturgical, catholic types of service. For instance, here in Westminster, London, on Good Friday evening, there is to be a procession of all the churches. I must qualify that 'all', because this church will not be involved, but all the churches of Westminster are expected to join in a procession from Trafalgar Square to the Roman Catholic cathedral not far away from here where a service will be conducted by Cardinal Heenan and the Bishop of London and the Methodist minister of Westminster Central Hall. That is the kind of thing that is happening, and it is for that reason that it is our bounden duty, as Christian people, to have some understanding of these matters.

The Church of England and the Presbyterian Church of England, who have been holding a series of conversations, have recently issued a report, and these are some of the things they say: 'No church as it now exists is adequately prepared and equipped in its theological formulations, or in its forms of worship, or in its methods of evangelism, for the tasks to which the Holy Spirit is summoning it in the future.' They say that all these things must be considered, and at the moment we ourselves are considering forms of church worship.

In connection with that, here is another statement from the report: 'The signs are too numerous that the denominations are aware of the judgment of history, and of the need to find new patterns of church life, witness and service.'

Whether we want it or not, we are involved in all this. Here are these churches saying that they must re-examine every-thing. If they are saying that, how much more should we say it, especially when we know beforehand that though they talk about 'examining', what they really mean is that they have already made up their minds. What they really mean is that the Free Churches must re-examine themselves and adopt the Catholic type of church service. There is no question about that. Statements have been made in which this is assumed. As the government of the church is going to be episcopal, so the service will be Catholic, liturgical in its form. That is why we must go out of our way to inform our minds and have a true understanding of these issues.

Now let us be quite clear. We are not judging anybody else. That is not my object at all. I am not concerned even to judge

[318]

the Catholic type of worship, but I am concerned to examine it, and to examine it in the light of Scripture. And we ourselves must be ready to admit and confess that we also are in danger. We all develop traditions, and it may be that we also will find that we are not as fully in conformity with the teaching of the Scriptures as we sometimes imagine ourselves to be. We have seen in our historical review that men and women, with the best intentions in the world, have departed from scriptural teaching; and we, too, are still in the flesh, and are subject to the same dangers.

So now, having looked at the matter historically, let us go on and ask ourselves this question: What is the general impression you get as you read your New Testament? This is always important. There is a danger, sometimes, of missing the wood because of the trees, of concentrating so much on particular texts that we forget the general tenor of the Scripture, the atmosphere or spirit of the New Testament as a whole. As we have no specific injunction from our Lord or the apostles to offer particular prayers, or to conduct services in a particular way, this general atmosphere or spirit becomes correspondingly very much more important.

Now I think that there can be no doubt at all that the kind of worship offered by the New Testament church is the kind indicated in our three verses. The apostle here, without setting out to do so, incidentally describes what was done in the church at Rome. In the corresponding verses in 1 Corinthians 14 we read that when the church met for worship, one member brought a psalm, another a prophecy, and so on [verse 26]. And notice, too, Colossians 3:16 where Paul tells us that they sang to one another in 'psalms and hymns and spiritual songs'.

So I would argue that the impression given is of a free and spontaneous worship. Indeed, in the church of Corinth this element of freedom and of spontaneity was so evident that it led to a certain amount of disorder and the apostle had to tell them, 'Let everything be done decently and in order' [*1 Cor.* 14:40]. But if you are tied in your service to a definite form, you cannot have disorder, it is all controlled. So I would argue that the New Testament teaching about the disorders that were arising in certain churches is, in and of itself, a proof that the

worship of the New Testament church was free and spontaneous.

But, secondly, let us go on beyond that. That disorder is
something that one would expect because it is consistent with
and conforms to the teaching in the Bible as to the difference
between the New Testament and the Old Testament. Now
this is a subject about which we must be careful. We need the
two Testaments, and yet there is a difference between the new
dispensation and the old. We have the same God, the same
grace, the same salvation. As we have been seeing at great
length, in working through chapters 9, 10 and 11, the Christian
is, after all, a child of Abraham, who is the father of all the
children of faith. So there is an identity and continuity
between the two, and yet there is a difference.

This, to me, is an extremely important point, because there
are two great possible errors with regard to this matter, and
many have fallen into one or the other. The one is to divorce
the New Testament entirely from the Old and to say that the
Old has nothing to do with us, that the New is entirely new.
That is wrong. We could easily prove that from quotations in
the New Testament, and from the way in which the New
looks upon the Old. Such an idea also violates the whole
principle that there is one grace of God, and one way of
salvation, and one eternal covenant of salvation.

But we must beware of the opposite danger of saying that
there is no difference between the Old and the New, with the
corresponding fallacy that comes out of that of governing the
New by the Old. This is a very real danger for certain people, in
particular those who belong to the Reformed tradition. They
know the value of the Old but their danger is to exaggerate and
to overestimate it and so they tend to control the New by the
Old.

Now I am suggesting that that is wrong, that there is a
difference between the New and the Old but that it is a
difference in degree, not in kind. Let me illustrate what I
mean. People are often perplexed by some words which our
Lord spoke about John the Baptist. Our Lord said in Matthew
11:11: 'Verily I say unto you, Among them that are born of
women there hath not risen a greater than John the Baptist:
notwithstanding he that is least in the kingdom of heaven is

greater than he.' Does that mean that John the Baptist is not to be regarded as a saved man and a child of God? That is patently wrong. What, then, is the difference between John the Baptist and 'the least in the kingdom of heaven'? I suggest that it is a difference not in his relationship to God, nor in his standing before God, but it is very much a difference in his understanding. John the Baptist, because he belonged to the old dispensation, was perplexed and uncertain. The Christian, on the other hand, should be rejoicing 'with joy unspeakable and full of glory' [*1 Pet.* 1:8], and be filled with a great spirit of assurance. If you take John the Baptist and contrast him with the apostles on and after the day of Pentecost, you will see exactly what I mean.

Now that is the difference between the Old and the New. But we also have the prophecy of Joel, quoted by Peter in his sermon on the day of Pentecost, which puts it still more clearly. The apostles and the others were baptized with the Holy Spirit and they became a phenomenon. Some of the people in Jerusalem, mocking, said, 'These men are full of new wine' [*Acts* 2:13]. Then we are told: 'But Peter, standing up with the eleven, lifted up his voice, and said unto them, Ye men of Judaea, and all ye that dwell at Jerusalem, be this known unto you, and hearken to my words: For these are not drunken as ye suppose, seeing it is but the third hour of the day. But this is that which was spoken by the prophet Joel' [*Acts* 2:14–16].

And what did Joel say? It was this: 'It shall come to pass in the last days, saith God, that I will pour out my Spirit upon all flesh' – not upon certain selected, special people only, it was to be a profusion upon all flesh, and notice – 'and your sons and your daughters shall prophesy' – they did not prophesy in the Old Testament; some people did, but they were exceptional; now there was a great profusion – 'and your young men shall see visions' – people who saw visions under the old dispensation were very few and rare, the seers and the prophets – 'your old men shall dream dreams: and on my servants and on my handmaidens I will pour out in those days of my Spirit; and they shall prophesy: and I will shew wonders in heaven above, and signs in the earth beneath' [verses 17–19].

Now there, surely, is the essential difference between the

new and the old and we ignore it at our peril. Inevitably it leads
to a different type of worship. Look at the Old Testament
worship – the temple, the tabernacle were more or less
essential. Why? Well, it was an external type of worship with
an appointed priesthood. It was very formal. Instructions were
given as to the furnishings, down to the smallest detail.
Everything was ordered, everything was prescribed exactly.
And God, having given the detailed instructions for the
tabernacle to Moses, said to him, 'See . . . that thou make all
things according to the pattern shewed to thee in the mount'
[*Heb.* 8:5].

But the New Testament is entirely different; it is an inner,
internal type of worship; it is free and informal. Our Lord
would sit down in a boat or on the side of a mountain and start
preaching. Or he would preach in a house – anywhere. You
have moved out of the realm of the formal and the external
into a living, vital, spiritual type of worship. And no longer are
you to recognize only certain people as priests. My friends, we
need to remember the Protestant Reformation – the universal
priesthood of all believers. That is why we do not walk in these
processions; we do not want to go back to a priesthood. We
believe, we assert, the universal priesthood of all believers. As
Christians, we are a kingdom of priests, 'a royal priesthood' [*1
Pet.* 2:9].

That is what I mean by saying that there is an essential
difference between the new and the old. So when you read
about the kind of church life revealed by verses like these in
Romans 12, you are impressed at once and say, 'This is the very
thing that I would expect from the fulfilment of the prophecy
of Joel. This is what I would expect as the result of the
"shedding forth", in great profusion, of the blessed Holy Spirit
of God.'

Now I move on to my third reason for opposing a liturgical
form of worship. I indicated in my historical review that one of
the arguments for the set forms of worship was that they were
essential because of the ignorance and the inability of most of
the priests who had become Protestant ministers. I admitted
that it was an argument that had a certain cogency. Yet I want
to suggest to you that it is an argument that you must handle,
very, very carefully, from this standpoint: Is not our Lord and

Saviour capable of giving ability to men? Is it not possible for the Lord to raise up men and give them gifts which will enable them to conduct worship, to pray and to preach, and so on?

And, of course, the answer to my question is the three verses that we are examining. Our Lord does give these gifts through the Spirit and He can give them to anybody. That is one of the glorious things that we find in the New Testament. 'Having then gifts differing according to the grace that is given to us . . .' And there is no limit. He can give them, as Joel prophesied, to the servants and the handmaidens, the young men as well as the old. He is not restricted. And this is something that you find not only in the New Testament but fulfilled so many times during the subsequent history of the Christian church.

Obviously God gave gifts and raised men up in the early churches. Try to think back to the conditions in those days. Here were the apostles and others. They were travellers who went around and preached the gospel. People were converted, and the apostles formed them into churches and then moved on. What happened to the churches? There is an obvious answer which, in a sense, we have already considered. In each church the Spirit gave gifts to different men and they stood out according to these gifts. They were elected as elders, and some of them became teaching elders, because they had the gift of teaching.

Now in recent years the church has been realizing this truth more and more. Take the books written by that excellent man Roland Allen on *St Paul's Missionary Methods and Ours* – I think his views are now generally accepted. As far back as 1913 Roland Allen pointed out that the western churches had been adopting a wrong method in their missionary work. The missionaries would go out to various countries, people would be converted, and then the missionaries would stay as the ministers. But Roland Allen points out that the apostles did not do that. The ministers arose out of the local people. How? Well, they did not raise themselves. The Spirit gave the gifts and so there developed, out of the churches themselves, the type of ministry that was essential for that church. And to say that cannot happen, and that you therefore must get one or two men to write out prayers for everybody else to read, is surely a reflection on the power of our Lord to give gifts to His people and to provide the necessary gifts for his servants and ministers in the life of the church. I feel it is wrong scripturally, therefore, to argue like that, and also wrong historically. As I said, I am prepared to grant it as a very temporary expedient, but it must not be continued.

Let me illustrate that. John Owen said that to ask men to go on reading these set forms and prayers perpetually is like a man being taught to swim. Since at first the man cannot swim, you do not throw him straight into deep water and tell him to get on with it, no, you provide him with what we now call water-wings. In those days two bladders were blown up and tied together on the man. When he entered the water the two bladders kept him afloat, enabling him to learn the strokes. But, as Owen pointed out, he does not go on using the bladders for ever – otherwise he would never learn to swim. A similar illustration is this: If a man should break his leg, then for a while he will have to use a crutch, and it is right that he should. But he must not go on using the crutch for the rest of his life. In the same way, set prayers are justifiable as temporary expedients but must not be continued.

Or let me put it like this to you – this is my fourth point – surely to create a written liturgy is ultimately the wrong way of facing the problem of the absence of gifts. Now you may say, 'What has all this got to do with us? Is this not ancient history?' It is not. I know churches in different parts of this country where prayer meetings or any other weeknight meetings can no longer be held. Why not? 'Because,' we are told, 'there is nobody here who can pray.' I have known churches which used to have well-attended, flourishing prayer meetings where now there is not even one. The people say, 'We've nobody who can pray, nobody who can give an address, nobody who can guide us, nobody who can conduct a Bible class. Nobody seems to have the ability.' So this is a very real and modern problem.

How, then, do you face this problem? Well, I am sure that the way to face it is not to provide a book out of which anybody can read. The way to face a problem like that is to get the church to examine itself and to say, 'Why can nobody pray here in public? What's the matter? Is the modern Christian different from the early Christian? Why do people not pray today as they used to pray?' You face it like that, and you say, 'Get down on your knees and ask God to forgive you.' Then without knowing it, the church members have started praying. Merely to ask forgiveness in public is a prayer. So the way to face this problem is not to provide a kind of permanent crutch, but to repent and ask God to have mercy and to shower down His blessing.

Here, again, is a principle that has a wider application. I see a tendency in the modern church to repeat this fallacy in different areas, not only over forms of prayer. For example, the way in which a church or churches face a period of dryness and ineffectiveness is very different today from times in the past. Nowadays, when the church is in such a state, its leaders decide to call in some evangelistic organization to put things right. But it used not to be done like that. There was a time in the Christian church when, if there was not much blessing and very few people were being converted, church members and leaders would say, 'Why are people not being converted? What is wrong?' They would say, 'Why has the Spirit of God left us? Let us appoint a day of prayer and humiliation and fasting. Let us go before the Lord and confess to Him that we are failing Him. Let us ask Him to show us where we have gone wrong and ask Him to come back among us.' And they would go on doing that until revival came. Surely that is the scriptural method, not calling in some expedient from the outside.

Let me give you a still more practical illustration of what I mean. Let me put it in personal terms – forgive me for that. I have a very great problem. I want to pass this on to you, and I would be glad if you would think about this and somehow or other give me your answers. As I speak here, what I am saying is being recorded on a tape-recorder, and that happens on Friday nights and twice on Sundays and we receive letters from different parts of the country asking us for these tapes. Here is my problem: Should I allow these tapes to be sent out? There are preachers who do allow this but on the whole I do not. Why not? The argument that I am given is this: 'But think of these people in different parts of the country with nobody to preach to them on Sundays, or perhaps with men preaching against the truth. Is it not your duty to send out the tapes?'

But I have a reply, and it is based upon the principle that I am putting before you. I am afraid that we will eventually reach a stage in which there will be perhaps just about half-a-dozen preachers in this country and everybody else will be listening to the tapes of these preachers. It is not impossible. There is a tendency in that direction and it is increasing. And I say that is wrong. Cannot God the Holy Spirit give gifts to men in these churches? So there can be a danger in providing ready-made sermons.

And that is the argument against liturgical forms of service. It is already there and all you do is read the words. One man prepares it, and hundreds, or thousands, perhaps, read it. And it seems to me that this practice does tend to violate the teaching, so plainly set forth in the Scripture, that the same Lord who could raise up men among slaves and the servants of the first century can surely still do so. But we seem to have forgotten the Holy Spirit and we say, 'Send us tapes', or, 'Provide us with sermons', or, 'Provide us with prayers'. Surely it is somewhat of a reflection upon the power of the Spirit to provide the necessary people and the necessary gifts.

But let me go on to my fifth argument. Is there not something about these prescribed forms of worship which contradicts certain very plain statements in the New Testament? You can read one of them in the interview between our Lord and the woman of Samaria in John chapter 4. The woman says to Him – and this is typical of the argument that is made – 'Our fathers worshipped in this mountain; and ye say, that in Jerusalem is the place where men ought to worship.' That, I say, is the old dispensation, and here is our Lord's answer: 'Woman, believe me, the hour cometh, when ye shall neither in this mountain, nor yet at Jerusalem, worship the Father' – you must not of necessity have these set places; you may have them, or you may not; you must not confine yourselves to that – 'Ye worship ye know not what: we know what we worship: for salvation is of the Jews. But the hour cometh, and now is, when the true worshippers shall worship the Father in spirit and in truth: for the Father seeketh such to worship him. God is a Spirit: and they that worship him must worship him in spirit and in truth' [*John* 4:20–24].

And if you also read Acts chapter 7 you will see that the

martyr Stephen had to develop precisely the same argument with those 'stiff-necked' Jews who would confine worship to the Old Testament form. Then take another example which we have already come across in our study of this Epistle – Romans 8:26–27: 'Likewise the Spirit also helpeth our infirmities: for we know not what we should pray for as we ought'– you cannot say that if you rely upon written prayers, can you? So what is the provision for us? Prayers prepared by certain great men? No, no – 'but the Spirit himself maketh intercession for us with groanings which cannot be uttered. And he that searcheth the hearts knoweth what is the mind of the Spirit, because he maketh intercession for the saints according to the will of God.' The answer to our inability is not prepared prayers, it is the Spirit. It may be a groan, something almost inarticulate, but it is a prayer – 'with groanings which cannot be uttered'.

And there are several exhortations about prayer in the New Testament. I think of Paul's words, for instance, in the last chapter of the Epistle to the Ephesians: 'Praying always with all prayer and supplication in the Spirit' [verse 18]. That is how you pray. You do not pray through forms, you pray 'in the Spirit'. The Spirit will give you the prayer and He will give you the facility and the power and all that you need. So I feel that we must consider those three texts very seriously without adducing any further ones, before we come to a final decision about this matter.

But then my sixth argument is that there is a very grave danger here of interfering with the freedom of the Spirit to give sudden, immediate inspiration. Now I could illustrate this point from preaching. It is a great problem which every preacher must have met at some time or other. We are not all equally gifted in the matter of speech and there are some men who almost seem to be incapable of preaching unless they write out every word. The great Dr Thomas Chalmers really could not preach without his manuscript. But this, it seems to me, is a very important point. I am not going to go so far as to say that a man should never write a sermon, I do not believe that, but I do say that the preacher must always be free. How many times have I personally found that what has been used of God is something that I had never thought of until the moment I uttered it. It was given me as I was preaching, not in my preparation. The freedom of the Spirit! We must be very careful lest we put limits upon the freedom of the Spirit. If you are tied to a particular written text, where does the Spirit come in?

These are the things that we have tended to forget. I remember once, some twenty years ago, speaking to the then Religious Director of the BBC. We were having a discussion about these matters and I was trying to explain to him why I did not preach on their programmes. I put it in the form of a question: 'If the Holy Spirit suddenly came upon the preacher, what would happen to your programmes?' And he admitted that it was a fair question.

But, again, look at it like this. Is there not a danger of our doing something which is antagonistic to revival? In revival there is an essential element of freedom. There must be an opportunity for the Spirit to break in. Let us be careful about our desire to have 'dignified' services. This has been the tragedy of Nonconformity. In the middle of the nineteenth century there began to be talk of dignity and learning – and Nonconformity has gone down ever since. The test of a service is not whether or not it is dignified, but whether or not the power of the Spirit is in it.

Why has there not been a revival for so long? Is not this partly the answer? The Spirit is not being given an opportunity. There is a danger of quenching the Spirit. John Owen, to quote him again, says quite specifically that in the light of verses 6, 7 and 8 of Romans 12, liturgical services and read prayers are definitely guilty of quenching the Spirit. But though there is that danger, I personally think Dr Owen is going a bit too far because the Holy Spirit is so powerful that He can even break in through a read service. He has done so many times. One of the greatest preachers at the Methodist Awakening in Wales two hundred years ago was a man called Daniel Rowland, and the Spirit came upon him as he was reading the communion service out of the Book of Common Prayer.

Now there are people who say, 'So, doesn't that justify the use of the Prayer Book?' It does not. That is the exception. The Holy Spirit can come in spite of our quenching Him, and in spite of our forms which put limits upon Him, but that does not justify our continuing in that procedure. There is the danger, then, of limiting the freedom of the Spirit. How often have you heard of a revival breaking out in a cathedral service? That is the test.

And, lastly, is it not a simple fact that a condition of low spirituality in the Christian church always leads to the use of forms? When men cannot preach, they begin to read their sermons; when they cannot pray, they begin to read their prayers. Low spirituality in the church always leads in the direction of the Catholic type of service, with an emphasis upon what is called 'the beauty of worship', by which people invariably mean 'set forms of worship', and that has been increasingly happening in the twentieth century. In contrast, whenever there is a revival, there is always a revival of extempore praying and freedom in the act of worship.

Now Evangelicals in all the denominations have always proved this. Evangelicals who normally use the set forms of prayer always pray freely and without prior preparation in evangelistic campaigns. So why should they not do the same in all church services? There is a contradiction there. The more evangelical a man is, the more he desires freedom, and the more he will introduce extempore prayers into his official service, even though it may mean that he is breaking the law in doing so. An evangelical who has the Spirit in him will inevitably be free and express himself freely with the whole of his spirit.

I will just leave you at this point with a question which seems to be the extension of the argument that I have been working out with you. Does not the whole question of hymn singing come in here as well? There are people who say you should not sing hymns but only psalms. Are the psalms adequate to express the fulness of the New Testament experience? Can the psalmists, who only saw these things 'afar off', give full expression to what is felt and experienced and thought by those who have known salvation in the fulness of the Spirit? I suggest we need to re-examine this whole area of worship very carefully and very seriously lest we limit the new dispensation by the old. You can become legalistic and literalistic, and that is always wrong. So I think that the principles we have been discussing apply to hymns also.

[329]

And so, again, you will find that in all great times of
movements of the Spirit, tides of the Spirit, there is always an
outbreak of the composition and singing of evangelical hymns
and tunes. Singing has always been one of the great characteristics of a true movement of the Spirit of God. We are told that
once, in the very early days of the Separatists, in the reign of
Queen Elizabeth, some went so far as to forbid all singing.
They said that even singing psalms was wrong. But they were
soon corrected about that. The Old Testament teaches us to
sing, and to sing psalms. But over and above that, obviously,
in the New Testament believers began to sing hymns
and 'spiritual songs' [*Col.* 3:16], which clearly were given by
the inspiration of the Spirit. And this, I repeat, has been a
characteristic of the church in all great periods of revival and
quickening when new life has come into the people through
the gracious operations of the Holy Spirit. Christian people, let
us again, openly, pray in the Spirit and ask Him to enlighten us
and to lead us and to guide us. Let us examine all we are and all
we do, our forms of worship as well as our faith and church
government, in the light of the teaching of the Scripture. May
God bless us to that end, and bless us individually and
collectively.

Twenty-four

*

*Let love be without dissimulation. Abhor that which is evil;
cleave to that which is good. Be kindly affectioned one to another
with brotherly love; in honour preferring one another; not
slothful in business; fervent in spirit; serving the Lord; rejoicing
in hope; patient in tribulation; continuing instant in prayer;
distributing to the necessity of saints; given to hospitality. Bless
them which persecute you: bless, and curse not. Rejoice with
them that do rejoice, and weep with them that weep. Be of the
same mind one toward another. Mind not high things, but
condescend to men of low estate. Be not wise in your own
conceits. Recompense to no man evil for evil. Provide things
honest in the sight of all men. If it be possible, as much as lieth in
you, live peaceably with all men. Dearly beloved, avenge not
yourselves, but rather give place unto wrath: for it is written,
Vengeance is mine; I will repay, saith the Lord. Therefore if thine
enemy hunger, feed him; if he thirst, give him drink: for in so
doing thou shalt heap coals of fire on his head. Be not overcome
of evil, but overcome evil with good.*

Romans 12:9–21

We come now to a new subsection in Romans 12 which goes
on to the end of the chapter. And as we look at this subsection,
it is very important that we should remind ourselves of the
context. In this chapter the apostle begins to deal with the
practical application and outworking of the great doctrine that
he has been laying down in the first eleven chapters. That is
his method. Doctrine first, then application; and we have spent
time in seeing how important it is that we should always
follow his method.

Primarily, Christianity is a way of life. The Christians were
first of all called the people of 'the way'. This was not merely

[331]

because they thought in a particular way, but also because they lived in a particular way, and because they died in a particular way. So it is vital that we should always proceed from doctrine to practice. 'Faith without works is dead' [*James* 2:20].

We have seen that this chapter can be divided up as follows. The first two verses lay down the great overriding principles that govern the Christian's conduct. They are a general introduction to the remainder of the Epistle.

Then the subsection that runs from verse 3 to verse 8 deals with Christians in the church exercising the various gifts that the Spirit of God gives for the edification, and the proper functioning of the church, which is the body of Christ.

This is the point at which we have arrived. But from verse 9 Paul is concerned to deal more with the general conduct and behaviour of Christians as individuals and in their relationship to their fellow Christians, and beyond that in their relationship to people in general in the world in which they still find themselves So there is a very definite break at the end of verse 8.

We are now confronted by a series of statements, about which commentators ask: Has the apostle just laid down a number of maxims for our guidance, without being concerned to have any arrangement? Did he just put down a number of things as they occurred to him, or even as they were suggested to him by the Spirit, or is there some order and arrangement here?

The majority of the commentators seem to be agreed that there is no discernible order here, and that it is very difficult to have the classification that we have had hitherto in the whole of this Epistle. But I must confess that I am not quite in agreement with them. I agree that from the standpoint of subdividing into headings, this is the most difficult subsection that we have come across in our studies of Romans.

But of all the apostles, Paul had a very orderly mind. That is one of the great features of his style. He was a logical man. He thought clearly and systematically. We know that there have been many times when he breaks into his theme, and forgets it and is carried away, but that does not matter, he always comes back to it. He has a fundamental order and system in his mind. You could easily contrast him in that respect with the Apostle

John. However, the question is whether he has any order or arrangement here, and I am contending that even here there is a classification, and we can suggest a division of the matter. I am not pretending that it is absolute. There are one or two difficulties. But I think that on the whole there is a sequence and I suggest that it is as follows.

In the ninth verse the apostle lays down two great principles which must govern the whole of the life and behaviour of the Christian. Now that, of course, is very typical of him. He has done that already in this chapter and it was his method. He has some great, fundamental undergirding, or overriding, principles which govern the whole of what he is going to say.

In the tenth and eleventh verses he is concerned, I suggest, with our general spirit, our general attitude as Christians, towards what we are, towards one another, and our work.

In verses 12 and 13 I believe he moves on to show us how we should react to varying circumstances, both our own and other people's. Having dealt with our action and activity, he is now turning to our reaction. First, what you do; secondly, what you do when things happen to you. Action! Reaction!

Then in verses 14 to 16 Paul deals with our reaction to other people. In verses 12 and 13, it was reaction to circumstances, but now he deals with our reaction to people, their behaviour, their conduct and their circumstances.

From verse 17 to the end of the chapter, there is clearly one special theme, and that is our reaction to wrong and evil. Somebody has been dealing with you in a wrong way, in an evil manner – how do you react to that? How do you treat them? The apostle takes that up and expands it more fully than any other single theme.

Then he ends the passage with, again, a general principle or maxim: 'Be not overcome of evil, but overcome evil with good' [verse 21].

There, in a very general way, is the analysis of this subsection and I think it is important to realize that there is a progression in the thought here, that there is a measure of order. What confuses people and makes them say that, perhaps, no such analysis is possible, is that, having said in verse 14, 'Bless them which persecute you; bless, and curse not,' instead of going on immediately to verse 17 where he says, 'Recompense to no man evil for evil,' the apostle seems to go back again to our relationships. And he does not talk about those who are persecuting us, or are unkind or malicious, but about people more generally: 'Rejoice with them that do rejoice, and weep with them that weep. Be of the same mind one toward another. Mind not high things . . .' This does seem to be an interruption in that logical sequence. And yet, I think, if we put it in the broad way that I have suggested, we have a solution to the problem.

As we saw, in verses 12 and 13 Paul refers first to our reaction to circumstances, then in verses 14 to 16 he goes on to our reaction to people, and finally, in particular, from verse 17 he turns to our behaviour with respect to definite evil and wrongdoing on the part of others with respect to us.

That, then, is our analysis. I think it is clear, is it not, that the apostle here is really putting, in his own way, our Lord's own summary of the commandments. You remember how a man came and asked our Lord, 'Which is the first commandment of all?' And our Lord replied, saying, 'Thou shalt love the Lord thy God with all thy heart, and with all thy soul, and with all thy mind, and with all thy strength: that is the first commandment. And the second is like, namely this, Thou shalt love thy neighbour as thyself' [*Mark* 12:28–31]. That is what we have here from verse 9 to the end of the chapter. Love of God – love of neighbour, even if your neighbour happens to be your enemy. It is a perfect statement of our Lord's words. Or, if your prefer it, it is a statement of the leading principles of the Sermon on the Mount. Once more, love of God, and love of your neighbour. That is the summary of the whole of the law.

Now, as we come to a detailed consideration of this subsection, there are two things, it seems to me, that stand out at once and should strike us. The first is that once more we have a final answer here to those people who would have us believe that there is a contrast between the teaching of our blessed Lord and the Apostle Paul. That view is still heard and is still fairly popular. People contrast what they would call the ethical, practical teaching of our Lord as you have it in the Sermon on the Mount, with the theological teaching of the Apostle Paul. They are always contrasting the simple gospel of Christ – which they say was always concerned with the practicalities of living – with all this theological superstructure which they say the Apostle Paul has incorporated into and imposed upon that simple gospel. Well, here is the final answer to that. The apostle was as concerned as the Lord was with the practicalities of the Christian life. Here he is dealing with exactly the same thing. This is his way of expounding the law as given to the children of Israel through Moses, even as our Lord had already taught it in the Sermon on the Mount.

The second comment is this: We cannot possibly understand the teaching of this subsection and profit by it, unless we constantly bear in mind the teaching of the first two verses of the chapter – 'I beseech you therefore, brethren, by the mercies of God . . .' If you do not know what they teach, and if you have not experienced them, it is no use your dealing with this subsection, you will not be able to do it. It is only an appeal to those who are born again. No man or woman can live the Sermon on the Mount without being born again, born of the Spirit, without having a power which is greater than the power of human nature.

'I beseech you therefore, brethren' – in the light of the great doctrine he has been laying down – 'by the mercies of God.' If we do not know that motive, if it does not appeal to us, if that is not what moves us, then it is idle to consider these injunctions, these maxims, if one may so describe them. It is as ridiculous to do so, as it is to talk about obeying the Sermon on the Mount. Our Lord, I believe, preached the Sermon on the Mount to show us our absolute need of the new birth and of the Spirit of God. The theory that people can take the Sermon on the Mount and make it the basis of their social gospel or of the life of the state is a sheer impossibility in practice. The idea that people who cannot even keep the law of England could live the Sermon on the Mount – is there anything more fantastic than such a notion?

We start, then, with verse 9: 'Let love be without dissimula-tion.' That is number one. Two: 'Abhor that which is evil; cleave to that which is good.' What a wonderful, what a perfect summary of the whole life of the Christian man and woman! These two things cover everything, and if we are only right about these two principles we cannot go wrong. That is why the apostle starts with them. There is no basis to Christian living apart from this verse, and the Christian life must always be thought of in these terms. Love! There is the great first principle. But it must be 'without dissimulation'. Now we shall find that Paul goes on repeating this. You will find, in chapter 13:10 that he says, 'Therefore love is the fulfilling of the law.' That is just another way of saying, 'Let love be without dissimulation.' It is the whole basis, the only thing, that makes the law possible; it sums up the whole of the law.

What is the law of God? Of course, the Jews, the Pharisees in particular, completely misunderstood it. There they were with their six-hundred-and-thirteen detailed rules, and they were experts, as our Lord said, on the minutiae of the law. He said, 'Ye pay tithe of mint and anise and cummin, and have forgotten the weightier matters of the law' [*Matt.* 23:23]. What are these? Oh, the love of God! The whole tragedy of the Jews was that they had reduced the true conception of the law of God to a matter of rules and regulations and details and subsections, thus losing themselves and forgetting the great principle.

And the apostle again deals with all that in his extraordinary manner, as we see it before us here. The law is summed up in this – love to God, love to your neighbour. That is the way to think of law; not to miss the wood because of the trees; not to be just little moralists, concerned about particular things. That comes in, of course, but first we must start with the great principle, we must start with the right idea of the law. If we do not, we shall go astray. And it seems to me, so often, that as Christian people we do fail in our behaviour because we approach these problems directly instead of indirectly. We start with a particular problem instead of with these two fundamental principles – loving God, loving our neighbour.

The apostle, therefore, starts with his great emphasis upon love, and when you are dealing with converts you start in the same way. It is not actions that matter but relationships. And it is because people forget this, that they get into trouble over the detailed actions. We must never forget that we are dealing with persons, and that it is personal relationships that matter above everything else; and in this there is nothing that counts save love.

There are many words which are used in the New Testament to deal with love and the apostle here uses the strongest, the deepest and the greatest word that was available – *agape*. *Agape* is the word that Paul uses to express God's love to us, and he is saying here that we should be animated in our living by the kind of love with which God has loved us. In 1 Corinthians 13 the apostle gives us what is sometimes called his 'hymn of love'. And people are undoubtedly right when they say that he had to write that chapter because the Greek language had not got a word which conveyed the Christian concept of love. So he had to say a number of things about love to safeguard it from debased or inadequate ideas.

So this is what the apostle lays down at once – your whole conduct is to be governed by the kind of loving outlook which characterizes God's outlook upon you. What is that? Well, first, it is unconditional love, love without reservation. Love is something that is totalitarian. It is, therefore, a call to us to give to God our allegiance, in all ways and with the whole of our being. We are to regard ourselves, therefore, in terms of love and within the terms of this whole relationship of love: love to God, love to the neighbour.

Then, secondly, the apostle hastens to say, 'Let love be without dissimulation.' This means that we must not be playing a part, we must not be pretending. It means that we must not be hypocrites. We must be honest. It must be true love, not some kind of artificial product which simulates love. And here I think it is very important for us to realize that in this matter of love not only must we not deceive others, we must not even deceive ourselves.

I believe there is a great deal of self-deception at the present time. Today, there is an emphasis on love and fellowship. Everything is to be done by means of 'love'. But the question is: Is it really love, or are people just fooling themselves? Is it genuine? Is it true? Is it real? Is it free from dissimulation? Is it merely a façade, an appearance, something that is 'put up', or is there a real love? Now the apostle is concerned that love must be 'without dissimulation' – play-acting or assuming, a love which comes from the depths of our being.

Let me give you some more negatives. When the apostle talks about love, he is not merely talking about politeness or affability. How often these things are confused! If people are affable, it is said that they are gracious and loving. But affability and courtesy are poles apart from love. Affability is merely putting on a manner, rather like putting on a suit. It is polite, an appearance. It is a superficial thing. But grace and love are very deep.

Again, love, according to the Bible, is never sentimental, it is never weak. Of course, we are living in an age which abuses the word love more than any other word. That is the influence, is it not, of the cinema and the television and the newspapers, and the way in which people talk about 'falling in love'? They do not know what it means. Though they call it love, they mean lust. So it is important that we should be clear about these things.

And thirdly, and most important of all, love must never be contrasted with law. We are living in a lawless age. Its motto is, 'Not law but love'. Today, people dislike the whole notion of law. But that is a fundamental fallacy. The apostle says in verse 8 of the next chapter that love fulfils the law. Or, as our Lord puts it, 'Which is the first and the greatest commandment? Thou shalt love . . .' To put love and law up as contrasts is a failure to understand the basic and elementary teaching of the whole of the New Testament. And yet that is being done at the present time. People deny the doctrine of the atonement because, they say, 'It is to do with law.'

But the atonement *is* to do with law. It is because the law had been broken that the Son of God had to die on the cross on Calvary's hill; his death was a great legal transaction. As Paul puts it in Romans 3:26: '. . . that [God] might be just, and the justifier of him which believeth in Jesus.' Without a fulfilment of the law there is no salvation for anybody. And the glory of the love of God is that it fulfils the law. It does not deny it, it does not set it on one side, it 'fulfils' it. So there is nothing more fatal than to think of love as something which is contrasted with law.

So what does Paul mean by saying, 'Let love be without dissimulation'? We can put it like this: It means that we must keep God's commandments. You remember how our Lord Himself has defined this in the fourteenth chapter of John's Gospel: 'If ye love me, keep my commandments' [verse 15].

[338]

How do you show that you love God – by singing hymns and choruses? All right, that comes in, but it is not enough, it does not guarantee that you really love God. 'If ye love me, keep my commandments' – there you are giving proof of love.

He says it again in John 14:21: 'He that hath my commandments, and keepeth them, he it is that loveth me'. If men and women do not keep God's commandments it is idle for them to talk about loving God. You do not love God in words, but in deeds, and in truth. Take the twenty-third verse of the same chapter: 'Jesus answered and said unto him, If a man love me, he will keep my words: and my Father will love him, and we will come unto him, and make our abode with him.'

Let us be clear, then, about this. Love is something that always shows itself in conduct and in action. It is not a mere sentiment. It is not weak but very strong, and it is a carrying out of the law, a fulfilling of the commandments of God. John is so concerned about this that he comes back to it. In 1 John 2:4-5 he says, 'He that saith, I know him, and keepeth not his commandments, is a liar, and the truth is not in him. But whoso keepeth his word, in him verily is the love of God perfected: hereby know we that we are in him.'

That is the teaching of the whole Bible. The Bible never merely asks for our mechanical obedience. Its teaching can be summed up in a phrase like this: 'My son, give me thine heart' [*Prov.* 23:26]. It is the heart that God wants. In other words, we are not only to keep God's law, we are called upon, as we are reminded here, to love it. The psalmist could rise to that height; he said, 'O how love I thy law!' [*Psa.* 119:97]. 'Thy commandments are my delights' [*Psa.* 119:143]. That is what God wants and Paul is saying that in his own way here in the words: 'Let love be without dissimulation.' This is what is to govern the whole of our behaviour. It is the keeping of the commandments of God, and not only keeping them, but loving the law and loving to keep the law.

So you not only keep the letter of the law, you keep the spirit. If you merely keep the letter or just keep within the law and are not true to the spirit, your love is with dissimulation. That means that you really hate it, you wish it were not there, but because you do not want to suffer punishment, you just keep on the right side of it.

We start by recognizing that the law of God is, after all, an expression of God's being. God does not give laws merely for the sake of doing so. He expresses His own nature in the laws. He says: I am like this. 'God is light, and in him is no darkness at all' [*1 John* 1:5]. And because that is true, certain things cannot happen in the presence of God, and the law simply tells us what they are. We must realize this and therefore love the law. 'Ye shall be holy' – why? – 'for I the Lord your God am holy' [*Lev.* 19:2]. Holiness is the expression of the being and character of God.

So when the apostle says, 'Let love be without dissimulation', he is saying: Oh, let your life of obedience to the commandments of God be wholehearted, entire, with no reservations. Do not obey God in order to please yourself or merely to please others. Now, alas, we know what these negatives mean, do we not? So often we live the life we do in order to please ourselves, to pander to pride and to feed it, or because we want the praise of others. There is a lot in the New Testament about not being 'men-pleasers'. If our motive for living the Christian life is either to please ourselves or to please others, our love is not 'without dissimulation', because the moment we start thinking of ourselves and our reputation, and what other people are thinking and saying about us, we have departed from the principle of love. Indeed, it is nothing but sentiment, and that is always with dissimulation.

In other words, we are being called here to please God above all else and to live to His glory and to His praise. 'The chief end of man is to glorify God.' 'Now,' says the apostle, 'please God with the whole of your being because of God's love for you. 'We love him, because he first loved us' [*1 John* 4:19]. If you know anything about the mercies of God, then this will be your response.

There are many ways in which Paul's teaching here can be put; there are many warnings in the Scriptures. The Scriptures come to us and they say, 'Be not deceived; God is not mocked: for whatsoever a man soweth, that shall he also reap' [*Gal.* 6:7]. 'Let love be without dissimulation.' If you do not practise that, then you are a fool, apart from anything else. If you think you can deceive God, then you know nothing about Him. Do not deceive yourself. Do not think that you, as it were, can take

God in and that you can act a part before Him. 'Be not deceived; God is not mocked.' Be aware of that – it is repeated so many times in the New Testament.

Or take the words of our Lord to the Pharisees: 'Ye are they which justify yourselves before men' [*Luke* 16:15]. Of course! 'They make broad their phylacteries' [*Matt.* 23:5]. And they made a great impression upon people, and people praised them. 'Wonderful men!' they said. Ah, it is an easy thing to take the world in, but our Lord says, 'Ye are they which justify yourselves before men; but God knoweth your hearts: for that which is highly esteemed among men is abomination in the sight of God.' Do not be fools, says the author of the Epistle to the Hebrews: 'All things are naked and opened unto the eyes of him with whom we have to do' [*Heb.* 4:13].

There are the warnings of the Scripture, and they are right. They are telling us not to be foolish or to try any dissimulation where God is concerned. It just does not work. For a while we may think it has worked. God does not always strike us down immediately, and the world may applaud us. But it is no good. The end always comes and death and judgment, and God knows all. Dissimulation is madness.

But Paul does not leave it at the negative. True love lifts us up above all this. So this phrase, 'Let love be without dissimulation,' is a great text for 1 Corinthians 13, and that is the real working out of this. That is how you love, and there you see the great positives. You have come to the realm of love, out of the realm of calculation and diplomacy and pretence and dissimulation. You are away from all that. You are living in a pure realm. You are positive in your loving, not because you want to create an impression, but as an expression of your heart's love to God who has shown such mercy towards you. And so the apostle is telling us here: Let this be the basis of the whole of your life, everything you do. And if you have love at the start and at the end and everywhere, then you will never be acting a part, you will, in turn, be loving God as He has loved you.

You notice that this is a command, and that again reminds us that love is not just a sentiment or a feeling. Get rid of that notion. It is not something you can create or work up when you like. Love is always the result of something else – the result of understanding. So this is a commandment. '*Let* love be without dissimulation.'

But how do you do that? How do you make sure that your love is without dissimulation? Now the apostle has already answered the question for us and I have often quoted this verse to you. It is the seventeenth verse in the sixth chapter of this great Epistle. 'But God be thanked, that ye were the servants of sin, but ye have obeyed from the heart' – what? – 'that form of doctrine which was delivered you.' There it is in a nutshell. If you really understand the doctrine that has been delivered to you, and if you believe it, then it will move your heart and you will practise it with the whole of your life. And, of course, it is not only a matter of understanding. The Holy Spirit in us creates this love within us. We are told in Romans 5:5: 'And hope maketh not ashamed; because the love of God is shed abroad in our hearts by the Holy Ghost which is given unto us.'

So we make sure that our love is without dissimulation by making sure that we are not just governed by our whims and feelings, our likes and dislikes – when I am in the mood, I will be nice; if I am in a bad temper, I will be difficult! No, love is always thinking it out, always realizing, always coming back to the 'therefore' of Romans 12:1: 'I beseech you *therefore* brethren, by the mercies of God'. Apply this great logic; examine your love in the light of the truth. And as long as you do, your love will be 'without dissimulation'.

There, then, is the first great maxim. Let me say something about the second: 'Abhor that which is evil; cleave to that which is good.' Now again watch the terms here: 'abhor' and 'cleave'. This second maxim follows of necessity, of course, from the first. The opposite of love is to hate, and that is the very term that the apostle uses. 'Abhor' means 'to have a horror of', 'to dislike utterly'. The Greek word the apostle uses has a prefix which means, a 'separation from', 'away from'. The word means, 'shrink from evil with abhorrence'.

Now evil is not something abstract. It is active opposition to good. I need not expand this. Unfortunately the world in which we are living is giving us a very clear demonstration, day by day, of the meaning of evil. Evil is not just the absence of good. It is a positive thing. It hates the good and is militant against it. Think of the evil in the world, in pleasure and in all the entertainments. Cannot you see this positive force that is ruling and guiding the world, the organization that is behind it, and the delight people have in making money out of it all? That is evil. You are to have a horror of that, says Paul. This very strong word means shying away from evil, as a horse shies away from something that he does not quite understand, something that frightens him.

Now the terms more or less explain themselves, so let me emphasize the principle. Notice the feeling that the apostle introduces into this – the strong feeling – 'Abhor!' He says: Have a positive hatred, an utter dislike. He tells us that we must not merely not do things that are wrong and evil, we must hate them. It is possible for someone to avoid doing evil things while having great pleasure in them in his mind and in his imagination. If that is his position, he is not abhorring evil. It is not merely that we keep on the right side of the law by not doing the wrong thing; but we find evil revolting. That is Paul's exhortation. Evil is unthinkable, in mind, in imagination, in thought, and in action.

How does one become capable of reacting like this to all evil? Again, it demands thought, and this is most important in all these matters. You will never 'abhor evil' unless you have an understanding of the doctrine. Go back again to verse 1: 'I beseech you therefore, brethren, by the mercies of God.' You may have recognized that certain things are bad and you may dislike them and feel a righteous indignation about them; you may even write letters to the newspapers about them. But if you are only a moralist and not a Christian, you will not be 'abhorring' evil. There is only one thing that can ever make you 'abhor that which is evil', and that is a positive love for God. You will never understand the nature of evil until you understand something of the doctrine of the holiness of God, for evil is the opposite of that. And so you only realize what evil actually is when you see what it is in God's universe. When you think of that holy God who made a perfect universe 'and saw that it was good', and when you think of this other thing that came in, then that makes you abhor it.

That is the biblical teaching. Read Psalm 104 for yourselves, and you will find that in that psalm the psalmist gives a great account of God's universe, of nature and creation, and of how

God controls everything. Then he ends in a most amazing way: 'Let the sinners be consumed out of the earth, and let the wicked be no more.' He suddenly brings in the wicked. Why does he do this? It is because he has looked out at the glory and the perfection and the marvel of it all, and then he sees this miserable sin marring the glory and the perfection, and he says, 'Get rid of it. Abhor it. Root it out, as it were. It has no place here.'

Now that is the apostle's meaning, and the only way to react like that is to have a knowledge of God in His glory and in His holiness, and in His majesty. The Bible is full of this kind of contrast. Psalm 97:10 says: 'Ye that love the Lord, hate evil.' The two are bound to go together. If you truly love the Lord, you will hate evil, not because you suffer when you do the evil thing, not because people will condemn you for doing it – that is morality – no, no, you hate evil because you see it in the light of God and His purpose.

Or take Amos 5:15: 'Hate the evil, and love the good, and establish judgment in the gate.' Or see how the apostle Peter puts it: 'He that will love life, and see good days, let him refrain his tongue from evil, and his lips that they speak no guile: let him eschew evil' – shy away from it – 'and do good; let him seek peace, and ensue it' [*1 Pet.* 3:10–11]. Or take the way Jude puts it in the twenty-third verse of his Epistle: 'Others save with fear, pulling them out of the fire; hating even the garment spotted by the flesh.' That is it! Those who love God must hate evil, and the more we know God and love Him, the greater will be our hatred of evil. We will not just refrain from doing things, we will not just be nice little moral people who do not do certain wrong things, we will have a positive hatred of evil.

In other words, the command is that we are to be like God Himself – 'Be ye holy; for I am holy' [*1 Pet.* 1:16]. Habakkuk says, 'Thou art of purer eyes than to behold evil, and canst not look on iniquity' [*Hab.* 1:13]. Or take the great contrasts in 2 Corinthians 6:14-15: God and Belial; righteousness and unrighteousness; light and darkness. There is no communion between them; they are eternal opposites.

So we abhor evil because we love God and our love is entire and 'without dissimulation'. We are not told just to put down a little list of things which we are not to do. How often has all this been put in such miserable terms? 'Because you have become a Christian you do not do this, that and the other.' Now I am not objecting to the list, probably everything is true, but a list is inadequate, taken by itself. It is legalism. Here we are in the realm of love. Do not merely look at these things *per se*. Look at them always in the light of God, in the light of His holy nature, in the light of His love to you and what He has done for you by His grace and mercy. Your love for Him should lift you up to that realm so that you look down upon evil, and hate and abhor it.

The opposite of the command to abhor evil is, 'Cleave to that which is good.' Now 'cleave' is a most interesting word. The Greek word conveys the idea of sticking two pieces of wood together with glue. So it means, 'Stick yourself to the good with glue'! Cement yourself, if you like, to that which is good. Join or fasten yourself so firmly to the good that you cannot be separated from it. And 'good' means that which is good in the sight of God.

So here are the two fundamental principles governing the whole of conduct. Cannot you see that we are obviously in a realm here which is entirely removed from that of mere morality? This is not a negative but a positive outlook. We are being called to a passion for holiness, and a passion for truth. If you regard the Christian life and the commandments of God as hard and grievous and narrow, and are sometimes tempted to give them all up, then it is because you know nothing about God and about His love. What you need is not to be reminded of the commandments but to be reminded of Him and His holy nature and His love for you – His grace to you who deserved nothing but punishment and hell. You 'love', and 'hate'; you are consumed by a passion to serve the God who has done so much for you through His dear Son, the God who did not even spare His Son but delivered Him up for you. And you show your gratitude to Him by doing everything you can to please Him and to be well-pleasing in His sight.

And, lastly, notice that here again we are given a command. Holiness is not something that is done for you. A teaching which says, 'Let go and let God', is the opposite of this. These are commands: 'Let your love be without dissimulation.' 'Hate evil; cleave to that which is good.' There is no such thing as

entire sanctification in this life, for these are perpetual exhortations and commandments. You cannot suddenly have all
sin taken out of you in one experience. No, holiness is a
commandment that you have to go on fulfilling and obeying;
you must work it out.

And thank God we are told how we can work it out. 'I
beseech you therefore, brethren, by the mercies of God . . . '
Consider it. Dwell upon the doctrine. If you want to know how
to live, do not start with the practicalities, start with the truth,
with the doctrine. Understand it, grasp it, see what it means in
terms of God's love to you, and then you will find a great love
welling up in your own heart and the Spirit will come and will
shed the love of God abroad in your heart [*Rom.* 5:5], and, filled
with that love, you will desire above everything else to keep
the commandments of God. They will no longer be grievous to
you. You will be hating evil, and you will be 'cleaving',
sticking fast as by glue, to that which is good and well-pleasing
in the sight of God. 'The chief end of man is to glorify God, and
to enjoy Him' – and to enjoy the glorifying of Him – 'for ever.'

Twenty-five

*

Let love be without dissimulation. Abhor that which is evil; cleave to that which is good. Be kindly affectioned one to another with brotherly love; in honour preferring one another; not slothful in business; fervent in spirit; serving the Lord.

Romans 12:9–11

We have begun to consider the two principles that govern the whole of this question of Christian conduct. But the apostle never stops at just laying down his general principles. He was a great teacher and he knew his people. He knew that it was not enough merely to lay down principles and then move on, so now he comes down to details. And that is what we must do.

I suggested in my general analysis of the section that in this tenth verse the apostle is dealing with our general relationship to one another. I deliberately put 'general', because, once more, he will come down to particulars. The Authorized [King James] Version says: 'Be kindly affectioned one to another with brotherly love; in honour preferring one another.' Now let us deal with the exact statement first, before we come to consider how we can carry it out. Probably a better translation would be this: 'in brotherly love to one another, loving warmly', or, 'with warmth'.

The word that is translated 'kindly affectioned' is most interesting. The root and original meaning conveys the whole notion of natural affection, not an affection which is called forth by circumstances, but something which is innately there because of the relationship in which we find ourselves. It is the word that is used to describe the love we have for our relatives, the kind of instinctive love which we feel towards members of the family to which we belong, the natural love of kindred. Now this is most interesting and important. The apostle is saying that in our relationships as Christians with one another, in the church and elsewhere, our love is not to be merely superficial or official. It is not just the liking that comes from being associated together in the same church. It must go beyond that. Paul says: Your brotherly love should really take on something of the character of the love that you have for members of the natural families to which you belong. Somebody, therefore, translated it like this: 'Love the brethren in the faith' – that is brotherly love – 'as though they were brethren in blood'. And I think that brings out the meaning very well.

So the question that confronts us at once is this: What does this mean? Again, you notice, it is a command: 'Be kindly affectioned one to another with brotherly love'. I have always been amused at the way in which some of the commentators handle this whole section. They seem to say, 'Well this, of course, is all quite obvious, we need not stay with it.' I was recently reading an article on this very section, and the writer actually said that. He said, 'These things are so obvious that we need not go into details here.' Now I have only one comment to make about that. That is a man who has not understood the section at all.

Of course, I know it is very easy to read these verses and say, 'Quite obvious! "Let love be without dissimulation." ' But though it may seem obvious, how do you do it? That is the question. And the same is true of Paul's command, 'Be kindly affectioned one toward another with brotherly love.' But we must stop and say, 'Am I doing that? Is that true of me? If not, why not? How can I conform to this? And the moment we do that, we find that it is not quite as obvious and as simple as we had thought, because there is one thing we cannot do and that is to create feelings. It is just impossible. And sometimes the more we try, the more bereft we are of feelings. Yet here we are confronted by a commandment: Let your love of the brethren in the faith be as though you were brethren in blood. Can you not see how different the life of the Christian would be, and would have been throughout the centuries, if only everybody had practised this?

[348]

So how can it be done? And to me, once more, there is only
one answer. We saw it before, we see it again, and we will
continue to see it with every one of these separate injunctions.
The only way to be sure that you are 'kindly affectioned one
toward another with brotherly love' is to pay attention to, and
to respond to, the exhortation in the first verse of the chapter: 'I
beseech you therefore, brethren, by the mercies of God . . .'
You must work out the meaning of that 'therefore', and 'the
mercies of God'. This is the only way. You cannot obey the
commandments otherwise.

It is always fatal to approach the question of feelings
directly. Feelings are always the result of something else, the
result, ultimately, of understanding and of thought. So the
apostle is exhorting us here not to try to put on some cloak of
feelings which we do not have. That would be sheer hypocrisy.
He is saying, 'Face these doctrines in such a way that you will
find that you do love your brethren in the faith as if they were
also brethren by blood.'

So you must work out your doctrine, and you do that like
this. You realize that as a Christian you are born again, that
you have a new nature; and you realize that the same thing is
true of all other Christians. You have started a new life, you
have been born into this life. Yes, but you have also been born
into a new family; so has every other Christian. So now you see
that you and every other Christian are members of the same
family and that you really are related in this extraordinary
manner.

Let me put this plainly to you by showing you how our Lord
dealt with this, and how the Apostle Paul does it at greater
length elsewhere. In Mark 10:29–30 we read, 'And Jesus
answered and said, Verily I say unto you, There is no man
that hath left house, or brethren, or sisters, or father, or
mother, or wife, or children, or lands, for my sake, and the
gospel's, but he shall receive an hundredfold now in this time,
houses, and brethren, and sisters, and mothers, and children,
and lands, with persecution; and in the world to come eternal
life.'

Now in effect, our Lord is saying: 'Because you have become
followers of me, it may mean that you will be ostracized by
your family. In that sense, you will lose your husband or your

wife, your father, or your mother, or your children, or your relatives; they will have nothing more to do with you. But it is all right,' says our Lord, 'you will get brothers and sisters and fathers and mothers and husbands and wives. You will not lose, it will all be made up to you. You will have many more than you had before.' Why? Because you have now entered into this amazing family of God, and there you have these new relationships.

And then you find the Apostle Paul saying the same thing in that well-known statement at the end of Ephesians 2. Writing to Gentiles, he says, 'Now therefore ye are no more strangers and foreigners, but fellowcitizens with the saints, and of the household of God.' You are members of God's household and of God's family. And that lies at the back of the teaching of the apostle in this verse in Romans 12. Christians belong to the same family. Now this is not something merely in thought. The terms regeneration and rebirth do carry a real meaning; there is something new. There is a new nature and we belong to a new family. So Paul is saying, therefore, that with regard to your fellow-Christians, you should feel what you did feel and still feel, perhaps, in the natural, human sense, for your own brothers and sisters because you belong to this spiritual family in as real a way as you belong to your physical family.

So the apostle is exhorting us to work this out. He is not just telling us to be polite to our fellow Christians because we are now members of the same society or institution, or the same church. He says, 'No, your relationship must be altogether deeper than that. You must feel this bond, you must feel that you are brothers and sisters. This does not just mean that you start calling everybody, 'brother'. As far as I am concerned, that always makes me feel less brotherly! That is not what Paul is talking about; that is superficial, a dissimulation; it is pretence or play-acting. That is not it at all. But what Paul does mean is that having realized the truth of the doctrine, you begin to be conscious of this, and you must not be content with anything less.

And so it works out in practice in this way: as human beings, we are always ready to do things for and with our relatives that we would not do with other people. We are ready to correct other people's children for doing certain things which we do not correct our own children for doing. That is human nature. We defend our own; we make excuses; we are always on the defensive for our own; we can always understand what they are doing. And Paul is saying that this should be equally true of our relationship to one another as Christians. We should feel this same innate desire.

To put this truth in another way, take the analogy of the body that the apostle has been using here, and which is elaborated in 1 Corinthians 12. There, you remember, the apostle says, 'And whether one member suffer, all the members suffer with it' [verse 26]. That is true of us as Christians and it should become more and more true. Because of our consciousness of this family relationship, we suffer together and we rejoice together. Nothing can happen to any one of us but that we are all in it. Why? Because we are not only members of the same body, we are members of the same family. And then if we find that at certain times and points some brothers and sisters are difficult, and do things which we cannot quite understand, then we do not condemn them as outsiders, but treat them exactly as we would treat natural relatives who were doing the same sort of thing. And it is in this way that the life of the church is harmonious; it is in this way that we all together minister to the glory of God and show to the world our relationship to one another because of our relationship to Him.

But let me add just one other note to this. You notice that the apostle says that it is our 'brotherly love' that is to show itself in this way. It is important that we should draw the distinction between liking and loving. Even in the natural sense, you do not like some members of your family as much as others. Now I am not here to justify this, or to criticize it. I am just saying that it is a fact that though you may be in exactly the same relationship to two people, you do not of necessity like them equally. Similarly, though we are commanded to love our fellow Christians to the same extent, we are not ever commanded to like them to the same extent. We are not told here that we have to like every other Christian, but we are told that our brotherly love to every Christian is to have the quality in it that characterizes our natural love and affection for those with whom we share the same family and its likes and dislikes and privileges.

I have sometimes even put it like this: Can you say quite honestly that you have a deeper affection for, and a deeper understanding of, your fellow Christians than you have for your natural relatives who are not Christians? That is a very good test of our position as Christian people. It is a proof of your regeneration, and it is also a proof that you have paid heed to this exhortation and are putting it into practice. A Christian should feel a closer bond with another Christian than he feels with a relative who is not a Christian. This is true of necessity. The new nature is in us. We are all children of God and belong to the family of God. And this is a relationship that will not only last while we are in this world of time, but will last throughout eternity.

In view of these things, says the apostle, make certain that your brotherly love one to another is being manifested more and more. And this happens by meditation, by grasping the truth, by applying this 'therefore', by reminding yourself of all the doctrine that has gone before, and realizing that this is true of you. And you pray that the Spirit may not only so enlighten you, but may so fill your heart with love – love to God and your fellow human beings – that you find that this becomes increasingly true.

That is the first part of the statement, but the apostle goes on and adds to that. He says, 'in honour preferring one another'. This, again, appears to be obvious, but the more you analyse it, the profounder you will find it to be. What is meant by 'honouring'? It is a word that was once much used but it is not found so often today. The Greek word referred to the price that was fixed for an object after you had gone to the trouble of having it evaluated. Think of something that is in your possession – a watch, perhaps. You decide to examine it, and as a result of your examination you assess its value and put a good price on it.

Now Paul applies that word to our relationship with others. It refers to what we think of others, our evaluation of them and of their gifts. And this, in turn, becomes the respect that we show to one another as the result of our estimation of one another. This is what the apostle means by 'honour': 'In honour preferring one another.' It carries the idea of reverence and of respect. And that, of course, in turn, determines our behaviour towards them, how we treat them, and especially how we treat them in terms of ourselves. This is very important. Once again, the failure to implement this exhortation has so often wrought havoc in the church. Read 1 Corinthians 4, where the apostle had to deal with this issue. There the trouble was mainly the way the Christians were quarrelling among themselves as a result of their evaluations of Paul and Apollos. That was bad enough, but the situation became still worse when trouble arose as a result of their evaluations of one another and of themselves.

What, then, is the meaning of the word 'preferring'? Here the commentators make two points and both are undoubtedly right. The word means 'to go before', 'to lead', 'to lead the way', and that can be interpreted in two ways. One is that Paul is saying that sometimes we show our respect for others by walking before them, as it were. We show our deference by leading them forward and by opening doors for them – 'preferring' them in that way. We do not walk after them but show respect and honour by preparing the way for them. That is a part of the meaning.

The second suggestion is that the word means to give a lead in offering respect. Make sure that you are always first in according honour to the other person. Go before others, not physically, but metaphorically. Go ahead of one another in your desire to show respect and honour to one another. Now those are the two meanings, and I believe that both ideas are involved here.

Here we are as members of the Christian church, and we have already seen in the earlier part of the chapter that we have all received gifts from God. 'I say', says Paul earlier in this chapter, 'through the grace given unto me, to every man that is among you, not to think of himself more highly than he ought to think; but to think soberly, according as God hath dealt to every man the measure of faith' [verse 3]. Then he goes on in verse 5: 'So we, being many, are one body in Christ, and every one members one of another. Having then gifts differing according to the grace that is given to us, whether prophecy . . .' and so on. We all have gifts, and the apostle says in effect: ' Learn to evaluate these aright and give respect and honour one to another. Go ahead of one another in doing that.' The two ideas can be mingled together. It comes down, therefore, to this: What is our attitude to one another and what is our attitude to ourselves? We cannot separate these two questions.

So how foolish those commentators are who say, 'This is so obvious, we need not stay with it, but will go on to something more important.' More important? Throughout the centuries nothing has done – or still does – so much harm in the life of the Christian church as the failure to put this injunction into practice. Even in the New Testament we can see the harm caused by this failure. But how can we do what Paul says? In this way: each one must give a lead to the other, and all others, in showing honour and respect to the gifts that each has received from God. But is the apostle inculcating a kind of mock modesty here? Is he teaching us to be a succession of Uriah Heeps? Of course, such a suggestion is just ridiculous.

I have already referred to 1 Corinthians 4. To me it is a most fascinating chapter, and on this particular subject it is the classic passage because in his own exhaustive manner the apostle deals with troubles caused by a lack of respect for other Christians. What, then, are the principles? Well, you can say at once that to prefer one another in the matter of giving honour does not mean for a moment that you abandon your canons of judgment. It is false modesty to say, 'Well, of course, I'm nobody, I'm nothing.' You know the type of people who do that – they are often the most conceited people alive. You know that they do not mean it. You are to have a true evaluation of yourself.

For instance, here is the apostle in 1 Corinthians 4, working out this great principle, but then towards the end of the chapter he says this: 'I write not these things to shame you, but as my beloved sons I warn you. For though ye have ten thousand instructors in Christ, yet have ye not many fathers: for in Christ Jesus I have begotten you through the gospel. Wherefore I beseech you, be ye followers of me' [verses 14-16].Now how can a man who says, 'in honour preferring one another' – and he includes himself in the injunction – how can he at the same time say, 'Be ye followers of me'? Is he contradicting himself?

Of course not! There must be no pretence. You do not do away
with facts. In one sense, for the great apostle to say that he
gives greater honour to some insignificant member of the
church is just to be ridiculous.

Because of their utter folly, Paul uses sarcasm in teaching
the Corinthians. He says, 'I think that God hath set forth us as
the apostles last, as it were appointed to death: for we are made
a spectacle unto the world, and to angels, and to men. We are
fools for Christ's sake, but ye are wise in Christ; we are weak,
but ye are strong' [verses 9-10]. Now that is nothing but
sarcasm and do not lose sight of that. Paul does not mean
for a moment – he could not mean – that the Corinthian
Christians are 'strong' whereas he is 'weak', that they are
'honourable' and he is not. No, no. He is dealing here with
the impression that they are giving, the attitude and mentality
that they have fallen into. So he reprimands them. He is the
apostle, he is their 'father', he is their teacher, and he does not
deny that. He speaks to them as their father. He instructs them
and guides them.

So this injunction does not mean that you abandon all
standards. For instance, if a man happens to be unusually
gifted with intelligence and understanding, this injunction
does not tell him to keep quiet and not offer his opinion, but
give the floor to someone who is equally a Christian with him
in the matter of regeneration, but has not been gifted by God in
the same way. It does not mean that a man like Paul should sit
quietly while somebody who has not got the capacity or the
gift expounds some Old Testament passage in the church at
Corinth; that would be ridiculous. And if we pretend it means
that, then we are not only not using the gift which we have, we
are bringing the whole of the teaching into disrepute.

No, what the apostle is inculcating in Romans 12:10 is this:
there is no place for pride in the Christian life. That is what he
is concerned about – we must never be guilty of pride. It is
another way of saying what our Lord taught us in the
Beatitudes: 'Blessed are the poor in spirit . . . Blessed are the
meek' [*Matt.* 5:3, 5]. Or take the way in which our Lord puts it
very plainly in Luke 7:7-10: 'And he put forth a parable to
those which were bidden, when he marked how they chose out
the chief rooms; saying unto them. When thou art bidden of

any man to a wedding, sit not down in the highest room; lest a more honourable man than thou be bidden of him; and he that bade thee and him come and say to thee, Give this man place; and thou begin with shame to take the lowest room. But when thou art bidden, go and sit down in the lowest room; that when he that bade thee cometh, he may say unto thee, Friend, go up higher: then shalt thou have worship in the presence of them that sit at meat with thee.' That, I believe, is the teaching that the apostle is putting before us here.

Or, let me put it in terms of the apostle's own statements – he has said some extraordinary things! Take 1 Corinthians 15:8-9: 'Last of all' – Paul is dealing with the resurrection appearances – 'he was seen of me also, as of one born out of due time. For I am the least of the apostles, that am not meet to be called an apostle, because I persecuted the church of God.' When the apostle says that, he means it literally. That is exactly and precisely what he felt. Mark you, he says in Galatians – and here you get the balance – that he is not inferior to any of the apostles, that he went up to Jerusalem to see the apostles, 'lest by any means I should run, or had run, in vain' [*Gal.* 2:2]. And when he went there and listened to these men, he said that he had discovered that he was not inferior in any way at all. There is no contradiction there. He knew the gift he had received, he knew the ability he had been given, and he could not make little of that, because then he would have been criticizing the gift of the Spirit!

But take the truth again as you find it in Ephesians 3:8: 'Unto me, who am less than the least of all saints, is this grace given, that I should preach among the Gentiles the unsearchable riches of Christ.' That is not mock modesty. Again, that is exactly what the apostle felt and said. These words are a kind of exposition of this phrase that we are looking at together.

Or take it in those words which I have often felt are perhaps some of the most poignant words in the whole of the New Testament. In the First Epistle to Timothy the apostle has been talking about anything which is 'contrary to sound doctrine' [*1 Tim.* 1:10]. He then writes: 'According to the glorious gospel of the blessed God, which was committed to my trust. And I thank Christ Jesus our Lord, who hath enabled me, for that he counted me faithful, putting me into the ministry; who was before a blasphemer, and a persecutor, and injurious: but I obtained mercy, because I did it ignorantly in unbelief. And the grace of our Lord was exceeding abundant with faith and love which is in Christ Jesus.' And later: 'Howbeit for this cause I obtained mercy, that in me first Jesus Christ might shew forth all longsuffering, for a pattern to them which should hereafter believe on him to life everlasting' [*1 Tim.* 1:11–14, 16].

That is 'in honour preferring one another'. And, you do this by coming to a true estimate of yourself. Self is the greatest curse of all. A wrong view of self is the source of nearly all evil. So when you are told, 'in honour preferring one another', you do not start by looking at others, you always start by looking at yourself. You will never be right in your evaluation of others until you have made a true assessment of yourself.

Again, the apostle puts this so plainly in 1 Corinthians 4. He was aware of the quarrel in the church at Corinth about Apollos and himself, and he puts it like this: 'With me it is a very small thing that I should be judged of you, or of man's judgment: yea, I judge not mine own self. For I know nothing by myself' – by that, he means that he cannot justify himself or speak against himself – 'yet am I not hereby justified: but he that judgeth me is the Lord' [*1 Cor.* 4:2–4]. The man has finished with himself, he is not sensitive, not over-sensitive, not hyper-sensitive, waiting for an insult. Is not this the curse of life? It is the most prolific cause, I would say, of all the troubles in the church and in the world. But here is a man who has been delivered from that. He has finished with himself. He can say quite honestly, 'But with me it is a very small thing that I should be judged of you, or of man's judgment: yea, I judge not mine own self.' I do not spend my time looking at myself and saying what a wonderful fellow I am, and admiring what I have done. I do not do that; I have finished with it.

But then Paul has a second argument. This is what he brings out in the seventh verse of the same passage. Here is the cure for this particularly horrible disease, one of the most terrible of the spiritual diseases – this overestimation of self, and under-estimation of others, which is the exact opposite of 'in honour preferring one another'. Now this is the answer: 'For who

maketh thee to differ from another?' Answer that question!
You are pleased with yourself. You say, 'I've got wonderful
power, and that other person is beneath contempt.' But who
has made you different? How do you explain the difference?
'Who maketh thee to differ from another?' And then go on:
'And what hast thou that thou didst not receive? now if thou
didst receive it, why dost thou glory, as if thou hadst not
received it?' Can you answer that? There is nothing to be said,
is there? So we see that we are not only unworthy and
shameful, but on top of it all, we are fools, we cannot answer
those questions.

So what is the doctrine that is put before us in these various
verses we have just looked at? Well, this is how the apostle
clearly works it out in his own case. First, he marvels that he is
a Christian at all; and we all ought to marvel at this. If we ever
lose our sense of wonder at the fact that we have ever become
Christians, we are, in a sense, already victims of this disease of
pride. We must never lose the sense of wonder. Why are we
different? There is only one answer: It is entirely the result of
the grace of God.

Furthermore, the apostle is amazed that he, of everybody,
should ever have been called to be an apostle. It is nothing in
him. He has not done it. It is not because of his wonderful
achievements, or his great insight and understanding. It is all
in spite of him. It is all the grace of God – 'But by the grace of
God I am what I am' [*I Cor.* 15:10]. And the more spiritual you
have become, and the more knowledge you have of God and of
the Lord Jesus Christ and of the Holy Spirit, the more you will
see your own sinfulness and the depth of evil that is in you.
The trouble with people who do not see this and who have a
high opinion of themselves is that they are ignorant of God and
ignorant of God's character and of His being. The apostle says,
'Christ Jesus came into the world to save sinners; of whom I
am chief' [*I Tim.* 1:15]. And he really felt that. He cannot
imagine anybody to be a greater sinner. So he has nothing to
boast of. Boasting is excluded, as he is so fond of saying [*Rom.*
3:27]. All that he has boasted of, he has seen to be dung and
refuse and entirely useless.

So you start with that, and then you are already seventy-five
per cent on the way to the solution of this problem – 'in honour

preferring one another'. Once men and women have really seen themselves as they are, as the result of the Fall and their own actions, once they have got to know something of the plague of their own hearts, they are humbled and nobody can say anything too bad about them. They can always say worse things about themselves than anybody else ever knows. They say, 'Thank God, people do not know all the truth about me!' There is your starting point.

But then you go on to the second point, which is your gift for service. Here were these foolish Corinthians comparing Paul and Apollos as if they were two actors on the stage, using their own natural powers and faculties. 'Don't you realize', says Paul in effect, 'that I and Apollos, and all the others, are only what we are because of the gift that has been given to us? One has been called to plant and the other has been called to water; one has been called to lay the foundation, others are called to build upon it. But it is not us at all, it is the great Master Builder. He is the one who counts, and we are nothing.'

We can do nothing in and of ourselves, we can only do harm. We have been given gifts – we have not produced them, we have not generated them – they are entirely given, as Paul has been showing in the earlier part of this twelfth chapter of Romans. So for people to boast of their gifts is, in a sense, almost a denial of the gift, it is so ludicrous. Now, as you realize these things, you will find, inevitably, that you are 'in honour preferring one another'.

And add this third and last consideration: look at your service. Let all of us look at our service – how poor it is! You can only boast of it if you are not really examining it. Examine your service: realize exactly its character and its quality. What do you find? Our Lord put our attitude to our work right once and for ever in His teaching to the disciples who were always ready to boast and compete with one another, to be animated by wrong, ugly, and false feelings. He told them: Do everything you can, but, 'When ye shall have done all those things which are commanded you, say, We are unprofitable servants' [*Luke* 17:10].

Oh, I have often tried to put it like this from the pulpit: the danger is always to compare ourselves with people whom we think have inferior gifts and qualities. But the thing to do is compare and contrast ourselves with the saints of the centuries, with the men and women depicted here in the New Testament, and, above all, with our blessed Lord Himself. What pygmies we are! What small creatures! This is the best antidote to this false feeling. It is the best way to encourage what the apostle inculcates in this phrase, 'in honour preferring one another'.

Read about the saints! Have you ever heard of what Charles Haddon Spurgeon once said about his own preaching – that great preacher who preached for all those years here in London in the nineteenth century, and whose name people have almost forgotten today, whose principles they have certainly denied, almost every one of them, even when they still use his name – do you remember what he said about his own preaching? He said he would not cross the street to listen to himself – and he meant it. When men and women have a true conception of this gospel and see what it is and what it deserves, they are bound to feel that their best efforts are utterly unworthy, poor and feeble. Charles Wesley was a great singer, was he not? He was a poet and wrote great hymns, and yet this is what he says: 'O for a thousand tongues to sing' – he only had one and he felt it was so feeble. 'This poor, lisping, stammering tongue,' as Philip Doddridge puts it. What is adequate? What can ever be adequate?

Now as you view yourself, your gifts and your service in that way, you begin to see that you have nothing to boast of. You are 'less than the least of all saints' [*Eph.* 3:8]. And once you feel like that about yourself, it follows that nobody can insult you. 'He that is down need fear no fall . . .' Nobody can ever know the worst about you; you alone know that. So they cannot insult you – it is impossible. But not only that, you feel sure that no one can be quite as bad as you are, no one can have the ugliness within that you have, and you see the gifts that God has given them – and so you maintain this perfect balance. You never say anything derogatory of the gift you have been given. And when you are tempted to boast and to despise others you say, 'Who maketh thee to differ from another? And what hast thou that thou didst not receive?' [*1 Cor.* 4:7]. And it is not you at all, it is God! And He is the same God who has given to you, as he has given to others, and you glorify God by recognizing His gifts in others, and paying honour and respect and reverence and deference to them.

Twenty-six

*

Not slothful in business; fervent in spirit; serving the Lord.
Romans 12:11

When we were considering the first two verses of chapter 12, we saw that they really give a summary of the whole of the remainder of the teaching of this great Epistle. Doctrine is not something merely to be contemplated intellectually; it is something to be applied, something to be put into practice. And there is no point or purpose in our knowledge of doctrine, unless it leads to a radical change in our lives. And there in two verses the apostle gives us all the great motives for Christian living.

Then the apostle moves on to deal with the Christian believer in the realm of the church and now, in this section, from verse 9 to the end of the chapter, he is dealing with Christians in their more general relationships. So we come to verse 11. And here the apostle is dealing with our general spirit, our attitude to our calling as Christians, how we do our work, the spirit in which we do it. And he puts that in these ringing words: 'Not slothful in business; fervent in spirit; serving the Lord.' We are all members of the body of Christ, so how are we to function? How are we to do the work to which we are called? What is to be the characteristic of our lives as Christian people?

Now let us look at the terms Paul uses: 'Not slothful in business . . .' Here we must agree with what is pointed out, it seems to me, by all the commentators and by most of the translations: that it is better not to use this word 'business', although in a sense it conveys the right meaning. But the Greek word that is translated here as 'business' has already appeared in the eighth verse where Paul says, 'He that ruleth, with diligence', and the word translated there as 'diligence' is exactly the same word as that translated here as 'business'. So you might translate these words in verse 11 like this: 'in diligence, not slothful'; or, 'in zeal, not slothful'. The meaning is very much the same but using the exact translation as in the eighth verse does help us to concentrate on what the apostle is concerned to teach us here, and that is what may be called 'moral earnestness'. We are to be earnest; we are to be alive; we are to be vigorous.

Now once more we discover that this is something that must be dealt with in terms of our understanding of doctrine. I need to say that about every single injunction in this chapter. It is no use taking these phrases in isolation. You must not look at any one of them except in the light of verses 1 and 2, otherwise you will go wrong. And that is something that can happen very easily with regard to this particular injunction. The apostle is not just saying, 'Pull yourselves together.' He *is* saying that, but he is also saying much more. And this is the point that we must bring out and that demands thought. This command must be considered, as I shall show you again, in the light of the 'therefore' and 'the mercies of God' of the first verse. If we do not understand this command in terms of that original pronouncement, we may obey the injunction but merely become busy people in the sense of busy-ness.

Now Paul's words do not mean that you are just to become 'fussing' people, mere activists rushing about in all directions. Here Paul is telling us that in this question of moral earnestness, we must work out the doctrine, otherwise we will never obey the injunction at all. Let us approach it, therefore, like this. He is telling us that we must not be slothful. We all know what sloth is. It is laziness, slackness. It is half doing a thing. It is the opposite of being energetic and vigorous.

There are undoubtedly many causes of sloth, and the apostle here and everywhere else does not exclude a natural cause. It is a very false interpretation of Christian doctrine to exclude the natural. We are all different temperamentally and constitutionally. All these factors have an effect upon our Christian lives and living, and we must be aware of that. So many people, in neglecting their own temperaments, try to produce a stereotyped, standard kind of Christian, and that seems to me to be quite wrong. God's work is always characterized by variety and it is equally true in the Christian church. We do not all have the same problems in life; and sometimes the main cause of sloth is temperamental and constitutional.

Let me illustrate this. There are some people who are born energetic and active; others are more the lethargic, phlegmatic type. Now you do not determine that, you are born like that, and must recognize it. There are some people who are born with a bilious disposition, and with a kind of constitutional, physical slackness. They cannot help it. Though essentially the same, wide variations are possible in the working of the circulation and nervous systems. And these, of course, do affect us.

Sometimes a particular temperament may almost be a national characteristic. Paul in writing to Titus says, 'One of themselves, even a prophet of their own, said, The Cretians are always liars, evil beasts, slow bellies. This witness is true' [*Titus* 1:12–13]. It is said, I do not know with how much real justice, that the southern nations of Europe tend to be more slothful than nations in the north. I think that is probably right – it is a question of geographical conditions. The colder the climate, the more invigorating it is and the more energetic we feel, whereas heat tends to be enervating. So all these factors must be taken into account, and we start with that.

Then you must include, of course, the work of the devil. The devil's supreme ambition is to ruin or to mar the work of God. What he did in the first creation, he tries to repeat in the second, the new creation. And the devil can attack us, as we know, in many different ways. He can attack us in the body, in the mind, and in the spirit. He can depress us; he can make us feel slack. And if he can produce lethargic, slothful Christians, he is very pleased indeed.

There are endless illustrations of this. Demon-possession is a gross manifestation of this influence of the devil. But, short of that, he can influence us in very many different ways, and he has often caused grievous trouble in the lives of many Christians just through producing a kind of slothfulness, a disinclination for work, a kind of heaviness of spirit, this feeling, 'Well, I can't do anything today, I don't feel like it. I hope I'll feel better tomorrow.' But you do not feel better tomorrow, and it goes on, and the result is that you are always like that. Now that is slothfulness, and the devil, I repeat, is often extremely active in producing that condition in us.

And then, on top of that, discouragements tend to produce slothfulness. Read the first chapter of the Second Epistle to Timothy, and you will find that Timothy seems to have been a remarkable example of this very thing. I think that probably he was also temperamentally and constitutionally like that. He was certainly a man who was easily depressed. When things went against him, and they were going against him when Paul wrote, he became very discouraged, and someone who is discouraged will soon be slothful and half-hearted. And to try to do something in a half-hearted manner is the most killing thing of all. So discouragements and trials and tribulations can lead to sloth. That was the trouble with the Christians to whom the Epistle to the Hebrews was written.

There, then, are some of the causes – we need not delay with them any longer. We all know something about this in experience and the great thing for us to discover is the answer to the question: What are we to do about it? And this is what the apostle deals with here. He says, 'In zeal, in diligence, do not be slothful.' But how are we to do this? It seems to me that three answers are given in this one verse, and I keep myself to that and to that alone.

Paul's words are an injunction. The apostle is very fond of this approach. We see it very much in Paul's epistles to Timothy. He seems to issue an order of the day, or, at times even, he almost seems to crack the whip, stirring Timothy up: 'Remember', he says, 'that Jesus Christ of the seed of David was raised from the dead according to my gospel' [*2 Tim.* 2:8]. 'God hath not given us the spirit of fear; but of power, and of love, and of a sound mind' [*2 Tim.* 1:7].

Now all these injunctions were designed to stimulate Timothy. There is a natural or a general answer to the question of how we are to deal with slothfulness, and it may be put in this way: Rouse yourselves. Now when he says this, the apostle is not asking you to try to turn yourself into something that you are not by nature. You cannot change your nature or your temperament. So he is not trying to get someone, who is, perhaps, a bit lethargic by nature, to put on a mask and play a part. It is not that. But he is telling us to rouse ourselves. We are never quite as bad as we think we are, any one of us, and that is an important psychological principle. Sometimes people who claim great results in what is called 'faith healing' are simply doing this very thing. When we are ill, we are never quite as ill as we think we are, we always add on a certain proportion. And it is, therefore, an easy thing to get rid of that extra bit that we put on psychologically.

So we can always do this much – we can rouse ourselves. We need to do this and it is one of the great and important lessons in life. You must know and understand yourself. You must deal with yourself and talk to yourself. You must reprimand yourself and think for yourself. This is part of Christian preaching. Slothfulness is bad in and of itself, and therefore you start by saying that you should not be like that. Now I am not saying that you should be like someone who is born brim-full of energy. All I am saying is that you can shake yourself so that you are functioning as yourself, and not as you have been doing recently. You rouse yourself, and apply various arguments to yourself.

The body, for instance, is always at its best when it is in a good condition and when it is being exercised. If you do not take sufficient exercise, you will soon become lethargic and that means you will become slothful. One morning, perhaps, you do not feel like work, or like reading the Scriptures, or praying, and the danger is to say, 'Well, of course, I'm not well today and I can't do this.' Now that is where you say to yourself, 'Now I must rouse myself. Perhaps I'm in this condition because I've been too slack. I've not been getting enough exercise.' So you apply that argument to yourself.

And as that is true of our body, it is true of the mind or any part of us, our spirits included. They are always at their best when they are being exercised and used. For example, if you do not exercise your mind, then you will find it more difficult to exercise your mind Moreover, you will not want to. And that is one of the modern problems, is it not, one of the great modern diseases? The newspapers and the television are discouraging people from using their minds, so that they have now got into a state in which they do not like to think and they do not like to be asked to think. I have been talking to ministers this week and they have been saying that their congregations no longer want to be taught; they always want to be entertained. That is slothfulness of the intellect.

And then you can go further and point out to yourself that there are dangers in sluggishness. If you allow all the organs of your body to fall into disuse, or if you do not use them as they should be used, then eventually this sluggishness will turn into a diseased condition. It has recently been said by research workers that if you take a bit of muscle of living tissue and keep on changing the medium in which it is kept, it can go on working and acting for ever; and I can believe that is true. Many diseases are the result of sluggishness. You can get crippled in your joints if you start protecting them. The more you use them, the better they are likely to be and the more supple.

Now apply all this in the spiritual realm. You say to yourself, 'If I go on like this much longer I shall be diseased spiritually.' And you undoubtedly will. Anyone with pastoral experience will know that it is the sluggish Christian who eventually becomes the diseased Christian, and his problem is then more difficult to deal with.

But then there is another argument. Remember that you are a part of a body: 'We, being many, are one body in Christ.' And therefore it follows, as we saw in working out that analogy, that if there is something wrong with one part, all the other parts will suffer. You cannot isolate yourself. 'None of us liveth to himself, and no man dieth to himself,' as we shall find the apostle saying in chapter 14. So you cannot say, 'I'm an independent unit.' If you are lethargic and slack and slothful, you will affect your neighbouring members and eventually the whole will be involved in this condition. So for these various reasons – and there are other arguments which you can adduce and work out for yourself – you turn upon yourself and you say, 'Away, dull sloth and melancholy.' You literally have to rouse yourself, and I am asserting that this is a part of one's Christian duty.

Now we are still on the natural level, remember, for

Christianity does not exclude the natural. How many heresies have arisen in the past because of that! So you start on the natural level and it is surprising, when you do that, to find how much you really can do. You think you need this, that and the other, but sometimes you need just to take yourself in hand. If you are always, as the wise man puts it in the Old Testament, observing the wind and so on, you will never sow, and the result is that you will never reap. So you just get up and begin to do things, whether you feel like it or not. You say, 'It's my duty to do it', and so you begin.

But let us go beyond that because the apostle does. Having just said, 'not slothful in zeal', he goes to the second point, which is much more important: 'fervent in spirit'. Here is a most important and, at the same time, a very interesting statement. There has been a good deal of arguing about what the 'spirit' means here. In the Authorized Version it is spelt with a small 's', but then in other translations you will find it has a capital 'S'. The whole question is: Is the apostle referring to a person's natural spirit, or is he referring to the Holy Spirit who is in the believer? And I have no hesitation whatsoever in saying that it is the second – that he is referring here to the Holy Spirit who resides in every Christian. 'If any man hath not the Spirit of Christ, he is none of his' [*Rom.* 8:9].

Now the argument which is adduced by the people on the other side comes from Luke's account of Apollos in Acts chapter 18, verses 24 and 25: 'And a certain Jew named Apollos, born at Alexandria, an eloquent man, and mighty in the scriptures, came to Ephesus. This man was instructed in the way of the Lord; and *being fervent in the spirit*, he spake and taught diligently the things of the Lord, knowing only the baptism of John.' And there, I am prepared to agree, we see a reference to the natural spirit. Apollos was one of those men who are naturally fervent – an energetic, mercurial man, a 'high-pressure type', as we tend to call that sort of person. I say that because we are told specifically that he had only known the baptism of John. That was the defect in that man and in his ministry, and he was put right by Priscilla and Aquila. They told him about the baptism with the Holy Spirit, as Paul himself had to tell the people at Ephesus [*Acts* 19].

So I think it is right to say that in Acts 18 there is a reference to Apollos' natural spirit. But I reject that explanation here in Romans 12 because this is a command, and, as I have already been explaining, you cannot change your temperament. If you are born 'fervent in spirit', that is what you are; but if you are born with a phlegmatic kind of temperament, you will not be fervent in spirit in a natural sense. Yet here we are all told to be 'fervent in spirit'. Therefore, I say that the words must refer to the Holy Spirit who is in us, because here is something that is true of all of us as Christians, whatever we may be by temperament. Do not forget that it is a command, and therefore it is possible for us.

What, then, does the apostle tell us to do about this? What does he mean by 'fervent in Spirit'? Now the apostle's word, translated here as 'fervent', means 'to boil', 'to be hot', or 'to be aglow'. It is a very strong word: 'always be on the boil in the Spirit'. Here is something which surely is expounded to us in Paul's letter to Timothy. First of all, he puts it negatively: 'God hath not given us the spirit of fear' [2 *Tim.* 1:7]. Timothy was in a state of fear, and the apostle says, 'That is not the spirit God has given us.' And he goes on to say that God has given us a spirit 'of power, and of love, and of a sound mind' – not slackness, indolence, slothfulness, lethargy, but instead, discipline, power, love, a sound mind!

In other words, Paul is reminding Timothy (and I suggest he is doing exactly the same thing in this eleventh verse of Romans 12) that the Spirit is a Spirit of power and energy. He is the Holy Spirit of power. And that is the term that is used about the Spirit right through the New Testament. Take it as Paul puts it to the Philippians: 'Work out your own salvation with fear and trembling' [*Phil.* 2:12]. How can I do that? The answer is: 'For it is God which worketh in you . . .' and that is through the Spirit. 'It is God which worketh in you both to will and to do' [*Phil.* 2:13]. There is your energy.

Paul takes the ground from beneath our feet if we are trying to explain our indolence away in natural terms. He says in effect, 'Whatever you are by nature, as a Christian you have the Spirit in you, the Holy Spirit, and He is a Spirit of power. He is a Spirit of energy.' So now there is some point and meaning in this exhortation. Paul is entitled to address it to all of us. You may be lethargic and phlegmatic, but it does not matter. If you are a Christian, the Holy Spirit is in you, and so, says Paul, in this life in the Spirit, be energetic.

In that case, the question that comes again to us is: How are we to do this? And there again we have the answer in the apostle's words to Timothy: 'Wherefore I put thee in remembrance', he says, 'that thou stir up the gift of God, which is in thee by the putting on of my hands' [2 *Tim.* 1:6]. He says, 'This gift is in you, so stir it up!' There, again, is a great phrase! Somebody else translates it: 'Fan the flame'! Fan the flame of the Spirit that is in you. You have received this gift. The way in which Timothy received it is not the important point. The important point is that 'the flame of the Spirit', 'the fire of the Spirit', has been given to Timothy, and he is being exhorted to fan the flame, to stir it up, and keep it alive. A very good way of looking at this is found in 1 Thessalonians 5:19 where the apostle puts the point negatively by saying, 'Quench not the Spirit.' The Spirit is thought of as fire, the energy of fire. Think of the things that fire can do, for instance, a steam engine operates as the result of the power of fire. 'Don't dampen down the fire', says Paul.

But how are we to fan the flame? How are we to stir up the gift? Again, we start with a negative – rake the ashes. You have allowed ashes to gather, you have been lethargic, you have not attended to the fire and there is more ash than fire. There is only just a little bit of redness to be seen. So the first thing you must do is to shake it and rake it. Now this is something that you and I can do. The apostle is not asking you to produce the fire – you cannot do that. And when men and women try to produce the fire there is chaos; it is a false fire. There is a lot of that about in evangelical circles – a false fire, a carnal zeal. But the apostle here is thinking of the exact opposite. The fire has been given – and that is always the great teaching – and what we can do is get rid of the ashes.

But then that is not enough. You have to make sure that there is a plentiful supply of air – a current of air. What is that? It is prayer. Then you add a little more fuel. You and I can do that, and we do it by reading the Scriptures. And when you have read the Scriptures, another very good thing to do is to read about revivals. That is the fuel that this fire likes. Read the lives of saints; read the lives of the great revival preachers.

Have you not found that there is nothing that so fans the flame of the Spirit within you, as to read about men filled with the Spirit whom God has used in the past? I have always said this, and I say it now with more urgency than ever: next to the Bible itself there is nothing more profitable, more stimulating, more invigorating, than to read such accounts.

I remember reading once about Anatole France, that infidel novelist. He used to say, 'When I am tired and jaded, I never go for a change to the country, I always go to the eighteenth century.' And I say exactly the same thing! The finest tonic I know, better than any change of scenery or climate, is the eighteenth century. When I am tired and jaded and feel slothful, I have never yet in all my life read anything about Whitefield and the Wesleys and Jonathan Edwards, but that I am immediately restored and the flame is fanned again.

Now these, then, are the things which you and I are called upon to do. But then the great point is this: remind yourself of the gift that is in you. We constantly forget this, even as Christian people. We think of ourselves in natural terms, in terms of natural abilities. It is all wrong. We must remember that the Spirit of God is in us. 'Know ye not . . . that the Spirit of God', Paul says, 'dwelleth in you?' [*1 Cor.* 3:16]. We have already seen that in the eighth chapter, from which I have already quoted. The apostle keeps on saying that the Spirit is 'in you': 'But you are not in the flesh, but in the Spirit, if so be that the Spirit of God dwell in you. Now if any man have not the Spirit of Christ, he is none of his. And if Christ be in you, the body is dead because of sin; but the Spirit is life because of righteousness' [*Rom.* 8:9-10].

It is all the same teaching. Here, the apostle is summing it up, enforcing it, driving it home once more. And you and I must realize that the Spirit that is in us is a spirit of power, the spirit of strength. We are not expected to do these things ourselves, and we cannot. But we are told that we can 'put on' - take unto us - 'the whole armour of God' [*Eph.* 6:11]. 'Be strong in the Lord, and in the power of his might' [*Eph.* 6:10]. However weak and lethargic you may be by nature, however slothful by temperament, you must remind yourself of this: stir up your mind.

Or take it as Peter puts: 'I think it meet . . . to stir you up by

putting you in remembrance' [2 *Pet.* 1:13]. And this is something that we all stand in need of. The devil is very busy with
us and he makes us forget these things, and we say, 'Oh, how
can I do this? Who am I to do this?' And the answer is, 'It is not
you, you have forgotten the Spirit who is in you. The flame, the
power of the Spirit, the energy of the divine Spirit is in you. So
you must remind yourself of that, and that is one of the ways in
which you are 'fervent in spirit'. The moment you remember
Him, and think of Him, you already begin to feel the heat
within you.

Now, thank God, we do know something about this, all of
us, do we not? I have already referred to John Wesley. The thing
that made that man an evangelist was, he says, that his heart
was 'strangely warmed'. That was the Spirit coming in. And it
is not only the warmth of comfort, it is the warmth of energy.
This is the motive power, this is what drives us along. And the
apostle is constantly putting this fact before us. At the end of
Colossians chapter 1 he gives a description of himself as a
minister and as a preacher of Christ: 'Whom we preach,
warning every man, and teaching every man in all wisdom;
that we may present every man perfect in Christ Jesus:' – and
now here are the two sides – 'whereunto I also labour, striving
according to *his* working' – that is the power, it is 'according to'
or 'as the result of' – 'his working which worketh in me
mightily.' The energy of the Spirit! And the way to be filled
with that energy is to remind yourself that the Spirit is in you,
and that He is a spirit of power and of love and of discipline, of
'a sound mind'.

So you overcome your natural nature. We all have our
different problems. The man who is lethargic has the problem
of sloth, but the naturally energetic and fervent man, like
Apollos, has always to guard against human zeal. He has to
make sure that he is not confusing his own natural energy with
the energy of the Spirit, and sometimes it is not easy to
differentiate. But we must realize that it is the energy of the
Spirit that matters, and you do that by reading, and by
reminding yourself of these things, by prayer, by meditation,
and so on.

And then another excellent way of remaining 'fervent in
spirit' is to remind yourself of the work to which you have

been called. We are given the great dignity of being co-workers with God: 'Workers together with him' [2 *Cor.* 6:1]. We are in His kingdom, and we are workers in His kingdom. There are many ways in which this is put. Our Lord Himself tells us, 'Ye are the light of the world' [*Matt.* 5:14]. He is the light of the world, but because we are in Him we become 'the light of the world'. 'A city that is set on an hill cannot be hid', he says [*Matt.* 5:14]. Here is a way to rouse yourself when you are feeling slack, feeling you have no energy, and doubting whether you will read your Bible, whether you will pray, or whether you will go to God's house to study the Scriptures, or to worship Him and sing His praises. When you feel like that, remember what you are called to, remember the state of the world in which you are living.

> *Men die in darkness at thy side,*
> *Without a hope to cheer the tomb;*
> *Take up the torch and wave it wide,*
> *The torch that lights time's thickest gloom.*
> Horatius Bonar

That is the way to rouse yourself. Think of the people in this great city of London who are in utter darkness. They just do not know. They do not know their condition; they do not know what is facing them. They do not know their awful plight. They know nothing about the hell to which they are going. And you and I are called to be 'the light of the world', together with Him. That is how Paul always thought of himself. He was the man who planted, and Apollos watered [see 1 *Cor.* 3:6]. But remember, they were but being used – God always gives the increase, and, indeed, does everything.

Or take the way in which the apostle puts it to the Philippians: 'Do all things without murmurings and disputings' – but 'do all things', remember, do not be slothful – 'that ye may be blameless and harmless, the sons of God, without rebuke, in the midst of a crooked and perverse nation, among whom ye shine as lights in the world' – as lights or luminaries in the heavens, as stars on a dark night [*Phil.* 2:14–15]. That is what you are, Paul says, as Christian people.

Now the moment you realize these things, you cannot

remain lethargic and slothful. You say, 'I must get up. I think of these people in the darkness and they are all watching me, and judging Him by what they see.' Therefore you rouse yourself. The nature of the work itself helps you to be 'fervent in spirit'. You have been given the Spirit in order that you may function, and then you think of what the function is, and that, in its turn, stimulates the fire and the power of the Spirit within you.

Or take it in one other way – and I have often, as I am sure we all have, fallen back on this kind of argument. It is the famous story about Nehemiah doing his work and building the wall. A man came to him and said, 'Look here, this is extremely dangerous. Don't you think that you and I ought to go and hide ourselves in the temple, otherwise we shall be killed.' Now of course that was, and always is, a very tempting suggestion. It appeals to the natural desire to protect yourself, to save your life, or, if you are feeling a bit lazy, it is a good excuse: 'You'll be needed again, so don't do anything now.' But there is only one answer to that, and it is the answer Nehemiah gave: 'Should such a man as I flee?' [*Neh.* 6:11] It is unthinkable! And so you apply this argument to yourself, and as you do, you remind yourself that the Spirit of God is in you. 'Know ye not that . . . ye are not your own? For ye are bought with a price' [*1 Cor.* 6:19–20].

So let us sum it up by putting it like this: We must realize that we are called to work for God. I remember a remark made by the saintly William Chalmers Burns, a man greatly neglected, it seems to me, whom God used so much to bring about revival in Scotland round about 1840 – you will find his name in connection with the biographies and memoirs of Robert Murray M'Cheyne. One of his favourite expressions, at least, he used it very frequently, was this: Putting his hand on the shoulder of a brother minister, he would say, 'Brother, we must hurry!' He realized the shortness of the time. And you and I should realize that. We see the world as it is, round and about us, and the time is short. 'Redeeming the time,' says the apostle, 'for the days are evil' [*Eph.* 5:16]. That was true in his day, is it not true today? The times are out of joint, the days are evil.

This is not an exhortation to tell you only to rouse yourself on the natural level. Paul is not asking you to turn yourself into something that you are not. He is not just asking you to be a fussy, busy kind of person. No, no! All the great doctrine is behind it, the doctrine of the Spirit, the doctrine of the new nature, the Spirit dwelling within you, the work to which you are called as a member of the body of Christ. Paul is telling you to let the energy of the Spirit work in you and manifest itself through you, to turn away the hindrances and the obstacles and to maintain the glow. We cannot produce the fire, but we can maintain the glow. We must not quench the Spirit. We must take these positive and active steps and work it out on the basis of verses 1 and 2. And then we realize the need of 'hurrying' and not wasting time. Because of the awfulness of the problem, and the condition of men and women, we must buy up the opportunity.

So let me sum it up for you in the words of a well-known hymn:

Take, my soul, thy full salvation;
Rise o'er sin, and fear, and care;
Joy to find in every station
Something still to do or bear.
Think what Spirit dwells within thee,
What a Father's smile is thine,
What a Saviour died to win thee;
Child of heaven, shouldst thou repine?

Haste then on from grace to glory,
Armed by faith and winged by prayer;
Heaven's eternal day's before thee;
God's own hand shall guide thee there.
Soon shall close thy earthly mission;
Swift shall pass thy pilgrim days,
Hope soon change to glad fruition,
Faith to sight, and prayer to praise.

Henry Francis Lyte

Twenty-seven

*

Not slothful in business; fervent in spirit; serving the Lord; rejoicing in hope; patient in tribulation; continuing instant in prayer.

Romans 12:11–12

So far, we have considered Paul's two great general statements: we must not be slothful and we must be fervent in spirit. But now the apostle goes on and adds a third element to the way in which we deal with our tendency to sloth, and it is this: 'Serving the Lord'. He rises here, of course, to a climax. He starts on the natural, general level and tells us to remember that the Spirit is within us and that we must not allow anything to 'quench the Spirit' or to keep the flame of the Spirit burning low; we must not 'grieve the Spirit'. But then he rises to the highest height, and gives us the ultimate antidote to any tendency to slothfulness in the Christian life: 'Serving the Lord'.

This is a most wonderful thought. In a sense, it is the key to everything else, and it certainly is the supreme motive, always, in Christian living and service. It is something that we always tend to forget, and it is when we forget this that we get into trouble. If we think of our Christian lives and work in terms of ourselves, and one another we will soon be in trouble. If the preacher is concerned about himself and his own reputation, he will soon be miserable; he will be jealous or envious, or he will feel that people are not praising him enough. And the antidote is that we are 'serving the Lord'. It applies to everyone in the Christian church and to every aspect of our activity.

There is only one answer to all the troubles that arise from looking at ourselves – serving the Lord.

In 2 Corinthians 4, this same great apostle expresses this wonderfully. The foolish Corinthian Christians were indulging in comparisons and criticisms, and the apostle was forced to defend himself, so he wrote there about himself, something that was very unusual for him. He says in this passage, 'We preach not ourselves, but Christ Jesus the Lord' [verse 5]. He did everything honestly as in the sight of God. He was not in the preaching business in order to gain anything for himself. He had been called there, and his one desire was not to 'handle the word of God deceitfully' [2 *Cor.* 4:2]. And he succeeded in his aim, he tells us, by 'preaching Christ Jesus the Lord' [2 *Cor.* 4:5]; self did not come into it. Paul says this in many other places also, and here it is again in Romans 12, put in the form of a summary. But, oh, how vital it is, and how foolish we often are in rushing over a statement like this. The glibness with which we use these terms is really quite alarming and appalling.

What, then, does 'serving the Lord' mean? Well, we must remind ourselves of certain principles, and, surely, the first that is suggested by this statement is that, after all, we are nothing but slaves. How often the apostle says this, and in so many different ways! 'Know ye not that . . . ye are not your own? For ye are bought with a price' [*1 Cor.* 6:19–20]. Look at the way in which he starts most of his epistles. 'Paul,' as the Authorized Version puts it, 'a servant of God', or, 'of the Lord Jesus Christ'. But what he really wrote was, 'the bond-slave'. He says he is a slave, a 'bond-slave'. He has been 'bought out', he has been 'redeemed', he has been 'ransomed'. He does not deserve anything. Read the first chapter of the First Epistle to Timothy, and there you will find Paul expressing his amazement that he, of all people, should ever have been put into the ministry, he, who was formerly, 'a blasphemer, and a persecutor, and injurious; but,' he says, 'I obtained mercy, because I did it ignorantly in unbelief' [*1 Tim.* 1:13].

Now that was the apostle's whole attitude. He was the 'bond-slave' of Jesus Christ, and a slave does not do anything for himself, he does it for his master. He has been bought, he has no right to think of himself or his own interests, because he belongs entirely to the other. So we remember that we are 'serving the Lord', and that is how we start working out this injunction.

But then we add something further. It is the fact that this is not our cause; it is not our business. That is the trouble, is it not? People talk about 'my church'. It is the besetting sin of ministers, of all of us who are in a position of leadership in the church. It is an attitude we must fight against – 'my church'! The idea is so monstrous; it is so ridiculous. You find it revealed in a denominational spirit – 'my denomination'. All sorts of rivalries and quarrelling and hatred come through regarding the church as if it were our own. There are chapels which compete with one another, even going so far as to compete in missionary collections, so that they can boast that they are always on the top of the list.

You see, the motive is no longer love for God, but something purely selfish and personal; it is self-adulation. People say, 'Look at what our church is doing!' and they publish the figures. But what a denial this is of the very essence of Christianity! And how widespread it is, and how terrible, especially when it is done in a subtle way as if it were not being done. In the same way, politicians 'leak' information when they give away facts while pretending that they have not revealed anything. There is only one answer to that attitude: the church is not yours; it is not ours; it does not belong to us.

You remember that great message from God which the prophet made to King Jehoshaphat? 'The battle is not your's, but God's . . . Stand ye still, and see the salvation of the Lord' [2 *Chron.* 20:15, 17]. And I have often pointed out from this pulpit that that is to me one of the most interesting and wonderful things about the life of the early church. Look at the way in which those spiritually-minded men and women responded to the first persecution of the early church recorded in Acts 4. This is their prayer: 'Lord,' they said, 'thou art God, which hast made heaven, and earth, and the sea, and all that in them is: who by the mouth of thy servant David hast said, Why did the heathen rage, and the people imagine vain things? The kings of the earth stood up, and the rulers were gathered together' – against whom? Against us? Not at all! – 'against the Lord, and against his Christ. For of a truth against thy holy

[378]

child Jesus, whom thou hast anointed, both Herod and Pontius
Pilate, with the Gentiles, and the people of Israel, were
gathered together . . . And now, Lord, behold their threaten-
ings' [*Acts* 4:24–27, 29].

These people had the wisdom and the spiritual perception to
see that the Jewish authorities, the Sanhedrin, were not against
them. Who were they? They were nobodies, 'ignorant and
unlearned men'. They realized that the authorities were not
against them, but against God. They were against the church
because the church was the church of God! And this is what
we so constantly forget. It is all His, and not ours at all. The
battle is against 'thy holy child Jesus'. God's great plan of
redemption and His great purpose with regard to the world –
that is what is being emphasized here. Thus in Romans 12, the
apostle says, 'serving *the Lord*': not yourself, nor your own
cause. That is the second way in which you work it out – it all
belongs to Him.

And then let us add to this, in order that it may really grip
and enthuse us. Think of the privilege of being given a part in
this work at all! Have we ever thought of that? In that
quotation which I gave you from 1 Timothy 1:13, the apostle
brings that out. He is amazed at the great privilege of being
given a part in God's work, and we must always remind
ourselves that 'we are workers together with him [God]' [2
Cor. 6:2]. Here is something that we cannot understand and
never will. God could have done everything without us. But He
has chosen to act through people like us.

And that, as we have seen, is the antidote to self-importance
in any church work or in any position in connection with the
Christian life. He has given us the honour; He has chosen to
work in this way. 'We, being many,' as Paul has told us, 'are
one body in Christ' [*Rom.* 12:5]. We are parts of this mystical
body of which Christ is the Head. And no greater honour can
ever come to human beings than to know that they are a part of
this body, that they belong to Him, and that they are sharing
something of His great work.

Another way in which you work out this principle of
'serving the Lord' is this: you realize that it is a very wonderful
way in which to show your gratitude to Him. We owe everything to Him. 'By the grace of God I am what I am,' says the

apostle in 1 Corinthians 15:10. Consider what He has done for you; consider who He is. And then think that He deserves your very best. The psalmist cries out, 'What shall I render unto the Lord for all his benefits toward me?' [*Psa.* 116:12]. And you and I should cry out like that even more, for we look back upon the sacrifice of the Son of God on the cross on Calvary's hill. That is what He has done for us. You remember the famous story about Count Zinzendorf and the great experience he had as the result of looking at a picture of the crucified Christ? It was as though the picture were saying, 'I have done this for thee. What hast thou done for me?'

That is the kind of argument that is here: we are 'serving the Lord'. And that realization rids us of all that hinders us and cripples us, and it certainly gets rid of all dejection and slothfulness, and all laziness and every tendency to do our work half-heartedly. We remember that we are serving Him, who gave Himself even unto death for us, gave all for us - gave Himself. And we, in turn, want to serve Him in order to show our gratitude.

But then we must add yet another argument: that God's honour is involved in all this, and here, again, is a most potent motive and argument. As we have seen, whether we like it or not, if we are Christian people, and if we are members of the Christian church, we are joined to Him. We are 'in Christ' and Christ is in us, and we are members of His body. Therefore, He is involved in the life, in the activity and in everything that happens to the church.

In other words, we must always pause to realize that He is involved in our failures. '. . . Ye are not your own . . . ye are bought with a price' [*1 Cor.* 6:19-20]. 'None of us liveth to himself,' the apostle says in Romans 14:7. You cannot act as an individual; you cannot isolate yourself. As a Christian, you belong to the community, the people of God. You are a part of the church of God. He is the Head, and He is involved, therefore, in everything you do and in everything that happens to you. And that is why we should always remind ourselves that we are serving Him.

If you are doing something entirely on your own, then, if things go wrong, nobody is involved except yourself. But that is never the position of the Christian, and the world is always, of course, very careful to observe this. If a Christian should be arraigned in a court, the newspapers will always point it out, and, as I have often indicated from this pulpit, you will see this kind of heading: *Sunday School Teacher On Trial.* If you read the facts, you will find that the man was a Sunday school teacher twenty years ago, but that does not matter, the reporters will drag it in. Why? Oh, it is a way of attacking Him and His honour! We are serving the Lord and He is involved. His name and His cause can be brought into disrepute by us.

We know what the world thinks of the Christian church today. It thinks of her as something weak and contemptible, and it thinks that most of the people who go to church go because they are afraid not to, and because they do not have enough intelligence to stop! People in the world despise the Christian church. Yes, but that is because *we* are slothful and make no impact. They are not aware of any power. And that is why we must say to ourselves: We cannot be slothful any longer. My behaviour affects not merely what they think of me, but what they think of Him, and the truth that comes from Him. That is the reason for rousing myself and making sure that the Spirit is having free play in my life.

But if He is involved in our failures, He is equally involved in any success that may come to us. Peter writes, 'Dearly beloved, I beseech you as strangers and pilgrims, abstain from fleshly lusts, which war against the soul; having your conversation honest among the Gentiles' – why? – 'that whereas they speak against you as evil-doers, they may by your good works, which they shall behold, glorify God in the day of visitation' [*1 Pet.* 2:11–12]. That is it! And our Lord has really said the same thing: 'Let your light so shine before men, that they may see your good works, and glorify your Father which is in heaven' [*Matt.* 5:16]. And we do that by reminding ourselves that we are 'serving the Lord' and not ourselves.

I have often used the illustration of the great message sent out by Lord Nelson on the morning of the Battle of Trafalgar – 'England expects that every man this day will do his duty.' The honour of England is involved, the honour of the country. You are not fighting a personal fight against the French, you are fighting for England – 'England expects . . .' This is what rouses you. You cannot be slothful when you hear such an appeal. You are immediately electrified, as it were, into activity, and you are anxious to do your best because of your country. Multiply that by infinity and we are given an idea of what it means that we are serving the Lord.

This is a great theme which runs right through the Bible. It was the appeal of all the prophets of the Old Testament. It was the cardinal failure of the children of Israel that they kept on forgetting who they were. They would persist in regarding themselves just as one nation among a number of nations, and they always had to be reminded that they were the people of God – God's own chosen people – and thus that His honour was involved in all they did.

And then another argument is that because we are serving the Lord, His eye is always upon us. What a salutary thought this is! I use the obvious illustration – unfortunately we are all too familiar with it – of how a man employed by another often behaves. If his master is about, he works very hard and is keen and enthusiastic, but when his master goes away, he slouches. But we are reminded here that His eye is always upon us – always, in all places and in all situations. He sees us when we are slacking, indolent, slothful. He sees it all. So we remind ourselves of those lines of the hymn:

> *Still walking in your Captain's sight*
> *And watching unto prayer.*
>
> Charles Wesley

'All things are naked and opened unto the eyes of him with whom we have to do' [*Heb.* 4:13]. You are not a private individual. You may say, 'Ah, well, I don't feel like it now, so I don't think I'll do this today. I won't go to church on Sunday. I won't read my Bible. I won't pray.' And you think it is a purely private matter, though you may, perhaps, be a little concerned about what other people may say. But that is not the thing that really matters. What really matters is that He sees it all. 'I know thy works,' He said to the churches in Revelation 2 and 3. And He does. You cannot get outside the scope of His all-seeing eye – the eye of the Captain of our salvation. And therefore we remind ourselves that He has put us as 'labourers into the vineyard'. The vineyard is His and it is for His glory.

And then there is a final appeal that is often found. It is expressed especially by the Apostle John – you get it more than once in his First Epistle, and it is also in the writings of the Apostle Paul. The argument is that we must rouse ourselves, and we must never be slothful, in order that we may not be ashamed at His coming, for He will come and we shall all stand before Him. As Paul says in 2 Corinthians 5:10, 'For we must all appear before the judgment seat of Christ; that every one may receive the things done in his body, according to that he hath done, whether it be good or bad.' That is why Paul preached as he did. It was not merely that 'the love of Christ constraineth us' [*2 Cor.* 5:14], but he knew that he would have to stand before the judgment throne of Christ, and give an account of all that he had done. 'Knowing therefore the terror of the Lord,' he says, 'we persuade men' [*2 Cor.* 5:11].

Christian people, how often do we think of this when we are tempted to this indolent slothfulness, slackness and half-hearted way of doing things, so that we say, 'Oh, I'll do it again some time!', instead of being always alive and alert, using all our energy, maintaining the glow in the spirit. On top of all the arguments that I have adduced, and the reasons I have put before you, I must add that you, too, will appear before the judgment seat of Christ, and you will have to give an account of yourself. You will be told, 'You saw the world in the state it was when you were there on earth. You saw the godlessness and vice and rampant evil. What did you do about it? Did you just lie back and say, "That's a job for the preachers" – or did you pray without ceasing? Were you an intercessor? Were you doing everything that you could in order to hold up the hands of the preachers and enable the gospel to be proclaimed?' We must all give an account of this, for we are serving the Lord, not ourselves. He is the Master and we shall all have to render up an account to Him. Look how our Lord put it Himself in the parable of the talents and in other parables. This great teaching is everywhere in the Bible.

And here it is all summed up for us in Romans 12. We must remind ourselves in all these ways that we are 'serving the

Lord'. So when you are tempted to slothfulness, listen to something like this:

> *From strength to strength go on;*
> *Wrestle, and fight, and pray;*
> *Tread all the powers of darkness down,*
> *And win the well-fought day.*
> *Still let the Spirit cry*
> *In all His soldiers, 'Come',*
> *Till Christ the Lord descend from high,*
> *And take the conquerors home.*
>
> Charles Wesley

'Whether therefore, ye eat, or drink, or whatsoever ye do, do all to the glory of God' [*1 Cor.* 10:31]. Be all-out in everything you do, realizing that you are His servants and that you are 'serving the Lord' and not merely pleasing yourself or other people.

The next thing Paul tells us is this: 'Rejoicing in hope'. Now you notice the intimate connection between all these things. As I have already indicated, Paul did not put these injunctions down haphazardly, just adding the next one that came to his mind. There is a logical sequence here. They are all inter-related and each one leads to the next.

Now here Paul is dealing with us from the standpoint of our outlook upon our lives as Christians, our whole attitude towards our life and our understanding of it. This, again, is a vital matter, especially at this time. Of course, you must start with the great principles which we have been laying down, but then you go on and apply them to yourself in this way: 'Rejoicing in hope'. What does this mean? I would say that the point at which we left off the last statement helps us to understand these words, for we have been reminded of the day when we will be standing before Him, and before His judgment seat, and that has led the apostle to think of how Christians view their lives in this world. And here it is: 'Rejoicing in hope'.

The apostle has already dealt with this subject, but here in this chapter he is summarizing many of the things that he has said in greater detail earlier in the Epistle. As far back as the fifth chapter, he wrote: 'Therefore being justified by faith, we have peace with God through our Lord Jesus Christ: by whom also we have access by faith into this grace wherein we stand, and rejoice in hope of the glory of God' [verses 1-2]. In the eighth chapter, Paul took up this theme still more definitely in that resounding statement: 'I reckon that the sufferings of this present time are not worthy to be compared with the glory which shall be revealed in us' [verse 18]. And in verses 24 and 25, he continues: 'We are saved by hope [in hope]: but hope that is seen is not hope: for what a man seeth, why doth he yet hope for? But if we hope for that we see not, then do we with patience wait for it.'

Now when the apostle says here, 'rejoicing in hope', he is not inculcating a general spirit of cheerfulness and rejoicing. There has been a great stress on that in the Christian church during this twentieth century – in a foolish reaction against a misunderstanding of Puritanism, there has been a cult of cheerfulness. Nothing is further removed from the rejoicing that the apostle is dealing with here. This is not something that we work up. Paul is not merely telling us to put on a smiling face. That is carnal rejoicing, something that the apostle never teaches.

Nor is he telling us here to cultivate a hopeful outlook. Today there is also a great emphasis on that. Where there are wars you hear people say, 'Cultivate the cheerful, hopeful outlook, the sanguine temperament. Don't look at the black side; always look for the silver lining in the cloud.' So is 'rejoicing in hope' a spirit of hopefulness, a hopeful outlook? No, no.

Nor is the apostle telling us to expect great things in the future of this world. You know the optimistic idealists who feel that we only have to apply Christian teaching and the world will get better and better. So they expect great things and are full of hope for the future of the world, or they are hoping to put the world right. 'Rejoicing in hope' – things will get better and better!

When the apostle talks of 'rejoicing in hope' he is referring to the great New Testament doctrine of 'the hope'. *The* hope – rejoicing in the hope. Here, again, we are reminded that none of these injunctions in Romans 12 can be understood, still less implemented, unless we are clear about Paul's teaching in the first two verses of this chapter. 'I beseech you therefore, brethren . . .' The 'therefore' links us with the whole of the doctrine that he has already been laying down. You cannot rejoice in hope if you do not know your doctrine. It is impossible. The only person who rejoices in hope is the one who is clear about the doctrinal teaching of this great Epistle – and the other epistles, too, of course.

So, first of all, rejoicing in hope means that we must have a right view of this world in which we find ourselves. And the view that the apostle teaches everywhere is that this is what he calls 'the present evil world'. According to New Testament teaching, a Christian is a man or woman who is saved 'out of the world', 'delivered from this present evil world' [*Gal.* 1:4]. Of course, if you do not regard the world in this way, you will not know what the apostle is talking about when he speaks of 'rejoicing in hope'. The whole teaching of the Bible is that this is a fallen world; it is a world under judgment; it is doomed; it is a world of evil and of sin and of wrong. And the Bible goes further and says that there is no hope for the world as it is. None at all. It cannot be improved.

Today, all that idealistic and humanistic, optimistic teaching of past years has been made to look ridiculous. It is a terrible thing, is it not, that it takes two world wars to make men and women see the truth of what has always been taught in the Bible. Think of the optimism of the nineteenth century. The Victorians forecast the coming of a parliament of man and federation of the world. Knowledge! Science! Progress! The whole world moving on to its destined goal, getting better and better and better. What makes most of those 'great Victorians', as they are sometimes called, so pathetic is that they were so completely, entirely wrong. They have been proved wrong by history. The twentieth century is the answer to the Victorians. But it is what the Bible has always said.

The truth, I repeat, is that we do not begin to understand the New Testament doctrine of 'the hope' until we realize that this present world is completely under condemnation. There is nothing in the Bible to suggest that this world can ever be improved. On the contrary, there is quite a lot to suggest the exact opposite. We are told that 'evil men . . . shall wax worse and worse' [*2 Tim.* 3:13]; that 'ye shall hear of wars and rumours of wars' [*Matthew* 24:6]. Our Lord even put this question: 'When the Son of man cometh, shall he find faith on the earth?' [*Luke* 18:8]. And yet it used to be believed that each generation began where the previous one ended, and that each one was advancing, and the gospel would Christianize the world.

There has been nothing so fatuous, quite apart from nothing so unscriptural, as the 'social gospel' that was so popular in the early years of the twentieth century. It was a complete denial of the basic, central teaching of the New Testament, and, as I say, has been proved false by history. No, you must start by realizing that you cannot rejoice in hope while you have any hope for this world.

So, then, having been put right about this world, the next step is to realize God's purpose with respect to it. Why did the Lord ever come into this world? Why did He live and die, and do all that He did? And the answer is that He came to redeem it. But His method of redemption was not one of gradual improvement. The programme is this: that in this present age people are being gathered out of the world, saved out of it, delivered out of it as individuals, and are being put into this new kingdom of God – the kingdom that is the continuation of the children of Israel. There it was in the Old Testament form; here it is in the New Testament form – the church. Our Lord Himself said, 'The kingdom of God shall be taken from you, and given to a nation bringing forth the fruits thereof' [*Matt.* 21:43]. The church is the present form of the kingdom, and people are being gathered into it. We have seen all this in chapter 11. Jews and Gentiles together are all being brought into this one olive tree. 'There is no difference' [*Rom.* 10:12]

And this calling out will continue until a given point. Nobody knows when. Many people have tried to determine the date, but they have always been wrong, and always will be, because we are not supposed to be concerned about 'the times or the seasons' [*Acts* 1:7]. But what we do know is that we are being prepared for a great event which is coming: the return of the Son of God to this world. As the angels told the disciples on Mount Olivet, 'This same Jesus, which is taken up from you into heaven, shall so come *in like manner* as ye have seen him go into heaven' [*Acts* 1:11]. Every eye shall see him. He will return and His coming will be visible. He will return to judge the world in righteousness. He will destroy all His enemies [see *Heb.* 10:13]. He will purge the cosmos of evil and all its effects. We 'look for new heavens and a new earth, wherein dwelleth righteousness' [*2 Pet.* 3:13]. This will be a cataclysmic event, not a gradual improvement. There will be a great crisis. When He is least expected, He will come. Far from everything leading optimistically up to our Lord's return, it will be the exact opposite. People's hearts will fail them. Even the elect will be in trouble. Then He will come, and He will set up His eternal kingdom of glory.

So here in Romans, the apostle is saying: Rejoice in that. That is what you must keep your eye on. Our Lord had taught the same thing: 'In the world ye shall have tribulation: but be of good cheer; I have overcome the world' [*John* 16:33]. According to the teaching of the whole of the New Testament, this is the thing in which we are to rejoice. Take the typical and glorious Christian statements made by the apostle in 2 Corinthians 4 and 5. Here is this great apostle, passing through a period of terrible trial and tribulation, and notice what he says. This is Christianity – not the world getting better and better and liking us because we are Christians. It is the exact opposite. Paul says, 'We have this treasure in earthen vessels' [*2 Cor.* 4:7] – and we are not promised that they will be anything better than earthen vessels in this world. He has already told us in the eighth chapter of this Epistle to the Romans, '. . . the body is dead because of sin; but the Spirit is life because of righteousness' [*Rom.* 8:10]. And while we are in this world, the body will be frail, subject to disease and decay.

'We have this treasure in earthen vessels.' And then the apostle adds: 'We are troubled on every side, yet not distressed; we are perplexed, but not in despair; persecuted, but not forsaken; cast down, but not destroyed; always bearing about in the body the dying of the Lord Jesus' – in the body, remember – 'that the life also of Jesus might be made manifest in our body. For we which live are alway delivered unto death for Jesus' sake' [verses 8–11]. He was surrounded by trials and troubles and tribulations. The apostle had a hard time and a difficult life – sickness, persecution, disappointment in friends. What a catalogue of trials! And yet the marvellous thing is that he rejoiced in the midst of it all. Not rejoicing in this world, but 'rejoicing in hope'.

And Paul sums everything up at the end of that chapter, and here is the exposition of this phrase that we are looking at here in Romans 12. Listen to him. He has given us the list of all his trials but he then looks at them all and says, 'For our light affliction, which is but for a moment . . .' What does he mean by 'but for a moment'? Is he pulling out a chronometer and measuring a moment? Not at all! He is measuring time in terms of eternity. He is not saying, 'I'm going to die tomorrow.' He says, 'No, no, it doesn't matter how long I'm in this life, it is only a moment.'

How is it that Paul can say 'but for a moment'? Well, you see, if you look at your life in this world from the perspective of eternity, it is nothing but a moment. If you measure your life in this world in terms of minutes and hours and days and weeks and months and years – oh, how long it seems! But Christians do not do that. Christians know that this is a temporary life, a passing phase. What is of interest to them is this life which is to come, this glory which is to come, 'This world to come, whereof we speak,' as the author of the Epistle to the Hebrews puts it [*Heb.* 2:5]. That is the thing.

And so Paul says to the Corinthians, 'Our light affliction' – light? Look at the list! Yet he says: But it is only light. Why? Because he is putting it all in another context. 'Our light affliction, which is but for a moment, worketh [produces] for us a far more exceeding and eternal *weight of glory*.' Where? Here and now? Not at all! Where, then? Oh, he says, 'While [as long as] we look not at the things which are seen' – not at this life, not at this present world – 'but at the things which are not seen: for the things which are seen are temporal; but the things which are not seen are eternal' [*2 Cor.* 4:17–18]. He is looking to the glory that is coming.

That is the thing! The hope! This is 'the blessed hope' that all the New Testament is looking forward to, and, Paul says in effect, 'Whatever may be happening to me in the here and now, it does not get me down.' Why? 'Because I know that *that* is coming for certain, and I am rejoicing at the thought of that and the anticipation of it.' It is going to be so marvellous that language fails him. 'Our light affliction . . . worketh for us a far

[389]

more exceeding and eternal weight of glory.' Somebody says those words should be translated, 'worketh for us an exceeding exceedingly abundant weight of glory'. Quite right! You can add on all the superlatives in the world and they will be inadequate to describe this 'weight of glory' for which we are being prepared.

That is the teaching; that is what you rejoice in. You cannot rejoice in the present world. Look at it – who can rejoice in it? Now you must not try to isolate yourself and say, 'I'm not concerned with what is happening outside, as long as I'm happy.' That is the antithesis of Christianity. No, no! You recognize what sin has done to the world and you realize what God's plan and purpose for the world is. You know that that is certain. So you rejoice in God's plan, and that is more than enough to keep you going. Listen to Paul again, in a great exhortation at the beginning of Colossians 3: 'If we then be risen with Christ, seek those things which are above, where Christ sitteth on the right hand of God. Set your affection on things above, not on things on the earth. For ye are dead, and your life is hid with Christ in God.' That is what you look to. Things above!

And Paul says exactly the same thing in writing to Titus: 'The grace of God that bringeth salvation hath appeared to all men. Teaching us that, denying ungodliness and worldly lusts, we should live soberly, righteously, and godly, in this present world; looking for that blessed hope, and the glorious appearing of the great God and our Saviour Jesus Christ' [*Titus* 2:11–13]. That is why the first Christians were ready to be martyred. They thanked God even as they were being martyred because of the hope that was set before them. This is the thing. Not this world, but the world to come and the glory that awaits us there.

Peter has exactly the same teaching. 'Hasting unto', he says; 'looking for'. 'Hasting unto the coming of the day of God' [2 *Pet.* 3:12]. 'Every man that hath this hope in him,' says John, 'purifieth himself, even as he is pure' [*1 John* 3:3]. What is he talking about? The improvement of this world? The Christianization of civilization? My dear friends, have people read the New Testament? What are they talking about? No, this is what John is talking about: 'Behold, what manner of love the

Father hath bestowed upon us, that we should be called the sons of God: therefore the world knoweth us not, because it knew not him' [*1 John* 3:1]. And it will never know us. The world will always be 'the world' and Christians are men and women who are taken out of it, saved from it, though they are still in it. 'Beloved, now are we the sons of God, and it doth not yet appear what we shall be: but we know that, when he shall appear, we shall be like him; for we shall see him as he is. And every man that hath this hope in him purifieth himself, even as he is pure' [*1 John* 3:2–3].

And so the Bible ends with the last chapter of Revelation looking forward and saying, 'Even so, come, Lord Jesus.' It is the only hope for us. That is the thing to which we should be looking forward. We 'rejoice in hope of the glory of God' [*Rom.* 5:2], in anticipation of it. And you can do that, whatever the world may be like and whatever it may be doing to you. And this is to be the permanent condition of Christian people. They remind themselves that they are 'serving the Lord', this Lord who 'sitteth on the right hand of God' [*Col.* 3:1] in the glory everlasting, who is 'expecting till his enemies be made his footstool' [*Heb.* 10:13], and who will most surely come and take His captives home. And we shall see Him as He is and be made like Him; and we shall share in His glory for ever and for ever.

These are the antidotes to sloth, to laziness, half-heartedness, pessimism, or fear of modern infidels and their writings. Read your Scriptures, consider the plan of God, look unto your Captain, keep your eye on Him: 'Looking unto Jesus, the author and the finisher of our faith' [*Heb.* 12:2]. Look at what He has done, look at what He is doing, look at what He is yet going to do. There will be no sloth then.

Twenty-eight

Rejoicing in hope; patient in tribulation; continuing instant in prayer.

Romans 12:12

We are dealing, you will remember, with the last section in this chapter, beginning at verse 9, where the apostle is considering our general relationship to other people. And now, in the twelfth verse, he is asking us to take a total view of our lives in this world. We began to do this in the last study, when we took up that first phrase, 'Rejoicing in hope', and saw that that is something that is absolutely vital to our whole position as Christians. There is nothing so fatal to Christian people as to fail to realize the nature of their lives in this world, and the antidote is to believe what the Bible teaches us about 'this present evil world'. There is no hope for it, it is under judgment, and all who belong to it will be involved in the judgment. Christians, on the other hand, are told, 'Set your affection on things above, not on things on the earth' [*Col.* 3:2], and we are, therefore, to 'rejoice in hope of the glory of God' [*Rom.* 5:2].

This is, of course, basic and fundamental, because if we do not understand it, we cannot possibly understand or put into practice this second injunction which we are now going to consider – 'patient in tribulation'. I have reminded you several times that these injunctions were not laid down haphazardly by the apostle. There is a very definite sequence here, he has an order in his mind. And 'patient in tribulation' follows of necessity upon 'rejoicing in hope'. Here you are: you are a saved person, a Christian, delivered out of this present evil world, and you have your eye set on that hope. So the question is: How are you going to live while you are left in this world?

[392]

And the apostle, this great authority on doctrine, this mighty genius, always descends to the practicalities, and enables us to apply all this doctrine in order that we may live our lives as we are meant to live them as Christian people –'Patient', he says, 'in tribulation.'

Now to prove my point about the logical connection between these injunctions – the ones that have gone before and the ones that follow – I would point out to you that the apostle does exactly the same thing here as he has already done in the fifth chapter. 'Therefore', he says there, 'being justified by faith, we have peace with God through our Lord Jesus Christ: by whom also we have access by faith into this grace wherein we stand, and rejoice in hope of the glory of God. And not only so, but we glory in tribulations also' [*Rom.* 5:1–3]. The moment he mentions 'rejoicing in hope of the glory of God', he comes to tribulations. 'Not only so, but we glory in tribulations also: knowing that tribulation worketh patience; and patience, experience; and experience, hope: and hope maketh not ashamed.' There is an inevitable connection between these things, and so each time they are mentioned, they go together.

What, then, is 'tribulation'? Now the commentators are very rightly interested in this word. Its original meaning is something that puts pressure to bear upon you, something that crushes. A *tribulum* was used to crush the corn in order to get flour, so 'tribulation' means that things are pressing heavily upon you almost to the extent of crushing you. Trials and tribulations come upon us in various ways. They may happen as the result of circumstances over which we have no control at all, or sometimes through temptations and sometimes through persecutions. They are sent to try God's people. I need not take time to elaborate this. Tribulations of many kinds bring pressure to bear upon your spirit, upon your mind, and upon your heart – they tend to crush you, and flatten you, and get you right down.

Now no one knew more about tribulations than the apostle Paul. In many places he gives pictures of the kinds of sufferings he had to endure. You must not think of him as a man seated in a study with books all round him, living a wonderful intellectual life. It was the exact opposite. He was a traveller; he was an evangelist, travelling on land, travelling by sea, undergoing shipwrecks, being maligned, persecuted and mis-represented. In the Epistles to the Corinthians in particular, especially in 2 Corinthians 4 and 11 where he gives us several lists, we read of the trials and tribulations which he had to suffer. He knew all about suffering, and he knew that all Christian people, in a measure, have to endure trials.

So here now the apostle tells us how to react to tribulations. Watch the order – it is so vital. First of all, get a right view of life in this world. The Christian never says, 'Isn't life wonder-ful!' Never! He sees through it all. 'This is the victory that overcometh the world' [*1 John* 5:4]. The world is to be over-come because of its evil. You have to be right in your whole view. You must be right about this question of 'the hope'. It is only then that you can proceed to argue in the way Paul does about tribulations.

So how am I to react to tribulations? First, I must not be shaken by them or give way under tribulation. That is the negative aspect, but it is most important and it must be emphasized. If I allow tribulations and trials to get me down, I have failed as a Christian. We must never grumble or com-plain. That is what we tend to do, is it not? When we are tried, when these things come to us, we say, 'Why should this happen to me?', or, 'Is Christianity not true after all?'

Now if you react like that, you are doing the opposite of what the apostle says here. That is what human nature does: it grumbles, it complains. People say, 'I thought that when I became a Christian, I would never have this sort of thing any more, but here it is happening to me.' There were many people saying that in the first centuries – you will find it dealt with in the New Testament epistles. But it is all due to ignorance: ignorance of this world, ignorance of the fact that 'we are saved by hope' [*Rom.* 8:24], that we 'walk by faith, not by sight' [2 *Cor.* 5:7]. That is the whole teaching. We are strangers and pilgrims, journeymen and travellers, passing through an evil world, on the way to the glory that God has prepared for His people. So we must not grumble; we must not complain; we must not feel that things are unfair. To sum it up, we must never allow tribulation to do us any harm at all.

Tribulation has often done Christian people great harm. There have been people who seem to be wonderful Christians

– but it is only as long as everything is going well. The moment trials come, they collapse. Oh, what poor Christians, and what poor representatives of the Christian faith! They are poor people from any standpoint, are they not? There are poor people even in the natural realm – fair-weather friends. In trouble they are no use. The expression is proverbial. 'Well, don't be fair-weather Christians', says the apostle in effect. 'Don't fail under testing and trial.' No, no – you must do the exact opposite.

So what must you do? Well, secondly, here it is positively: be *patient*. I agree with those who say that the English word 'patient' is too weak, too negative a word. There is something positive about the word that the apostle uses. It carries the notion of endurance – patient endurance. That is much stronger. But someone may say, 'It's all very well saying, "Have patient endurance. Be steadfast in tribulation." But how?'

Well, it works out like this. The first thing is: do not be surprised at tribulations. I think that is what gets most people down. They had never expected this to happen. They had a false view of salvation, a kind of romantic view that is not realistic. They did not get that idea from the Bible, but from somewhere else, perhaps from some psychological teaching masquerading under Christian terminology. The Bible is always realistic. Indeed, we can go so far as to say you should not expect anything different in this world; you should not expect anything better.

If you are 'rejoicing in hope', it means you have a true view of this world, and you will know that it is a vale of woes; it is an evil world. When I put it like this, I am quite deliberately testing you. If you do not like this sort of emphasis it is because you are not a Christian. The view we take of this present world is one of the finest tests as to whether or not we are Christians. These tribulations should not depress us because this is what the Bible teaches everywhere. As we have already seen, our Lord Himself said this just at the end of His life: 'In the world ye shall have tribulation' [*John* 16:33]. How would you like to evangelize with that? But that is how our Lord puts it.

To me, that message of tribulation in this world is the most glorious form of evangelism – and I am speaking from my experience. When I was a young man, I always disliked the kind of preacher or evangelist who seemed to be jovial and happy. 'Come and join us', he would say. 'Come into this, this is marvellous.' I knew it was not true. The man who always appealed to me was the man who told me the truth about life and about myself. I liked him because he spoke the truth, and then I discovered that he was also being scriptural. 'In the world ye shall have tribulation.' Very well, then, do not be surprised when you get troubles. To be forewarned is to be forearmed. You will never be taken by surprise. If you expect much of this world, you are doomed to disappointment. If you expect nothing of it, then you will not be disappointed when you get nothing or when you get evil. 'He that is down need fear no fall', as old John Bunyan put it.

But listen to Peter saying the same thing: 'Beloved, think it not strange concerning the fiery trial which is to try you, as though some strange thing happened unto you' [*1 Pet.* 4:12].Do not regard it as strange; do not think it odd. If you understand the Christian gospel, the Christian message, says Peter, then, when you are tried, you will not think that some strange, unexpected thing is happening to you, but you will be ready for it.

Of course, the Book of Revelation, the last book in the Bible, is virtually exclusively devoted to the theme of tribulations and trials. Look at the beasts arising, the persecutions, God's people almost crushed out of existence, hardly any of them left at all. The idea that Christianity grows from century to century as if it is going to fill the whole world by some evolutionary process, is a complete denial of the whole of the teaching of the New Testament. Hebrews 12 puts this very strongly. It even says that not only should you not be surprised if, as a Christian, you get trials and tribulations, you should really be surprised if you do *not* get them, and you should not only be surprised, you should be rather worried. If everything is going well with you, if everybody praises you, if you never get any persecution, then it is about time you seriously questioned whether or not you are a Christian. It is not the bastards but the children who are disciplined [see *Heb.* 12:7–8].

'The servant is not greater than his lord,' said our Lord [*John* 13:16]. Paul writes to Timothy, 'Yea, and all that will live

godly in Christ Jesus shall suffer persecution' [2 *Tim.* 3:12].
'Woe unto you, when all men shall speak well of you' [*Luke*
6:26] – that is the dangerous condition to be in. And, indeed,
these things are most important at the present time, are they
not? At a time like this, I cannot imagine anything more
terrible than to be popular in the Christian church viewed as
an institution. That would be most alarming. So there is the
first part of the argument: do not be surprised.

Secondly, we are enabled to be patient in tribulation when
we realize that what is happening to us is just the very thing
that happened to our blessed Lord and Master – the Saviour.
That is how the world treated him. He was 'a man of sorrows,
and acquainted with grief' [*Isa.* 53:3]. Look at His life, look at
the trials, look at the tribulations.

> *It was the way the Master went;*
> *Should not the servant tread it still?*
> Horatius Bonar

He has prepared us for tribulation. He said, 'If the world hate
you, ye know that it hated me before it hated you' [*John* 15:18].
Very well then, let us take that to heart and work it out like
this: to endure these things means that we are indeed following in His steps, and it is a very great privilege.

Peter expresses it like this: 'Servants, be subject to your
masters with all fear; not only to the good and gentle, but also
to the froward. For this is thankworthy, if a man for conscience
toward God endure grief, suffering wrongfully. For what glory
is it, if, when ye be buffeted for your faults, ye shall take it
patiently? but if, when ye do well, and suffer for it, ye take it
patiently, this is acceptable with God. For even hereunto were
ye called: because Christ also suffered for us, leaving us an
example, that ye should follow his steps: who did no sin,
neither was guile found in his mouth: who, when he was
reviled, reviled not again; when he suffered, he threatened not;
but committed himself to him that judgeth righteously' [*1 Pet.*
2:18–23]. What a privilege it is!

In the same way, the author of the Epistle to the Hebrews
says in the great twelfth chapter: 'Seeing we also are com-
passed about with so great a cloud of witnesses' [verse 1]. He

has been talking in the eleventh chapter about the 'heroes of the faith' of Old Testament times. Look at what they had to endure. Look at the suffering, at the misunderstanding! They often stood alone with everybody against them. Look at Moses; look at Abraham. Look at Noah standing alone. So, 'Seeing we also are encompassed about with so great a cloud of witnesses, let us lay aside every weight, and the sin which doth so easily beset us, and let us run with patience [patient endurance] the race that is set before us, looking unto Jesus the author and finisher of our faith' [*Heb.* 12:1–2]. That is it. Look at what happened to Him. 'For consider him that endured such contradiction of sinners against himself, lest ye be wearied and faint in your minds. Ye have not yet resisted unto blood, striving against sin' [verses 3–4]. You have not been called to do that.

What a privilege it is! We belong to the same company as the saints, martyrs, apostles, prophets and, above all, our blessed Lord Himself. This is the way to face tribulation. You see how we are applying the doctrine to all aspects of our Christian living. We are not ruled by our feelings, but are working out this great doctrine that has been set before us in the earlier chapters.

But, in addition to that, what does it mean to 'be patient' in tribulation? Well, it means we must allow tribulation to teach us things which nothing but tribulation will probably ever teach us. We are all recalcitrant children; we all need to be taught many things. We all have rough edges, even as Christians, and there is a process that we must go through in order to get rid of them. Be patient while the process is taking place, says the apostle here, and, again, it is the teaching right through the New Testament. We need to be taught – so be patient.

Let tribulation teach you first and foremost about yourself. Is there anything that ever teaches you so much about yourself as trials and troubles? When things are going well, you do not think, you take life for granted and feel you are all right. The moment tribulation comes, you are humbled. You discover your weakness. You discover your pride and self-interest. You discover the rebellious spirit that is in you. You may not have known that it was there. You may have thought that your faith was well-nigh perfect, but trials come and you find yourself feeling a grudge against God. Then you see what a poor Christian you have always been. It just took the trial to bring it out. So, says the apostle, let tribulations do you good in that way – let them teach you about yourself.

Tribulation will also teach you about the world as it is. It will teach you about other people. It will teach you what to expect from them. It will teach you to take a right view of others. Nothing does that so well as observing their behaviour under trial and their reactions to your trials. Things are not what they appear to be and people are often not what they appear to be. But you will learn and you will get experience. As Paul says, 'Tribulation worketh patience; and patience, experience' [*Rom.* 5:3–4]. Experience is a wonderful teacher.

Tribulation will teach you about other people in another way also: it will teach you to sympathize. The people who are most sympathetic to those who are ill are those who have been ill themselves. Those who have never known illness are not very sympathetic towards people who are ill. I have seen many men and women like that, and I have known an illness or an operation do such people great good. It has introduced a new note into them, a note of sympathy and of understanding. It is tragic, is it not, that it takes tribulation to teach us these lessons, but that is the sort of people we are, because of what sin has done to us. We are saved, but we are not perfect. There is a good deal of the old nature that has to be sloughed off, and tribulation is a wonderful medicament for doing that. So it will teach us to bear with other people in their trials and troubles; it will teach us to 'bear one another's burdens' [*Gal.* 6:2], and to have a word of sympathy and of understanding for others as they pass through trials.

So as a result of tribulation we go through a great process of education. 'Whom the Lord loveth he chasteneth' [*Heb.* 12:6]. Sometimes He does it directly, sometimes He just permits it; sometimes He allows the devil to bring about trials, as with Job, and, 'the latter end of Job', you remember, was 'more than his beginning' [*Job* 42:12]. God allowed it all. Poor old Job! Look how he struggled, but oh, he came out all right at the end. God had been dealing with him. And so if we are only wise and allow tribulation to deal with us, if we are only patient under the treatment, we shall find that we will come well out of it.

[399]

In other words, our experience will be that of the man who wrote Psalm 119. This is how he puts it: 'Thou hast dealt well with thy servant, O Lord, according unto thy word. Teach me good judgment and knowledge: for I have believed thy commandments. Before I was afflicted I went astray: but now have I kept thy word' [*Psa.* 119:65–67]. And then he goes on actually to say: 'It is good for me that I have been afflicted; that I might learn thy statutes' [*Psa.* 119:71]. This has been the testimony of God's people throughout the centuries. Nothing has done them more good than their trials. This was the experience of some of the German Christians in the things they had to suffer during the last war, and even before the war, in concentration camps. They were purified and purged and they thanked God for it, because this was the method by which they were brought to an understanding of the real nature of the Christian life and, above all, to a deeper know-ledge of God.

And again, the twelfth chapter of Hebrews puts it very well, does it not? It says, 'No chastening for the present seemeth to be joyous, but grievous: nevertheless afterward it yieldeth the peaceable fruit of righteousness unto them which are exercised thereby' [*Heb.* 12:11]. There is pain for the moment, but, oh, you are much better for it afterwards. Picture an athlete in a gymnasium with his trainer. The trainer will put him through it. His muscles will be aching and he will feel terrible, but afterwards he will find that he is stronger than he has ever been.

The apostle James was enabled to put it like this: 'My brethren, count it all joy when ye fall into divers temptations [tribulations].' Count it all joy! Why? Because, James says, 'Knowing this, that the trying of your faith worketh patience. But let patience have her perfect work' [*James* 1:3–4]. His precise argument is that trials are the way in which your faith is being truly tested.

Peter, again, when he is reminding the Christians of the great hope of the resurrection, writes, 'Wherein ye greatly rejoice, though now for a season, if need be, ye are in heaviness through manifold temptations [trials]' – why? – 'that the trial of your faith, being much more precious than of gold that perisheth, though it be tried with fire, might be found unto praise and honour and glory at the appearing of Jesus Christ' [*1 Pet.* 1:6–7]. Wonderful!

So we go on to the final step in this little bit of argumentation, which is this: trials and tribulations are the very things that make us think more of heaven and of the glory that awaits us. This is because of our imperfection. When things are going well, with no trials and problems, we live for this world only, and some would even teach that you get the whole of your salvation in this world. But Scripture does not say that. You only get an 'instalment', a 'first fruit'. We only get 'the earnest of our inheritance' [*Eph.* 1:14]. But many people seem to think we have everything here; they never think of the world to come. That has been evident even in some evangelical preaching and teaching, which is subjective and inward-looking. But the New Testament is always talking about heaven and the glory of heaven. And there is nothing that makes us look at that so much as tribulation. 'The world is too much with us', wrote Wordsworth. And when the world shows its teeth, you really begin to see what it is, and that drives you to look at what is coming.

That is how the apostle puts it to the Corinthians: 'Our light affliction, which is but for a moment' – note the word – '*worketh* for us a far more exceeding and eternal weight of glory.' The 'light affliction', this trouble and tribulation, produces for us, actually creates for us, in the way I have been showing you, 'a far more exceeding and eternal weight of glory; while we look not at the things which are seen, but at the things which are not seen: for the things which are seen are temporal; but the things which are not seen are eternal' [*2 Cor.* 4:17–18].

So, be 'patient in tribulation' and it will do you the world of good, you will even thank God for it. You will say, ' "Whom the Lord loveth he chasteneth," and He evidently loves me.' And you will thank Him for all that He has taught you by allowing you to pass through a period of trial. 'All things work together for good to them that love God' [*Rom.* 8:28]. Do you know that? Have you experienced that? If you have not, you are but a child, a tyro in the Christian life. Thank God that He knows us better than we know ourselves. He knows what is good for us.

Christian Conduct

The bud may have a bitter taste,
But sweet will be the flower.

William Cowper

Be 'patient in tribulation'.

That, then, brings us to the last injunction in this verse, which is this: 'continuing instant in prayer'. Do you see the connection? I have said that tribulation makes us think of the world to come, and that reminds us of Him. And that, of course, therefore leads at once to the whole question of prayer. Here, again, is something that is emphasized throughout the New Testament. It is amazing to notice the frequency with which this very point is made. Our Lord said, 'Men ought always to pray, and not to faint' [*Luke* 18:1]. And the apostle Paul towards the end of the Epistle to the Ephesians, when he has been dealing with 'the whole armour of God', concludes like this: 'Praying always with all prayer and supplication in the Spirit, and watching thereunto with all perseverance and supplication for all saints' [*Eph.* 6:18]. And in 1 Thessalonians 5:17, he writes, 'Pray without ceasing.' Never stop praying; never quit praying. It is a universal injunction.

And again I would demonstrate to you the inevitable connection of all these statements. Hope! Tribulation! Prayer! We have already seen this connection in the eighth chapter of Romans where the apostle writes: 'We are saved by hope: but hope that is seen is not hope' [*Rom.* 8:24]. He has been dealing with tribulation, and then comes to the hope. But, having dealt with this hope, he says, 'If we hope for that we see not, then do we with patience wait for it. Likewise the Spirit also helpeth our infirmities: for we know not what we should pray for as we ought' [verses 25–26. Tribulation, hope and prayer always go together in the New Testament and it is a very good way of testing ourselves to ask whether they always go together in our experience. They should.

In other words, the teaching is this: Why should we 'pray without ceasing'? Why should we be 'instant in prayer'? And our Lord's answer in Luke 18:1 is clearly that praying is the only alternative to fainting. 'Men ought always to pray, and not to faint.' If you want to avoid fainting, keep on praying. That is the only way you remain on your feet in a world like this, governed as it is by the devil. Keep on praying – 'continuing instant in prayer'. Never stop.

Now these things are very practical and again I must ask a question: Do you realize your need of prayer to that extent? If not, why not? Are you praying without ceasing? The teaching of the entire New Testament is that we should be instant in prayer. Is it true of us? If it is not, I ask again, why not? Is it because we are lazy, or is it because we are spiritually dead and are not aware of the conflict? Is it due to spiritual ignorance? Have we a wrong view of the Christian life? This life is depicted by the great saints as a fight. 'The good fight of faith', the apostle calls it in 1 Timothy 6:12. 'We wrestle not against flesh and blood, but against principalities, against powers, against the rulers of the darkness of this world, against spiritual wickedness in high [in heavenly] places' [*Eph.* 6:12]. A tremendous conflict! And Christians are people who pray, and pray constantly. If we do not, it is because we are ignorant, or slothful, or else we are just foolishly self-confident, which is the consequence of ignorance. We have a wrong view of regeneration and think we can now do everything.

What, then, does the apostle mean by being 'instant in prayer'? What is this prayer process which he is talking about? First, let me hurriedly say what it is not. It is not some psychological treatment. There is nothing more unspiritual and unscriptural than the way in which many people use prayer as just a method of therapy. What they mean by prayer is having beautiful thoughts – 'positive thinking', it is sometimes called. But that has nothing at all to do with prayer. That is people talking to themselves, and if you are talking to yourself, you are not praying, because praying means talking to God. Prayer is not psychological thinking, nor auto-suggestion.

Neither does Paul mean that we just pray as a duty. Some Buddhists and others have their prayer wheels and they think, like the Pharisees, that 'they shall be heard for their much speaking' [*Matt.* 6:7], by which is meant the number of hours they put into praying. And there are people who count their beads. That is mechanical; it is not prayer at all, but the very reverse. Prayer is entirely spiritual. No, by prayer, Paul means approaching 'the throne of grace' [*Heb.* 4:16]. To pray means to

[403]

go into the presence of God, to have a personal communion with Him, to 'draw nigh to God' [*James* 4:8]. And that is what Paul is talking about here. 'Be instant in prayer': always keep in touch with Him.

Why is this essential? Why should you be 'instant in prayer'? Let me give you some headings. One good reason is that when you turn to God in prayer you have the great comfort of knowing that He is there, that you are not alone. Children do that sort of thing, do they not? If you are walking with a child in the dark and the child is frightened, he will talk more than usual. Why is he doing that? Just to reassure himself that you are still there with him – it gives him wonderful comfort. We are all children, and even if prayer did nothing else, that in itself would be wonderful. Take the hymn, 'O Jesus, I have promised'. The writer says:

> *I shall not fear the battle*
> *If Thou art by my side,*
> *Nor wander from the pathway*
> *If Thou wilt be my guide.*
> John Ernest Bode

In a time of trial, it is wonderful, is it not, to be able to talk to the right kind of person? In a sense, the conversation may make no difference to the circumstances, but it does make a tremendous difference to you. So keep on talking to God. Be 'instant in prayer'.

And all that, in turn, reminds you of God's protecting care and His protecting power.

> *I need Thee every hour;*
> *Stay Thou near by;*
> *Temptations lose their power*
> *When Thou art nigh.*
> Annie Sherwood Hawks

Again:

> *I fear no foe, with Thee at hand to bless.*
> Henry Francis Lyte

Or listen to another hymn:

> *O let me feel Thee near me;*
> *The world is very near,*
> *I see the sights that dazzle,*
> *The tempting sounds I hear:*
> *My foes are ever near me,*
> *Around me and within;*
> *But, Jesus, draw Thou nearer,*
> *And shield my soul from sin.*
>
> *O let me hear Thee speaking*
> *In accents clear and still,*
> *Above the storms of passion,*
> *The murmurs of self-will*
> *O speak to reassure me,*
> *To hasten and control;*
> *O speak, and make me listen,*
> *Thou guardian of my soul.*
>
> John Ernest Bode

These are the prayers of the saints, and they show what prayer means. You are aware of difficulties outside you and inside you, and you know that you are weak. So you speak to Him and ask Him to be with you and to deliver you.

> *O Lamb of God still keep me*
> *Close to thy wounded side,*
> *'Tis only there in safety*
> *And peace I can abide.*
>
> *With foes and snares around me*
> *What fears and lusts within,*
> *The grace that sought and found me*
> *Alone can keep me clean.*
>
> James George Deck

So prayer means going to Him for these reasons, and feeling you want to keep near to Him. It is instinctive in the child, and we are all the children of God. That is why we should be praying without ceasing. And as we do so, we shall be receiving strength from Him. We must ask Him. James puts it like this – having asked, in effect, 'Why are you people in trouble?', he gives the answer quite simply and plainly, 'Ye lust, and have not: ye kill, and desire to have, and cannot obtain: ye fight and war, yet ye have not' – why? – *'because ye ask not'* [*James* 4:2]. Grace is not something that is given to you in a packet. It is not something in a machine. You do not put your coin in and pull out a packet. No, no, it is a personal relationship, and you must go on asking. You are not given everything in one great donation and then left to go drawing on that. No, you keep on going to the Giver.

So you ask Him, and you go to Him, and you receive strength from Him. The apostle says, 'I can do all things through Christ which strengtheneth me' [*Phil.* 4:13]. 'Be careful for nothing,' he writes, 'but in every thing by prayer and supplication with thanksgiving, let your requests be made known unto God. And the peace of God, which passeth all understanding, shall keep your hearts and minds through Christ Jesus' [*Phil.* 4:6–7].

Now that is the essence of prayer. It is not just mechanically working through a list, ticking the items off as you put up one request after another. Oh, there is such a lot of praying by rote today, and people think it is wonderful. But that is the Buddhist type of prayer. Real prayer is intimate, personal communion; it is desiring the Person because you know, 'It pleased the Father that in him should all fulness dwell' [*Col.* 1:19]. So you can say with another hymn-writer:

> *From Thee, the overflowing spring*
> *Our souls shall drink a fresh supply;*
> *While such as trust their native strength*
> *Shall melt away, and droop and die.*

That is good old Isaac Watts. That is why you pray. Or, as another puts it:

> *Strong in the strength which God supplies*
> *Through His eternal Son;*

Romans 12:12

Strong in the Lord of hosts
And in His mighty power,
Who in the strength of Jesus trusts
Is more than conqueror.

To keep your armour bright
Attend with constant care
Still walking in your Captain's sight
And watching unto prayer.

Charles Wesley

Here it is, my dear friends. We are saved. We no longer belong to this world, but we are still in it. We are left here. We are 'strangers and pilgrims' [*1 Pet.* 2:11]. We are travelling through, and this world is all against us – against everything that belongs to God. How can we go through? We have been told the way. Yes, you will get your tribulations: 'In the world ye shall have tribulation: but be of good cheer; I have overcome the world' [*John* 16:33]. And as He has overcome it, He will enable us to overcome it, too. In Him we shall be more than conquerors. 'Who shall separate us from the love of Christ? Shall tribulation . . .' – you remember the list that Paul puts up – 'or distress, or persecution, or famine, or nakedness, or peril, or sword . . . Nay, in all these things we are more than conquerors through him that loved us' [*Rom.* 8:35, 37]. Keep in touch with Him. Get the wonderful feeling as often as you can. Be instant, always! Make sure that He is there. Speak to Him – He will speak to you. You will feel His presence, feel His strength, and He will give you strength. Then you will be able to say with the great apostle, 'I can do all things through Christ which strengtheneth me [*Phil.* 4:13]. 'Men ought always to pray and not to faint' [*Luke* 18:1].

Twenty-nine

*

Distributing to the necessity of saints; given to hospitality.
Romans 12:13

Now we come here to the last of what I have called 'general injunctions'. Paul has just reminded us that we are subject to trials and troubles, and that we must have a clear view of our life in this world, otherwise we shall be sadly disappointed and will soon be in trouble in our life of faith. Our Lord has warned us and prepared us, and Paul has told us how we are to face our own personal tribulation.

But immediately he goes on. He cannot leave it at that. We are not the only ones who are subject to trouble. All our fellow believers are subject to exactly the same conditions. So here Paul reminds us that we must realize our responsibility with respect to them and he shows us how we should help them to deal with the same problems. That is what we have in this thirteenth verse, and here, I suggest, Paul finishes a subsection. So far he has been looking at our Christian life positively and has been indicating to us what we have to do. Then from verse 14 onwards he deals with our reactions to what other people do, whether unpleasant or pleasant.

So as we come to the end of this little subjection, we must be clear about the exegesis of the words. This is most important. There are two statements here – we have a balance. You notice that Paul has been doing that all along, and here the first injunction is: 'Distributing to the necessity of saints'; then the balancing portion is: 'Given to hospitality'. And the second is a kind of interpretation or elaboration of the first, in the form of a principle.

So let us look at the terms. 'Distributing' is an interesting and important word. Literal distribution is, of course, a part of the meaning, but it is not enough. It is too weak, and it does not bring out the fulness of the meaning conveyed by the Greek word used by Paul. It really means 'entering into fellowship with the necessity of the saints'. You enter into fellowship with them as they have these necessities. It is the same word that is often used of a 'sharer'. Indeed, it is essentially the word that you have in the apostolic benediction: 'The grace of the Lord Jesus Christ, the love of God, and the *fellowship* [the *communion*] of the Holy Ghost.' So Paul is saying that you do not merely distribute to the necessities of the saints, but that you enter into fellowship with them; you become partners with them; you share with them.

In other words, you must feel that their burden is your burden, that you are in the hardship with them, and that you really are feeling it yourself. You have entered into a kind of partnership with them in their predicament. It is important that we should realize that, because if we do not, we shall miss a great deal of the teaching which Paul gives here.

But let us go on to the word 'necessity', which means 'needs', and that means the basic necessities. The apostle is not saying that we should enter into partnership with our fellow believers in their desires or in their likes or wishes. But we must enter into fellowship and partnership with them with regard to their needs. The distinction, of course, is important. We are all still in the flesh, and there are some people who are not always quite clear as to the difference between absolute necessities on the one hand, and luxuries on the other. There is all the difference in the world between being short of the necessities of life and wanting more than we need. You are to enter into partnership with fellow believers when they really are in trouble and need.

Then, further, you notice that the apostle says, 'Entering into partnership with the needs of the *saints*'. This, too, is an interesting word. 'The saints' are the holy ones, the ones who have been set apart. So the apostle is not talking about everybody, but about people who have been set apart by God. Here is something which might very well detain us, but we will not allow it to do so at this point. Let us, however, remind ourselves that in the New Testament every member of the church is regarded as a saint. In Romans 1:7 Paul is writing to those 'in Rome, beloved of God, called to be saints', and you find that expression 'called saints' or 'called to be saints' in most of the epistles.

In an age which is being increasingly governed in its thinking by Roman Catholic teaching, I think we need to remind ourselves of the New Testament meaning of the word 'saint'. Roman Catholic teaching is that only some are saints – the vast majority of church members are not. Saints are only those people whom the Church decides to 'canonize', and there are certain tests which must be passed before any one may be so described. Now we must protest against that. People are called saints, not because of anything they do, but because of what God has done to them. They have been 'separated' by God through belief of the gospel.

This teaching is not confined to the Apostle Paul. Take, for instance, the Apostle Peter. He expresses the same thought at the beginning of his first letter: 'Peter, an apostle of Jesus Christ, to the strangers scattered'– and then he names the countries – '. . . elect according to the foreknowledge of God the Father, through *sanctification of the Spirit*, unto obedience and sprinkling of the blood of Jesus Christ' [*1 Pet.* 1:1–2]. Now that is not the sanctification that follows justification, but the sanctification that precedes even believing, the sanctification that means 'set apart'. No one can believe without being set apart, without being taken hold of, by the Holy Spirit. People do not make themselves saints. No church makes a man or woman a saint. Saints are made by God, and, I repeat, all Christians are saints. We have all been taken out of the world and put into this new kingdom, this new condition. We are God's people, and Paul is telling us here that we must enter into partnership and fellowship with all people, like ourselves, who are suffering need.

The second half of verse 13 is in the form of a general principle: 'Given to hospitality'. What is hospitality? This is a word that we use frequently, do we not? But the word used by the apostle is, again, much stronger than our word hospitality.

We have debased it, as we tend to debase most words. The word that the apostle uses means 'loving strangers'; 'stranger-loving'. Paul says in effect, 'You must have fondness or affection for strangers.' This is exactly the same word as that used in Hebrews 13:2: 'Be not forgetful to entertain strangers.' You might translate that verse in this way: 'Be not forgetful of hospitality.'

Paul says that we are to be '*given to* hospitality' and here again it is extraordinary how almost every word we are considering at this point causes us to express a measure of criticism of the Authorized Version. The other versions are, however, no better here. It is unfortunate that the English words are much too weak. 'Given to hospitality' really means *pursuing* hospitality, seeking after it.

Let me give you some examples of the same Greek word translated in a better way. Take 1 Corinthians 14:1. You remember how, after the great hymn of love in 1 Corinthians 13, the fourteenth chapter starts with these words: '*Follow after* charity'. That is the idea in Romans 12:13 – not 'given to charity', but, 'following after it'. Some still more striking examples are found in Philippians 3 where the same word appears three times. Take verse 6: 'Concerning zeal, *persecuting* the church'. 'Persecuting' is the right translation there in Philippians, but the whole idea is of pursuit – going after the church in order to harm it. The word indicates eagerness. Or again in Philippians 3:12: 'Not as though I had already attained, either were already perfect: but I *follow after* . . .' I am not just 'given to' these things, I follow after them. And then Paul elaborates that idea – 'if that I may apprehend that for which also I am apprehended' – and later he elaborates it still further. Then, in the fourteenth verse, he says, 'I *press toward* the mark' – that is the same word again.

Now this is undoubtedly an inspired translation here in Philippians. You notice how the translators vary the terms to bring out the force of the Greek. But all of them together give us this tremendous idea of zest, and zeal, and keenness, and pursuit of something. Not just 'given to' hospitality, but really going after it, going out for it, pursuing it, seeking it, following after, pressing toward the mark, as it were.

Now a very good way of enforcing this injunction is to show

you its opposite, and here Peter is of help to us because in 1 Peter we find what is almost the negative of this injunction. There Peter says, 'Use hospitality one to another without grudging', and he is describing people who were not exercising hospitality in the right way. 'Do not grudge the hospitality as you give it', he says. There were Christians who felt that they had to offer hospitality, but they would rather not. So they gave it grudgingly. Peter says: Do not offer hospitality half-heartedly, with an ill grace, as if it goes against the grain.

The kind of behaviour that Paul is expecting from us (it is not the same word, but it is the same principle) is that which we find in his reference to Onesiphorus in 2 Timothy 1:16-18 where he says, 'The Lord give mercy unto the house of Onesiphorus; for he oft refreshed me, and was not ashamed of my chain: but, when he was in Rome, he sought me out very diligently, and found me.' You 'seek out'; you buy up the opportunity.

Those, then, are the words of this injunction. What do we have to say about them? Now nobody who knows the Bible at all can fail to notice that here in Romans 12:13, the apostle is teaching us something that is very frequently taught in the New Testament. Let me just give you some examples. The apostle comes back to this subject in verse 26 of Romans chapter 15: 'For it hath pleased them of Macedonia and Achaia to make a certain contribution for the poor saints which are at Jerusalem' – and he was very pleased about that. 'It hath pleased them verily; and their debtors they are.'

Then you find generosity and hospitality urged in several places in the form of positive injunctions. Here it is in Galatians 6:6: 'Let him that is taught in the word communicate unto him that teacheth in all good things.' 'Communicate' – that is the same idea. It means to give to him, to support him, to help him. Later, Paul goes on to tell us to 'do good unto all men, especially unto them that are of the household of faith' [*Gal.* 6:10]. The same idea reappears in Philippians 4:15: 'Now ye Philippians know also, that in the beginning of the gospel, when I departed from Macedonia, no church communicated with me as concerning giving and receiving, but ye only.' And he commends the Christians in Philippi for this. The same thought is to be found in 1 Timothy

6:18 and again, as I have reminded you, in Hebrews 13, not
only in that second verse but also in the sixteenth verse where
it is put in these terms: 'But to do good and to communicate' –
notice that word 'communicate' – 'forget not: for with such
sacrifices God is well pleased.' We are also told that elders,
presbyters and bishops must be people who are 'given to
hospitality' [see *1 Tim.* 3:2], and must enjoy exercising it.
These are some of the terms that are used with regard to such
people.

So you can see that this was obviously a most important
point in the early church and I think there was a special reason.
Christians were being persecuted bitterly, and at any time they
might have to leave their homes and districts and go elsewhere. Now all the Christians were alive to that, and in your
reading of the New Testament you must always bear it in
mind; it is part of the background of the New Testament. If we
do not know the historical circumstances of the first believers,
it is sometimes difficult to understand why great emphasis is
placed upon particular subjects, and this is an important
example. It was persecution that led to the need for hospitality.
There were very few inns or places to stay so that, naturally,
in the life of the early church Christian people had to be
reminded very frequently of the importance of offering hospitality.

So what is the general teaching for us? What is the application to ourselves? The first thing we must realize once more is
that Paul is not just giving a vague general injunction to be
kind. I have pointed out, with regard to all these injunctions,
that they are the outcome of doctrine, and that they must
always be considered in the light of the doctrine. That is why
we spent such time on the first and second verses of this
chapter 12. They are the key to the whole conduct of the
Christian and they govern the rest of this Epistle, right to the
end of chapter 16. Do not forget that 'therefore': 'I beseech you
therefore . . .' If you ever find that any of these injunctions go
against the grain, it is because you have gone wrong somewhere in your doctrine; you have somehow not understood the
full content of this 'therefore'. If you really have grasped the
teaching of the first eleven chapters, all these things should
come naturally and almost inevitably.

But not only that, to understand these injunctions, and this one in particular, we must realize also the full content of the teaching which we have had in verses 4 and 5 of this chapter: 'As we have many members in one body, and all members have not the same office: so we, being many, are one body in Christ, and every one members one of another.' Now it is because that is true that Paul says here, 'Distributing to the necessity of saints; given to hospitality'. We only see the relevance of this injunction and feel its force as we grasp that central teaching of the doctrine of the church as the body of Christ.

And there is nothing more wonderful than this. Why should we do what the apostle tells us here in this thirteenth verse? The answer is that all of us are these separated people. You remember how Peter puts it: 'But ye are a chosen generation, a royal priesthood, an holy nation, a peculiar people; that ye should shew forth the praises of him who hath called you out of darkness into his marvellous light. Which in time past were not a people, but are now the people of God: which had not obtained mercy, but now have obtained mercy. Dearly beloved, I beseech you, as strangers and pilgrims . . .' [*1 Pet.* 2:9–11]. That is the appeal.

This is not a general injunction to Christian people to be generous to all those who are in need. No, no, it is much more particular. As we saw, we are to help the saints who are in need, and, therefore, we must carry with us the previous teaching, especially that teaching about the Christian as a member of the body of Christ. And also we must bear in mind the teaching of verses 9 and 10: 'Let love be without dissimulation . . . Be kindly affectioned to one another with brotherly love.' This injunction in verse 13 is one of the ways in which we do that. So the teaching here assumes the teaching that has gone before, it must be understood in its context.

So Paul is saying that we are all the family of God. We are all brothers and sisters. And is not this a marvellous thought? You and I belong to the same family. Indeed, we are more closely related than we are by natural ties, because we are members of the family of God, and the moment you realize that, there is no difficulty about this injunction. If a member of your family is in trouble, you are there. 'Blood is thicker than water', you say.

Well, I say, 'The Spirit is thicker than blood, because He is the Holy Spirit of God.' It is inevitable. You remember Paul's argument in 1 Corinthians 12, where he uses the analogy of the body. He says, 'Whether one member suffer, all the members suffer with it.' You see your brother in trouble – well, you are in it with him, you are in partnership with him. Paul puts that as an injunction. Yes, but it is an injunction that comes out of an established position. Realize the relationship, he says, and therefore put it into practice.

There is another illustration of this which has always fascinated me and I have always enjoyed reading it. We are told in the twelfth chapter of Acts that Peter was arrested and put into prison. First of all, King Herod had taken James, the brother of John, and had killed him, and then, 'because he saw it pleased the Jews, he proceeded further to take Peter also. And when he had apprehended him, he put him in prison, and delivered him to four quaternions of soldiers to keep him; intending after Easter to bring him forth to the people' [verses 3–4]. Then notice: 'Peter therefore was kept in prison: but prayer was made without ceasing of the church unto God for him' [verse 5]. Only one of them, Peter alone, was literally in the prison, but every member of that church was in the prison with him. They were suffering with him. Why? Because he was one of the family, he was a brother, and nothing can happen to a brother without our all feeling it and being involved in it with him.

Again, take the way the author of the Epistle to the Hebrews puts it. Let us go back to that thirteenth chapter – indeed, my difficulty here is to know what not to quote! 'Let brotherly love continue. Be not forgetful to entertain strangers: for thereby some have entertained angels unawares.' Then: 'Remember them that are in bonds, as bound with them; and them which suffer adversity, as being yourselves also in the body' [*Heb.* 13:1–2]. You are bound with them, in the same body with them. I know that it means that you are also in a physical body and that the same thing can happen to you, but it also has this other meaning. In other words, there is a solidarity, an identity. Nothing can happen to any one of you without it happening to all. That is the teaching and the doctrine is absolutely essential. If you give grudgingly, you are showing that you do not understand the doctrine of the church as the body of Christ, and your own place in it.

So the apostle is telling us: Recognize Christians when you meet them. Here they were, scattered abroad because of persecution, and some would arrive in Rome, as Paul himself would, and as Priscilla and Aquila had done. He says, 'Distribute to the necessity of saints.' So how do you know them? You have to recognize them, have you not? And this, again, is a wonderful thing. Do you recognize Christians when you meet them for the first time? You should. Thank God one does. I have often met people whom I recognized as Christians the first time I saw them. They may have come a long way, some of them across the ocean, but we recognized one another.

But not only do you recognize them, you are glad to see them, and you are most anxious to help them. 'Bear ye one another's burdens, and so fulfil the law of Christ' [*Gal.* 6:2]. Be eager to do this. This is expressed wonderfully in 2 Corinthians 8. Notice how the apostle puts it: 'Moreover, brethren, we do you to wit of the grace of God bestowed on the churches of Macedonia.' Then: 'How that in a great trial of affliction' – that was their position – 'the abundance of their joy and their deep poverty abounded unto the riches of their liberality' (verses 1–2). You cannot add to that, can you? It is as though Paul is describing a mighty river. Their 'deep poverty' is as deep as the depths of the river, yet equally deep are 'the riches of their liberality' in a great trial of affliction. Their riches rise up from the depths. And 'the abundance of their joy' rises to the heights. Here is this tremendous stream flowing along between these banks.

Now the apostle is exhorting us to follow that example of generous self-giving: 'For to their power, I bear record, yea, and beyond their power they were willing of themselves; praying us with much intreaty that we would receive the gift, and take upon us the fellowship [the partnership] of the ministering to the saints. And this they did, not as we hoped, but first gave their own selves to the Lord, and unto us by the will of God' [2 *Cor.* 8:3–5]. That whole chapter, as you notice, deals with this marvellous theme.

In other words, it comes to this: 'Love thy neighbour as

thyself' [*Mark* 12:31]. 'Thou shalt love the Lord thy God with all thy heart, and with all thy soul, and with all thy mind, and with all thy strength' – and then – 'Thou shalt love thy neighbour as thyself.' Love your brother especially because he is your brother, and this injunction in Romans 12 becomes a very good test of our whole position, of ourselves as Christians. John argues, 'For he that loveth not his brother whom he hath seen, how can he love God whom he hath not seen?' [*1 John* 4:20]. This is how it works.

But John puts this very strongly. People sometimes think that John was the loving apostle and much more tender than the Apostle Paul. I always find them the other way round. John with his bluntness frightens me much more than Paul does. Listen to this: 'Hereby perceive we the love of God, because he laid down his life for us: and we ought to lay down our lives for the brethren. But whoso hath this world's goods, and seeth his brother have need, and shutteth up his bowels of compassion from him, how dwelleth the love of God in him? My little children, let us not love in word, neither in tongue; but in deed and in truth' [*1 John* 3:16–18]. Paul never said anything as severe as that. He is much the gentler of the two.

John's words, of course, are perfectly true. Paul makes a more general appeal. John says quite simply, 'Do not merely talk about loving God. If you shut up your bowels of compassion to a brother who is in need, you must not talk about the love of God; you are a hypocrite.' John is a man who calls us liars if we say that we know God while living in sin. He puts this point very plainly to us: 'We know that we have passed from death unto life, because we love the brethren [*1 John* 3:14]. Yes, says John, but do not love the brethren 'in word, neither in tongue' but 'in deed and in truth' [*1 John* 3:18]. You must be ready to lay down your lives for the brethren, if needs be, as Christ laid down His life for you.

Paul here is exhorting us to do the kind of thing that we read of in the very beginning of the church. In Acts 2:44–45, we read, 'And all that believed were together, and had all things common; and sold their possessions and goods, and parted them to all men, as every man had need.' We read exactly the same thing again in chapter 4:34–35, 'Neither was there any among them that lacked: for as many as were possessors of lands or houses sold them, and brought the prices of the things that were sold, and laid them down at the apostles' feet: and distribution was made unto every man according as he had need.' And Paul is here just calling us to that kind of life.

There are one or two matters of interest which I must raise at this point. First, I think that this injunction of the apostle casts great light on those two portions from Acts in this way. Some people have thought that Acts 2 and 4 describe an attempt at some sort of Communism which was later abandoned. Indeed, some would say that it was a mistake to have abandoned it. But it seems quite clear to me, from this injunction of the apostle and from other passages that I have already quoted to you in the New Testament, that Christianity does not teach Communism.

Christianity does not teach that we should sell all that we have and put it into a public pool so that nobody has any private property or any private possessions. No, it teaches *stewardship.* You still have your possessions but you are governed by the spirit of love, so that if you see a brother in need, you give to him from what you have. It is the equality which Paul speaks of in 2 Corinthians 8 – nobody lacked, nobody had too much. The others contributed according to the need which arose among the brethren.

This is a most important point and we could have spent a long time on it. We cannot do that, but let us put it like this. It is sometimes, indeed, I would say always, easier to get rid of all you have than to act as a steward. If you give all you have and have nothing left, then you have no problems. But if you still retain your possessions and, as a Christian, know that your brother has a right to them when he is in need, then your responsibility and your difficulties are greater. But it is that to which we are called by the New Testament. You are a steward of all that you have, and you must feel that it belongs to your brother and sister as much as to you if they are in need.

Now that is not Communism. Communism operates by acts of law; it compels people. It is the opposite of this law of love. Paul's words are an appeal which is made to men and women

[418]

in the light of the doctrine. Communism simply forces everyone to be levelled out. The law of love urges us to level one another out in a spirit of love, so that we are all, always, in a position where none of us is suffering from need. It is good, therefore, that we should know this when we meet people who talk about Communism and either say that Christianity should be like it, or that Communism is superior. The New Testament teaching is the answer to that argument.

Secondly, the appeal the apostle makes to us here is not just a general social appeal of the kind that is made very often at the present time. He is not asking us to be part of some vague secular philanthropy. There is starvation and need in certain countries, and a general appeal is made to relieve this suffering, to which the churches respond. But that is not what we have here.

Now let us be clear about this. The primary call on the Christian is to his fellow Christians. 'Let us do good unto all men, especially unto them who are of the household of faith' [*Gal.* 6:10]. They come first. Of course, if you are in a position to help others beyond that, do that also. But churches receive requests from various secular societies which are doing a lot of good – Red Cross, Famine Relief and various others. Now I would argue that we are not involved in those general appeals. It is our business to seek out the Christians, the saints, in these needy countries, and to do what we can to help them. They have priority, and they are often the people who are most neglected. Paul is not referring here to indiscriminate giving, and I think the church should be more jealous of her prerogatives in this respect, and not submit meekly and at times unintelligently to a general appeal.

People in the world say, 'You Christians, of course, of all people, should be giving to this appeal.'

We say, 'Now wait a minute, do you know what a Christian is? Christians are separated men and women. They are saints and we are bound to certain people in needy countries more than we are to the generality of people in those countries. Anything else we can do we will do readily and gladly as an act of charity and compassion, but our first call is always the call that comes from the saints, our fellow believers in Christ.'

Thirdly, there are difficulties about carrying out Paul's injunction in Romans 12:13 and one of the biggest is (I am sorry to have to use such language) the professional beggar. Churches know something about such people – poor men and women who for various reasons have gone wrong. Let us always be sympathetic towards them. But they have no right to become professional beggars, especially at a time like this when the state makes provision for such people. Of course, what they usually want, though they do not say so, is money for drink and so on.

But what do we do about them? Sometimes these professional beggars are a little bit arrogant and they are ready to quote a verse like this verse in Romans. They do not know the words, but they quote what they think is the spirit. They think a church is an institution that gives to anybody who asks, anybody who is in need. They almost insist upon being given something.

Now it is quite clear that the early church had exactly the same problem, not only in this matter of giving to beggars, but also in connection with people travelling from city to city throughout the Roman Empire who would arrive at a church and announce that they were great preachers and wanted an opportunity to preach in return for hospitality. What do you do with men like that? Not every man who thinks he is a great preacher is right, in fact, most are certainly not! But there were such people travelling round the early church and Christians clearly had difficulty about this. So they had to adopt a method, and we are told what it was at the beginning of 2 Corinthians 3: 'Do we begin again to commend ourselves to you? or need we, as some others, epistles of commendation to you, or letters of commendation from you?' Because of the abuse of this exhortation that we are considering, the early church had to resort to the expedient of letters of commendation. When a brother said, for instance, that he had to go to Rome on business, he was given a letter confirming the truth of his claims – a very good practice.

But what do you do if a man does not have a letter? Now this is where the whole question of discrimination comes in – and there is such a thing as 'the gift of discrimination'. I mentioned it earlier, in passing. How do you recognize a Christian? Well, there are various ways in which this can be done, and, remember, it is a part of our stewardship. A steward is not a man or woman who gives to the first person who asks. You must assess the person. A good steward can calculate and assess and make computations. It is a very simple thing indeed just to empty your pockets to the first person who comes along; but it can be very bad stewardship. You may be helping someone to continue in sin by doing that, and then when the right person comes along you have nothing to give.

No, stewards must know what they are doing. And the way in which you test people is by listening to them speaking; let them talk. I often have had to do it and still do in my vestry at the close of services. After a number of years you can generally tell the kind of person with whom you are dealing. An impostor will generally start with a kind of spiritual introduction, perhaps thanking you very profusely for the sermon. Yet you feel uneasy. If this man is as spiritual as he maintains, why is he dressed as badly as he is? Why is he unwashed? Why is he unkempt? Can someone who is as spiritual as this one seems to be from his speech, really be what he is representing himself to be?

So you let him go on talking and you hurry him a little bit, and soon you will find that what he really wants is to ask you for money, and then you have an opportunity of talking to him about his soul. You try to show him the error of his ways, and you may give him something to help him in order to show that you are not condemning him. But you expose the sham and the hollowness and the pretence, and then you act with charity with respect to him. But we have all made mistakes. We have all been taken in; we have given to frauds. I trust that we have never refused a deserving case. But you need to pray for discrimination so that you will be able to recognize a true Christian and a truly worthy case.

How, then, do you actually put all this into practice? Now in a very wonderful way the thirteenth chapter of the Epistle to the Hebrews tells us all about it. The writer talks about three kinds of love. First: 'Let brotherly love continue.' Then, in the second verse, 'love of the stranger', which is translated in the Authorized Version as, 'Be not forgetful to entertain strangers.' You love your brother; you love this stranger.

The best way to show this love is to obey what the writer says in verse 5: 'Let your conversation be without covetousness.' Now a better translation of that would be something like this: 'Let your manner of life be free from the love of money.' If you want to love your brother and to love the stranger, be sure that you do not love money, for if you love money, you will not love your brother or the stranger. So there you have three kinds of love, with two positive instructions and one negative. Start with the negative: do not be a lover of money, and then you will be well on the way to being a lover of your brother, and a lover of the stranger.

Let me give you some encouragements to the putting into practice of this general exhortation: 'distributing to the necessity of saints; given to hospitality'. Why should you do this? Because as you do, you can be quite sure you are always doing it unto Him. Do you remember how our Lord puts it towards the end of the twenty-fifth chapter of the Gospel according to St Matthew? He says, 'When the Son of man shall come in his glory . . . before him shall be gathered all the nations . . . and he shall set the sheep on his right hand, but the goats on the left Then shall the King say unto them on his right hand, Come, ye blessed of my Father, inherit the kingdom prepared for you from the foundation of the world: For I was an hungred, and ye gave me meat: I was thirsty, and ye gave me drink: I was a stranger, and ye took me in: naked, and ye clothed me: I was sick, and ye visited me: I was in prison, and ye came unto me. Then shall the righteous answer him, saying, Lord, when saw we thee an hungred, and fed thee? or thirsty, and gave thee drink? When saw we thee a stranger, and took thee in? or naked, and clothed thee? Or when saw we thee sick, or in prison, and came unto thee? And the King shall answer and say unto them, Verily I say unto you, Inasmuch as ye have done it unto one of the least of these my brethren, ye have done it unto me' [*Matt.* 25:31–40]. So love your brethren. Enter into fellowship and partnership with them in their needs and love the stranger, because you are not only doing it for them, you are doing it 'unto Him'. He is the One you are pleasing, and He is the One you are serving.

Let me give you a second exhortation: 'Be not forgetful to entertain strangers' – why? – 'for thereby some have enter-

tained angels unawares' [*Heb.* 13:2–3]. And there is no higher
experience than that. You have taken in a stranger because you
are following this injunction. There was not much to look at in
this stranger, but you discover later that you have taken in an
angel, you have entertained an angel unawares. There are great
stories on this in the literature of the church. We read of how a
great saint would be travelling and in need, and would be taken
in, and how his arrival would turn out to be the greatest
blessing that had ever come to the family because it had
obeyed the injunction of the Apostle Paul.

But here is a third and a final argument for you. Think of
the reward that will come to you – I have already given it you
from Matthew 25. Think of the day when He will say,
'Inasmuch as ye have done it unto one of the least of these
my brethren, ye have done it unto me' [verse 40]. 'Well done,
thou good and faithful servant . . . enter thou into the joy of
thy lord' [*Matt.* 25:21]. 'Inherit the kingdom prepared for you
from the foundation of the world' [*Matt.* 25:34]. What a
wonderful thing!

But listen to our Lord Himself urging and exhorting and
encouraging us to do this very thing the apostle tells us to do.
Here it is in Luke 16:8–9. It is the parable of the unjust steward.
'The lord commended the unjust steward, because he had done
wisely: for the children of this world are in their generation
wiser than the children of light. And I say unto you, Make to
yourselves friends of the mammon of unrighteousness that,
when ye fail, they may receive you into everlasting habitations.' It means, make the right use of your money. Do not be a
miser. Help others. Use this 'mammon of unrighteousness',
your money, to make friends for yourselves, so that when the
day may come that you fail, and it will certainly come when
you die, and arrive on the other side, those friends who have
gone before you will be in the front ranks waiting for you,
welcoming you.

Let the Apostle Paul put this in his own way in 1 Timothy 6.
This whole chapter, in a sense, deals with this one matter that
we are considering. Paul says: There are certain people from
whom we should withdraw. Who are they? Well, these are
people 'destitute of the truth, supposing that gain is godliness'
[*1 Tim.* 6:5], or who go in for godliness in order to get gain.

'But', he says, 'godliness with contentment is great gain. For we brought nothing into this world, and it is certain we can carry nothing out. And having food and raiment let us be therewith content. But they that will be rich fall into temptation and a snare, and into many foolish and hurtful lusts, which drown men in destruction and perdition. For the love of money is the root of all evil: which while some coveted after, they have erred from the faith, and pierced themselves through with many sorrows. But thou, O man of God, flee these things; and follow after righteousness, godliness, faith, love, patience, meekness' [verses 6–11].

But then listen to Paul at the end: 'Charge them that are rich in this world, that they be not highminded, nor trust in uncertain riches, but in the living God, who giveth us richly all things to enjoy; that they do good, that they be rich in good works, ready to distribute, willing to communicate' – why? – 'laying up in store for themselves a good foundation against the time to come, that they may lay hold on eternal life' [verses 17–19].

It is exactly the same teaching as our Lord gives in Luke 16. Teach them, Paul says, in their use of money, to be ready to distribute, willing to communicate; and teach them that in this way they are really laying up in store for themselves in the world to come this great 'balance', as it were. They are doing it here, they will reap the reward there. Give them this right view, this right perspective. If they do this, tell them, they will have a firm hold, a certain hold, they will have absolute assurance of eternal life itself.

And that is the great encouragement to all of us to implement this injunction of the apostle here in Romans 12:13. Enter into fellowship with all saints who are in need. 'Pursue', 'seek after' this love of strangers. Practise hospitality, kindness to others. And as you do, you will be pleasing your Lord and Master. You will be certain of receiving from Him that final encomium beyond which nothing more can be desired: 'Well done, thou good and faithful servant' [*Matt.* 25:21]. You will have entertained many an angel unawares, even in this life, and you will have made certain of your eternal bliss in the glory everlasting. And you will be welcomed there not only by the Lord Himself but by these people whom you helped when they were in this evil world, who have gone on before you, and they will receive you into your 'everlasting habitations' [*Luke* 16:9].

Thirty

*

Bless them which persecute you: bless, and curse not. Rejoice with them that do rejoice, and weep with them that weep.

Romans 12:14-15

Perhaps I ought to remind those interested in statistics that this is our three-hundred and twenty-sixth study in this great Epistle. When we finished at the end of May we had come to the end of the thirteenth verse, so we start now with the fourteenth verse.[1] That was a kind of junction, the end of a little subsection in this chapter, but it is important, as I am constantly reminding you, that we bear in mind the general arrangement of the subject matter here.

Some of us are tempted to stop with doctrine, and to feel that when we have come to the end of chapter 11, we have all we really want out of the Epistle to the Romans. That is fatal. We must take the whole of the Scripture, otherwise we shall miss its balance. And here in this whole section, as we have seen,, the apostle is concerned with our practical, daily living.

Why should we be so concerned about this? One great reason is that the glory of God in His great salvation is involved. If we say that we are people who believe what we read in the first eleven chapters, and then live in a manner that is opposed to that teaching, we bring the very doctrine in which we claim to glory into disrepute. People – particularly today – are much more concerned with what we do than with what we say, so

[1] These studies resumed on Friday 7 October 1966 following a break since the end of May that year. See also the footnote at the beginning of the first study in this volume.

[426]

the glory of God and of His great salvation is, in a sense, in our hands and people will judge it by what they see in us. If we talk learnedly about justification, sanctification, and glorification but still live like everybody else in the world, then men and women who observe us will inevitably react by turning away from the gospel. But not only that, these truths are so interrelated and intertwined that we can never enjoy the benefits of our great salvation if we do not obey its precepts.

Many people go astray here. They are seeking blessings, seeking experiences, but fail to realize that it is in the way of ordinary practical duty that they are most likely to get the blessings they are seeking. If we do not implement this 'therefore' in verse 1, it is no use praying for or expecting some unusual experiences. God has always granted His greatest blessings to those who have been obedient to His command-ments – the instructions of the gospel as well as the law in the Old Testament. So if we really are concerned about our own happiness, we should take the path of obedience. This is the high road that leads to our enjoyment of the blessings of salvation. 'If ye know these things,' says our Lord, 'happy are ye if ye do them' [*John* 13:17]. There it is, once and for ever. If you know them – all right; but that will not make you happy. You are only happy when you do them.

And, in the same way, as I have been indicating, surely the best form of evangelism is Christian people manifesting the Christian life in their daily lives and occupations. This has been God's way throughout the centuries. That is how the gospel spread in the early centuries. It was this that conquered the ancient world. Often the first believers were not allowed to preach, especially not in great meetings. It was the life of the individual, average Christian that had such an impact that it shook the ancient world. Of course, there was the preaching of the apostles and others, but it was this further factor, it is generally agreed, that was most responsible for the spread of the gospel. It is the best form of evangelism. It is when people see in us this peculiar something that marks us out that they will come to us and say, 'What is this you have? I wish I could be like that.' That has been so often demonstrated in the long history of the Christian church.

Now we are reminded of all that here. We see here that

theoretical Christianity is useless, to individual Christians, and certainly to those who are outside. And, indeed, I will go further. A theoretical Christianity is a contradiction in terms, for the whole object of salvation is to do something to us, to bring us to God, to bring us to perfection, to ultimate glorification. There is nothing so wrong, so foolish and harmful, as a mere theoretical Christianity.

So, bearing all this in mind, we come now to the beginning of verse 14, and from here to the end of the chapter we have a further series of particular injunctions. It is, let me remind you, rather difficult to classify these. Some commentators would say that the apostle is here only dealing with people outside the church. But I think that that is quite unjustifiable – I do not think it applies to verses 15 or 16. This really does not matter, but I would prefer to put it like this: Up until now the apostle has been telling us how we should behave towards other people, the initiative is ours, as it were. But here, I think I will be able to show you, in each case he is dealing with our reaction to what other people are like and to what they do to us.

So verses 14– 21 really form a new section. They look from a different angle at the position of Christians living their lives in the world. Here we are, living among certain types of people who tend to do things to us. So the apostle tells us how we should conduct ourselves in the light of this. What is to be our reaction to them?

Here, again, is a most important subject, so let me make some general comments. First of all, notice once more the wonder of the Scripture. Is it not perfect? It deals with everything – and let me say once more that there is no more fallacious way of looking at the Scriptures than to regard them as just something theoretical, just an idealistic view of life. No, the Scriptures are intensely practical, and here in Romans 12 one cannot but notice their stark realism. They never paint a rosy picture or give the impression – which is sometimes given, particularly in evangelism – that if we will only come to Christ, nothing will ever go wrong again, but we will go walking down the road of life with our heads up, free of trouble. In fact, they tell us the sort of thing that we find in verse 14, 'Bless them which persecute you.' The Scriptures face the worst, and tell us how we can face it.

This is, of course, a part of the doctrine. As we have seen, the message of the gospel is not that the world is going to be made better but that you and I are saved out of it. Our blessed Lord Himself, with the great honesty and realism that we find everywhere, said, 'In the world ye shall have tribulation: but be of good cheer; I have overcome the world' [*John* 16:33]. The apostles said exactly the same thing. We read towards the end of Acts 14 that the Apostle Paul and his companion, as they went around the churches, reminded the people that 'we must through much tribulation enter into the kingdom of God' [verse 22].

To me, this is so wonderful. The gospel does not mislead us or try to wheedle us into the kingdom or entice us by giving a false prospectus. No, no, it is utterly, absolutely, honest, and this, again, is one of the great differentiating characteristics of the gospel as over against the cults. The cults offer an instant panacea. 'Wonderful!' they say. 'Everything is going to be all right!' But the Scriptures enable you to be prepared for the worst and tell you how to face it.

Again, as we come to look at this particular injunction that is before us here, we see the all-importance of remembering verses 1 and 2. Christians are new people, and they must live an entirely new kind of life. I will go further – they are the only ones who can live the kind of life that is depicted here. The instructions and injunctions that we have in Romans 12 are not just a collection of moral maxims such as those of ancient pagan writers – Seneca and others – or those written in later centuries – the writings of La Rochefoucauld or the letters of Lord Chesterfield, and so on. This is quite remote from all that. We have here a standard that the natural person is entirely incapable of reaching. Human beings cannot possibly live in the way that we are instructed to live here unless they are born again, unless they have the life of God in their souls, unless they are the possessors of new natures. There is no greater heresy – and it has been very common in the twentieth century – than the heresy of thinking that you can get Christian conduct from people who are not Christian. Incidentally, the essence of the heresy of pacifism is that it expects nations and people who are not Christians to implement these instructions. They cannot do it; it is impossible. In other words, once more, you must never separate practice from doctrine.

So, with that in our minds, let us look at Paul's words: 'Bless them which persecute you: bless, and curse not.' Here we are reminded that because we are Christians, we are certain to be persecuted. This same apostle would later write to Timothy: 'All that will live godly in Christ Jesus shall suffer persecution' [*2 Tim.* 3:12]. Our Lord had said it all before him: 'The servant is not greater than his lord' [*John* 13:16]. 'If they have called the master of the house Beelzebub, how much more shall they call them of his household?' [*Matt.* 10:25]. He says repeatedly: If they have treated me in this way, how much more are they likely to treat you like that [see *John* 15:18–20].

This, again, is a profound piece of doctrine. Its truth is constantly proved by the things that happen to us. Christian people are persecuted in some shape or form. Why? Simply because they are Christians. The world only persecutes the true Christian. You can be a church member without ever suffering any persecution. The world does not object to church members. But if you are truly Christian, born again, with the new nature in you, you will be attacked because of your new nature. So the world, without realizing it, can, by persecuting you, pay you a great tribute and do you a great kindness. By treating you in the same way our Lord was treated, it is giving you an absolute proof that you are a child of God. Our Lord said, 'If the world hate you, ye know that it hated me before it hated you . . . because ye are not of the world, but I have chosen you out of the world, therefore the world hateth you' [*John* 16:18–19].

The world recognizes this same thing in us that it recognized in Him. That is the astounding thing that we are told in the pages of the four Gospels. Here is the Son of God come from heaven to earth. He did nothing but good. He 'went about doing good' [*Acts* 10:38], relieving suffering and sickness, being kind to people, preaching the message of the love of God to a fallen world, and yet the world hated Him, rejected Him and in the end crucified Him. There you see the state of the world exposed, confirming what the Bible always says about it.

And the same thing happens to those who are His people.

There are abundant statements to that effect in the New Testament –we have just looked at some. Persecution takes many, many different forms. Sometimes it can be open, blatant, physical, even military. At this moment, in different parts of the world there are people in prisons simply because they are Christians. There are people in the modern world who are being killed because they are Christians.

But persecution does not always come like that. It can be very subtle indeed. It can just mean people looking at one another when you go into a room or into an office. It can mean people working against you. They may discriminate against you in a profession or in business – a lot of this happens. It can be a sneer or a suggestion, a curl of the lip – all sorts of things. I need not spend time in describing them. Never forget that persecution is not bound to be open or physical. Perhaps it is the subtle and the intellectual and the emotional forms of persecution, that are the most cruel. But in various ways persecution will come and the apostle deals with it in this amazing way.

So what is to be our reaction to persecution? And here the instruction is quite plain: 'Bless them' – bless them! – 'which persecute you: bless, and curse not.' The literal meaning of the word translated 'bless' is 'speak them good'. It comes to this: pray for those who persecute you; 'speak them good', even to God. Ask God to deal with them and to be merciful to them. Do them good in the highest way that you know of, which is to pray for them.

Then the apostle puts this negatively, and he must do this. 'Curse not', he says, which would be better translated by saying, 'Bless them which persecute you, and stop cursing them.' Paul puts it positively and negatively, as is so often his way. The instinctive tendency is to curse your persecutors, but Paul says: Stop cursing. Rather, you must bless them.

Now it is important that we should understand what the apostle means by 'curse not'. He is not referring to swearing. Christians are not tempted to swear at people; that is not our temptation for we are not swearing people. No, it means this: 'Stop calling down a curse upon them.' That is our danger. The danger for the Christian is not the use of expletives or bad language but of asking God to curse these people. So I can put

Paul's meaning like this: 'Call down God's blessing upon them instead of calling upon God to curse them.'

And in saying this, of course, the apostle is repeating something that our Lord Himself had already taught us in the Sermon on the Mount. You find it in Matthew 5 from verse 43 onwards: 'Ye have heard that it hath been said, Thou shalt love thy neighbour, and hate thine enemy. But I say unto you, Love your enemies, bless them that curse you, do good to them that hate you, and pray for them which despitefully use you, and persecute you.'

But there is an even clearer statement of this whole subject in Luke chapter 9 verses 51 to 56. This is an example of what we are not to do, and it indicates, therefore, what we should do. We read: 'It came to pass, when the time was come that he should be received up, he stedfastly set his face to go to Jerusalem, and sent messengers before his face: and they went, and entered into a village of the Samaritans, to make ready for him. And they did not receive him, because his face was as though he would go to Jerusalem.' Now listen: 'And when his disciples James and John saw this, they said, Lord, wilt thou that we command fire to come down from heaven, and consume them, even as Elias did?'

These men said, in effect, 'Do you want us to curse these people in your name?' That is what they meant. 'Shall we call down a curse from heaven upon these people and destroy them? They are refusing to receive you. They are opposed to you. They do not realize who you are.'

Then we read: 'But he turned, and rebuked them, and said, Ye know not what manner of spirit ye are of. For the Son of man is not come to destroy men's lives, but to save them. And they went to another village.' Now there it is perfectly. Our Lord says to James and John: Do not do that. I have not come into the world to do that. I have come to save men and women, so stop cursing and do the exact opposite: Ask God to send down a blessing upon them.

This is obviously a most important matter. And the essence of it is that our attitude to persecution must be positive. Now this is very difficult. There is nothing more trying, perhaps, than the endurance of persecution. But we must behave as Christian people and this tests the reality of our Christianity in a most thorough manner. God's people have suffered and endured persecution throughout the centuries. We all know something of it, which makes it so important that we should be clear about this particular teaching.

So, I repeat, the essence of the teaching is that our attitude and reaction to persecution must be positive. It is not enough merely not to retaliate. Many people think that that is enough. Others do something to me – ah, I instinctively want to get my own back on them. But I do not. All right, that is included, but Paul's injunction means more than that.

Again, it does not just mean that you say, 'Very well, I'll bear this,' and then bear it by ignoring it. You say, 'Let them do what they like, I'll just put up with it. I'll suffer. I'll endure it.' But that, again, is entirely negative. It is resignation; it is not doing anything at all positive about it. Again, it is quite right – we are not to retaliate and we are to bear it. But we must go beyond that also. We must positively desire the good of these people who are treating us like this. 'Bless them' – desire good to come to them from God. Pray that God may bless them.

But how can this be done? Is there anything more difficult than this? I say once more, only Christians can do this, and they can only do it because they alone can think in the one way that makes this possible. You see, this is not a matter of feeling. You can only bless those who persecute you as you follow out a certain argument, as you go through a certain process of reasoning. And nobody can do this except the Christian. That is why I want to expound it to you.

But let me point out something else which, I trust, will also be of practical help and value to you. This is that the principle laid down here about blessing those who persecute us also governs our reaction to people who are related to us, or with whom we are very friendly, but who are not Christians – persecution is an extension of this situation. Though these people do not necessarily persecute us, they do not understand us, and that leads to difficulties. You have all had this problem. You have become a Christian, but they are not. What do you do about them? Now the danger, of course, is to be impatient with them, even, sometimes, to get annoyed with them. The danger is, as it were, metaphorically to shake them and to react almost violently to them because of their failure. Have you not found yourselves in trouble just at this point? How exactly are you to handle these people, about whom you are so concerned and in whom you are so interested, who just cannot see the truth? You are amazed at them and, as I say, you are almost annoyed with them. What are the rules?

Here, then, are the principles that should govern our action in both these cases. First of all, you must start by reminding yourself of God's reaction to you. You want to know how to react to other people so start by reminding yourself of how God reacted to you, and what God has done for you. You are a Christian now; all right. But remember what you once were! You were not born a Christian – you were born a sinner. We are told in many places in the Scriptures what we were. We were God's 'enemies' says Paul in Romans 5:10. He repeats this teaching in Ephesians 4:18: 'Being alienated from the life of God'. In Romans 8:7 he says: 'The carnal mind is enmity against God: for it is not subject to the law of God, neither indeed can be.' That was true of every one of us. Not only that, we were arrogant in our attitude to God; we were disobedient; we broke His commandments; we broke His laws. And not only that, we were 'hateful', says Paul, 'and hating one another' [*Titus* 3:3].

What was there in us to recommend us to God? The answer is, nothing – nothing at all. And yet we are Christians now. And we are Christians because God did not curse us because we were what we were. Instead, He loved us. 'God so loved the world – the world I have just described to you – that he gave his only begotten Son, that whosoever believeth in him should not perish, but have everlasting life' [*John* 3:16]. That is how God dealt with you when you were as these other people are now. You were even worse than my second group because you were, in a sense, persecuting God, working against Him, delivering opinions against Him, saying terrible things in your heart, if not always with your lips.

Or take God's love as our Lord depicts it in the father of the prodigal son. There it is to perfection. It is entirely in spite of the son that the father runs to meet him and embraces him and does all that he does for him. It is in spite of the son's lack of love, in spite of his utter selfishness, in spite of the contempt that he felt for his father and his home, in spite of all this – the fool that he was and everything else. 'By grace are ye saved through faith; and that not of yourselves: it is the gift of God' [*Eph.* 2:8].

So whenever you find yourself reacting or tending to react violently to the persecution you are receiving, or whenever you are on the point of calling on God to curse your persecutors, or feel you are close to imitating James and John with those Samaritans, then stop, and say, 'What if God had dealt with me like that, where would I be now?' This is Christian thinking and this is what the apostle is telling us to do. You can only bless as you have this background. You are what you are solely by the grace of God; it is nothing in you at all.

So that is the first principle. You stop yourself reacting to persecution as you would do instinctively and you put down this great postulate: my position is entirely the result of grace. Then the second point you must make is this. With this idea of grace firmly in the centre of your mind, you look at the people who are persecuting you, and say: Why are they behaving like this? Why are they doing this to me? I've done them no harm, indeed, quite the reverse. Why do they treat me like this?

This is most important because the moment you ask these questions, you are proving that you are a Christian, that you are born again. In 2 Corinthians 5:16 Paul says, 'Henceforth, know we no man after the flesh.' Before his conversion he looked at everybody 'after the flesh'. He was a Jew and he was proud of the Jews. He despised the Gentiles and looked down upon them and treated them as dogs. That was looking at men and women 'after the flesh', and we all do that by nature. But, 'If any man be in Christ,' writes Paul in the next verse, 'he is a new creature [new creation]: old things are passed away; behold, all things are become new.' And everybody else becomes new. The persecutor becomes new to me. I see the persecutor and everybody else in a new way, exactly as I see myself.

In this Christian way of thinking, you look at the persecutor and draw a vital distinction between the sin of which he is guilty and the sinner who is guilty of it. Now there is nothing to be said for the sin – it is always wrong to persecute. Sin is always evil, and it deserves to be punished. But the sinner must be differentiated from the sin. The danger is to look only at the sinful action and react violently. But when you ask the question: 'Why is he doing this? Why is he behaving in this manner?', you are looking beyond the action to the person who is guilty of it. And immediately you will come to the only correct conclusion. You will say, 'He's doing this because he's unregenerate, because he's in a state of ignorance, because he's blind to spiritual truth, because his mind is darkened. He's biased against God and all His ways.'

And you must press that to this point: you must realize that he really cannot help it. Let me give you a simple illustration. If a poor man who had lost his reason began behaving in a certain way and you treated him as if he were a sane person, then you would be very cruel. The moment you realize that this poor man is insane and cannot help himself, you make allowances for him. 'Answer a fool according to his folly' [*Prov.* 26:5].

So you must say of your persecutor, 'This man is behaving like this because he's the dupe of Satan. He's the slave of the devil. He doesn't understand. He's against me because I've become a child of God, because I believe in God and I'm a Christian. Yes, but they treated my Lord in exactly the same way.' What is it that led humanity to shout out, 'Away with him! Crucify him!'? There is only one answer: they were blind. As the apostle puts it in 2 Corinthians 4: 'If our gospel be hid, it is hid to them that are lost: in whom the god of this world hath blinded the minds of them which believe not, lest the light of the glorious gospel of Christ, who is the image of God, should shine unto them' [*2 Cor.* 4:3–4].

The Christian is judging people in this way all the time. This man, this woman, who is persecuting me, this group that may be persecuting me, they do not know what they are doing. They do not see; they do not know; they do not understand. And remember that this is equally true of that relative or loved one of yours who is not a Christian, with whom you are beginning to get annoyed. You say, 'But I put the gospel to them. I've done everything, and still they won't see it.' But instead of being impatient like that, say, 'They can't help it. They're blinded by the devil. They're victims – spiritually diseased – and it is as wrong for me to get annoyed with them as it would be for me to get annoyed with an insane person.'

You work out the Christian doctrine in that way. There is your second step.

Your third step is this – and when you have taken this second step it will have already happened – you will be feeling sorry for your persecutors. And you do not even stop at that. The next step is that you will desire their salvation. You will say, 'What a tragedy! They are still as I once was. Thank God, I've been delivered – oh, that they were delivered, too!' What are you doing now? Well, you have already started praying to God to bless them. 'Bless them which persecute you: bless, and curse not.' Having seen them as they are, you will pray that they may be delivered out of the snare of Satan, out of the condemnation of the law; saved from hell. You will say, 'I must pray that God will have mercy upon them, as He did upon me, and change them, that He will give them the new birth, give them a new nature, change them from being persecutors, as Saul of Tarsus was, into preachers and commenders of the gospel.'

'Bless them' – that is it. Having worked it out – and you cannot bless your persecutors unless you do; you cannot create a nice feeling; you must work it out – the moment you have, the logic becomes inevitable. If you are not sorry for them, it means you are not a Christian. If you are a Christian, you are bound to be sorry for them, and that will lead you to pray for their salvation, for their deliverance and regeneration.

Let me close, therefore, by giving you some quotations from the Scriptures. I have already quoted that portion from the ninth chapter of the Gospel according to St Luke. Read it again from verses 51 to 56: 'He turned and rebuked them, and said, Ye know not what manner of spirit ye are of.' You are not behaving like disciples of Christ. 'For the Son of man is not come to destroy men's lives, but to save them' [verses 55–56]. Have compassion on them; feel sorry for them; pray to God on their behalf.

But our Lord put this much more strongly in His parable of the servant who owed his master a very large sum of money. The lord took pity on his servant, and released him from his debts. But the servant would not have pity on his fellow servant who owed him a only small amount. Then we read: 'And his lord was wroth, and delivered him to the tormentors, till he should pay all that was due unto him. So likewise shall my heavenly Father do also unto you, if ye from your hearts forgive not you every one his brother their trespasses' [*Matt.* 18:34–35].

That expresses it very plainly, does it not? Or read from the Sermon on the Mount, that passage that I have already partly quoted: 'Ye have heard that it hath been said, Thou shalt love thy neighbour, and hate thine enemy. But I say unto you, Love your enemies, bless them that curse you, do good to them that hate you, and pray for them which despitefully use you, and persecute you; that ye may be the children of your Father which is in heaven: for he maketh his sun to rise on the evil and on the good, and sendeth rain on the just and on the unjust. For if ye love them which love you, what reward have ye? do not even the publicans the same? And if ye salute your brethren only, what do ye more than others? do not even the publicans so? Be ye therefore perfect, even as your Father which is in heaven is perfect' [*Matt.* 5:43–48].

That is our standard. We are to be like our blessed Lord. Do you remember Luke 23:34? Here is our Lord – they have already captured Him. They have led Him to His death and they have nailed Him to the tree. Then we read about the two malefactors, one on one side and the other on the other side. In verse 33 we read, 'When they were come to the place, which is called Calvary, there they crucified him, and the malefactors, one on the right hand, and the other on the left.' Then in verse 34: 'Then said Jesus' – here is the interpretation of Romans 12:14 – 'Father, forgive them; for they know not what they do.' And that is what you and I are to say about those who persecute us: 'Father, forgive them; for they know not what they do.'

'Ah, but,' you say, 'that's the Son of God! That's a standard that's too high for me! I can't aspire to that!' Well, you should! Do you remember the death of the martyr Stephen? In Acts 7:59–60 we read: 'And they stoned Stephen, calling upon God, and saying, Lord Jesus, receive my spirit. And he kneeled down, and cried with a loud voice, Lord, lay not this sin to their charge. And when he had said this, he fell asleep.'

It is possible for us, the disciples, to rise to the height of our blessed Master. 'Father, forgive them; for they know not what

[438]

they do.' 'Lord, lay not this sin to their charge.' 'Bless them which persecute you: bless and curse not.' And so you will show that you are children of your Father who is in heaven, and that something of the divine nature that was in your blessed Lord is also in you.

Thirty-one

*

Rejoice with them that do rejoice, and weep with them that weep. Be of the same mind one toward another. Mind not high things, but condescend to men of low estate. Be not wise in your own conceits.

Romans 12:15–16

In the last lecture, we were considering, in terms of verse 14, how we are to react to persecution, and now we come to Paul's next injunction which is: 'Rejoice with them that do rejoice, and weep with them that weep.' Here, again, Paul is concerned about our reaction to other people, this time to people who are either rejoicing or weeping. The really interesting point in this verse is the order in which the apostle puts these two things – he puts the rejoicing before the weeping – and I think that he does this deliberately.

The question that occurs at this point and that has often been discussed is this: Which is more difficult, to rejoice with those who rejoice, or to weep with those who weep? On the surface, one might think that the first is the easier, but it seems perfectly clear, the moment you examine it, that rejoicing with those who rejoice is the more difficult of the two. But why?

Now this brings us, I think, to the very heart of the Christian life. To 'weep with those who weep' is more or less natural. It is a most exceptional person who is not touched by the sight of someone else weeping. By nature, by constitution, the natural man or woman, however bad, feels some kind of response when someone is weeping. Of course, there are certain people who are so hardened that even weeping does not touch them. They are quite immune and seem to be entirely lacking in any kind of sympathy. But there are not many such people. There is something in us all that tends to respond to weeping and we are ready, as it were, to weep as well.

Not only that, when a person is weeping it means that for the time being he or she is humbled and in difficulties. Something or other has got this person into a state of defeat. And this, again, makes it very much easier for us to weep. It is simpler for us to be sympathetic towards those who are down than it is to rejoice with those who are up. But why is this? It is because the ultimate problem with every human being with-out a single exception is the problem of self, the problem of pride. The self is always looking at itself. It wants to be considered great and important. That has been innate in human nature ever since the Fall. One of the first and main things that happened to man and woman as a result of the Fall was that they became proud and self-centred. And involved in pride, of course, is jealousy and envy. Now when a person is rejoicing, then he has some cause. He has been successful or he has had a piece of good fortune. Something good, something uplifting, has happened to him and he feels he is on his feet – so he is very pleased. And we are correspondingly jealous. All that is worst in self is involved at this point. It is certainly not natural to rejoice with those who rejoice.

Now if you examine yourself and your experience of life, I think you will find that it is easier to weep with those who weep because of the element of pity that comes in when people are suffering. Failure, or lack of success, or anything which gets someone down, stops that person being in competition with us. Indeed, for the time being we feel that we are in a better position. We are not weeping – they are. We are up and they are down, so we can afford to weep with them. That is why it is more or less natural. So the apostle, I suggest, puts rejoicing first in order to emphasize it and to challenge us with what is more difficult before he puts the less difficult.

Now one takes it for granted, of course, that in both cases, in both the joy and the sorrow, the apostle is assuming that the causes of the joy and the sorrow are legitimate and true. If a man is rejoicing because he has succeeded in doing something wrong; if a woman comes along and is very happy because she has stolen a sum of money, then obviously we do not rejoice. Or again, a man or woman may be weeping because their ambition has been thwarted. In that case, we do not weep with them, but reprimand them. People can weep in anger and for very selfish reasons, because the self has been hurt, and we do not weep with them either.

Once more, the apostle's emphasis is positive. He does not leave it at: 'Don't envy happy people' – which is about as far as the world can go. This is, of course, at the very root of the whole of life. We see it when political parties have their meetings.[1] You would think that people in the same party would all love one another and rejoice in one another's success. But do they? Now that is where biographies are so important, and autobiographies, too – these smiling people, all applauding one another, are envious and are plotting and scheming behind one another's backs. They appear to be rejoicing, but they are not. It is the very exceptional man or woman who genuinely rejoices at another's success, and this is the case not only among politicians, but also among members of the learned professions and among academics, and right through all social circles.

The greatest problem of all is the problem of jealousy and envy. About the highest the natural person can ever attain is to refrain from envy, and even that is well-nigh impossible. People can get to the stage of not showing their envy, but there is a very real difference between not showing it and not feeling it. The point is that we must not even feel it. But that is negative, whereas the apostle is very positive. He says you must take positive pleasure in the rejoicing of your fellow Christian; you must really enter into his happiness and be pleased with the success or whatever it is that leads to his rejoicing. The negative is not enough.

There are many negative ways of dealing with envy. Many people have cultivated a kind of detachment. I could elaborate this. This is the story of humanity and it shows you the difference the gospel makes. There have been men who have

[1] This sermon was preached in October when the British political parties have their annual conferences.

been famous because of their so-called stoical calm which has given them the reputation of not being jealous and envious. But the more you learn about such men from their biographies and autobiographies, the more you find that what really happened was that, after much effort, they were able to arrive at some kind of philosophical calm where nothing could move or disturb them and where they seemed to get rid of all passion. There are systems which can achieve this – yoga, for example. You cultivate a kind of resignation, a passivity, so that you are not affected by anything that happens.

But that is always negative and it never approaches what we are dealing with here, it never knows what it is to 'rejoice with them that rejoice'. All it can do is either not show the envy or produce what is sometimes described as 'the Roman attitude'. I could very easily illustrate this from the history of the twentieth century. And your great 'Romans' are not quite as unmoved and dispassionate as their public image would lead you to believe. There is a rancour deep within, and sometimes it can show itself in the form of disease. I am one of those who is ready to believe that the death of certain well-known persons from cancer, for instance, is to be easily explained by this very thing that we are considering. Thwarted ambition harms the whole system, even leading to illness. I must not go into that. All I am emphasizing is that the apostle's injunction is positive: Christian people are positively to 'rejoice with those that rejoice' as if the success were their own.

Once more, is it not obvious that no man or woman can ever do this for themselves? You can put on an artificial smile, but your happiness is not even skin deep. You can put on an assumed pleasure and joviality and mouth congratulations, but we are not being cynical when we say that it is well known that the pleasure is not real, it is not true. A man or woman of the world, the 'natural person', cannot carry out Paul's injunction. There is only one way whereby it becomes possible, and that is by the work of the Holy Spirit in us.

And how does the Holy Sprit do it? Well, this is the glory of Christian salvation. The Holy Spirit deals with all that is involved in self, and does this by means of the new birth and the new nature. The new birth is the one thing that resolves the problem of self. Nothing else can do it, and that is why our gospel does not teach a modification of the self, but a doctrine of regeneration, of a rebirth, a new being, a new person. Only this gospel of salvation in Jesus Christ our Lord can ever deliver us from our self and all that is involved in that horror. It works like this: We are not only delivered from self, we are also identified with others. That is the marvellous thing. We become members of the same family, we belong to the same Head, we belong to the same body.

The same thought is brought out in several places in the first chapter of Philippians. The whole doctrine of the church as the body of Christ implicitly carries this point within it. This is, indeed, one of the ways in which we show that we do belong to the one body. Earlier in Romans chapter 12, the apostle has said, 'As we have many members in one body, and all members have not the same office: so we, being many, are one body in Christ, and every one members one of another [*Rom.* 12:4]. We spent time with that great doctrine because, I say again, you cannot do anything about these injunctions unless you are clear about the doctrine. Indeed, we need to go back to verses 1 and 2. You must be not only 'not conformed to this world', but also 'transformed by the renewing [of the very spirit] of your mind' before you can possibly 'rejoice with those who rejoice'. But under the influence of the Holy Spirit, and as the result of His operation, you are given a new nature and you share it with others, and it is this that enables you to obey Paul's injunction in Romans 12:15.

How? Well, according to this teaching, nothing can happen to your fellow Christians without its affecting you, both negatively and positively, both as regards the weeping and the rejoicing. In 1 Corinthians 12, where Paul deals in great detail with the idea of the church as the body of Christ, he says in verse 26: 'And whether one member suffer, all the members suffer with it; or one member be honoured, all the members rejoice with it.' You cannot help yourself because whatever happens to the other is really happening to you. The human body, as we saw when we discussed the illustration, is not something that can be divided into disparate segments which have nothing to do with one another and are only connected by means of some strings or by bars of iron or something. No, no; the body is one, it is organic, and whatever happens to one part

[444]

of the body involves the whole. As I told you, get an infection in the tip of your little finger, and you will soon have a headache. The unity leads of necessity to this. You cannot help yourself, you feel the pain. And that is how it is with the church, the body of Christ.

Now there are many examples of this in Scripture. Take, again, for instance, the incident in Acts 12 when Herod, after killing James, the brother of John, arrested Peter and threw him into prison. But we read: 'Prayer was made without ceasing of the church unto God for him' [verse 5]. The believers were with Peter in prison. In the fourteenth chapter of Romans, where he is talking particularly about Christians, Paul writes, 'For none of us liveth to himself, and no man dieth to himself [verse 7]. We cannot. If we are truly Christians we cannot live independent, isolated lives. It is not we who decide this, it is God who has decided it in planning His salvation; and the Spirit makes us one body. What happens to the other affects and influences me. So if one member is honoured we all rejoice with him. It is not only happening to him, it is happening to the body of Christ, it is happening to the Head, so we are rejoicing with our great and glorious Head.

Now the apostle has another very interesting way of putting this same thing. I always feel that this is one of the most moving things he ever wrote, considering what a strong man, what a virile personality, he was. Listen to him in 2 Corinthians, this time in chapter 11. He is describing his troubles and problems and anxieties as a minister, as an apostle. 'In weariness and painfulness, in watchings often, in hunger and thirst, in fastings often, in cold and nakedness. Beside those things that are without, that which cometh upon me daily, the care of all the churches' [verses 27–28]. And then in verse 29: 'Who is weak, and I am not weak? who is offended, and I burn not?' That is it – this great and mighty man! I burn in righteous indignation; I burn in sympathy. Though he has all the care of all the churches, nothing can happen to any individual without his feeling it with all the intensity of his big and glorious nature.

So it works out like this: there is no more thorough test of our profession of the Christian faith than just this ability to feel with other Christians. And oh, it is very much easier for me to be right about every dot and comma and tittle of the faith to which I adhere, than it is, in actual practice, to rejoice with them that do rejoice, and to weep with them that weep. But this is a part of the gospel; it is a part of the teaching. It is no use talking if we fail at this point. This includes the doctrine. The great doctrine of the work of the Holy Spirit in regeneration and in baptizing us into the body of Christ is implicit here. It is 'the unity of the Spirit in the bond of peace' [*Eph.* 4:3]. There is not much point in saying that we believe the doctrines unless we are aware that they must be worked out in the realities of our daily life.

I am staying with this and emphasizing it because I am more than ever convinced that it is the lack of practical obedience to Paul's injunctions that accounts for the state of the church, and for the fact that the masses are outside. It was a taunt hurled at the early Christians, but it was also a great compliment – the jibe, 'See how these Christians love one another.' And that is the kind of thing that still impresses the world. So never divide doctrine and practice; the one always goes with the other. And you test the reality of your doctrine by what you do in your daily behaviour.

Now what a different story the story of the Christian church would have been if all Christians had implemented this injunction in Romans 12:15. If you read church history, you will see how the devil has constantly crept in and so twisted Christian people as to prevent them from keeping Paul's words. And people on all sides who have been zealous for the faith have been guilty in this respect. I am not pitting the one against the other, I am putting them together – doctrine and practice, doctrine and experience. Here it is, let us face it.

Then let us go on. In the next verse the apostle tells us, 'Be of the same mind one toward another.' That is the main injunction in verse 16. But then he helps us to understand that and to practise it by going on to say, 'Mind not high things, but condescend to men of low estate'; and, secondly, 'Be not wise in your own conceits.' Now all these things are intimately related. Rejoicing! Well, you say, that is a matter of the emotions. I agree, but of course, you cannot divide a person's feelings from their thinking. Thinking and feeling and action are all inextricably mixed up together, so Paul, having said to

the Roman Christians, 'Rejoice with them that do rejoice, and
weep with them that weep,' now tells them – and this will help
you to obey the earlier injunction – 'Be of the same mind one
toward another.'

What does this mean? It means to mind the same things, to
agree with one another, to be united in feeling, in interests,
and in the objects of your interests. Or, put negatively: Let
there be no discord among you. The New English Bible, which
translates these words, 'Have equal regard one for another',
seems to me to have missed the meaning completely. That
applies much more to the previous verse than to this. What
they really mean by their translation is this: 'Have the same
opinion about others as you have about yourselves and so treat
them well.' That is a perfectly right thing to do, but I suggest
that that is not what this particular injunction is saying to us.
This verse refers to the mind; it is telling us to have a common
mind.

Now Paul does not mean that as Christians we are bound to
agree together about everything. He means we must have a
unity with respect to the truth. And, of course, in pleading for
this, the apostle is doing something that he does in almost
every epistle he ever wrote. Let me show it you in 1
Corinthians 1:10: 'Now I beseech you, brethren, by the name
of our Lord Jesus Christ, that ye all speak the same thing, and
that there be no divisions among you; but that ye be perfectly
joined together in the same mind and in the same judgment.'
That is a perfect commentary on this injunction in Romans
12:15.

Or again, Paul puts it like this in 1 Corinthians 11:17–19:
'Now in this that I declare unto you I praise you not, that ye
come together not for the better, but for the worse. For first of
all, when ye come together in the church, I hear that there be
divisions among you; and I partly believe it. For there must
be also heresies [schisms] among you, that they which are
approved may be made manifest among you.' The apostle is
dealing with exactly the same thing there. Or take it in
Philippians 1, particularly in verse 27: 'Only let your conversation' – your manner of life and behaviour – 'be as it becometh
the gospel of Christ: that whether I come and see you, or else
be absent, I may hear of your affairs, that ye stand fast in one

spirit, with one mind striving together for the faith of the gospel.' That is what Paul is after.

Or again in Philippians 3:15–16: 'Let us therefore, as many as be perfect, be thus minded' – let us think like this – 'and if in anything ye be otherwise minded, God shall reveal even this unto you. Nevertheless, whereto we have already attained, let us walk by the same rule, let us mind [think] the same thing.' That is what Paul is appealing for. It is the same thing all along.

Or take it again in a striking statement in the Epistle to the Colossians in the second chapter. The apostle says, 'I would that ye knew what great conflict I have for you, and for them at Laodicea, and for as many as have not seen my face in the flesh; that their hearts might be comforted, being knit together in love, and unto all riches of the full assurance of understanding, to the acknowledgement of the mystery of God, and of the Father, and of Christ; in whom are hid all the treasures of wisdom and knowledge' [verses 1–3]. And he goes on with this. He says, 'As ye have therefore received Christ Jesus the Lord, so walk ye in him: rooted and built up in him, and stablished in the faith, as ye have been taught, abounding therein with thanksgiving' [verse 7].

This is the main idea in this particular injunction of the apostle. We are all to be minding – thinking – the same things. Our minds are to be working in the same way and along the same channels so that there may be no division, no schism, but unity as Christian people. But how is this to be done? Paul goes on to tell us in the two following injunctions which are explanations or expositions of this first one and also indicate to us how it can be achieved. The first is this: 'Mind not high things.' Here is an important statement. Paul has already told us something very similar in Romans chapter 11 verse 20: 'Well; because of unbelief they were broken off, and thou standest by faith. Be not highminded, but fear.' It is the same thought exactly.

There is some dispute over what Paul means by his words, 'Mind not high things.' Some say the phrase refers only to our thinking, to intellectual pride and haughtiness, and I tend to agree that that is certainly its first meaning; but it means more than that. I think it also refers to high desires, to ambition, socially or in any other realm. Here, again, is a warning that one finds running right through the Bible. Take, for instance, Psalm 131 which puts this before us in a very interesting and appealing manner. 'Lord,' says the psalmist, 'my heart is not haughty, nor mine eyes lofty: neither do I exercise myself in great matters, or in things too high for me. Surely I have behaved and quieted myself, as a child that is weaned of his mother: my soul is even as a weaned child. Let Israel hope in the Lord from henceforth and for ever.'

Now there is a man who realizes the danger of 'minding high things'. What a wise man he was! What a great deal of misery people have brought upon themselves because they have not followed that example. Intellectual pride is a devastating thing and it has been a curse in the church throughout her long history. What harm has been done because people have set themselves up as authorities, people who are not authorities at all but have succumbed to the spirit of haughtiness, and have become inflated with their own ideas. Let me give you a New Testament counterpart. It is 1 Corinthians again, and chapter 8, which is virtually devoted to this from beginning to end. The chapter begins, 'Now as touching things offered unto idols, we know that we all have knowledge. Knowledge puffeth up, but charity edifieth [builds up]. If any man think that he knoweth any thing, he knoweth nothing yet as he ought to know' – and so on.

In that eighth chapter of 1 Corinthians Paul is dealing with the whole question of the 'weaker brother'. Now in the church at Corinth there were some Christians who were more intelligent and intellectual than others, and they had come to an understanding about the whole question of meats offered to idols. But there were other Christians who had not yet seen this truth and the high-minded people, the clever people, despised these 'weaker brothers', who were therefore hurt. As a result of all this, there was great trouble in the church. Now that is what Paul is dealing with here. He says: Don't become high-minded. Don't become haughty. Don't become intellectually proud. Paul deals with the same point in 1 Timothy 6:17: 'Charge them that are rich in this world, that they be not highminded, nor trust in uncertain riches, but in the living God, who giveth us richly all things to enjoy.'

[449]

That is the negative injunction, but positively, instead of doing that, says Paul, 'condescend to men of low estate'. Now the translation here is a bit unfortunate. The word 'condescend' has become an objectionable word today, and rightly so. It would therefore be better to have a different translation. The word that the apostle used is a word that means 'to be carried away by'. So he is saying: Do not be high-minded, but rather allow yourselves to be carried away by men of low estate.

Now let me show you why this is the correct interpretation. In Galatians 2:13, the apostle uses exactly the same Greek word. He is talking about an occasion when he and Peter were both at Antioch, and he says, 'The other Jews dissembled· likewise with him; insomuch that Barnabas also was carried away with their dissimulation.' Now 'carried away with' is a much better translation. Do not let yourself be carried away by things that inflate you and lead to arrogance – intellectual arrogance and pride and haughtiness; allow yourself to be carried away in a different manner.

We must also watch our translation of the second part of this injunction. It reads here in the Authorized Version, 'by men of low estate'. But that is a slight interpretation by the translators because the word 'men' is not there. All we have in the Greek is 'the humble': 'Allow yourself to be carried away by the humble'. And the commentators have argued throughout the centuries as to whether 'humble' means humble things or humble people. Now once more it seems to me that it means both, because people and things are so mixed up and involved in one another that you cannot separate them.

So Paul means, first, that we are to avoid becoming intellectual. We are to use our intellects, but God forbid that any of us should ever become intellectuals! You are to try to understand the doctrine, yes, but the moment you become proud of your understanding, it is of no use to you. That is 'minding high things', being rather pleased at yourself for your learning and your understanding and your knowledge. No, no, says Paul, go in for humble things.

But, secondly, this also applies to people, because the inevitable effect of becoming proud of your knowledge is, as we are shown in 1 Corinthians 8, to despise people who do not have your understanding. The apostle therefore says here, 'Allow yourself to be carried away by people and things which are humble'. But we must never be guilty of condescension. There is a way of mixing with humble people by patronizing them, and that is despicable; it is thoroughly bad. That is why this word 'condescend' must be taken right out. Sometimes great people will deign to visit some lowly person but that is the antithesis of Christianity. No, no, Paul means 'become one with them'. You must allow yourself to be carried away by humble things and humble people without being patronizing, with not a suspicion of condescension, none whatsoever.

Once more, we are facing one of the most thoroughgoing tests of our profession of faith. Here is something that cannot be imitated by the world. Often the world does not even try to live humbly, but it does sometimes, and even then it is a dismal failure. Only the Spirit of God can bring one into this condition. You find it in King David, so highly exalted and such a brilliant man, who said, 'I would rather be a doorkeeper in the house of my God, than to dwell in the tents of wickedness' [*Psa.* 84:10]. He did not 'mind high things'.

Or take the apostle himself in the first chapter of this very Epistle: 'I long to see you, that I may impart unto you some spiritual gift . . .' [verse 11]. 'Ah,' you say, 'he's put himself on a pedestal, hasn't he? He says, "that I may impart unto you some spiritual gift, to the end ye may be established."'

Is Paul patronizing them? No! See how he continues: 'That is, that I may be comforted together with you by the mutual faith both of you and me' [verse 12]. This mighty man, this greatest of all Christian teachers, sits down with them on the same seat. It is an exchange, he says. You and me! 'Mutual faith'! I have something to give you, you have something to give me. Paul could learn from them. This is the great apostle putting his own injunction into practice. And he deals with the same thing exactly in 1 Corinthians 3:18: 'If any man among you seemeth to be wise in this world, let him become a fool, that he may be wise.'

But so that you do not feel that this teaching is confined to the Apostle Paul, listen to James who has exactly the same doctrine, especially in his second chapter: 'My brethren, have not the faith of our Lord Jesus Christ, the Lord of glory, with respect of persons. For if there come into your assembly a man with a gold ring, in goodly apparel, and there come in also a poor man in vile raiment; and ye have respect to him that weareth the gay clothing, and say unto him, Sit thou here in a good place; and say to the poor, Stand thou there, or sit here under my footstool: are ye not then partial in yourselves, and are become judges of evil thoughts?'

Then notice: 'Hearken, my beloved brethren, Hath not God chosen the poor of this world rich in faith, and heirs of the kingdom which he hath promised to them that love him?' [*James* 2:1–5]. That is the only thing that matters to Christian men and women. They do not care whether people are rich or poor, high or low, intelligent or unintelligent – whatever the world may say. No, their question is: Is this person a Christian? Are these people rich in faith? Are they children of God? If so, I belong to them and I like talking to them; I like meeting them. Peter's teaching is the same. In 1 Peter 5, he reminds the elders that he is himself 'an elder', but he says in verse 3: 'Neither as being lords over God's heritage, but being ensamples to the flock.' That is it.

And you see this, of course, to perfection in our blessed Lord Himself – 'a friend of publicans and sinners' [*Matt.* 11:19]! He sat down with them, He ate with them and as a result He was misunderstood. There was no condescension, no patronizing, it was natural. That was His holy nature. You remember how He took a towel and washed the disciples' feet and then said, 'I have given you an example, that ye should do as I have done to you' [*John* 13:15]. That is the way He did things. That is the way He lived. And he says that one of the great tests of the gospel is this: 'The poor have the gospel preached to them' [*Matt.* 11:5].

So we must listen to this injunction: 'Mind not high things, but be carried along with humble things and humble people.' There is nothing more incongruous than social distinctions in the Christian church. Yet that has happened, and I believe that this partly accounts for the present state of the church. The Christian church, as you see her generally throughout the running centuries, has been a travesty of the New Testament church. Its leaders have been called 'princes of the church'. Princes of the church! There is no such thing. 'Spiritual lords' –

what a denial of the injunction here in Romans 12:16! This is what has done such harm to the Christian faith.

Why are the masses, the so-called 'working-class people', untouched by the gospel and outside the church? The answer they give you is that the church is a snobbish society – the society of the middle classes and some of the upper classes – that it is a class-conscious society! So often the impression is given that the ministry consists of those who are in some kind of continuing Oxford and Cambridge club and that the people are, as it were, down below somewhere. This is what destroys the Christian faith and is, indeed a denial of the gospel.

This has been happening in the twentieth century. It was our grandfathers who made the mistake. I saw this in South Wales where the working man had the impression that the chapels belonged to the bosses, to the owners and managers, and that as institutions they were against the common man. You saw these distinctions still more clearly in the Church of England where the vicar was often a local squire, perhaps a son of the aristocracy, and mixed with the aristocracy and patronized the people.

These social and intellectual divisions were found in every section of the Christian church. There is a famous story about a poor old woman going out of a morning service in Edinburgh, after she had been listening to a learned sermon from one of the great 'pulpit princes' as they were called in the nineteenth century. Oh, how we are suffering today because of those popular pulpit princes who did not preach the gospel but entertained the people and did not sow the seed for the future! They were too great to be evangelists, too great to preach in a way that everybody could understand. But you remember the story? The poor old woman was going out and somebody said to her, 'Did you enjoy the service?'

She said, 'Yes, I did.

Then she was asked, 'Well, what was it exactly he was preaching about?'

Her response was: 'Far be it from me to claim that I can understand or follow the mind of such a great man.'

I again recommend that you read the history of the church in the nineteenth century and compare it and contrast it with the eighteenth century. I am referring chiefly to the Free Churches

– the Church of England did not change much, but there was a great change in the Free Churches. In the eighteenth century, as the result of the Evangelical Awakening, you had in practice the very spirit that the apostle is inculcating here. But then a subtle change took place. People said, 'We must have a learned ministry.' So along came these great men with their great minds – I am thinking of people like Dr Dale of Birmingham – and the people did not know what they were talking about. They took their problems into the pulpit and talked about affairs of state. I have a kind of admiration for many of them, but these are the men, it seems to me, who did the harm. The church went wrong when this snobbish element came in.

Nothing more devastating can enter into the life of the church than pride. And it is not confined to the church. This snobbish element is to be found in religious movements also. Not everybody is admitted; you have to belong to a certain class or to have attended a certain school.

So I not only ask where you find that kind of thing in the New Testament but I go further and say it is denounced completely and strongly in the whole of the New Testament. When you meet people your only interest should be this: Are they children of God? Are they heirs of eternity? Are they spiritually minded? They are the people to talk to, they are the people with whom you want to mix, whether or not their grammar is perfect. Now I am not putting any premium on ignorance or on bad grammar. All I am saying is that this is not the way in which you assess people. It is the business of the man with the bad grammar to improve his grammar, but in the church you do not judge people by such standards. No, you assess them in spiritual terms. You look for this fundamental life of the spirit that is in us all and should make us all say with David that we would rather spend the rest of our lives in the humblest position in the church of God than move in the so-called 'high circles' where Christ is not known or loved or honoured. 'Mind not high things, but be carried along with lowly things and lowly people.'

Thirty-two

*

Be of the same mind one toward another. Mind not high things, but condescend to men of low estate. Be not wise in your own conceits.

Romans 12:16

We have seen that in verse 16 the apostle makes a special appeal to us to have a common mind: 'Be of the same mind one toward another.' He is emphasizing the importance of agreement among God's people because it is the only way to have harmony in the church.

Now I must remind you again that the two statements that govern the whole of this section are verses 9 and 10: 'Let love,' Paul says, 'be without dissimulation. Abhor that which is evil; cleave to that which is good. Be kindly affectioned one to another with brotherly love; in honour preferring one another.' These are the controlling principles and from there on he works them out and shows us how they are to apply in the particular details of our lives.

Verses 9 and 10 are the basis for Paul's great appeal for the 'common mind' that he talks about here in the sixteenth verse. Then, as was his custom as a very wise teacher, he goes on to show us that there are two things that tend to militate against Christian people having 'the same mind one toward another'. The first he puts in these words: 'Mind not high things, but condescend to men of low estate.' We dealt with that in the last lecture and saw that haughtiness and high-mindedness militate against this harmony, this agreement, this unity in the church.

[455]

But now the apostle says something else. The second danger is this: 'Be not wise in your own conceits.' This, again, is most important. The apostle has already said it in chapter 11:25: 'I would not, brethren, that ye should be ignorant of this mystery, lest ye should be wise in your own conceits.' There he was telling these Gentiles not to become puffed up because the Jews were failing for the time being. 'Don't exaggerate your own importance', he says in effect. 'Don't overestimate yourselves.'

And now here it is once more. The literal translation of these words is: 'Be not wise with yourselves.' Paul means by that, 'Don't talk to yourself about yourself and congratulate yourself on your great wisdom.' You remember how, in putting up his defence before Agrippa and Festus, the apostle says that before his conversion, 'I verily thought with myself . . .' [*Acts* 26:9] and that was his whole trouble. That is the whole trouble with unregenerate, unconverted people. Each person always 'thinks with himself'; he is always talking to himself. Every unconverted man or woman is a kind of mutual admiration society. They talk to themselves about themselves, and especially, as the apostle indicates here, about their own wisdom. This is a great warning against intellectual pride. We see men and women boasting of their wisdom, glorying in it, wise with themselves. The whole history of the church shows the damage that has accrued as the result of Christian people not observing this injunction.

Let us look at these words like this: I lay it down as a first proposition that the greatest of all sins is the sin of intellectual pride. I do not hesitate to assert that it is a greater sin than the evil which John calls 'the pride of life'. In his First Epistle, he talks about 'the lust of the flesh, and the lust of the eyes, and the pride of life' [*1 John* 2:16]. That, of course, is another danger – worldliness, a worldly-mindedness – and it is a terrible sin; but this is greater. There is something rather foolish, I feel, about the pride of life. It is ostentatious and that always makes it look rather ridiculous, a kind of vain show. But intellectual pride is much more subtle.

So why do I say that this is the greatest of all sins? First of all, it was the sin of the devil himself, leading him to pit his wisdom against that of God. He was a created being and God had endowed him with a mind and understanding. But he became proud. He inflated his mind and his own idea of it, and that was the cause of his downfall.

Secondly, as you remember, intellectual pride was the first sin in the Garden of Eden. The devil in his subtlety tempted Eve along that very line: he gave her the idea that they could become as gods knowing everything – wisdom! And as it was the first sin and the cause of the original fall, for that reason, it has continued to be the greatest of all sins.

But, further, it is also the most serious of the sins because it is the abuse of God's greatest gift to humanity. When I say that, I am not thinking of the spirit as such, but of the gifts and propensities and faculties that we have as human beings, the things that especially differentiate us from the animals. This, undoubtedly, is the greatest gift that God has given to us – this gift of reason, the gift of understanding, the gift of thought, the gift of being able to assess things. Obviously, therefore, to abuse this greatest gift is the greatest sin.

Or look at it in this way: it is our minds that ought to be saving us from most of the mistakes we make and most of the wrong things we do. That is where an adult is more inexcusable than a child. You can excuse a child who does certain things that are wrong. Children do not understand and it would therefore be very cruel and wrong to expect adult behaviour from them. But when we cease to be children and grow up, then it is right to expect us to think and reason and understand and be responsible.

So of all the faculties that we have, it is the mind that should enable us to live in a worthy, true and sensible manner. If you abuse this gift, then obviously you are abusing that which God has given you to safeguard you from your troubles, and there is no greater sin than that. So here, in this aphoristic, pithy manner, the apostle is putting before us one of the most important things we can ever consider together: 'Be not wise in your own conceits.'

Now intellectual pride can take two forms and it is important that we should consider both. The one form is knowledge, and the other is wisdom, and it is important to be able to draw a distinction between the two. We read in James 3:13: 'Who is a wise man and endued with knowledge among you?'

[457]

'A wise man – but there is something else – 'endued with knowledge'. Wisdom and knowledge are very closely related, of course, but they are not the same.

The difference can be put like this: Knowledge is information, awareness of things, discovery of things, becoming acquainted with things. It is something that can be taught. There is no need for me to elaborate this because we are living in an age that is given over to the acquiring of knowledge – the age of encyclopaedias, the age in which people are listening to instruction and in which they get information in many different forms. This explains the popularity of these television quiz shows, as they are called. They are all giving you knowledge – they further the gathering and acquiring of a certain number of facts, large and small.

But what is wisdom? Ah, here is the important point! It is something essentially different. You can have great knowledge and yet be entirely lacking in wisdom. And, on the other hand, you can be a man or woman of great wisdom, but have very little knowledge. So it is important that we should be clear as to the relationship between the two. You can define wisdom as 'the power and the capacity to use and to apply your knowledge'. You see the distinction? You may have great knowledge, but you may lack the capacity to make use of it.

Perhaps the simplest way of putting this is to say that the whole tragedy of the world at this present moment is that it has vast knowledge but is terribly lacking in wisdom. Look at the scientific knowledge we have. Why, then, is the world as it is? Why is it nervous? Why is it in a state of tension? Because human wisdom is not commensurate with its knowledge. Men and women have acquired vast knowledge but, because they lack wisdom, they do not know how to use their knowledge. Wisdom is the power, the faculty, the ability to put what you know to good and worthy ends.

I remember many years ago, when I was trying to practise a little medicine, I had a friend and colleague who was a perfect illustration of the difference between having knowledge and being able to use it. This man was an excellent student in the sense that he was good at reading text books. He had an amazing photographic memory, and was a good examinee because he could answer theoretical questions. But when that man was confronted by an actual patient with a not-very-difficult disease, he seemed quite incapable of applying his great book knowledge. On many occasions I observed his inability to treat a particular case that was in front of him. He was a very learned man but a poor clinician, a poor doctor. And you will know of similar instances in almost every walk of life.

Now the whole trouble in the world today is that it is exalting men and women of mere knowledge. Very clever though they may be, that is not enough. It should be the case that the more they know the wiser they become, and it is because of sin that that does not follow. Hence the troubles of the human race. So people who are wise in their own conceits can be proud of their knowledge or proud of their wisdom. Those in the first group, not able to draw the distinction between wisdom and knowledge, think that their knowledge means wisdom, so they go wrong. The second group, though they do not have much knowledge, think they are wise. They may, indeed, be wise and receive praise, but then they become conceited and proud.

But what makes this so wrong? Why does the apostle say, 'Be not wise in your own conceits'? There are a number of answers. First, you must not be wise in your own conceits because it really is not justified. You have nothing to be proud of; you are deluding yourself. Take a man who is very proud of his knowledge. The question to ask him is this: What do you really know?

'Ah,' he says, 'but I know this, that and the other.'

But then point out to him what he does not know! You will always find that the truly great scholar is modest. The old adage puts it perfectly: 'A little learning is a dangerous thing.' It is a little learning that tends to turn our heads and make us think we know everything. The more people know, the more they realize what they do not know. So the greater the scholar, the humbler the person, almost invariably. Now the apostle puts this very well when he deals with this very problem in 1 Corinthians 8:1-2. 'Now,' he says, 'as touching things offered unto idols, we know that we all have knowledge. Knowledge puffeth up, but charity edifieth. And if any man think that he knoweth any thing, he knoweth nothing yet as he ought to know' – and that is the simple truth. So when you are tempted to be proud of your knowledge, just remind yourself of what you do not know.

Paul refers to this again, in 1 Corinthians 13, where he says: 'Now we see through a glass, darkly; but then face to face: now I know in part' [verse 12]. 'For we know in part, and we prophesy in part. But when that which is perfect is come, then that which is in part shall be done away' [verses 9-10]. How little our knowledge is! It is only as 'through a glass, darkly'. At the very best, it is only a partial knowledge. And again, in Philippians 3, Paul, with his wonderful knowledge of the Lord, says, 'I count not myself to have apprehended' [verse 13]. He thanks God for what he has got, but, he says, 'I press toward the mark' [verse 14]. Oh, there is so much to be possessed and he has so little!

That, again, is where the world goes mad at the present time, boasting of its knowledge. Knowledge is wonderful as long as we do not boast about it. But despite the little we know, our ignorance is appalling. And, of course, it is exactly the same with regard to wisdom. Who is there who has not made many a mistake in life? The wise man often behaves like a fool. One of the wisest men in the whole of the Old Testament is Solomon, but look at the end of his life. What a fool he made of himself, this wise man! Remember how he began and the amazing wisdom he displayed – as in the story of those two women and their children [1 *Kings* 3:16–28]. Solomon, the man of the Proverbs and probably of Ecclesiastes, was famous for his wisdom, and yet in his personal life, how unwise, how foolish, he was!

The moment you tend to be proud of your wisdom and to boast of it, just look back across your life and see the mistakes you have made, and it will humble you and keep you in order. In Romans 1:22 the apostle says that this is what has happened to the whole human race: 'Professing themselves to be wise, they became fools.' And look at the world with all its supposed wisdom; has it ever been madder than it is today? It boasts of its understanding and knowledge, but look at what it is doing. Men and women in the learned professions, people of great knowledge, indeed, people who can often give very good advice to others, turn their own lives into tragedies. The failure of wisdom! So if you tend to boast about your wisdom, you are probably doing something that is not true, so do not do it.

And then, secondly, consider this: whatever wisdom, whatever knowledge, you do have, you have nothing to boast of because you have not produced them. If you have that blotting-paper kind of mind that can absorb facts and makes you a good student, well, you did not produce it; you were born with it. You may have taken up schemes to develop it, but if you do not have the capacity to start with, your schemes will not take you very far. And with your wisdom, too – you may have a natural gift for wisdom, but you did not produce that either, so do not boast of it. Read 1 Corinthians 3 again, and you will find that there the apostle deals with this at great length.

But let me go on to something still more important. 'Be not wise in your own conceits' – because if you are, it will do you great harm. As we have seen, in 1 Corinthians 8:1 Paul says, 'Knowledge puffeth up.' Inflates! But what is it inflated with? What is it that inflates? Gas! Air! It is not real, it is not solid, it does not 'build up', he says. As love builds up, knowledge puffs up. It appears to be very big but it is nothing but a balloon, just an inflated tyre with no real substance. And it is a very bad thing when someone becomes like a balloon and is puffed up with pride. It is devastating to the personality, to one's whole outlook upon oneself and upon life.

But I can perhaps best put it in this way: When we are proud we become guilty of the very things that the apostle tells us in 1 Corinthians 13 are not true of love. That sounds complicated, does it not? 1 Corinthians 13 is sometimes called Paul's hymn of love, and there he tells us negatively and positively about love. So if you are proud of your own wisdom, if you boast of your knowledge, if you are wise in your own conceits, you will be the opposite of what the apostle says there about love: 'Charity suffereth long, and is kind.' But a person who is puffed up never suffers long and is never kind. 'Charity envieth not.' But conceit is always full of envy. 'Charity vaunteth not itself.' But knowledge puffs up, vaunts itself, exaggerates itself, makes itself bigger than it really is, becomes a lie.

And then, charity 'is not puffed up'. There it is, the same phrase. Charity is not blown up, inflated. And charity 'doth not behave itself unseemly'. Truly wise men and women never behave in 'unseemly' ways, but those who think they are wise are proud of their wisdom, and that makes them lose their balance, and then they do things that are 'unseemly'.

Charity 'seeketh not her own'. But those who are proud of their intellects are always seeking their own. They seek admiration; they seek applause; they want everybody to say, 'Look at you! How clever you are!' Charity 'is not easily provoked'. The wise are not easily provoked, but those who have some pseudo-wisdom can be very easily provoked. And then: 'thinketh no evil; rejoiceth not in iniquity, but rejoiceth in the truth; beareth all things, believeth all things, hopeth all things, endureth all things. Charity never faileth . . .'

Now that is a very good description of love, but it is equally true of true wisdom. And therefore men and women who are puffed up prove that they do not have true wisdom. And their conceit does them very great harm. And that, in the fourth place, leads them, of course, to do harm to others, as we are told there in 1 Corinthians 13. Proud men or women are always difficult to live with; they behave badly and others suffer because of this.

But then there is a fifth reason for observing this injunction of the great apostle, and this is that being wise in our own conceits puts us in an extremely dangerous position. Again, a proverb puts this perfectly: 'Pride goeth before destruction, and an haughty spirit before a fall' [*Prov.* 16:18]. It is invariable. You find this teaching in many places in the Scriptures. Take 1 Corinthians 10:12. Here is a verse for people who are in this danger: 'Wherefore let him that thinketh he standeth take heed lest he fall.'

Or again I would remind you of Galatians 6:3: 'If a man think himself to be something, when he is nothing, he deceiveth himself.' People who are proud of their wisdom deceive themselves. Or go to James 3:1 'My brethren, be not many masters.' That means: Do not be authorities. Do not regard yourselves as wise men, as leaders. Do not set yourselves up in positions of leadership. Why not? '. . . knowing that we shall receive the greater condemnation. For in many things we offend all. If any man offend not in word, the same is a perfect man, and able also to bridle the whole body' [verses 1–2].

Now this is James' argument. 'Do not be many masters.'

Why not? For the good reason that you are setting up a standard for yourself. You are saying, 'I'm a wise man. I *know*.' And you will receive the greater condemnation because God will take you at your own evaluation. He will say: Now then, you used to claim, when you were on earth, that you were very wise, a person of great learning and knowledge and understanding and wisdom. That is what you said about yourself. But I will test you. I will examine you in terms of the very claims you have put forward for yourself. So if you have set this very high standard for yourself, your fall, your failure, your condemnation, will be correspondingly great.

And, of course, in saying that, James is but echoing the words of our blessed Lord and Master who puts it like this in the Sermon on the Mount: 'Judge not that ye be not judged. For with what judgment ye judge, ye shall be judged: and with what measure ye mete, it shall be measured to you again' [*Matt.* 7:1–2]. There it is once and for ever. You set up a standard for yourself as a man or woman of great wisdom, you condemn others and show their failures in knowledge or in wisdom, but you yourself will be judged by the very standard that you have been applying to those people. You are bringing judgment of the severest kind upon yourself. I repeat, those who are proud of their own wisdom are putting themselves in the most dangerous position possible. They will have to meet their own standard at the bar of eternal judgment.

But the final answer is the most important answer of all. Anyone who is wise in his or her own conceits is the exact antithesis of our blessed Lord and Master. He is eternally different. He says, 'Take my yoke upon you, and learn of me; for I am meek and lowly in heart' [*Matt.* 11:29]. That is how he describes Himself and that was His character – 'A bruised reed shall he not break, and smoking flax shall he not quench' [*Matt.* 12:20]. There he was, Son of God incarnate, and yet He said: I know nothing of myself. 'For I have not spoken of myself: but the Father which sent me, he gave me a commandment . . . even as the Father said unto me, so I speak' [*John* 12:49–50]. I do not generate My words. I do not produce them.

This was our Lord, living life as a man, and He said that He was utterly dependent upon the Father. What He said was given to Him, what He did was given to Him in every single respect. He did not do anything of Himself. Far from boasting of His wisdom He was 'the meek and lowly Jesus'. That is the astounding fact that one finds as one looks at Him in these portraits in the four Gospels. We see the lowliness and the meekness, the humility of the Son of God incarnate. He is the perpetual rebuke to all who are tempted to feel 'wise in their own conceits'.

For all these reasons we should avoid the sin of pride with all the power that we are capable of. But that leads me to the last general matter. How do we deal with this danger? We all differ in many respects. Some are more in danger at this point than others, but it is a danger that to some degree confronts all of us. What can we do about it? How are we to avoid being wise in our own conceits? Well, negatively, it does not mean false modesty. It does not just mean that you must go about trying to give the impression that you are an ignoramus and entirely lacking in wisdom. That is no good. The Uriah Heep type of person is never commended anywhere in the Scriptures. If you are someone with ability and wisdom, then that is who you are, and it is nonsense to say that you are not. The affectation of humility is always abominable.

So what do we do? Now there is abundant teaching in the Scriptures about this. There are certain general things that can safeguard us. First: 'Walk humbly with thy God' [*Mic.* 6:8]. Remind yourself of the things I mentioned earlier – all you do not know and the mistakes you have made and your fallibility. But above all, 'Walk humbly with thy God.' Look unto Jesus, follow Him in this respect as in every other respect.

What else? Well, remember Paul's injunction in Philippians 2:12: 'Work out your own salvation with *fear and trembling.*' We have rather tended to forget this, have we not? This has not been popular in the twentieth century. We are bright and breezy Christians. But Paul says, 'with fear and trembling'. It is not that you are uncertain of your salvation, rather, you are in fear and trembling because you *are* certain of the end, because you know you are under the eye of God. You know that you are His child and that your responsibility is tremendous, and you are afraid of letting your Father down, letting your family down, letting your home down. If you are truly wise, you will know the evil that is in this world, you will see 'the world, the flesh and the devil' [*1 John* 2:16]. Yes, the devil and his subtlety and his insinuations! Because you realize that this is a terrifying world to live in, you walk in fear and trembling.

And then remember the other words of the apostle, how he tells us that when he first went to preach in Corinth he went 'in weakness, and in fear, and in much trembling' [*1 Cor.* 2:3]. Look at this great man, this mighty man, this Apostle Paul, this outstanding genius – I cannot praise him too highly. And yet this man did things in fear and trembling – he was not self-confident and assured in his evangelism or in anything else. 'Fear and trembling'! Why? Oh, it was the sacredness of the task! His blessed Lord and Master had entrusted him with the wonderful treasure of the gospel and he feared lest he stand between the people and this gospel or detract from it in any way, or make it more difficult for them. He realized the forces that were meeting together when he was preaching the gospel and he was fearful in case in any way he might fail. He could not rely on anything in himself. He came 'not with enticing words of man's wisdom', but 'in demonstration of the Spirit and of power' [*1 Cor.* 2:4].

These are general things that we ought never to forget. They ought to control the whole of our outlook and all our activity. Or, as James puts it again in a wonderful phrase: 'Let him shew out of a good conversation his works *with meekness of wisdom*' [*James* 3:13]. That is the opposite, you see, of being puffed up with knowledge and wise in your own conceits. Which leads me to this – that the best way I can help you to safeguard yourself against this particular danger is to give a very hurried exposition of James chapter 3 verse 13 to the end of the chapter. The best commentary on the Scripture is the Scripture itself, in another passage, and James seems to have written these words here in order to expound the wonderful aphorism that we have in Romans 12:16.

James says: 'Who is a wise man and endued with knowledge among you? let him shew out of a good conversation his works with meekness of wisdom. But if ye have bitter envying and strife in your hearts, glory not, and lie not against the truth. This wisdom descendeth not from above, but is earthly, sensual, devilish. For where envying and strife is, there is confusion and every evil work. But the wisdom that is from above is first pure, then peaceable, gentle, and easy to be entreated, full of mercy and good fruits, without partiality, and without hypocrisy. And the fruit of righteousness is sown in peace of them that make peace.'

Now a brief exposition is this: The way to safeguard yourself against being proud of your wisdom is to learn the difference between true wisdom and false wisdom. Then you reject the false and seek the true. How do you do it? You look at the two types of wisdom – the false and the true. How do you tell the difference. First of all, consider their origin. Where does true wisdom come from? The apostle tells us that true wisdom comes from above, which means, from God. And the other? Well, you can start by saying that it comes from the earth. It is human wisdom, worldly wisdom.

But let James himself expound the characteristics of these two types of wisdom. The wisdom that comes from below is, first of all, as we have said, always earthly. It is clever, but it never rises above the human; it belongs to this world and knows nothing about the eternal. Secondly, James says that the wisdom from below is 'sensual'. It belongs entirely to the animal part of our nature. For instance, our brain, our intellectual ability, is a part of our animal nature. This wisdom is psychical or 'soulish' and lacks the spiritual element.

But, thirdly, James even goes so far as to say that this wisdom is 'devilish'. There are people who are given the credit for being wise but, says the apostle, the wisdom they have comes from the devil, it is demon-like. That is what 'devilish' means. This wisdom is given by evil spirits, and the evil spirits can be very clever. As Paul says, the devil can transform himself into an angel of light [2 *Cor.* 11:14], and, he says, the devil's agents can do exactly the same thing. In 1 Timothy 3:6, therefore, Paul says that when electing elders, a novice must not be appointed: 'Not a novice, lest being lifted up with pride he fall into the condemnation of the devil' – and that, as I said earlier, was pride of wisdom. So this wisdom that puffs itself up and is proud of itself can be very clever; it can appear to be wonderful, but really it is always not only earthly or soulish, it is even devilish. It is that which turned Satan from being a bright angelic spirit into the devil.

And then James goes on to tell us how this false wisdom reveals itself – and it will always come out; it cannot be hidden. You never know exactly when, but sooner or later this wisdom is certain to show itself in what James calls 'conversation' – the habit and way of living. It shows itself in pride, in envying, in bitterness, in strife. And, of course, above everything, as he has been telling us earlier in the chapter, it shows itself in the failure to control ourselves, and, especially, in the failure to control our tongues so that we say things we should not.

That is the message of this third chapter of James, is it not? Beware the wisdom of the world, the false wisdom. And remember that this warning applies to men and women who are truly Christian because the moment they become puffed up about their wisdom, they are proving that they have worldly wisdom and not the true wisdom. It eventually gives itself away, with tragic consequences.

What about true wisdom? Ah, what a difference! It is 'from above'! It comes from God, the only 'wise' God, and, of course, it bears the characteristics of God. The first thing is that it is pure – there is no admixture, no adulteration, nothing false, nothing pseudo. It is a whole, not an alloy.

And then it is 'peaceable'. True wisdom is always peaceable because it always leads to meekness and humility. People who have true wisdom are people of peace. They are also 'gentle', not puffed up, not proud. The wise man is truly a gentleman.

The truly wise are 'easy to be entreated'. They are not intolerant. You can approach them and speak to them. They are ready to listen to you and are ready to take advice. They know the dangers. They do not say, 'I know everything – nobody else does.' No, no, they are easy to be entreated, and you can get on with them.

And they are 'full of mercy and good fruits'. Of course! 'Without partiality'. They are not prejudiced. They are prepared to listen to the other side of an argument and consider it carefully without bias. They have a spiritual, open mind. 'Without hypocrisy': they do not pretend to be better than they are, or to have more wisdom than they really have.

Then James ends by saying: 'And the fruit of righteousness is sown in peace of them that make peace.' In other words, it is this great phrase at the end of verse 13: 'meekness of wisdom'. Men and women who have true wisdom are humble. They have self-control; they are in charge of themselves and control their thinking and everything else about themselves. They are loving and peace-making. And this is shown in their lives. 'Who is a wise man and endued with knowledge among you? let him shew out of a good conversation' – wisdom is not theoretical, but always shows itself in practice, in conduct, in daily life and living – 'his works with meekness of wisdom.' Here are people who do not boast of themselves but boast in God and say, 'By the grace of God I am what I am' [*1 Cor.* 15:10].

So the way to safeguard ourselves against this terrible danger of being wise in our own conceits is to understand the difference between the false and the true wisdom, and then, having realized the difference, to seek for the true wisdom with the whole of our being. James has already told us how to do that: 'If any of you lack wisdom' – and we all do – 'let him ask of God, that giveth to all men liberally, and upbraideth not; and it shall be given him. But let him ask in faith, nothing wavering. For he that wavereth is like a wave of the sea driven with the wind and tossed' [*James* 1:5–6]. Ask in faith, without wavering, and you will be given this true wisdom from above which is 'first pure, then peaceable, gentle, easy to be entreated, full of mercy and good fruits', and all the other glorious things that characterize it.

Let old John Bunyan, in his usual practical, down-to-earth manner, enforce this teaching by a last word: 'He that is down need fear no fall.'

If you are already on the ground, you cannot fall. If you are already humble, you are in a very safe position. It will save you many a bruise, many a hurt, many a trouble.

> *He that is down need fear no fall;*
> *He that is low, no pride;*
> *He that is humble ever shall*
> *Have God to be his guide.*

'Blessed are the meek.' May God give us grace to understand these things and to put them into practice. This is all, as I said at the very beginning, only a part of the original appeal to 'be of the same mind one toward another'. We will never be that if we are proud in our own conceits. May God therefore give us understanding and so fill us with His Holy Spirit that we shall be meek and humble and lowly, and our blessed Lord will not be ashamed to own us as His brethren.

Thirty-three

*

Recompense to no man evil for evil. Provide things honest in the sight of all men. If it be possible, as much as lieth in you, live peaceably with all men.

Romans 12:17-18

When we were making a general analysis of this chapter, I suggested that here, in the seventeenth verse, we come to the final subsection. From verses 9 and 10 onwards the apostle deals with our attitude towards other people and the way in which we conduct ourselves in general. Then from verse 14 onwards he turns to our reaction to what other people do to us, and we have seen how, in verses 14, 15 and 16, he has been laying down some general principles.

But here, at the seventeenth verse, Paul goes beyond that. He is concerned about what we actually do in practice. The principle is that we must bless those who do harm to us and persecute us, we must bless them, and not curse them. We are told: 'Rejoice with them that do rejoice, and weep with them that weep.' But, above all, we are told: 'Be of the same mind one toward another.' The members of the church should always be characterized by a unity of mind and outlook. And, in order for that to happen, Paul says: 'Mind not high things, but condescend to [allow ourselves to be carried along by] men [and things] of low estate.'

Then in the last lecture we considered that final exhortation: 'Be not wise in your own conceits', which is, as we saw, a most important injunction. And we ended on this note: the way to avoid that is to seek the wisdom that comes from above, from

[470]

God. So you see the connection between that and verse 17 of this final subsection: 'Recompense to no man evil for evil.' In other words, we are, as the apostle goes on to show us, to try to 'live peaceably with all men'. So here, again, is the practical carrying out of what he has laid down for us. If we have wisdom from above, we shall have a wisdom that is first 'pure', and then 'peaceable', and you remember how James works that out in his description of this wisdom [see *James* 3:17–18].

So Paul continues on a very practical level. Men and women of true wisdom – not those who only think they are wise – are always peacemakers. But how do these peacemakers conduct themselves? Well, here is the answer, and I would again urge the importance of carrying in our minds the background of verses 1 and 2 and also verses 9 and 10 of this chapter, because these are the principles. It is only Christian men and women who can carry out these injunctions; the natural person cannot. We must always remember that these words are addressed to those who have new life in them, who have 'the mind of Christ', who have 'life from above'. These words are impossible for anybody else to keep.

Here, then, is the first statement: 'Recompense to no man evil for evil.' This is the negative aspect. Here is somebody who does you some wrong, who really has done something to you which is truly evil. What are you to do about it? Paul starts with a negative: Do not pay him back. Do not recompense evil for evil. Here at once we see that we are told not to do what we all instinctively want to do and feel that we must do. The natural instinct is to hit back. From the moment that Adam fell, this kind of spirit came in – enmity, self-seeking, hitting back, self-defensiveness. It is the whole tragedy of the story of humanity in its fallen state. So the apostle, knowing us as he knew himself, saw the wisdom of starting with a negative.

This is a wonderful principle that you will find constantly in the Scriptures. The Bible always starts where we are. It meets us on our own level, as it were, and gradually raises us up. It does not usually start with the positive, but almost invariably with the negative. You are told first of all what you must not do. This is your instinctive response, but do not do it! And for a while you may not be able to get beyond that, but even that is

[471]

something. Do not despise it. If you cannot get beyond that for the time being, well, at any rate, keep with that. We must not ignore this negative. It is a vital bit of teaching, and it cuts right across that which is natural.

Here, of course, the apostle is simply putting before us our Lord's own teaching in the Sermon on the Mount where he talks about turning the other cheek: 'Whosoever shall smite thee on thy right cheek, turn to him the other also' [*Matt.* 6:39]. I will come back to that later because I want to deal with it in a fuller manner. We also find this teaching in 1 Peter 2 where Peter refers to our Lord and to His example: 'Who, when he was reviled, reviled not again; when he suffered, he threatened not; but committed himself to him that judgeth righteously' [*1 Pet.* 2:23]. It is of the very essence of Christian teaching that you do not retaliate, you do not hit back, you do not 'avenge yourself'.

This attitude has often been the cause of much sarcasm on the part of men and women of the world who have not only rejected the Christian message but have ridiculed it. A famous example was Thomas Paine, who lived towards the end of the eighteenth century and was a well-known infidel. Tom Paine, in referring to our Lord's teaching about turning the other cheek, said, 'This is the spirit of a spaniel!' The taunt that Christian teaching produces flabby, sentimental people, lacking in virility, has often been made and is found especially in this twentieth century with the whole cult of self-expression. 'Believe in yourself,' people say. 'Exert yourself. Stand up for yourself!' And because of this, Christian teaching has often been despised.

But is turning the other cheek just weakness? And the answer, of course, is: 'A thousand times, no!' The apostle himself proves that by going on to the positive teaching. So, negatively: 'Recompense to no man evil for evil'; positively: 'Provide things honest in the sight of all men.' What does this positive aspect mean? Unfortunately, the translation in the Authorized Version is, again, not too good and people who have taken it as the true translation have often misunderstood it completely. Some, indeed, have interpreted it as being merely an injunction to us to provide for those who are dependent upon us. Of course, that is a right and a good thing to do, and we are told so elsewhere, but that is not what Paul is saying here. That idea does not fit into this context at all and is more or less meaningless at this particular point. No, the apostle here is giving the positive part of the injunction.

So not only do we not hit back, we are to do the opposite. Now to understand this, we must discuss the meaning of the words. Take the word translated here as 'provide'. 'Provide things honest in the sight of all men.' Now in the Elizabethan era and at the beginning of the seventeenth century, 'provide' was a good translation of the Greek, but over the centuries the word has acquired a different connotation, so we must give an alternative translation. The word used by the apostle means 'take thought in advance', or 'take thought for', or 'take thought in advance concerning things that are good in the sight of all men'. The whole key to understanding Paul's meaning lies in that phrase 'take thought in advance'. In other words, when somebody acts in an evil way towards you, the danger is to react instinctively, automatically. But Paul says: Do not do that. Stop! Before you do anything, think about it. Do not allow yourself to act in an instinctive manner.

Of course, this is absolutely vital and fundamental, and our great claim for the Christian life is that, in the last analysis, it is the only life which is based upon reason. Christian men and women, unlike all others, do not act instinctively; they always know what they are doing and they should always be able to give a reason for what they are doing. They always 'take thought in advance'.

But let us take that further and put it like this: The trouble both with us, as we are by nature, and with those who are not Christians, is that we tend to regard each problem that arises in and of itself, and that is something we must never do. Somebody does me evil, so I just think of that and react in the same way. But I must not do that. I must take this particular action and put it into a larger context. Before I do anything, I must take thought and work out my response in the context of my total position and outlook as a Christian.

There, then, is the meaning of the word 'provide'. Then, 'things honest'. In a way, it just means 'good things' as distinct from bad. So Paul is suggesting that since to retaliate is bad, we must provide good things. Here, again, the word is interesting and important. In the Greek New Testament two words are used to convey the idea of goodness. The first word describes inherent or intrinsic goodness, something which is good in its very nature, in and of itself. But that is not the word that is used here. The word here is a word that is always used to describe exterior or external goodness, goodness which is seen, goodness which expresses itself outwardly. It is the outward expression of an inner, inherent goodness.

Now the apostle deliberately chooses that second word. He is concerned here about a goodness which can be seen, a goodness which is visible and evident. So he says, in effect, 'Instead of retaliating, instead of hitting back, take thought and provide, produce, let there be evidence of, things which are obviously good in the sight of everyone. This, then, is the positive aspect of the injunction. This is how we are to conduct ourselves when somebody does evil to us.

Here is Christian teaching which we find in many parts of the Scriptures. The Authorized Version translates 1 Thessalonians 5:22 as, 'Abstain from all appearance of evil.' It is doubtful whether that is the best translation; it might be better translated as, 'Abstain from all forms of evil.' But there is truth in the other idea also – 'all appearance of evil'. Abstain from anything which may appear to be evil, have nothing to do with it. Or, as the apostle has told us here in this very chapter, 'Abhor that which is evil' – abhor it! – 'cleave to that which is good.'

But a very much better illustration, and a parallel with what we have here, is to be found in 2 Corinthians 8 where the apostle is dealing with the problem of helping the saints in Jerusalem who were suffering, and for whom the Corinthians were collecting money. He tells them that he is sending certain representatives to Corinth, including Titus, and with Titus, '. . . the brother, whose praise is in the gospel throughout all the churches; and not that only, but who was also chosen of the churches to travel with this grace, which is administered by us to the glory of the same Lord, and declaration of your ready mind: avoiding this, that no man should blame us in this abundance which is administered by us: *providing for honest things*, not only in the sight of the Lord, but also in the sight of men' [2 *Cor.* 8:18–21]. The words 'providing for honest things' are the words we have here in Romans 12:17: 'Provide things honest . . .'

But you see the point the apostle is making to the Corinthians. His purpose is, 'That no man should blame us in this abundance which is administered by us.' 'It is very important,' he says in effect, 'that we should administer this fund properly and honestly, and that we should do it in such a way that it will be obvious, not only in the sight of God, but also in the sight of men, that we have not been dishonest, or abused our position, that we have done nothing wrong in any way. Let us administer this fund', he says, 'in a way that will be open and plain to every one.' We are often reminded that it is not enough that justice should be done, but justice must be seen to be done. That is the principle involved here.

So that is the meaning of the words. What, then, is the teaching? What is our exposition of this injunction? We can put it like this: when somebody does evil to you, do not think about yourself only. 'For none of us liveth to himself' [*Rom.* 14:7]. That is a great word of Christian teaching. It is here, too. When this happens to you, think of the effect upon others of what you do in response, not only the effect upon Christians, but upon everyone. The principle is this: whatever may happen to us, we must always react in a responsible manner. We must always show that we realize that what really matters is the opinion other people form of Christianity as they see the way we live. The people outside will judge the gospel, judge the whole of the Christian message, by what they see in us. They say, 'It's very easy to talk; talk is cheap. But you people who make great claims, what are you like in practice?' They are always watching. Therefore we are always to 'Provide things honest in the sight of all men.'

So when somebody does evil to me, I must put it into the whole context of my life as a Christian. I am not to be concerned only about myself. I am to think this through. I must not act on my instincts or on my own feelings. I must not be concerned about my own reputation. What is involved here is the honour of the Christian faith. It is, indeed, the honour of the Lord Jesus Christ; it is the honour of God. At stake is the reputation of the family of heaven to which by the grace of God I now belong. I am a member of the body of Christ and must never act as an independent, isolated person . Now there is a type of person who tends to boast and say, 'I always speak my mind.' Well, you have no right to talk like that. You cannot isolate yourself in that way. If you do, others will suffer and you will bring the whole of the Christian gospel into disrepute. We must always be thinking this matter through and remembering who we are.

Let me give you some parallel examples of this same teaching. In the Sermon on the Mount, our Lord says, 'Let your light so shine before men, that they may see your good works, and glorify your Father which is in heaven' [*Matt.* 5:16]. They are watching you, and they know to whom you belong. You are to live in such a way, He says, that when they see what you are doing they will be amazed and astonished and they will have to admit, 'We cannot understand this. There's only one explanation – these are God's people. They could not do it if they were not.'

Later on in that same chapter, our Lord puts it in greater detail: 'Ye have heard that it hath been said, An eye for an eye, and a tooth for a tooth: but I say unto you, That ye resist not evil: but whosoever shall smite thee on thy right cheek, turn to him the other also. And if any man will sue thee at the law, and take away thy coat, let him have thy cloke also. And whosoever shall compel thee to go a mile, go with him twain. Give to him that asketh thee, and from him that would borrow of thee turn not thou away. Ye have heard that it hath been said, Thou shalt love thy neighbour, and hate thine enemy [the man who does evil to you]. But I say unto you, Love your enemies, bless them that curse you, do good to them that hate you, and pray for them which despitefully use you, and persecute you.'

Why do this? 'That ye may be the children of your Father which is in heaven: for he maketh his sun to rise on the evil and on the good, and sendeth rain on the just and on the unjust. For if ye love them which love you, what reward have ye? do not even the publicans the same? and if ye salute your brethren only, what do ye more than others? do not even the publicans so? Be ye therefore' – and put full weight on that 'therefore'; here is the appeal – 'perfect, even as your Father which is in heaven is perfect' [*Matt.* 5:38–48].

So when somebody acts in an evil way towards you, let all know that you are different from the people of the world. Let them see that there is something about you that differentiates you from all who are not Christians. Let it be evident, let it be obvious, let it be seen that you are different. Let it be seen that you are indeed 'children of your Father which is in heaven'. Or take it as Peter puts it: 'Follow his steps' [*1 Pet.* 2:21]. Do what He did. That is how He behaved when He was here, and you belong to Him, and His mind and His Spirit are in you. 'Follow [then] his steps: who did no sin, neither was guile found in his mouth: who, when he was reviled, reviled not again; when he suffered, he threatened not; but committed himself to him that judgeth righteously [verses 22–23].

There is no better, more direct way of showing that we are the children of God than this. This is what the world cannot do. It is by responding to this injunction and not recompensing to any man evil for the evil that he does – it is in this way that you show that you are born again. You have a different spirit in you. You have a new life in you. You are no longer a natural man or woman. You are, indeed, 'a partaker of the divine nature' [*2 Pet.* 1:4].

People have sometimes suggested, and I tend to agree with them, that the apostle himself may have first been convicted as he observed the death of the martyr Stephen. Paul had been in agreement with the verdict of death passed on Stephen. But as he saw Stephen dying with his face shining, was that the first thing that disturbed him? Was that a part of the meaning of, 'It is hard for thee to kick against the pricks' [*Acts* 9:5]? Was Paul first shaken out of his self-righteousness as a Pharisee when he saw how this man died – gladly, readily, offering that wonderful prayer to his heavenly Father not to lay this thing to their charge, just as his Lord had done on the cross on Calvary's hill? Was it this, I wonder, that disturbed the apostle?

This has often happened in the long history of the Christian church. Many people were first convicted of sinfulness, and first had a glimpse of the new life, when they saw some confessor, some martyr, being put to death in an evil manner simply because of his Christian faith. So that is the great injunction of this seventeenth verse, 'Recompense to no man evil for evil', but, on the contrary, take thought about these things and live in such a good way, showing such excellencies in all your behaviour before all people, that they see that you are essentially different.

Now let us go on to the eighteenth verse: 'If it be possible, as much as lieth in you, live peaceably with all men.' Paul is still on the theme of peace, you see. It started with, 'Be not wise in your own conceits.' Have this other wisdom which is always peaceable, which always maintains unity and concord and amity among God's people. That is the fundamental injunction. We are to be peace-seekers, and, again, we are to be like this 'with all men'.

But you notice that Paul introduces two qualifications, and they are interesting and important. The Christian faith, the Christian teaching, never asks us to do the impossible – never. So when you get a general injunction like this, you will find that it is often accompanied by certain qualifications. Here, the first is: 'If it be possible'.What does this mean? Some have misunderstood it and have said that it means, 'If you can': 'If it is possible for you, live peaceably with all men.'

But that is not what the apostle says at all. To maintain that, is to miss the whole point. That is a subjective view, whereas the statement is objective. What Paul means is this: Live at peace with all men unless they make it quite impossible for you to do so. The doubt is not in you, but in them. There are people who behave in such a way that peace is impossible. Whatever you may feel, whatever you may desire, whatever you may do, they are determined that there shall be no peace; they *will* quarrel. 'If it be possible' – there are circumstances in which it is not. That is the first qualification.

Then the second qualification is the important one: 'as much as lieth in you'. This means: You must never be the cause of trouble. Let strife never be because of you, because of what you are, because of what you do. That is quite plain, is it not? Paul says: If they do not make it impossible as far as you are concerned, as far as it rests in your control and power, 'live peaceably with all men'.

Does this mean peace at any price? This is the question that arises. These various injunctions speak to different members of a congregation. There are some people whose great trouble is the desire to hit back and to 'recompense evil for evil', and very often the great fight of their lives is the struggle not to retaliate, but to 'provide things honest'. At the opposite extreme there is another kind of person, the 'peace at any price' person. Not the militant, aggressive, warlike person, but the phlegmatic, flabby kind of person who says, 'Anything for a quiet life.'

This is a most important matter. Paul cannot mean that we are to put peace before everything else. He cannot mean that at all costs and at any price we must maintain this condition of peace. Why not? We find the answer in that statement made by James in his description of the wisdom that is from above. You notice that he goes out of his way to say this: 'The wisdom that is from above is first pure, then peaceable' [*James* 3:17]. He does not put peace first but purity; he puts truth first. To reverse the order and put peace first is a snare which is so liable to trap the second type of person.

But now let us go on to examine this a little further because I believe that at the present time this injunction is particularly important. There is great confusion in the Christian church on just this very question. The climate of opinion today is one in which people tend to say, 'Let us all come together whatever we may believe. Let us all be one.' This is an example of peace at any price and it is an issue that we must examine in a very practical way. We see it illustrated in Galatians chapter 2. Paul is dealing in that Epistle with the teaching of the Judaizers who said that unless a man was circumcised he was not a true Christian. In the second chapter Paul says, 'But when Peter was come to Antioch, I withstood him to the face, because he was to be blamed. For before that certain came from James, he [Peter] did eat with the Gentiles: but when they were come, he withdrew and separated himself, fearing them which were of the circumcision. And the other Jews dissembled likewise with him; insomuch that Barnabas also was carried away with their dissimulation. But when I saw that they walked not uprightly according to the truth of the gospel, I said unto Peter before them all . . .[verses 11–14]. Paul 'withstood him to the face'.

Now Peter, you see, was carried away here. In a spirit of fear, and in an effort to preserve the peace, he was compromising the truth, and the Apostle Paul dealt with that in a very strong and firm manner. Because this issue was so important, Paul took the risk of entering into a quarrel with Peter. And Paul took a similar risk in the case of Titus. He says earlier in that chapter, 'But neither Titus, who was with me, being a Greek, was compelled to be circumcised' [*Gal.* 2:3]. The apostle would not submit to that.

And this is teaching which we find running right through the New Testament Scriptures. We are not to compromise on matters of truth but are to do as the apostle did there in Antioch. Paul writes to the Ephesians (and there are many similar injunctions): 'Have no fellowship with the unfruitful works of darkness but rather reprove them' [*Eph.* 5:11]. If a man remains an heretic after the first and second admonition, says Paul to Titus, you are to have nothing further to do with him [*Titus* 3:10]. John also tells us that we are not to wish God speed to such a man. 'If there come any unto you, and bring not this doctrine, receive him not into your house, neither bid him God speed' [2 *John* 10].

But it is not quite as simple as it appears to be. People often like to bring up at this point the action of the Apostle Paul on one occasion when he was up in Jerusalem. In Acts 21:20–26 we read that at the request of the leaders of the church in Jerusalem, Paul submitted to Jewish purification rites in order to allay fears that he was teaching the Jews to forsake the law of Moses and no longer circumcise their children. He also agreed to pay the expenses of four Christian Jews who were going through similar rites. In verse 26 we read: 'Then Paul took the men, and the next day purifying himself with them entered into the temple, to signify the accomplishment of the days of purification, until that an offering should be offered for every one of them.'

Now has Paul gone back on his own principles? How do we reconcile that with what he says in Galatians 2 and in so many other places? I would suggest to you that the following principles should govern our actions in this respect. First, we must always contend for the truth and for the faith. We are exhorted to 'earnestly contend for the faith' [*Jude* 3]. We must 'stand in rank', we must be 'set for the defence of the gospel' [*Phil.* 1:17]. We must never shrink from speaking the truth. The truth is to be declared whatever the cost.

Now we all know what it is to feel like Jeremiah. Poor Jeremiah! He said in effect, 'Every time I speak I only get into trouble. All these other prophets are against me. I'll never say another word!' But, you remember, he could not stay quiet. The fire was burning in his bones. But we understand him – all for peace! 'I'm not going to say certain things. I know that if I do they will offend certain members of my church, or they will upset somebody else and I'll be in trouble. I may suffer, my wife and children may suffer, so I'll say nothing. I'll preach an inoffensive message.' You hold back portions of the truth because you know they are going to hurt and offend people.

Now this is always wrong; it is always condemned. We are to preach the truth. It is committed to us. We do not decide – it is given to us: 'The faith which was once [and for ever] delivered unto the saints' [*Jude* 3]. We must never compromise this truth. We have no right to, it is not ours. We are to declare it whatever the consequences. We are not to modify it; we are not to leave portions of it out; we are not to add to it. We are to deliver the truth as it has been delivered to us. On all vital matters of doctrine we are to be as uncompromising as Paul was with Peter.

Secondly, we must be patient and as helpful as we can in all other matters. We are not to be bigoted and unyielding. There are matters in connection with this faith that are not central and all-important. I would explain Acts 21 in those terms. Paul, on the central matter of circumcision, would not yield and never did, and even the authorities in Jerusalem held to that. But there were a number of Jews who had seen the truth of the gospel and had come to believe it, without seeing everything. It takes a long time to work these things out. There are examples of that everywhere in the Scriptures. Peter himself, you remember, had to be given a vision before he would go and preach the gospel to the Gentiles. He was converted, he had had the experience of Pentecost, but he had not worked it out. The old prejudices were there.

And it was the same with these people in Jerusalem. But the apostle saw that it was wise – in a matter that was indifferent, and for the sake of avoiding offence, and to make it easier for these people to work out their faith and to avoid a scandal – to do this thing which he knew was not essential. There are certain absolutes which we simply declare, come what may, but there are other matters which are not vital to salvation and there we must be prepared to be accommodating. We must remember the weaker brother. 'Conscience I say, not thine own, but of the other' [*1 Cor.* 10:29]. It is not merely a matter of what you know to be right; you must see where that other person is. You must try to help, to be patient, and long-suffering. If you can make a slight concession that will not compromise the truth, for the sake of your fellow Christian, do so. That is the principle which seems to me to be quite clear in the New Testament and which we must always remember.

But, thirdly, the way in which we assert and declare the truth is all-important. 'Speaking the truth in love' [*Eph.* 4:15] – that is the teaching, and you must not leave out any one part of that statement. 'Speaking the truth *in love*'. We cannot help it if the truth offends people, but we must always make sure that it is the truth that is offending them and not us. As a preacher, I must be careful that if there is offence, people are offended not by me, not by my person, not by my behaviour, not even by the way in which I speak and preach, but only by the truth itself. If it is the truth that is offending them, I am innocent, I cannot help it. I am anxious to be at peace. I have done my best to be persuasive, to present the truth in as attractive a manner as I can. So if they still resent it and reject it and react quite violently because of it, it is not my responsibility. I must declare the truth always but I must always declare the truth in love.

Fourthly, we must never make a personal issue of these things. We must never contend for ourselves, nor even for our point of view, still less for our own reputation. We must contend for the truth. Nothing has been more regrettable and deplorable in the long history of the church than the way in which men have made doctrines a personal issue, as if people who disagree with them are against them individually. The moment people are influenced and governed by personalities, they have departed from the truth and the spirit of the New Testament teaching. The truth is not a personal matter at all, and we must be very careful to keep the personal element right out of it. 'If it be possible, as much as lieth in you, live peaceably with all men.'

[482]

And finally – and this is the great text that I leave with you to work out for yourselves, this is the final answer to this great matter – 'Let the peace of God rule in your hearts, to the which also ye are called in one body; and be ye thankful' [*Col.* 3:15]. Paul is using the illustration of an umpire in the games, or an arbitrator in a dispute. Let the peace of God act as umpire, or as arbitrator, in your hearts, so that when someone does evil to you, you do not take the decision to act into your own hands. You do not decide. He does. So it does not matter what happens to you, it does not matter what you may suffer, what people may think or say, you should have only one concern: not only that you may enjoy the peace of God yourself, but that that peace may be in the church.

This is a wonderful injunction, a wonderful principle by which to live. Make certain that you always have the peace of God in your heart. Let nothing disturb you. Whatever happens to you or around you, you say, 'I will never do anything to disturb that peace.' You can state the truth, you can state it boldly, you can withstand a Peter to the face, but always do it in such way that you still have the peace of God in your heart. You are not trying to get the better of Peter, you are not trying to put him down and put yourself up. You are concerned about the whole state of the church and the peace of God's people. You want them to enjoy the benefits of salvation to the full. Let the peace of God always act as the umpire in all matters and you will never go astray. May God have mercy upon us all and enable us by His Spirit to implement these great and glorious injunctions.

Thirty-four

*

Dearly beloved, avenge not yourselves, but rather give place unto wrath: for it is written, Vengeance is mine; I will repay, saith the Lord. Therefore if thine enemy hunger, feed him; if he thirst, give him drink: for in so doing thou shalt heap coals of fire on his head.

Romans 12:19–20

We test our love for our Lord, not only by loving one another, but also by our reaction to such words as these in Romans 12. We turn now to verses 19 and 20. Paul has just been telling us that we should never be the cause of trouble or of dispute or any kind of warfare. He says: Do your utmost always to create and preserve an atmosphere of peace. And the nineteenth verse follows on with the injunction: 'Dearly beloved, avenge not yourselves.' Here is one way in which you can help to preserve peace. If somebody harms you, do not avenge yourself, for by not avenging yourself you are helping to preserve this peace of which he has just been speaking.

Now you notice that the apostle introduces these words in a very special way with a very special appeal – 'Dearly beloved'. He is concerned about these Christians in Rome and their welfare, and he knows that if you indulge in a spirit of revenge, whatever you may do to the other person, you will make yourself very miserable. So he tells them not to be vengeful. He pleads with them. He is anxious for them, and, of course, he is also concerned about the good name and welfare of the church. There is nothing worse than a quarrelling church, a church in dispute. History, unfortunately, demonstrates far too clearly that nothing does greater harm. So the apostle is moved and appeals to his readers to pay very special attention to this matter.

I think Paul also writes as he does because he knows the subtlety of the devil. He knows that on a point like this, as we have seen on previous points, this appeal, this standard, is so contrary to human nature that it is perhaps the greatest demand that is ever made of us. How much easier it is to preach than to carry out this exhortation! How much easier it is to give up everything and go right off to the heart of Africa or some remote island in the Pacific than to carry out this particular injunction. You are looking here at the Christian life and Christian living at its very acme, and the apostle, therefore, begins this urgent appeal with the words, 'Dearly beloved'. He says, I am not only telling you, I am pleading with you.

Now as usual Paul puts his teaching both negatively and positively, and always the negative first. 'Avenge not yourselves.' Somebody does wrong to you, does harm to you, and, of course, your immediate instinct is to hit back, to avenge yourself, to get your own back. That is human nature – you see it in children, you see it everywhere. We all have it in us, we all know it perfectly well. But you remember how we worked out the meaning of that expression, 'Provide things honest'? It means, think before you act; do not act impulsively. Christian men and women think; they pause. As Christians, they no longer act immediately, as 'natural' people. Animals live instinctively, and, because of the Fall and sin, human beings behave like animals. So they immediately hit back and avenge themselves. But the apostle says: Do not do it, you are Christians.

Now I want to say again, as I have been saying about some of these previous injunctions, it is good to attain the negative. If everybody in the church had always got as far as this negative, church history would have been very different. Do not despise the negative; it is very important. It is the first step, and if you cannot get beyond the negative, at least get as far as that. Do not hit back.

But, of course, the apostle does not leave it there – he goes on to the positive statement: 'but rather give place unto wrath'. Now the word 'rather', which is in italics in the Authorized

Version, is not in the original, but has been supplied by the translators. It is a good addition as it helps us to understand Paul's words. It helps to bring out the contrast. Instead of taking vengeance, go to the other extreme. But the contrast, of course, is implicit in Paul's words so I would justify the inclusion of the 'rather'.

So if we are not to avenge ourselves, what are we to do? Well, says Paul, we must 'give place unto wrath'. What does this mean? Now this expression 'give place' is most interesting. There are those who have thought that instead of avenging yourself in a state of rage, it means you let things pass, you cool down. They think it means that you should not act immediately, but give yourself a chance. You should give place unto wrath by giving it time. Later you will not be so excited and passionate.

Others have suggested that it means that you should let your adversary vent his rage upon you. Here is a person in a temper doing something to you which is quite unjustifiable, and they think the apostle is saying: Don't avenge yourself, don't hit back, but just allow him to continue. Just do nothing. Let him have his fling, as it were. Let him pour out his wrath upon you. Let him do anything he likes.

But we cannot for a moment accept those explanations. As we have said, whenever you are confronted by a statement like this, it is always good to look up similar usages of the word or phrase that you are considering. And you will find that elsewhere there are several interesting examples of the use of the Greek words translated 'give place'. Now one is in Luke's Gospel, in chapter 14 and verse 9. In verse 8 we read this instruction from our Lord: 'When thou art bidden of any man to a wedding, sit not down in the highest room; lest a more honourable man than thou be bidden of him.' And our Lord continues in verse 9: 'And he that bade thee and him come and say to thee, *Give this man place*; and thou begin with shame to take the lowest room.' You must get up out of the seat that you have taken at the top of the table, and make room for this other man who is more honoured than you.

Another example is found in Ephesians 4:27 where Paul gives an injunction: 'Neither *give place* to the devil' – do not give him room; do not give him any opportunity. It is exactly the same phrase. So it means 'make room for', 'give scope, or free scope, to', or, if you like, 'leave it to' the thing or person in question.

Then we come to the word 'wrath' – 'Give place unto wrath'. Here, unfortunately, the Authorized Version has left out a word which really is the key to understanding this statement. It should be translated like this: 'Dearly beloved, avenge not yourselves, but rather make room for *the wrath.*' And the moment you understand that, I think the explanation becomes perfectly plain and clear. Paul is talking about the wrath of God! Do not avenge yourselves, but make room for the wrath of God. Do not indulge your wrath, but like the man in the feast who has to get up and go somewhere else, make room for, give free scope to, make allowance for, prepare the way for, leave it to, the wrath of God.

That this must be the true meaning is established by the next words, for Paul immediately goes on to say, 'for it is written'. 'Do not avenge yourselves, but make room for the wrath of God' – why? – 'for [because] it is written, Vengeance is mine; I will repay, saith the Lord.' That is a quotation from Deuteronomy 32:35, and it means: 'Vengeance is mine – not yours.' The emphasis there is upon the word 'mine'. So the apostle brings in his quotation, as was his custom, to substantiate an argument. He says: Do not do that, because vengeance really does not belong to you; it belongs to God.

The next word, 'repay', is simple. It means 'requite', or 'give back' or 'pay back'. This is our Lord's teaching in the Sermon on the Mount. At the beginning of Matthew 7 we read this: 'Judge not, that ye be not judged. For with what judgment ye judge, ye shall be judged: and with what measure ye mete, it shall be measured to you again.' That is repayment. It is a kind of 'paying back in your own coin'. Another way of putting it is to say, 'Whatsoever a man soweth, that shall he also reap' [*Gal.* 6:7].

So, then, having understood the meaning of the various phrases and expressions, we are now in a position to consider the teaching. What is the apostle telling us? Let me put it like this: We must never seek personal vengeance – never. Why not? Because that is God's work and not ours. That is God's prerogative, that is God's business.

Now we come here to a very important principle. The apostle does not merely tell us these things. The explanation is implicit in his teaching. Why is this God's work and not ours? The answer is, because we are sinful; because we are all sinners; because we are unjust as the result of sin. Our judgment is inadequate. We are unfit for such a task, and especially, of course, when it happens to be our own case. We all know this. We are very bad judges of ourselves and of our own position and conditions, and of what happens to us. As the result of sin, we are all self-centred, always on the defensive, always shielding ourselves. We see a fault in another person and denounce it, but will always explain away the same sin in ourselves: 'Accusing or else excusing one another', as Paul has already said in Romans 2:15. So we are not fit to exercise judgment. We do not see the whole position. We are biased judges, incapable of arriving at a true judgment, and it is very dangerous for us to take the punishment into our own hands. No, no, God is the Judge of the whole earth, and He alone is the Judge. God's judgment, God's wrath, is always holy; it is always just; it is always righteous and it is always controlled.

So this word 'wrath' is used here with respect to God. Paul says, 'But rather give place to the wrath of God.' We have already considered this expression 'the wrath of God' in Romans 1:18, where the apostle says, 'For the wrath of God is revealed from heaven against all ungodliness and unrighteousness of men, who hold [down] the truth in unrighteousness.' And when we were dealing with that verse we emphasized the point that we must never think of the wrath of God as we think of the wrath of a human being. Our wrath is passionate and always lacking an element of control, but God's wrath is always judicial. It is never vindictive. It is never a passion that carries Him away, as it were. His wrath and His judgments are always just, always righteous and always holy, and therefore, says the apostle, because of our own condition and inadequacy, and because God is what He is, you must not repay, but leave it entirely to Him. Stand aside, as it were, and allow God to work.

But it is very important that we should obey this injunction in the right spirit, and this is where the subtlety comes in. The devil can appear as an angel of light, he can quote Scripture, and he comes to men and women when they are prepared to pay heed to this injunction. 'Yes, that's right,' he tells them, 'you leave it to God. God will give it him, and in a way that you cannot!' So you refrain from avenging yourself in order that the one who has offended you may receive a greater punishment than you could ever have given him. And the moment you say that, you have denied the entire spirit of this injunction.

This is very important and the rest of the exposition will make it still more plain. I am just emphasizing it at this particular point. We must never desire the harm of the person who has offended us – never! So you do not leave someone to God in order that he may receive a greater punishment. Quite the reverse. You leave him to God because you recognize that God alone is capable of giving a just judgment. So Paul is saying: Leave him entirely in God's hands; leave God to deal with him.

Our Lord Himself, you remember, acted entirely on this principle. Peter tells, you remember, that 'when he was reviled, [he] reviled not again; when he suffered, he threatened not' – what did He do? – 'but committed himself to him that judgeth righteously' [*1 Pet.* 2:21–23]. That is it. Our Lord left judgment entirely to God. He did not defend Himself. He did not avenge Himself. He just committed Himself and the whole case 'to him that judgeth righteously'. So when we make room for the vengeance and the wrath of God, it must always be done in the right spirit.

But if I left it at that, my teaching would be misleading. We must add a qualification at this point, and I want to show that this, too, is most important, particularly, perhaps, at a time like this. Many people have taken this injunction at the point at which I have just left it, and have gone no further. They have argued or deduced that the apostle is teaching a kind of flabby passivity, that we are just to do nothing at all. Furthermore, they press it so far as to deny any doctrine of punishment or retribution. They heartily dislike the whole teaching concerning the wrath of God. God, they say, is love, and that means that there is no punishment, no vengeance, no wrath. Believing they are reflecting the 'spirit of Christianity', they do not hesitate to take whole sections out of the Scriptures, particularly this verse in Romans.

Many times I have read, and I have heard people say, that they do not believe in a God who can say, 'Vengeance is mine.' The idea that there can be wrath in God is, to them, a contradiction of the entire spirit of Christianity. They would have us say, therefore, that we just bear everything, in all realms and in all respects, and that we should not be interested at all in the notion of punishment and retribution. Now it is important that we should realize how wrong that teaching is.

So let me put it to you in a number of propositions. First, as we have seen, you must never be concerned about personal wrongs or seek personal vengeance. That is an absolute. Never seek personal vengeance, no matter what has been done to you. 'Avenge not yourselves.'   .

And we must go further. We must, secondly, never even desire an enemy personal harm. This is the essence of Christian teaching. We have already considered a number of passages on this subject, including verses from the Sermon on the Mount. We have seen that Jesus said, 'Love your enemies' [*Matt.* 5:44]. Now you cannot love your enemy and desire him harm at the same time. You may have been treated abominably, it does not matter. 'Avenge not yourself'– not in action and not even in desire.

Now that is perfectly clear. Nevertheless, thirdly, though I am never to avenge a personal wrong or desire my enemy any harm, I am at the same time to be concerned about truth, about righteousness, about justice, and about the glory of God. This principle is important, not only in a practical way, but also from the standpoint of your handling of the Scriptures.

Fourthly, it is not only right, it is also our duty to desire that God's reign should be vindicated and extended, and that God's glory should be manifested over the whole earth.

And, fifthly, it is right that we should be comforted by the fact that God reigns supreme, and that He will ultimately vindicate Himself, and His reign and His rule over all, in the punishment of all those who are His enemies.

Now notice how I am putting it. I am saying that it is right that we should be comforted by the thought that in an evil age like this, when God's enemies are in the ascendant and rampant and seem to have everything under their control, it is right and good that as God's people, we should be comforted in the knowledge that 'the Lord reigneth' in spite of everything, and that He will finally vindicate Himself and His glory. And a part of this vindication will be the punishment of the wicked, the enemies of God. The distinction, you see, is between personal wrongs and wrongs to the name and the glory of God. I am not to avenge personal wrongs, but if I do not have a zeal for the name and the glory of God, then I am not behaving in a truly Christian manner.

Take, for instance, the imprisonment of the Apostle Paul and Silas at Philippi. Paul and Silas had been arrested quite unjustly – it was a scandalous action – and had been thrown into the innermost prison where their feet had been made fast in the stocks. You remember the story of how they were freed as the result of an earthquake and spent the night in the jailer's home. But then we read: 'When it was day, the magistrates sent the serjeants, saying, Let those men go. And the keeper of the prison told this saying to Paul, The magistrates have sent to let you go: now therefore depart, and go in peace.'

Then: 'But Paul said unto them, They have beaten us openly uncondemned, being Romans, and have cast us into prison; and now do they thrust us out privily? nay verily; but let them come themselves and fetch us out. And the serjeants told these words unto the magistrates: and they feared, when they heard that they were Romans. And they came and besought them, and brought them out, and desired them to depart out of the city' [*Acts* 16:35-39].

So you see how the apostle drew a distinction there. He was not avenging himself, he was not concerned about the personal wrong, the personal iniquity to which he had been subjected. But all law ultimately derives from God and Paul was concerned about the dignity and the honour of law and of justice. Here were men who were supposed to be administering justice and they were being most unjust. These magistrates were violating the law that they were meant to uphold and the apostle objected to that. He reprimanded them and showed them exactly how they should be behaving. Paul refused to leave the city like that and the magistrates had to come down and carry out the law.

We see another example of this principle when Paul was

arrested and taken before the Sanhedrin. We read: 'And Paul, earnestly beholding the council, said, Men and brethren, I have lived in all good conscience before God unto this day. And the high priest Ananias commanded them that stood by him to smite him on the mouth. Then said Paul unto him, God shall smite thee, thou whited wall: for sittest thou to judge me after the law, and commandest me to be smitten contrary to the law?' [*Acts* 23:1–3].

Paul was objecting to the injustice of being struck on the mouth by a man was who supposed to be administering law. Incidentally, the apostle had not been aware that this man was the high priest – not that that matters. What does matter is that here was a man who was abusing his position, and the apostle, not to vindicate himself or to get vengeance for himself, but in the interests of truth, of law, of justice, and righteousness, reprimanded this man and asserted the great principle that the law should not be broken.

But there is another still more interesting example which has always fascinated me. The Apostle Paul wrote to Timothy: 'Alexander the coppersmith did me much evil: the Lord reward him according to his works: of whom be thou ware also; for he hath greatly withstood our words. At my first answer no man stood with me, but all men forsook me: I pray God that it may not be laid to their charge' [*2 Tim.* 4:14–16]. Notice the different way in which the apostle reacts to Alexander the coppersmith and to his fellow Christians who all forsook him at his first trial. Here was the apostle up on trial for the first time, and they all suddenly disappeared, leaving him to stand alone. Christian people have tended to do that throughout the centuries and are still doing so. Such people are fair-weather friends who are not there when you need them, perhaps, most of all.

But the apostle did not react to the friends who had deserted him as he did to Alexander the coppersmith who was militantly opposing and hindering the truth. Of him, the apostle says, 'The Lord reward him.' This man had done Paul grievous harm – 'much evil' – and Paul knew that he was ready to harm Timothy and the others. But Paul did not try to get his own back on Alexander. He did not avenge himself. He did the very thing he is telling the Romans to do. He stood aside and said,

'The Lord reward him according to his works.' He was leaving it to God to judge the case and to decide the punishment.

As for the weak Christians who had deserted Paul, there was nothing really harmful in them, they were just rather feeble. 'At my first answer', said Paul, 'no man stood with me, but all men forsook me' – just cowards, weaklings. And the apostle's attitude to them was very different from his attitude to Alexander. He says, 'I pray God that it may not be laid to their charge.' He pleaded for them with God. He did not just leave them in the hands of God, but asked God to have pity and to have mercy upon them, to remember that they were weak. He interceded on their behalf.

Now why have I felt it necessary to show that the apostle's injunction here in Romans 12:19 does not inculcate a flabby kind of passivity and is not some vague talk about the love of God which does not believe in truth, righteousness and justice, discipline, punishment, retribution and the wrath and vengeance of God – why am I emphasizing this point?

My first reason is that when we understand this doctrine correctly, we understand the so-called 'imprecatory' or 'vindictive' psalms. There are many psalms where the psalmist prays for terrible punishment to come upon unbelievers. Take, for instance, Psalm 69 where we read this: 'Let their table become a snare before them: and that which should have been for their welfare, let it become a trap. Let their eyes be darkened, that they see not; and make their loins continually to shake' [verses 22–23]. Or the last statement in Psalm 104: ' Let the sinners be consumed out of the earth.'

People have often stumbled at these psalms, but there is no difficulty if you approach them along the lines that I have just been putting before you. In all those psalms, the psalmists are not writing from a personal standpoint. They are not writing from a desire for personal vengeance. No, no; they are writing entirely from the standpoint of the honour and glory of God. They are grieved as they see these people flouting God's laws, trampling upon the sanctities, speaking in arrogance. It is zeal for the Lord and the name of the Lord that makes the psalmists write as they do. That is the real and sole explanation of the imprecatory psalms. If you just draw the distinction between the writers and the glory of God, His justice and righteousness, you will have no difficulty. Remember, of course, that these men were men of their own time. Life was like that then and they expressed themselves in everyday images. But it is the principle that is important.

Now I have to admit that some teachers and preachers in the past have, it seems to me, gone much too far in stating the principle of God's retribution. There were old preachers two or three centuries ago who used to say that the righteous should greatly rejoice at the thought of seeing the torments of the ungodly in hell. That is carrying the principle too far. I repeat that we should never be concerned about personal vengeance but about the glory of God and His holy name; and if we are not concerned about that, there is something wrong with us. If you do not grasp this principle, you cannot really understand the Old Testament, and if you do not understand the Old Testament, you will not understand the New Testament, because they go together.

The second point is that this teaching is also the answer to pacifism. You are familiar with the teaching of the pacifists. Pacifism teaches that at all times and under all circumstances it is wrong to kill, and those who fought in the Second World War or in any war, were sinning grievously. When you ask pacifists for their reasons, their reply is that the commandment says, 'Thou shalt not kill.' They also say that our Lord said in the Sermon on the Mount, 'Whosoever shall smite thee on thy right cheek, turn to him the other also' [*Matt.* 5:39]. 'So,' they say, 'the explanation is quite simple.'

But it is not as simple as that, is it? That is an example of what I call extracting statements out of the Scriptures, instead of comparing scripture with scripture. God said, 'Thou shalt not kill', but the same God commanded the children of Israel to exterminate the Amalekites. We also read that King Saul actually got into terrible trouble because he had not fully carried out that commandment, but had spared some of the enemy. He was punished for not killing every one.

What, then, is the explanation? Again, it lies in the difference between the personal and the general. The commands not to kill and to turn the other cheek are addressed to the individual. They are not spoken to the state, nor to society at large, and I prove that by showing that the God who says,

[494]

'Thou shalt not kill', commands the Israelite nation to kill certain enemies who are His enemies as well as theirs.

And when we come to the thirteenth chapter of Romans, we shall find that the teaching in verse 4 about the magistrate not bearing the sword in vain maintains precisely the same principle. There is a difference between my seeking personal vengeance and my believing that it is my duty to uphold the law of God. And the law of God is expressed in the law of the land, as Paul wrote in Romans 13:1: 'The powers that be are ordained of God.' So we are not to misinterpret this teaching concerning vengeance as meaning that there should never be any vengeance at all. There should, but not ours. It is to be God's vengeance.

Then there is one other matter. You will often find that people say, 'That teaching about the vengeance and the wrath of God and so on, that's Old Testament teaching, not New Testament.' And you may have read in the press that people preaching from Christian pulpits have said that they have no use for the God of the Old Testament, but they believe in 'the God of Jesus'. Now there is nothing new about this teaching – it started in the first centuries of this Christian era – but it has been very popular in the present age because it seems so loving and wonderful

So what do we say in response? The first answer is that it is always wrong to create division or antagonism between the two Testaments. God is the same in the Old Testament and in the New. But if you want the best argument of all, it is that our Lord accepted the teaching of the Old Testament in its entirety. So you are not pitting yourself against the Old Testament, but against the Son of God.

But, further, if these people took the trouble to read the Old Testament, they would find that these Old Testament characters, whom they despise so much, were able to rise to very great heights indeed. Look at a man like Job who suffered so much from his false friends, yet look at his magnanimity; look at his readiness to forgive everything.

Or take the case of David. David, perhaps, was a man we understand still better, a man of strong feelings and passions. But read the story of David. It is amazing. Look at the way in which he was maltreated by Saul, the first king of Israel, who hounded him, as David points out, as if he were chasing a flea. Look at the indignities which Saul heaped upon him. The way David reacted to that is almost incredible. Many times he could have killed Saul but he would not. He said to Saul, 'The Lord judge between me and thee, and the Lord avenge me of thee: but mine hand shall not be upon thee' [*1 Sam.* 24:12]. Indeed, when David was told about the death of Saul and his son Jonathan, David's heart was broken. Now you would have thought that David would have rejoiced in view of the fact that Saul had insulted him in every conceivable manner, but, on the contrary, he was overwhelmed with grief. Read the first chapter of the Second Book of Samuel and his lament over the death of Saul.

Then take, too, the story of David's handling of that terrible man Nabal who deserved vengeance if ever a man deserved it. David listened to the pleadings of Abigail and he left judgment to God. And God dealt with Nabal and brought about his death in His own way. Now David was a man like ourselves who was ready to avenge himself; but he did not. And, to me, one of the most glorious statements in the whole of the Old Testament is to be found in the Second Book of Samuel, in verse 10 of chapter 4. When some of David's foolish men, who had killed a good man out of jealousy, came and reported it to David, they thought that he would rejoice. But this is what David said: 'When one told me, saying, Behold, Saul is dead, thinking to have brought good tidings, I took hold of him, and slew him in Ziklag, who thought that I would have given him a reward for his tidings.' No, no, says David. The man did not understand me, he did not know me. He came rushing to me and thought I was going to reward him when he told me what he had done to Saul, but I was not pleased.

So when you read the Old Testament, you find that these men were able to rise to the height of this injunction that we are considering together in Romans 12. But apart from that, the New Testament itself is full of this teaching about the wrath of God and the vengeance of God upon His enemies. If you read our Lord's parable of the tares in Matthew 13, you will see it very plainly. The master told the servants not to pull up the tares, but to leave them until the harvest – that is, the judgment of God. Read again the story of the rich man and

Lazarus. And read the parable of the sheep and the goats where you find our Lord, in the plainest language possible, talking about God's final retribution upon men and women who have disobeyed Him. Let me quote the words to you because they are so often forgotten today that we cannot afford to take the risk of assuming they are known.

'Then shall he say also unto them on the left hand, Depart from me, ye cursed, into everlasting fire, prepared for the devil and his angels: for I was an hungred, and ye gave me no meat . . . Then shall he answer them, saying, Verily I say unto you, Inasmuch as ye did it not to one of the least of these, ye did it not to me. And these shall go away into everlasting punishment: but the righteous into life eternal' [*Matt.* 25:41-42, 45-46].

So those who omit God's judgment are not only quarrelling with the Old Testament, they are quarrelling with the Incarnation of God's love. We have had this teaching already many times over in this great Epistle to the Romans. It is found, too, in an unmistakable manner in 2 Thessalonians: 'Seeing it is a righteous thing with God to recompense tribulation to them that trouble you; and to you who are troubled rest with us, when the Lord Jesus shall be revealed from heaven with his mighty angels, in flaming fire taking vengeance on them that know not God, and that obey not the gospel of our Lord Jesus Christ' [*2 Thess.* 1:6-8].

And what is the Book of Revelation but a great exposition of the wrath and the vengeance of God upon His enemies, upon those who have rejected His gospel, spurned the voice divine, and refused His great offer of love in His only begotten Son, the One crucified? In Revelation we are given a vision of the saintly beings under the altar, and there they are crying out, 'How long, O Lord?' And if you and I do not have a zeal for the name of God, if we do not have a zeal for the righteous judgment of God, our Christianity is seriously defective. You must never feel a desire for personal vengeance, but if you do not look for the day when God will vindicate Himself, and when all the scoffers and the sinners of today and of all ages will receive their just recompense, then your understanding of the Scripture is at fault, and your worship of God is seriously defective. Paul does not teach some flabby passivity or sentimentality, but inculcates the great principle of the difference between personal vengeance and the vengeance of Almighty God. May He by His Spirit give us wisdom in these matters.

Thirty-five

*

Therefore if thine enemy hunger, feed him; if he thirst, give him drink: for in so doing thou shalt heap coals of fire on his head. Be not overcome of evil, but overcome evil with good.

Romans 12:20–21

We have been considering how, in the nineteenth verse, the emphasis is mainly negative. We are not to avenge ourselves. But the apostle does not stop at that. He never, as we have seen, stops at a negative, though he generally starts with it, and it is always important. But Paul then goes on to the positive statement, and this is the glory of the Christian position. The Christian is not just a negative sort of person. It is a complete travesty of the gospel to suggest that the Christian is merely someone who does not do certain things. Christians are very positive people. Of course, there are things they do not do, but what really reveals them to be Christians is the positive element in their whole outlook and behaviour.

So the apostle goes on to the positive principle, and here it is at the beginning of this twentieth verse: 'Therefore if thine enemy hunger, feed him; if he thirst, give him drink.' Not only are we not to do our enemy any harm, we are to do him positive good. This is essential Christianity. And this is where we so often find the difference between Christian teaching and the morality of the world even at its best and highest.

This injunction proves, I think beyond any doubt, the correctness of our interpretation of the nineteenth verse in which we said that you do not refrain from vengeance simply in the hope that God's punishment will be severer than yours.

[499]

We dismissed that and said it was quite wrong because it is a contradiction of the spirit of the apostle's teaching. And now we have absolute proof of that: 'Therefore,' Paul says in effect, 'do not retaliate but leave judgment to God because God alone is just. He sees the whole, and will judge properly and rightly. Leave it to God because you must not desire harm to come to your enemy. Go on, therefore, and do good to him in this matter of food and drink, or any other need he may have.'

Now here Paul is quoting from Proverbs 25:21–22. So we find a further reason for describing as folly the pitting of the New Testament against the Old. Here, again, the apostle is establishing positive New Testament teaching by a quotation from the Old. As we saw, Christian people who dismiss the Old Testament are showing not only a failure to understand the Old Testament, but also a failure to understand the New. It is astonishing to see how frequently the apostle clinches an argument, or gives a final demonstration of a point he is making, by an apposite quotation from the Old Testament.

Generosity to our enemies is taught in the Book of Proverbs by the wise man. Let me emphasize that this is not confined to food and drink – they are illustrations. Do good to your enemy in any way you can, whenever an opportunity presents itself. Take advantage of the opportunity to do him good. Though he is your enemy, this is the way in which you are to treat him.

Then we come on to the statement in this second half of this twentieth verse, 'for in so doing thou shalt heap coals of fire on his head'. This is a part of the quotation from Proverbs, and, again, it has caused considerable discussion among the commentators. Some people say that it means: 'Do good in this way in order that you may make the punishment of your enemy all the greater if he doesn't respond to what you do for him.' You deliberately give him food and drink, knowing that he will not respond, in order that the punishment God gives him will be yet greater. Your motive, in other words, is the punishment of your enemy and the increase of that punishment.

But of course, we have to reject that interpretation absolutely, not merely in order to be consistent with our interpretation of the nineteenth verse and the previous verses, but also because it is entirely out of line with the whole spirit of the apostle's teaching here. And not only that, if you read the second half of Proverbs 25:22 you will find that it ends like this, 'and the Lord shall reward thee'. If you do give your enemy food and drink, 'Thou shalt heap coals of fire upon his head, and the Lord shall reward thee.' So it is something that is well-pleasing in God's sight, and a revengeful spirit, as we have already seen, is never well-pleasing to Him. So that cannot be the explanation.

It does seem to me, as indeed to the majority of commentators, that there can be only one explanation of this statement. The idea of coals of fire on someone's head obviously carries with it the suggestion of pain and of acute discomfort. Yes, but this is a metaphorical statement, and it does not mean actually putting coals of fire on the head. Nor does it mean calling down thunder and lightning from heaven, or anything like that. What it means, surely, is that you will cause pain, not physical pain, but the pain of shame, and the pain of remorse. It means that as the result of your kindness, your enemy will have an intense feeling of shame and of remorse. He will know a kind of burning, a keen anguish in his mind, heart and spirit and your hope is that he will feel this to such an extent that it will lead to self-examination and repentance. You will shock him and he will begin to reconsider what he has done to you, and then will see how terribly wrong it is. And this will lead to repentance.

Now that is surely the only meaning that these words can carry. In this metaphorical sense, you heap coals of fire on his head. He will probably be more miserable at that point than he has ever been before, certainly much more miserable than he was when he acted in an unkind and in an inimical manner. Remorse, repentance, can be extremely painful, and by treating your enemy in this truly Christian way you cause him to pass through this trial. He will condemn himself and not know what to do with himself.

This is something, of course, which cannot be guaranteed. Your enemy may not respond, but that is not your responsibility. Your task is to do everything you can to bring him to that condition. You must aim at that. And, thank God, this kind of behaviour on the part of Christians has often led to this most desirable result. There have been many, many examples in the history of the church of people even being converted as a result of Christian people putting into practice the apostle's injunction here. It has been used of God to lead to the salvation of those who have been most opposed to the gospel. But whatever the result, this is what we are told to do.

That, then, leads us to the twenty-first verse, the last verse in the chapter. Now this verse not only sums up the immediately preceding argument, it sums up the argument of the entire section. It is again very characteristic of the apostle's method. He generally does this, as we have been seeing so often in working our way through this Epistle. He works out the details of his argument, then crowns it all by a great statement in which he seems to put the whole case in a nutshell. And this verse, I feel, is an example of that. It is a most important statement: 'Be not overcome of evil, but overcome evil with good.'

This is one of these pregnant statements which puts before us the principle of the Christian life in its very essence. Notice that the apostle puts this teaching negatively and positively, and, as usual, gives the negative before the positive: 'Be not overcome of evil.' Do not allow evil to defeat you. The principle that Paul gives us here seems to me to be absolutely essential in a true living of the Christian life and I have tried to divide it up into a number of propositions. Here is the first. We must always put into the first position what happens to us as souls, not just as human beings. Everything in the life of the Christian must be subordinated to the interests of the soul. Here, of course, is something which is absolutely basic. It is the dividing line between the Christian and the non-Christian. The non-Christian does not think of himself as a soul, but as a member of society, as a member of a nation, a member of a family, or something like that. But the Christian does not and should not.

Why do wars happen?[1] It is because people think instinctively in terms of nations – 'My country right or wrong'. That is the way the natural person thinks – my country or my family. Other countries or other families may be wrong, but

[1] This lecture was given on 11 November, Armistice Day, when those who have died in war are remembered

yours, oh, no! That is why there are wars and that is why there is an Armistice Day. But the Christian does not think like that. The Christian thinks essentially, primarily, always, as a soul.

Our Lord laid down this principle once and for ever: 'For what is a man profited, if he shall gain the whole world, and lose his own soul? or what shall a man give in exchange for his soul?' [*Matt.* 16:26]. The enemy insults you or takes something from you or harms you, and as a natural human being you react. But the Christian must not do that. The Christian always remembers that it is the soul that matters. You may have gained the whole world, but it is useless if you have lost your soul. And though the world may rob you of all your possessions, if you have your soul intact, as it were, then they have not taken much from you. They have only taken some trappings that in any case you will lose sooner or later, when you come to die. This is the Christian way of thinking. And the moment you start along that line, you are on the road to victory. But it is only the Christian who can do this.

But then, secondly, it is not things in and of themselves that are important. What is important is the way in which they affect us as souls. The trouble with all of us by nature, the trouble with the natural man and woman, is that they only see the action of their enemy as an action *per se*. They say, 'He has insulted me! He has taken this from me!' They are interested in the particular action. But that is not true of the Christian. What interests Christian men and women is the effect of the action upon their souls, its spiritual effect.

Let me put it still more plainly. The Christian is not interested in the actions of another person so much as in the power behind the actions. This is the difference between the non-Christian and the Christian. The non-Christian simply sees an offensive person, and takes revenge. But the Christian sees the evil principle underlying the action. Christians see the devil prompting the action. It is as Paul puts it in Ephesians 6:12: 'We wrestle not against flesh and blood' – neither in ourselves, nor in other people – 'but against principalities, against powers, against the rulers of the darkness of this world, against spiritual wickedness in high places.'

In other words, the apostle does not say here in Romans, 'Be not overcome of men', but, 'Be not overcome of evil'. He does not say, 'Do not let men overcome you', but, 'Do not let evil overcome you', though he is talking about the actions of people. That is why I say that this is the principle – that Christians never take a superficial view. They do not just take events in and of themselves. They see what is behind what happens. They see the hand of the enemy, the hand of the devil, the hand of evil. That is what concerns them.

This is a most important principle for us to grasp in connection with the whole of the Christian life. I have often put it like this: All of us tend to be far too interested in particular sins, instead of being interested in *sin*. That is part of this danger of looking at things in and of themselves. People come and talk to me about a particular sin, and they always give me the impression – and it is a correct impression – that they really think that if only they could stop doing this, then they would be perfect. And what I have to tell them is this: Even though you get a complete victory over that sin, you will still not be perfect; you will still have to fight evil; you will still have to fight sin; you will still have to fight the devil. This is but one manifestation, a particular symptom. But it is not the symptoms that matter, it is the disease. It is the principle of evil that matters.

What, then, is the relevance of all that to this passage? It is this. Paul is saying that if you take vengeance you are allowing evil and sin to overcome you, to have a victory over you. 'Dearly beloved, avenge not yourselves.' If you allow what this other person does to you to get you into a temper, then you have been defeated, not by the person but by the devil. You are committing sin, for anger, and temper, and passion are always wrong. You should not be in that condition, whatever may have happened to you. Whatever the other person may have done to me, if I am in a temper and a rage, then the devil has got me. That is the important thing, much more important than the particular tool that the devil has used.

Let me put it like this: as Christian people we should not be disturbed in spirit; we should not be agitated. The Christian should never lose the peace of God and the peace of Christ. You remember that two lectures ago we ended on that note: 'And let the peace of God rule [act as umpire] in your hearts' [*Col.* 3:15]. Never lose it! We should never lose this central,

essential peace that we are given in our great and glorious
salvation. For a Christian to be agitated is always wrong; it is
sin. Whatever somebody else has done to you, the devil has got
you at that point if you have lost this glorious peace of spirit.
'And the peace of God, which passeth all understanding, shall
keep your hearts and minds through Christ Jesus' [*Phil.* 4:7].
The moment you lose control of yourself you have been
overcome by evil. It does not matter how great the provoca-
tion, it does not matter what somebody may have done, if you
have lost control and are saying or thinking or trying to do
wrong, then the devil has won, and you are defeated.

Or take it in the form of pride. If your pride is hurt, and all
your natural human nature rises up at once in self-defence and
a desire for revenge, it is again a defeat by the devil. We have
failed if, as Christian people, we are suffering from hurt pride;
that is always sinful. That is how men and women naturally
behave and we are to be essentially different.

Now our Lord Himself brings this out so clearly. It is not
enough if you do not actually retaliate. You remember how our
Lord puts it in the Sermon on the Mount: 'Ye have heard that it
was said by them of old time, Thou shalt not kill; and
whosoever shall kill shall be in danger of the judgment: but
I say unto you, That whosoever is angry with his brother
without a cause shall be in danger of the judgment: and
whosoever shall say to his brother, Raca, shall be in danger of
the council: but whosoever shall say, Thou fool, shall be in
danger of hell fire' [*Matt.* 5:21–22]. Hard thoughts, even against
an enemy, are sinful. There used to be a saying, 'Killing Kruger
with your mouth', and we have all committed murder in spirit
in that way. It is a terrible thing to be overcome by evil instead
of overcoming it.

I repeat: the desire for evil to come to someone else is sinful
in itself. If we are guilty of thinking of any one of the sins
which I have just been enumerating, we have been overcome
by evil, and that is altogether worse than anything that any
human being can ever do to us. There is a limit to what people
can do to us. They can harm us on the surface, but cannot
harm our souls. It is only evil that can do so. When evil
overcomes us, we are being overcome at the highest, the
noblest part of our being, indeed, in our very relationship to

God Himself. So, then, we must not allow this to happen to us. The power of evil is something which we should ever keep in the forefront of our minds. So the apostle says: Do not be overcome of evil. See evil, rather than persons; see the devil rather than particular things. That is the essence of the teaching at this point.

Now let us turn to the positive teaching, and again you see how important it is not to stop at the negative. So here it is: 'Overcome evil with good.' Now notice the word 'overcome'. Paul is not merely teaching us to hold a balance, as it were, to hold evil at bay, merely not to give in to sin. No, no, Christians are to *overcome* evil, they are to be 'more than conquerors' [*Rom.* 8:17].There is an overplus. They are to be victors. They are to get *it* down instead of allowing it to get *them* down. And remember that Paul says that we are to 'overcome evil *with good*'. There is nothing else that can overcome evil but good. This is the principle of antagonism and this positive good is so antagonistic to evil that it really can demolish it

We could so easily expand this. We are facing a mounting moral problem in Britain and in every other country precisely because of this failure to overcome evil with good. The moral systems can do nothing at all to overcome evil. Oh, I know the psychologists talk about sublimation, but it is all talk, they cannot enable you to do it. No, no, they can do nothing more than try to control the manifestations of evil, to keep it within bounds. That is all right, I am not disparaging that, but moralists must not talk about a radical cure they cannot bring about. Education, culture, all these things, fail completely at this point. No, no, there is only one thing that can overcome evil, and that is positive good. Take the famous phrase of Dr Thomas Chalmers – 'the expulsive power of a new affection'. Nature abhors a vacuum. Evil is driven out by the coming in of the good.

Now how does this happen? 'Overcome evil with good', says the apostle. He says: Do what I am telling you. Do not be defeated but get the victory. And Paul has already told us how we do this. One of the best ways is: 'If thine enemy hunger, feed him; if he thirst, give him drink.' Whatever it is that he is in need of, go to him and relieve him in every way that you can. But how does this overcome evil? It works out like this: You overcome evil in yourself by doing this. Every time you do good to your enemy you get a victory over the old nature that is still left in you. You are not responding to evil but mortifying it. You are putting into effect this great principle of 'the mortification of the deeds of the body' [see *Rom.* 8:13]. 'Mortify therefore your members which are upon the earth,' says Paul in Colossians 3:5. Every time you do this you are making yourself stronger and better, you are growing in grace, you really are overcoming evil in and of yourself.

Thank God, we all know something about this, do we not? Every time you have put this injunction into practice, you have known how much better, how much stronger you have been. What a difference there is between your state when you have avenged yourself, and when you have put Paul's words into practice. You know you are cleaner, you are purer and healthier, you are happier. You know it at once. You have done your own soul good; you have built up your spiritual stock. You are a better, stronger Christian, more ready to meet the enemy when he comes again. You are growing in grace and in the knowledge of the Lord. So you overcome evil in yourself.

But not only that, you also overcome evil in your adversary, this person who is acting towards you as an enemy. He acted impulsively, as a natural man, when he harmed you, but the moment you pulled him up you did him good. You made him think and re-examine his actions. All this is excellent. It is the treatment of his soul. You gave him an understanding of the wrong he had been doing. You promoted repentance in him. The greatest good, the greatest kindness, we can possibly do for another person is to help him or her come to repentance. You showed your adversary a new and better way. You opened his eyes to a possibility he had never realized, something that he could know and experience. So you are doing endless good, overcoming evil in your enemy as well as in yourself.

But add even to that – you are also overcoming evil in general, in itself. Every time we follow Paul's injunction we are defeating the devil, we are getting a victory over him, as our Lord won victories over him in the temptations in the wilderness and at many other points, supremely on the cross on Calvary's hill. Every time you feed your enemy or give him a drink, you are really saying, 'Get thee behind me, Satan', and he has to go. 'Resist the devil, and he will flee from you' [*James* 4:7].This is the way to resist the devil – not fearfully, negatively, but by positively doing something that causes him to run away.

Now this is real victory – victory over evil. And, of course, this is the high water mark of the Christian life. There is nothing more wonderful than this. Did you know that to put into practice this injunction about not avenging yourself but giving way, rather, to God, and feeding your enemy and giving him drink – did you know that a man or woman who can do this is able to do something that the greatest men of the world know nothing at all about? This is real achievement.

Now today is Armistice Day, and it is a day when people talk of valour, of outstanding achievements and of mighty victories won. Our history books remind us of the great people of the past. They overcame enemies, they conquered armies, they delivered countries. All right! You can praise them as much as you like. All I am saying is that the person who succeeds in carrying out the apostle's injunction is gaining a victory that so many of those people know nothing about at all and were quite incapable of achieving.

Again, the wise man in the Book of Proverbs puts this so well. We honour the men who can take cities – yes, but, says this wise man, 'He that is slow to anger is better than the mighty; and he that ruleth his own spirit than he that taketh a city' [*Prov.* 16:32]. Look at the great captains and kings of the past. They could capture other men, and they could control and take cities, but they could not control their own tempers. They were not in control of their own spirits. That is the tragedy. Alexander the Great! What a mighty man! He seemed to control the whole world. But he could not control his own lust and as a result he died of an aneurysm at a comparatively early age.

To be slow to anger is to rule your own spirit. Have we not all known something about this? It is always much easier to manage other people than to manage ourselves. But that is your job ultimately, and it is mine. I find it easier to control a congregation than to control myself. This is the challenge, is it not? There is no point in controlling people if you cannot control yourself. If you cannot control yourself, you are defeated; you are a miserable failure. But if you can, this is real achievement; this is glorious victory; this is true greatness.

What, then, is it that makes self-control possible? What is the secret? This is the glory of it all: 'Be not overcome of evil, but overcome evil with good.' The history of the human race is of one evil person defeating another evil person, but it is all evil in the end. One up, one down; one comes, and one goes. But this is God's victory. What is it that makes the maxims of Romans chapter 12 unequalled in all human philosophy? Why is this chapter unique in its glory and in its wonder? On what basis was the apostle putting this appeal and giving us this injunction?

No man or woman can rise to this level unless they have a right view of themselves. That is always the first thing. You remember how the apostle started the chapter: 'I beseech you *therefore* brethren, by the mercies of God.' It is all that Paul has been saying in his great doctrine of what has happened to us – justification, sanctification, glorification, adoption, our position as sons – it is all this that makes our obedience possible, and nothing else can do it. You have to have a right view of yourself.

Now remember, we are dealing particularly with what people do to us and how we react to that, but here is the principle: 'Know ye not . . . ye are not your own? For ye are bought with a price [*1 Cor.* 6:19–20]. So you start by reminding yourself of what you are and who you are; you think of your soul. And the difference between non-Christians and Christians is that non-Christians belong to themselves, while Christians belong to Christ and to God. So you must stop thinking in terms of yourself. You react violently because you are thinking of yourself. You have been insulted; you have been offended; you have been hurt; you have been deprived. Self! But that goes when you think in a Christian way.

You are not your own, so you must start thinking of yourself, and always keep on thinking of yourself, as a child of God. You are in this new relationship. Think of your Father; think of your family. This is the way to react in an entirely new manner to the things that people do to you. What really matters is not our little reputations, it is the reputation of the family, it is the reputation of God, it is the reputation of heaven. My defeat reflects upon the Head; my defeat is, in a sense, a defeat for the kingdom of God, and it causes great joy among the devil and all his hosts and forces.

But on the other hand, every time we get a victory, it commends the gospel and helps to win other people and take them from the kingdom of darkness into the kingdom of God's dear Son. This has happened often. As I was thinking about all this, an illustration came to my mind of a young lady I once saw as a candidate before a certain missionary society. She was eventually accepted and went out to work in the Far East, and this, in a nutshell, was her story. She had been a student in Cambridge where she was the secretary of the Communist Party. She happened to be in Cambridge during that very severe winter of 1946 to 1947 when everything was frozen up, in Cambridge and in most other parts of the country. She lived in a room off one of the staircases in the college, and, of course, there was a terrible shortage of water. You could only have a bath once a week and there was always a queue. There was one other girl on that staircase, a Christian, the only Christian on the staircase. The Communist girl noticed that instead of asserting her rights and always going to the front and always complaining, as the others were, the Christian girl bore with it all. She allowed people to be assertive and selfish while she just went on quietly. This shook the Communist. She said, 'Here's someone who really is practising and living what I claim to believe but do not do.' The attitude of the Christian not only opened her eyes and made her think, it led to conviction, to repentance, and to conversion, and she went out as a missionary. The simple action of this Christian girl led to that great result.

Now this is the attitude that we should always adopt. Our failure reflects upon the Head, our success commends the gospel. The apostle says, 'Let a man so account of us, as of the ministers of Christ, and stewards of the mysteries of God' [*1 Cor.* 4:1]. The foolish people in Corinth had been comparing and contrasting Paul, and Apollos, and Cephas, and dividing themselves up into silly factions. But Paul says: Do not think of us as men, but as ministers of Christ, and stewards of the mysteries of God. He goes on: 'Moreover it is required in stewards, that a man be found faithful. But with me it is a very small thing that I should be judged of you, or of man's judgment: yea, I judge not mine own self' [verses 2–3]. That is the position, and once you get there you do not avenge yourself. No, no! You have a right view of yourself in your relationship to your Father in heaven, to our Lord, and to the entire kingdom of God.

But you also have a right view of others, even of your enemies, those who do you harm. You do not see them as men and women but as souls, as lost souls. You see these people as the victims of sin and evil, as those who are blinded by the god of this world. You are sorry for them and pray for them. You do good in order to help them. You see them as men and women going to hell – you think of them in terms of their eternal destiny. You do not just say, 'This person has done this to me today!' but, 'This soul will have to stand before God in a final judgment and have nothing to anticipate but an eternal punishment.'

You also remind yourself that you are a soldier in a great war, that you are fighting 'the fight of faith', that you are wrestling against principalities and powers. So what matters? Oh, not what happens to me, but the defeat of the enemy and the triumph of the Lord and of His cause. I do not think of everything in terms of myself, but of evil and good, hell and heaven, the devil and God, this great cosmic fight. You see that, rather than yourself or other people.

And then you realize that as a soldier in this great battle, you must always fight in God's way and not in your way. You instinctively hit back, thinking you are defending yourself. But you must not do that. Listen to the apostle again: 'For though we walk in the flesh, we do not war after the flesh: (For the weapons of our warfare are not carnal, but mighty through God to the pulling down of strong holds;) casting down imaginations, and every high thing that exalteth itself against the knowledge of God, and bringing into captivity every thought to the obedience of Christ' [2 *Cor.* 10:3–5]. You will never defeat your Goliaths in Saul's armour. No, no, that is ridiculous. Fight the battles of the Lord in this spiritual way: 'Put on the whole armour of God' [*Eph.* 6:11]. 'Be strong in the Lord, and in the power of his might' [*Eph.* 6:10]. It is the only way. Give up the old carnal, selfish, personal way of fighting.

You must fight this battle in a spiritual manner – 'Overcome evil with good.'

And then think of the great privilege of being allowed to have any part at all in such a crusade, in such a fight, in such a battle. God is deigning to use us; we are admitted into the army. We are fighting in the army of the living God, and no privilege on earth is comparable to this. It does not matter what people may do to us as long as we are in God's army. They can never rob us of the dignity and the privilege and the honour and the glory of having our part to play in this mighty battle of God against hell, light against darkness, truth against lies.

And, finally, whatever people may do to you, whether they praise you or hate you, whatever terrible things they do – what does it matter? Keep your eye on the day of triumph that is coming, the certainty of the victory, the day when He will appear and will look at you and say, 'Well done, thou good and faithful servant.' He remembers the time when you did not avenge yourself for His sake, because you were thinking of Him and His kingdom and not of yourself. He sees it all; His eye is over it all. 'The crowning day is coming by and by.'

And looking at everything in this way, you soon come to see that what happens to you in this world is comparatively unimportant. 'What is your life? It is even a vapour' [*James* 4:14]. Keep your eye on the 'great recompence of reward' [*Heb.* 10:35]. It is only what He sees and what He will say to you at that great day that really matters.

Let me sum this up in a hymn that is often given to children to sing. It is good and right for children, but not only for children – for all of us. Here it is:

We are but little children weak,
Nor born in any high estate;
What can we do for Jesus' sake,
Who is so high, and good, and great?

Oh, day by day each Christian child
Has much to do, without, within;
A death to die for Jesus' sake,
A constant war to wage with sin.

Romans 12:20–21

When deep within our swelling hearts
The thoughts of pride and anger rise;
When bitter words are on our tongues,
And tears of passion in our eyes:

Then we may stay the angry blow,
Then we may check the hasty word;
Give gentle answers back again,
And fight a battle for the Lord.
Cecil Frances Alexander

'Be not overcome of evil, but overcome evil with good', and so 'fight a battle for the Lord'. May the Lord enable us in this way to bring glory and honour to His great and holy name.